Instant
DHTML Scriptlets

Dino Esposito

D1445559

Wrox Press Ltd.®

Instant DHTML Scriptlets

© 1998 Wrox Press

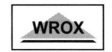

Published by Wrox Press Ltd. 30 Lincoln Road, Olton, Birmingham, B27 6PA.

Printed in CANADA

ISBN 1-861001-38-X

Trademark Acknowledgements

Wrox has endeavored to provide trademark information about all the companies and products mentioned in this book by the appropriate use of capitals. However, Wrox cannot guarantee the accuracy of this information.

Credits

Author
Dino Esposito

Development Editor
Anthea Elston

Editors
Jeremy Beacock
Sonia Mullineux

Technical Reviewers
Shawn Murphy
Rick Kingslan
Jon Bonnell
Andrew Enfield
Mark Harrison
Omar Khan

Design/Layout/Cover
Andrew Guillaume

Index
Donald Glassman

Cover image by David Maclean. Digital processing by Andrew Guillaume.

About the Author

Dino is a senior consultant who specializes in Windows and COM programming. He now works for Andersen Consulting focusing on the development of Web-based applications. He's a frequent speaker at industry conferences such as Microsoft Developer Days and occasionally teaches seminars for Infomedia Communications on Win32 programming, Visual Basic and Dynamic HTML.

He also has extensive experience developing commercial Windows-based software especially for the photography world and has been part of the team who designed and realized one of the first European image databanks.

He loves writing and is a contributing editor to *Microsoft Interactive Developer* and a regular contributor to *Windows Developer's Journal*. He has also co-authored *Professional IE4 Programming* published by Wrox Press.

Dino lives in Rome (Italy) with his wife Silvia. He likes dogs (mostly Alsatians) and tennis. Feel free to contact him at despos@tin.it.

Credits

Every book involves many more people than actually appear on the cover. This book is no exception. The first person my thoughts turn to, however, is not here. Or rather, is not here yet! Yes, Francesco, we all are waiting for you to arrive soon, sound, healthy and lively. We love you very much already, and hope you'll like sleeping too!

The destiny of all the women who fall in love with programmers is well-known. And sooner or later most of them are reconciled to their lot. They regularly have to face heaps of books and magazines scattered on the floor, flying modems, ubiquitous coffee cups and even the clicking of the keyboard in the middle of the night. Without such a woman to wake you in the night and ask *"Who's this model you're screaming about?"*, and then joke *"Let's stop applets and scriptlets, today we have omelet!"*, you can't sleep four hours a night and work one weekend after another. Believe me, you have neither time nor need to wonder why they call it ECMAScript, with such a woman. Yes, Silvia, don't worry—I love you much more than Dynamic HTML.

Whatever you do in your life—whatever you make of your life—a mom and a dad always have something to do with it. Even if they stay in the shadows, even if it seems they aren't there, they are always there when you need them. And they never go far enough to leave you alone. Thanks for your love. I love you too.

OK, OK. Now it's your turn to come on the stage. Ladies and gentleman, special thanks go to Marco Lucani and Raffaele D'Orsogna for being friends and personal consultants, and to Francesco Balena, Carlo Pescio, and Antonio Derossi who always have something to teach me (and learn from me). Not to mention Roberto Raschetti who never failed to give me both appreciation and the best advice I've ever had.

And now let me say "Thanks" to Josh Trupin, who gave me the chance to learn about scriptlets. As usual, I didn't stop there and, after learning, I wanted to write about it. Maybe you don't know, but you're somewhat "responsible" for this book. Thanks to Josh and everyone at *Microsoft Interactive Developer* for encouraging me to continue writing. Since I'm talking about computer magazines, it's simply impossible to forget all the people at Infomedia. Hey guys, what about the book?

Last but not least, Anthea Elston worked on this book with a devotion that surprised me, but I can easily guess that all the staff at Wrox did the same. Yes, I very much enjoyed writing this book and, above all, I enjoyed doing it with Wrox.

Thanks to you all
--Dino

INSTANT

DHTML
Scriptlets

Table of Contents

Chapter 15: Remote Scripting and the Microsoft Scripting Library.......... 381

Introduction

Scriptlets are the latest innovation in the released version of Microsoft's Internet Explorer 4.0. In simple terms, they are nothing more than ordinary HTML pages equipped with a special layer of script code that allows the authors to handle them as if they were programmable ActiveX Controls. Scriptlets introduce the concept of HTML code reusability and make it real, far beyond the usual cut-and-paste gestures. With scriptlets, you have a real software platform, with the extreme ease and usability of HTML language.

Scriptlets stem from the **Dynamic HTML** object model and are an important new tool in any Web developer's toolkit.

In addition, they are a key point in the short and mid-term evolution of the shell of Microsoft's operating systems. So stay tuned, whether you're a traditional Windows programmer or a Web developer.

What is this Book About?

When I started experimenting with the Dynamic HTML object model, one of the first negative aspects I noticed was the lack of an integrated mechanism to allow reusability with a minimum of effort.

I soon realized that with Dynamic HTML my Web pages could become much more dynamic, attractive and—of course—useful. Furthermore, the richness of the DHTML objects certainly encouraged the use of HTML outside the Web environment. But I still had to reinvent the wheel each time I wanted to take even a short drive. Some pieces of DHTML code lend themselves very well to being thought up and designed as separate and distinct components. They integrate into HTML documents in a natural manner and are as seamless as other standard elements. Thus, we have a powerful object model and an operating system's shell already prepared to provide full support to it via **Active Desktop**.

All this seems to prefigure a real new development platform and a new family of software components. What is missing in this idyllic scenario is just the right lever to lift the world (as Archimedes would have said). Scriptlets are the lever we have been waiting for.

The Book's Layout

This book is focused on scriptlets and provides a wide coverage of the topic in all its primary and secondary aspects. By reading it, you should get an excellent grasp of the whole topic. The first chapter of the book introduces the basics to enable you to understand scriptlets and their position in the context of Dynamic HTML programming. The rest of the book presents scriptlet fundamentals and several real-world examples, and the last chapter tackles the latest addition— Server Scriptlets. We will pay particular attention to showing how the original DHTML code—that you should be able to write and understand—evolves into scriptlets.

A key fact that we'll be emphasizing is that scriptlets are "objects" placed at a higher abstraction layer than just Dynamic HTML code.

Why Scriptlets?

Scriptlets are HTML pages that heavily exploit the DHTML object model. However, they require specific know-how to be well designed and become fully functional. At first glance, scriptlets may be considered as a subset of Dynamic HTML. However, they are one step beyond it and may well open an exciting new market for developers. At the moment of writing, scriptlets are just a product-specific feature of Microsoft Internet Explorer 4.0. Frankly, we don't know what's going to happen in the future. However, at least partially, the worldwide acceptance of scriptlets is tied to the acceptance of Dynamic HTML. Hence the question, why a book on scriptlets?

Overall scriptlets are a great idea aimed to give a better structure to all new and existing Web-based applications. They allow you to componentize your pages using HTML and scripting. Internet Explorer 4.0 makes them available on a variety of platforms, including Unix and Mac, as well as Windows 3.x, Win32 and Windows CE.

Scriptlets and DHTML are also part of the Active Desktop and part of the Windows 98 and Windows NT 5.0 shell. Consequently, they are not just new and dazzling toys for Web developers, but also a new and dazzling feature of the current and upcoming Windows-based operating systems.

Dynamic HTML on the Web

If we're writing HTML pages, or developing Web-based projects today, we should consider carefully the possibility of using Dynamic HTML and scriptlets. Internet Explorer 4.0 exposes a set of objects that differ from those offered by other browsers, particularly Netscape Communicator. We can bet that this kind of incompatibility between Internet Explorer and Communicator will continue in the future. Moreover, Microsoft and Netscape are not the only browser vendors on the earth.

However, Internet Explorer 4.0 at this time is undoubtedly the browser that gives you the most powerful and open implementation of Dynamic HTML.

This status-quo is supposed to continue throughout 1998, until the World Wide Web Consortium (W3C) ships a final standard for DHTML. The final specification will not necessarily be coherent with today's implementation provided by Internet Explorer 4.0.

The first public draft of DOM (Document Object Model) released by the W3C consortium is attempting to provide a universal standard for Dynamic HTML. Unfortunately, at this stage only generic directives are available, and there is no clear and precise information on how it will develop.

Dynamic HTML in the Windows Shell

Things are completely different if we look at life from a Windows perspective. Dynamic HTML and scriptlets are a concrete reality immediately after installing the Active Desktop that ships with Internet Explorer 4.0. Even if Microsoft changes its object model in the future it's a fair bet that it will remain backward-compatible. So we can make use of it without restrictions.

Scriptlets and DHTML for example can enrich the customized folders, the desktop itself, and be utilized to develop HTML-based modules that exploit the WebBrowser ActiveX Control.

The evolution of Scriptlet Technology

The final chapters of the book cover a couple of really advanced topics that are currently under development: Remote Scripting and Server Scriptlets. They relate only partially to the main focus of the book—which is DHTML Scriptlets. However, they are strictly tied to the more general world of scripting and are two really interesting innovations for Web developers. We've covered both in detail—or rather we've covered them to the best level of detail available today. Never forget that scripting technology (and scriptlets in particular) is evolving day after day and no one can say today what we can expect to happen tomorrow.

What Do I Need to Use This Book?

All you need to create scriptlets and Dynamic HTML documents yourself is a text editor capable of saving files in ASCII format, and Internet Explorer 4.0 (or higher) as the browser. To enable scriptlets, you must have the released version of IE4.

If you have a beta version or haven't IE4 at all, then you can download the shipped product freely from:

`http://www.microsoft.com/ie4`

If you use some specialized HTML editors like Microsoft FrontPage 97 when writing scriptlets or Dynamic HTML pages, be cautious. Sometimes it silently modifies the text you typed in, removing unknown and unsupported tag attributes. This happens more often than you could imagine with DHTML features. For this reason it's recommended that you use normal text editors or the newly released Microsoft FrontPage 98. The cheapest way to get both syntax highlighting and normal save options is using the text editor integrated in the Developer Studio 97 environment.

Apart from tools, to take advantage of this book you need a good understanding of the Dynamic HTML object model. This is covered with different slants and different levels of detail in other books published by Wrox Press. For example, you can check Instant IE4 Dynamic HTML Programmer's Reference *ISBN: 1-861000-68-5* for a primer and Professional IE4 Programming *ISBN: 1-861000-70-7* if you want more advanced coverage of the subject. The latter also includes a chapter entirely devoted to scriptlets, which is the optimal starting point for a book like this.

Since scriptlets are Dynamic HTML documents, you need to know at least the main elements of the hierarchy and their most common methods, properties and events. A handy knowledge of scripting languages such as VBScript and JavaScript will help. A basic understanding of COM interfaces and ActiveX Controls is useful, but not strictly required. As long as you have created Dynamic HTML pages before, and have done a little Visual Basic or VBScript programming, you'll have no problems keeping up with what we'll be doing here.

Who Should Read This Book?

You should read this book if you're interested in writing HTML-based applications or advanced Dynamic HTML pages that will be viewed best with Internet Explorer 4.0. Scriptlets simplify the process of creating tutorial or kiosk-based modules where you can reasonably assume or require the presence of Internet Explorer 4.0 with or without Active Desktop.

Where you'll find the Samples and Updates

If you want to try out the examples in this book, you can run them straight from our Web site or you can download them as compressed files from the same site. The index page can be found at:

`http://www.rapid.wrox.com/books/138X`

If you're located in Europe or in United Kingdom, or you find that the site in the United States is down for maintenance, then you may want to try our mirror site which can be found at:

`http://rapid.wrox.co.uk/books/138X`

What is the World Wide Web Consortium?

In the pages above, we've already encountered the World Wide Web Consortium, often shortened to the acronym W3C. It is a worldwide organization presided over by Tim Berners-Lee, who was the inventor of the HTML language, back in 1983.

The incredible success gained all over the world by HTML since 1992 (the year when it entered the public domain), made it necessary to create a moderating organization with the task of approving and promoting the various standards. Each vendor of HTML-related products—from browsers to editors—introduced its own custom tags over the years. This created several HTML variants, more or less incompatible with each other. Everyone was claiming that their own set of extensions was far better and definitely open. Everyone was pretending that competitors supported it, creating a de-facto standard.

The W3C is required to examine all the proposals for defining an up-to-date and possibly universal Web language. Once the consortium approves a proposal, all vendors interested in following that standard should adopt it. On the other hand, when it rejects a draft all the work done by vendors in the meantime risks being lost.

Although the W3C has the right to the last word, its activity is regularly driven by mainline manufacturers (Microsoft and Netscape above all) who never allow time for the standards to catch up with the browser versions

The W3C and Dynamic HTML

The scenario set out above describes perfectly what is happening with the Dynamic HTML specifications. Based on generic documents, Netscape released Communicator, which implemented Dynamic HTML through non-standard tags. Their implementation doesn't respect many of the current W3C suggestions, because they occurred after the product had shipped. You can visit Netscape's Web site to get more information on this and the future updates. Look at:

`http://developer.netscape.com/library`

for technical information and at:

`http://www.netscape.com`

for a general overview.

Internet Explorer 4.0 shipped after Communicator and is, therefore, closer to the most recent draft. However, the next paper to be released could reverse the situation.

It's likely too that when the W3C finally approves the DHTML standard, both the best known and most used browsers will be different from now. And, probably, both will be ahead of the specs again!

What is the Document Object Model?

Within the W3C there's a team working on the definition of a platform and language-neutral program interface. It will allow you to access any element in the currently viewed page both for reading and writing. The generic interface is called Document Object Model (DOM) and a public draft of it can be found starting from the following URL:

`http://www.w3.org/`

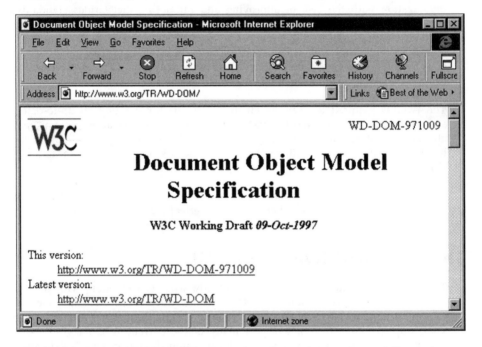

The ideal browser should build its own specific implementation of Dynamic HTML on top of this DOM. Dynamic HTML is a technology that includes the DOM and should use it as the public interface to access the page elements.

At present Internet Explorer 4.0 exposes a hierarchy of objects built according to the DOM directives. But will this be true when the final specification is released?

Following the DOM, any DHTML implementation must support any scripting language and must also expose the browser environment. Internet Explorer 4.0 does this via Microsoft's ActiveX Scripting Engine and ActiveX automation.

Of course, scriptlets aren't included in the Document Object Model since they are largely a browser feature. Will scriptlets ever become a standard? I don't know, but the ActiveX Controls and the Netscape plugins are both good samples of browser-specific features that were accepted and supported by all vendors.

Some Terminology

Before going any further, let's take a moment to enumerate and explain some terms that will be used often in the following chapters.

Scriptlets—the subject of this book. They are special HTML pages hosted in another HTML page. Scriptlets can be scripted since they expose properties and methods just like ActiveX Controls.

SOM (Scripting Object Model)—the Internet Explorer 4.0 object model that allows you to access the document currently viewed as well as the browser's infrastructure (window, location, navigator and so on). SOM includes the document object model, which is a subtree in the hierarchy and describes the content of page.

MIME (Multimedia Internet Mail Extension)—despite the name, it provides a description of the type of a given object. This information helps the browser to recognize the element and decide how to deal with it. The **MIME** type attribute plays an important role with scriptlets. In fact, they are hosted within the **OBJECT** tag, which is commonly used for ActiveX Controls. Scriptlets, however, require a different treatment and the browser distinguishes between them through the **MIME** type.

DHTML (Dynamic HTML)—an extended version of the HTML language that encompasses access to the Scripting Object Model. By this means, the page currently viewed can be modified without involving the server where it originally resided.

HTML and DHTML pages don't differ in content or file format. What changes is what the browser builds on the top of the page. A browser like Internet Explorer 4.0 parses the page content, creates it dynamically and exposes an object model that represents it. A page aware of this model which attempts to exploit it via scripting is called a Dynamic HTML page. But if you view the same page with a different browser, you'll probably get a bunch of script errors and an absolutely static and unmodifiable content.

Document container—a special ActiveX application capable of hosting documents created and displayed via an ActiveX server. For example, Microsoft Word 97 works as an ActiveX server (a.k.a. OLE server) creating and displaying Word (*.doc) documents. A document container, such as Internet Explorer 4.0 or Office 97 Binder, is able to host an ActiveX server module like Word 97 while displaying its own documents. There's a subtle difference from the old concept of OLE server and container. Now the document automatically uses the entire host client area as its own site.

Document server—as mentioned above, it's an ActiveX module, able to display documents the OLE way. A document server differs from an OLE server by the means of a few new COM interfaces it implements. Analogously, a document server can be an in-process module (DLL) or out-of-process (EXE). Examples of well-known document servers are all the Office 97 applications (Word, Excel, PowerPoint), the Visual Basic 5 ActiveX Documents and—of course—the **MsHtml** library which is the module that provides HTML browsing capabilities in Internet Explorer 4.0.

7

Conventions

We have used a number of different styles of text and layout in the book to help differentiate between the different kinds of information. Here are examples of the styles we use and an explanation of what they mean:

Advice, hints, or background information comes in this type of font.

Important pieces of information come in boxes like this

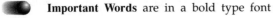 **Important Words** are in a bold type font

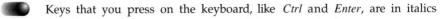 Words that appear on the screen in menus like the File or Window are in a similar font to the one that you see on screen

Keys that you press on the keyboard, like *Ctrl* and *Enter*, are in italics

Code has several fonts. If it's a word that we're talking about in the text, for example, when discussing the **For...Next** loop, it's in a bold font. If it's a block of code that you can type in as a program and run, then it's also in a gray box:

```
<STYLE>
... Some VBScript ...
</STYLE>
```

Sometimes you'll see code in a mixture of styles, like this:

```
<HTML>
<HEAD>
<TITLE>Cascading Style Sheet Example</TITLE>
<STYLE>
style1 {color: red;
    font-size: 25}
</STYLE>
</HEAD>
```

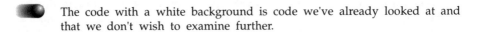 The code with a white background is code we've already looked at and that we don't wish to examine further.

These formats are designed to make sure that you know what it is you're looking at. I hope they make life easier.

Tell Us What You Think

We've worked hard on this book to make it enjoyable and useful. Our best reward would be to hear from you that you liked it and that it was worthy your money. We've done our best to try to understand and match your expectations.

Please let us know what you think about it. Tell us what you have liked best and what has made you regret spending your hard-earned money. If you think this is just a marketing gimmick, then test us out—drop us a line!

We'll answer, and we'll take whatever you say on board for future editions. The easiest way is to use email:

feedback@wrox.com

You can also find more details about Wrox Press on our Web site. There, you'll find the code from out latest books, sneak previews of forthcoming titles, and information about the authors and the editors. You can order Wrox titles directly from the site, or find out where your nearest local bookstore with Wrox titles is located. The address of our site is:

http://www.wrox.com

Customer Support

If you find a mistake, please have a look at the errata page for this book on our web site first. Appendix D outlines how can you can submit an errata in much greater detail, if you are unsure. The full URL for the errata page is:

http://www.wrox.com/Scripts/Errata.idc?Code=138X

If you can't find an answer there, tell us about the problem and we'll do everything we can to answer promptly!

Just send us an email to **support@wrox.com**.

or fill in the form on our web site: **http://www.wrox.com/Contact.stm**

How to Contact the Author

Please feel free also to send any question about the book directly to the author. Dino Esposito can be reached via email at one of the following addresses:

 desposito@infomedia.it

 despos@tin.it

Alternatively, you can also send messages to **feedback@wrox.com** specifying who is the real recipient of your email.

The Role of Dynamic HTML

Unless you spent the last year of your life in a solitary cave or lost in an inaccessible rainforest, you should know by now about Dynamic HTML (DHTML). Maybe you don't know exactly what it is. Or maybe you have just heard about it from your colleagues or your favorite newsgroups. Perhaps you're a programmer whose everyday work is miles away from the open and exciting world of the Internet. Alternatively, DHTML maybe heavily involved in the most recent project you were allocated to. In any case, whichever way you look at it, DHTML is today's hottest topic.

DHTML is a new and decisive step in the evolution of what was originally the HyperText Markup Language created by Tim Berners-Lee at CERN, about fifteen years ago. In recent months, we have observed a more and more creative use of static and animated images, that has made the pages we were facing on the Web increasingly active. In this scenario, scripting languages plays a central role. They provide interactivity by inserting a new layer between the users and the elements of the page. Thus, a click on a graphic object causes a piece of code to execute, giving some kind of responsiveness to the users.

This code is not written using any of the most common and complex programming languages, such as C or C++. Instead, it is written in scripting language, such as VBScript or JavaScript, most of which have simple, loose and easy-to-learn syntaxes.

A script procedure in most cases acts just like glue, holding together all the elements that actually form a Web page. From the user's perspective, an HTML page appears to be a collection of logical objects scattered on a surface. Contrary to appearances, these logical objects don't yet correspond to any software component that you can sensibly call an "object". Prior to the advent of Dynamic HTML, we had three types of actors on the stage: text, graphics and scripting. Their cooperation produced more attractive pages, capable of interactively responding to the users' activity. That's all, and nothing more than that.

The term 'object' usually refers to self-contained software components exposing methods, properties and events. Put another way, a real object would allow users and authors to drive it programmatically and take care of responding to external inputs by itself. ActiveX Controls, for instance, are objects.

What's really new about Dynamic HTML is that the whole page may be automatically seen as a collection of objects. At last we have a perfect match between what is logically perceived as being an object and its actual implementation.

In this section we're going to examine the context that DHTML comes from and the close relationship between DHTML and scripting. You need to understand the scope and the role of Dynamic HTML to be able to comprehend what scriptlets are and why they have been created. In particular, the next pages will tell you about:

- The birth of non-static and read-write Web pages
- The role of the browser
- Why ASP and DHTML are both dynamic but completely different things
- Why DHTML might greatly interest you, even if you're a traditional Windows programmer

In this book, we're not covering basic aspects of Dynamic HTML, neither will we provide an exhaustive programmer's reference for the myriad of properties, events and methods that feature in the object model. We'll assume you're already familiar with topics such as Dynamic HTML, Internet Explorer 4.0 and scripting languages. If not, please refer to the introduction for some useful hints and suggestions for further reading.

Configurable pages

On the road to fully programmable and dynamically modifiable pages, Cascading Style Sheets (CSS) are an important but intermediate stop. Basically, they are lines of text-based information that store the authors' preferences for the visual and graphic look of a single Web page or a group of HTML documents.

Internet Explorer 3.x, for instance, offers full support for CSS. It lets you define your preferences for the display of any HTML tag. In this way, for example, you can tell the browser that all the <H1> text should be drawn using a Tahoma bold font in blue color and right-justified. Of course, the same is true for any built-in element.

To be precise, instead of "you can tell the browser" I should have said, "you can recommend that the browser", since any browser holds its own set of default styles. The final settings are determined by mediating between what the author suggests and what the browser usually does for the given HTML tag.

Practical advantages of CSS

There are a number of practical advantages in using CSS. The most important is that you can collect all your "cosmetic" settings in a single file and associate it with any Web page you write.

Furthermore, you introduce a sort of abstraction layer that saves you from specifying the same formatting options each time, for each element.

If we look at it more closely, we realize that there's a double saving: first, you save time and avoid bother; second, and more important, you save space and earn precious downloading time. In fact, you only need to obtain a few KBs from the Web server instead of having the same information repeated over and over again, tag by tag. A nice side-effect of this is that sometimes you can avoid using bitmaps to make a given page more effective, but can resort to appropriate and predefined text formatting. Naturally, the Cascading Style Sheets work well because of the browser, which is interpreting the style information and adapting its own defaults.

Programmable pages with CSS

The implementation of CSS, though working perfectly, is quite rough and has nothing that could call to mind the concept of "object." Nevertheless, style sheets were the first example of programmable, and somewhat dynamic, pages. You don't explicitly assign a color or a font, but you issue a command that assigns a given style to a tag.

The CSS commands available don't form a full-fledged scripting language yet. For example, if you want to assign styles based on runtime conditions, then you need a real script language such as VBScript or JavaScript. To be able to utilize all of such a language's power, you also need an object model. In other words, you might want to expose all the formatting options and all the feasible tags through a hierarchy of objects. This is the essence of Dynamic HTML.

Once you produce something that can be somehow programmed, you have something that tends to assume a **dynamic** behavior.

You will certainly have noted that the adjective "dynamic" and the acronym "HTML" are often put together. You will also have realized that this began to happen a long time before Dynamic HTML came to light. But what is the real meaning of the word "dynamic"?

What is 'dynamic'?

'Dynamic' is code that changes its aspect and its functionality on-the-fly, responding to certain kinds of external, and sometimes internal, commands. Thus, when talking of dynamic HTML pages (note the word 'dynamic' without the uppercase D) you're addressing a number of topics, including changing the page content, modifying the graphical look and adding interactive behavior. Changing the behavior doesn't change anything in the page as a whole. A page, in fact, contains all the scripting logic from the time of its first download. Modifying the aspect or the content, however, implies real change in the page and the browser's settings.

Client and Server-side dynamism

The word "dynamic" is often also used to refer to Active Server Pages. In this case, the meaning of "dynamic" is completely different. An ASP document is an HTML page that doesn't exist on the HTTP server, but is generated on-the-fly responding to a user's request. You can still call it dynamic, but it's another kind of dynamism. Once an ASP document is created on the server-side, it is sent to and handled by the browser as an ordinary HTML page.

In short, there are two completely separate worlds to which the term "dynamic" applies. These are: the server and the client.

Active Server Pages occurs on the server side and creates HTML pages dynamically starting from a given set of templates and sometimes making use of special design-time ActiveX controls. Dynamic HTML occurs on the client side and consists of a hierarchy of objects that some specialized browsers build on top of the HTML file just downloaded from the Web or read from a local site.

So, don't get confused by the word dynamic and pay attention to the case of the D. Usually a lower case means HTML pages created dynamically just a moment before being sent across the net. The uppercase, on the other hand, indicates the Dynamic HTML object model, that is a set of components that represent the HTML page you're currently viewing. Since you can automate them via scripting, it results in dynamic update of the page content.

Dynamic HTML with IE40

An HTML document is mostly made up of text, images, controls, and script. In particular, script code is the means of controlling the behavior of the page. The advent of Dynamic HTML has begun to change the role of the scripting languages, giving them another level of importance. Scripting is not just the tool you use to co-ordinate the various page elements; it has evolved into a simple and more accessible development tool for creating real software components. The intrinsic simplicity of VBScript or JavaScript opens up the world of programming to many more people than C or C++, or even Visual Basic and Delphi.

The flexibility of DHTML, along with the concept of scriptlets, gives you a powerful platform for developing Web-oriented applications. Furthermore, the integration between Internet Explorer 4.0 and the Windows shell makes things much more interesting and exploitable.

Some Basic Concepts

In the Dynamic HTML world, a Web page is a surface on which a variety of objects are placed. Everything you can put in HTML code is seen as an object by DHTML-aware browsers like Internet Explorer 4.0. This applies to all elements identified by known tags, such as ActiveX Controls, forms, frames, tables, Java applets, images, anchors, or scripts. But things don't end here. In fact, you can see any piece of text that is part of the document as an object, even a substring.

So when we state that everything you can find in HTML code may be considered (and scripted) as an object with its own set of properties, we really do mean exactly this and aren't exaggerating! To identify the HTML code you need to provide it with a unique ID. An ID may be a string or a number and you can think of it as the name (or rather the moniker) of that object in that page.

The Document Object

As mentioned earlier, a Web page is a kind of container which holds the constituent elements. This surface is actually called a **document** and is represented in Internet Explorer 4.0 by the **document** object. If you like to put it in terms of windows, we could compare the document to the client area of the IE frame window.

The **document** object is part of the Internet Explorer 4.0 object model you can see in the figure on the right.

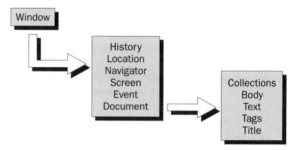

This hierarchy allows you to access all of the browser's internal information. The document object is the root of the collection of objects that form the page. From here, we can locate any single element defined in the HTML code, whether it is visible or not. The objects are organized in collections, namely associative arrays which you can index by name or position.

If the document is the surface where the output will show, then scripting is the machine that produces this output by manipulating the page components. By building a hierarchy of objects on the top of the HTML source code, Internet Explorer 4.0 gives scripting a collection of basic objects to work with in order to produce effects and any sort of output.

The inner relationship between scripting and the document object model is similar to the one we can observe between the C++ language and MFC or ATL classes for Windows programming. Although you're given the ability to build your own classes for writing programs from the ground up, you might want to take advantage of existing components to speed up development and save yourself some boring tasks. This framework offers you something that resembles an object model. Then, it's up to you to assemble and arrange the elements to produce a good result.

Document Collections

Collections are the standard way provided to get into the HTML code through the abstraction layer built by Dynamic HTML implementation. When authoring Web pages, you make calls into the objects and collections the browser builds for you at runtime

When a page is accessed through the Internet Explorer 4.0 address bar, the File|Open menu, a hyperlink, or in any other way, the browser caches it and extrapolates its content. Then it dynamically instantiates a set of Component Object Model (COM) objects and makes them work on the extracted data. Of course, the COM servers have been designed to expose the proper set of methods and attributes. This process may take a while to complete and its end is notified via a specific document event. From now on, accessing the document object is safe. In the meantime the browser fills out all the collections that will allow you to access your next required subset of page elements. Anything in the Web page can be reached via a generic or more specific collection.

Programming Dynamic HTML

To program Dynamic HTML means being able to fully exploit the document object model, once it gets correctly initialized. The best way to do it is by the means of scripting code. As you know, Internet Explorer 4.0 supports only two script languages as standard: VBScript and JavaScript, or rather a custom implementation of it called JScript.

If you're interested in Microsoft scripting technologies, then you can check the following address: **http://www.microsoft.com/scripting**
You can also find online technical reference for the latest versions of both VBScript and JScript there. The script code glues together the various elements giving our page a certain behavior. But what can we do with Dynamic HTML? What are the features we can implement? What's really new and exciting about it for all of us poor programmers?

Highlights of Dynamic HTML capabilities

There are a number of new features you can exploit with DHTML object model. However, the most important all refer to dynamic page modification. Updating a page is a process that takes place on the client-side and consists of changing an internal cache the browser builds from the actual downloaded sources. If you press the *F5* key or click the Refresh button on the Internet Explorer 4.0 toolbar, then the current page will be read back from the server and you'll lose all the dynamic changes you have made so far. The server is completely unaware of what happens between the browser and the user, whose interaction is governed by the script code the page authors have written.

What you can change in a page is summarized by the following points:

- Absolute Positioning and Z-Order
- Style of any Page Element
- Text of any Page Element
- Attributes of any Page Element

In addition, you can exploit multimedia and graphic effects by the means of a variety of filters and transitions already available. Another great feature of Dynamic HTML is data-binding. Let's give a brief overview of all these features.

Changing the Page

In a Dynamic HTML environment you can modify everything you want and everything you need. Of course, do remember that you don't have to do things just because they're doable. So make sure not to be affected by that mysterious FX syndrome that strikes the majority of first time Visual Basic programmers, when they discover how easy it is to give a red background to a poor textbox or an innocent listbox. Don't give in to color-mania; use them only when really necessary.

Absolute Positioning

This is the capability to assign an absolute position to the topleft corner of a page element. You can express it in pixels and be sure that the object will appear exactly where you require it. You can choose between absolute and relative positioning. The properties **posLeft**, **posTop**, **posWidth** and **posHeight** allow you to keep track of the exact location of an element.

Z-ordering or Z-indexing is another interesting feature which introduces different layers for text and non-text elements. Layers are like transparent slides you can pile one on top of another. The final page is formed by, say, some text and an image that overlap. By using the **z-index** property, you can choose which one to display in the background.

Style of the Elements

There are a great number of settable styles for the various page elements that support the **STYLE** tag. You access them through the **style** object. Among the options, we cannot forget the foreground and the background color, the border style, the font information (family, weight, height, effects, and so on) and even the cursor shape.

Text of the Elements

You have two ways of modifying the text of a page element. You might want to replace it as pure ASCII text or as HTML text. Moreover, you can modify it within the tag/endtag delimiters or completely replace the element, overriding the tag portion of its syntax at the same time. To do this you use four self-explanatory read/write properties such as **innerHTML, outerHTML, innertText, outerText**.

Using these properties you can alter virtually any component, ActiveX Controls—images and scripts included.

Attributes of the Elements

An HTML tag can have attributes. A classic example of this is the attribute **Classid** that you find inside the **<OBJECT>** tag for ActiveX Controls denoting the CLSID of the COM in-proc server. Another frequently encountered attribute is **Language**, which indicates the actual script language we're going to use. Using **setAttribute, getAttribute** and **removeAttribute** you can do practically whatever you want with them.

Other Special Effects

Visual and transitions filters are just special effects that make pages much more attractive. Unsurprisingly, they work only on text and images. By using filters you can obtain graphic enhancements such as transparency, grayscaling, mirroring, flipping, shading and various light effects.

Transitions, on the other hand, are effects that take place when displaying an image. You might want it to progressively materialize from a white background, or have it slowly fade to the background color. There's a large gamut of available effects, so you just need to try them out and choose the one that best fits your needs.

These special filters help greatly in producing interactive and live pages. Everything happens on the client-side and there is no further contact between the browser and the server. The functionality behind transitions and text updates is implemented in the browser itself, or, to be more exact, by the COM modules stored in the **msHtml.dll** file.

Data-Binding

Data-Binding is not really a special effect, at least according to the usual meaning we assign to this word. Data-Binding doesn't enhance the look-and-feel of the page or make it any more impressive. At this point, you might wonder why we're discussing it here. There's an obvious answer to this question, because data-binding might have a special impact on your customers, just as a shaded or animated logo would.

More importantly, data-binding establishes a special channel to the server. The connection remains active until the specified recordset has been completely downloaded. Data-binding relies on data-source objects, such as the Tabular Data Control (TDC), being able to connect and transmit asynchronously records from a database.

Where's the special effect? Your customer will see the page begin to take shape and become usable, even if the data-source component is still working and downloading records.

Data-Binding is the DHTML counterpart of Visual Basic's data-aware ActiveX Controls. You associate a **DataSrc** field to an HTML tag and have it display the content of the given database.

Practical advantages of DHTML

Now that we've taken a quick look at some highlights of Dynamic HTML, it's time to explore what its practical advantages are.

First of all, you get a richer and more powerful environment in which to display your Web pages. This feature wouldn't be so exciting if it didn't endow us with the capability of updating the page itself, dynamically and—above all—locally. Combine these two aspects and you realize how many new things you can do with Dynamic HTML.

Of course, the majority of these are concerned with the user-interface of the page, but don't forget that HTML is not supposed to be a programming language. HTML should be just an expressive language to be used for displaying information in a pleasant, interactive and possibly customizable way. So where's the improvement?

Scriptable Objects

Scripts can now affect HTML elements at a finer level of granularity, reaching any tag and identifying any tagged element with its own ID. This means that you have the tools to modify virtually any remote piece of the HTML source code. But when would you do this?

A mechanism called event-bubbling makes it possible for you to define specific event handlers for all the elements that have an ID. This was the missing piece of the jigsaw. With Dynamic HTML you can identify any piece of code as an object, and use that identification as a hook for the events that involve it. At last, if you need to, you can change its style or text using the properties and methods exposed.

The richness of the DHTML model is a good starting point for writing general and reusable functions. You can isolate specific pieces of code into separate routines, but you need a way to port them back and forth from between projects. A real programming language allows you to do this using libraries, DLLs or ActiveX code components. But HTML isn't a programming platform. Or rather, HTML wasn't a programming platform.

Now, with scriptlets you can develop fully reusable and structured HTML code made up of objects kept together and governed by scripting.

Summary

This chapter was intended to be a brief overview/reminder of Dynamic HTML. We've discussed configurable HTML pages and traced the evolution that brought us from static to active Web content, right up until the present day where the content itself has grown to become dynamic.

The use of the word dynamic can be a bit confusing and we tried to clarify the various contexts in which you can hear of it. Finally, we enumerated the highlights and main advantages of DHTML.
In particular, we've covered

- Differences between ASP and DHTML
- The document object model
- Highlights of Dynamic HTML
- Data-Binding
- Advantages of Dynamic HTML

In the next chapter we'll start to look at scriptlets themselves.

Chapter

2

Getting started with Scriptlets

The DHTML model gives you the opportunity to manipulate the elements that actually form an HTML page without restrictions. Therefore, you can see virtually any element of the HTML source code as an object, with its own set of properties, methods and events. DHTML defines a number of objects, and anything you can identify in an HTML document is expressed in terms of one of them.

All the objects are implemented inside the **msHtml.dll** library (a standard part of IE4), and made available to the programmers through COM interfaces. There are specific components for wrapping images, links, applets, and controls, but also for the body of a document, its style, the frames collection, any forms, and so on.

Scriptlets are a step beyond DHTML and provide a way to add new, completely custom built, objects to the DHTML standard objects. These objects aren't binary pieces of code like ActiveX controls, but represent an evolution of DHTML pages and are made out of script and HTML tags. As a result, they look like ordinary automation components that you should already be familiar with. Scriptlets are nothing more than HTML documents, with an additional layer of script code that makes them appear to be very similar to controls. On the other hand, since they are HTML pages they might also be seen as custom extensions to the standard DHTML object model.

In this chapter, we're going to present scriptlets. Our first aim will be defining the key aspects of the scriptlets architecture and exploring the differences and similarities between it and ActiveX controls.

Later on, we'll analyze scriptlets in order to evaluate their role and their power with respect to the construction of reusable HTML-based components.

The final goal of the chapter will be discussing some scriptlets portability and security issues. After that, we'll be ready to start talking about scriptlets programming.

In particular, the chapter is intended to cover:

- HTML code reusability
- Scriptlet architecture
- Code portability and compatibility
- Internet zones and related security issues
- Tools for developing scriptlets

By the end of this chapter, you should have a clear, if theoretical, understanding of the whole subject, and be ready for further discussion and more advanced programming topics.

Re-using HTML code

The power of the DHTML object model is emphasized by scripting code that adds a level of interactivity and flexibility. You should know by now about the advantages of scripting, since it's not a new issue.

However, what's really new is that scripting the DHTML object model provides a considerably larger range of choices, and—consequently—increases the possible applications by several orders of magnitude. Simply put, DHTML allows you to be much more creative when developing scripting code.

A primary reason for this increased expressiveness is the ability you now have to change the HTML source code dynamically. You can add new features or simply modify the attributes of existing tags. A revolutionary opportunity!

For instance, with DHTML you can have bitmapped anchors that look like buttons when pressed and released. To get this result, you no longer need specialized components such as ActiveX controls. Now, it can all be done in pure DHTML code.

The end point of this discussion is the reusability of HTML source code. Have you got the idea? You're given the opportunity to write powerful and commercial-quality code that can manipulate the structure and the events of any page at its leisure. It does it by adding, replacing and removing everything—from ActiveX controls to scripts, and from text to images and links.

So why not try to encapsulate these routines into reusable pieces of code? When a development language grows beyond a certain threshold, as for the number of basic objects and its general complexity, it poses the problem of writing really reusable code.

With the addition of DHTML object model, HTML has undoubtedly exceeded this limit. As a consequence, you cannot keep on cut-and-pasting handy utilities every time you need them: you need a quicker, easier and more elegant solution.

As you've probably guessed, scriptlets are just this: a clean, terse, and pretty cool way of designing full HTML objects, built on the top of DHTML object model.

Designing stand-alone Objects with DHTML

Let's now look at a concrete example of the power of DHTML, one where the need for code reusability arises and becomes a central issue. We'll then look at how scriptlets and scriptlet programming can start to solve our problems.

A few lines above, we stated that, using DHTML, you can have, say, bitmapped anchors that behave like buttons when pressed and released. Furthermore, the bitmap might be replaced to denote a 'hot' or disabled state—behaving exactly as the flat toolbars in many Windows 95 programs do.

How can we do this? Let's say you're using a bitmap as an anchor to reference something. No matter, at this point, whether it is a link to a paragraph inside the same page, to a remote URL or to another HTML page. What's important is that now you have a bitmap that represents a clickable object. In fact, when you move the mouse over it, the mouse pointer changes to the usual pointing-hand.

Suppose you are unsatisfied with it and want something more. At the moment, you have a simple clickable bitmap that sends you on to another page, as in the following picture.

You can download or run this page from our Web site at:
`http://rapid.wrox.uk.com/books/138X`

If you run the page and move the mouse over the WROX logo, you get something like the next picture, which is not standard behavior for a simple bitmap anchor: the picture raises itself, like a toolbar button:

The practical effect is the same as the usual underlined **hyperlink**, but a bitmap can be far more expressive than just a word. However, while the classic hyperlink is recognized all over the world, and is universally known as a clickable string, our bitmapped anchor is not. Or rather, not yet! For the moment, though, we just want to enhance its interaction with the user, making it a bit more responsive and lively. The model is the flat buttons of the new Windows toolbars: they seem to be static bitmaps, but animate and react when the mouse goes over them. A similar effect can be obtained even without DHTML. However, by using DHTML we can prepare it to be a scriptlet, reusable as a component in any other HTML page with just a line of code.

Exploiting DHTML events

DHTML exposes a number of events, and bubbles them up to any identifiable object. So if you want to catch a system notification, such as **onclick**, **onmouseup**, **onmouseover** and the like, when it occurs over a given object within the page, then you first have to give that object a unique ID. Such IDs may be numbers as well as descriptive strings. Usually, they are made up of a single word, like a Visual Basic control's name. Let's take a look at a small portion of the HTML code for the page seen above:

```
<html>
<head>
<title>Bitmapped Anchor Sample</title>
</head>
<body background="Tao.gif">

<p align="center">
<font face="Tahoma">
```

```
    The following object is a &quot;<strong>Bitmapped Anchor</strong>&quot; written
    in pure HTML code.
    </font>
    </p>

    <p align="center">
    <a href="anchor.htm">
    <img id="anchor" src="wrox1.gif" border="0">
    </a>
    </p>

    <p align="center">
    <font face="Tahoma">
    Try clicking on it and see what happens!
    </font>
    </p>

    </body>
    </html>
```

In the sample, the page simply links to itself, (provided the page is called a**nchor.htm**, but this is not at all a problem: just have the **href** property point elsewhere!) The most interesting part of this page is the following lines:

```
    <a href="anchor.htm">
    <img id="anchor" src="wrox1.gif" border="0">
    </a>
```

We defined an anchor around an image. The image is inserted using the **<IMG>** tag, as usual. We assigned this image an ID, in this case **anchor**. All over the page, this image can be referred to by means of it. But what would need to refer to this image, or any other element in the page? Elementary: the scripts!

Scripting comes into play when it's time to respond to events. Of course, this is exactly what we want our anchor to do. Wouldn't it be nice if the anchor itself was capable of reacting when the mouse passes over it, or when it gets pressed or released?

Isn't it true that this way such an anchor would begin to resemble a real—and above all, custom—object, rather than an ordinary HTML hyperlink?

But there is more! Let's expand our example:

```
    <html>
    <head>
    <title>Bitmapped Anchor Sample</title>
    </head>
    <script language="vbscript" for="anchor" event="onmousedown">
      anchor.src="wrox_down.gif"
    </script>
    <script language="vbscript" for="anchor" event="onmouseup">
      anchor.src="wrox_up.gif"
    </script>
    <script language="vbscript" for="anchor" event="onmouseout">
      anchor.src="wrox_flat.gif"
    </script>
    <script language="vbscript" for="anchor" event="onmouseover">
      anchor.src="wrox_up.gif"
    </script>

    <body background="Tao.gif">
```

25

```
<p align="center">
<font face="Tahoma">
The following object is a &quot;<strong>Bitmapped Anchor</strong>&quot; written
in pure HTML code.
</font>
</p>

<p align="center">
<a href="anchor.htm">
<img id="anchor" src="wrox_flat.gif" border="0">
</a>
</p>

<p align="center">
<font face="Tahoma">Try clicking on it and see what happens!
</font>
</p>

</body>
</html>
```

We've only added a few lines to the previous HTML page, all of which relate to event handling. We're basically interested in four different events:

- **onmousedown**
- **onmouseup**
- **onmouseover**
- **onmouseout**

We need to trace when the mouse is pressed or released over the element and when it enters or leaves the same area. All these events have been defined in the DHTML object model and are bubbled up from the element that has the event to its parent objects.

Responding to move events

As you can see, we don't need to do much responding to the events. To animate the anchor, all that we need to do is replace its bitmap as it responds to events .

The above picture shows four images we could use to simulate an animated push button. The second picture is the button's normal state, the third is its depressed state and the fourth is the 'raised' button you get when the mouse pointer is over the button. The first bitmap is useless at the moment, since it renders the anchor in a disabled state. (The reasons for this will soon become clear, so stay tuned!)

The picture presents the bitmaps side by side as if they form a single image. This happens sometimes in Windows programming through a common control called 'imagelist'. Such a component allows you to pack multiple little bitmaps into a single file. However, here we used such a notation only for ease of presentation. DHTML doesn't allow us to access portions of a single image as we could using Win32. Thus, in the code we're using bitmaps as distinct files.

```vbscript
<script language="vbscript" for="anchor" event="onmouseover">
anchor.src="wrox_up.gif"
</script>
```

The standard look of the anchor is given by the file **wrox_flat.gif**, which is transparent with respect to white—that is, no white pixels get drawn. When the mouse is moving over the anchor, IE4 fires the event **onmouseover**, which is handled by the code above. The **for** and **event** clauses link the code to the occurrence of the given event on the given element. The element is identified via its ID.

Changing the image is very easy, and is accomplished by:

```
anchor.src="wrox_up.gif"
```

The **src** property contains the name of the image to display for the **<IMG>** element. Each time it gets modified by the user, it causes an immediate refresh of the page. The effect is visible in the next figure.

With a little graphic work, you can simulate a pop-out frame around the image. Apparently, we simply draw a frame directly on the window's device context. Instead, we replace the bitmap with an identical one that includes the frame.

To get transparency, use GIF files, and set the transparency option when creating them. As you can see, the files we're using have a common background color. That color is set as the transparent color for the image. This means that when drawing the image IE4 will ignore all the pixels of that color. Consequently, any area in the image with such a color will result transparent with respect to the page background!

When the mouse exits, we're notified of an **onmouseout** event. The only thing that changes is the name of the bitmap. In this case, we've simply restored the original image.

27

Responding to click events

A mouse click is composed of two distinct events: a mouse-down and a mouse-up. Sometimes you just want to know about the global event (the click), but here we need more detailed information. We will keep on replacing bitmaps but we do need to distinguish between **onmousedown** and **onmouseup**. In the first case, we want such an effect to produce:

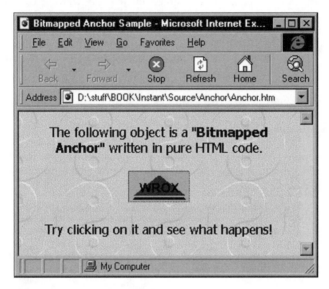

Responding to the mouse-up notification we don't restore the original bitmap, but the raised one, because the mouse is still over the element.

What is scripting for?

Technically speaking, what we have just designed and implemented is an enhancement of a normal HTML page, which exploits the power of the DHTML object model. It puts together and manipulates standard elements, in order to give us some non-standard, and even useful, behaviors. So, how does scripting relate to this?

Scripting languages are the glue for manipulating and automating these system objects. Thanks to the open architecture of the ActiveX Scripting engine, IE4 allows you to use literally any scripting language you may know. In fact, you can use and mix VBScript, JavaScript, Perl, maybe Python, or even Rexx, for writing scripts to be used in DHTML documents. This is not at all a secondary consideration, especially in the context of large scale Web-based projects. In addition, the language-independence is a precise requirement of the W3C, the standards authority for DHTML.

As you probably already know, IE4 only natively supports VBScript and JScript, which is Microsoft's implementation of JavaScript and is nearly identical to it. To find out more about both JScript and VBScript you might check the respective Web sites at:

`http://www.microsoft.com/jscript`
`http://www.microsoft.com/vbscript`

To be able to exploit other scripting languages, such as Perl, you need to install a proper parser DLL which supports the interfaces required by the ActiveX Scripting engine. Of course, to have your script code executed on other machines you should make sure that the same engine is installed on them.

It's worth asking 'what can scripting do for me?' Scripting plays a fundamental role in enhancing DHTML documents with customized and built-in behaviors. Don't forget that scripting lets you do what you want to do with your pages.

Combining scripts and objects

When programming, you have two distinct players on the ground: scripting and standard DHTML objects. By combining them, you can get attractive, useful behaviors from your pages. The previous example demonstrates just this.

Unfortunately, though, if you want to reuse that bitmapped anchor in another DHTML document, you have to cut-and-paste at least the four `<SCRIPT>` tags. Furthermore, some other minor code adjustments are also required, since you should adapt the scripts to the specific `<IMG>` tag they link to. In fact, it's reasonable to expect that a different ID is involved, and—above all—different images.

Scripts and DHTML objects are a powerful mixture, but we all need a better way to allow us to express and exploit their potential. Earlier we deliberately often used the term "behavior". In particular, at the beginning of this paragraph there's a sentence that sounds like this

> *By combining* [scripts and objects], *you can get attractive, useful behaviors from your pages.*

It's a great truth. Until you have more powerful and flexible tools, the best that you can get from your DHTML pages is specialized behaviors. Passing from document to document you can reproduce them, even quickly and easily, but nothing more than this. In fact, 'reproducing a behavior' is like cut-and-paste, and is more akin to recycling than reusing.

Instead, what we need is **object-oriented reusability**, which will allow us to build self-contained components by marrying up scripting and DHTML.

Introducing Scriptlets

A bitmapped anchor that behaves as shown above is conceptually quite a new object. From HTML's point of view, however, it could also be considered as an extended tag. Whatever you think, however, such a component is something that plugs into your pages and makes them richer.

If you think it over, it's easy to enumerate feasible properties and methods for it. For example, we can surely have some picture attributes, and a Boolean flag to let us know whether the anchor is enabled or disabled. In addition, we could endow it with the capability of changing state programmatically, passing from normal to highlighted and pressed. Finally, we can require it to fire specific events (say, at every state change) or reflect the DHTML standard events such as **onmousedown**, **onmouseup**, and the like.

Believe it or not, what we've just outlined is exactly the public interface of a scriptlet component.

What does "Scriptlet" mean?

What is a scriptlet? A scriptlet is what the word itself suggests. That is, it's a small software component made up of script code, written in a variety of languages. It exploits the facilities of the DHTML object model (as our bitmapped anchor does) in order to set up meaningful behavior. They are not like Windows DLLs or more generic libraries, which are collections of exported and reusable functions. Scriptlets, however, are a collection of **<SCRIPT>** tags hosted in the same HTML page.

In our bitmapped anchor example, to specify such a behavior we added an **<IMG>** tag and a bunch of related **<SCRIPT>** tags. If we want to move that component elsewhere, then we need to export just the images and scripts. So what about writing a new HTML page with this content only and attempting to host it elsewhere?

Reusability the Scriptlets way

Scriptlets reusability is obtained in the same way as the reusability of ActiveX controls. That is, you write a component with a specific behavior and host it wherever such a behavior is needed. A component has properties and methods to be driven and events to notify changes in its state. To write a scriptlet, you write a traditional HTML page and add all the script code that is required. To embed, and actually reuse, a scriptlet component, you simply refer to that HTML page in almost the same way as you refer to an ActiveX control. The scriptlet's source code is hidden in the page. So you don't need to rewrite it and can now reuse that functionality in a comfortable object-based fashion.

Scriptlets are mostly Web solutions, authored with HTML and script, that content providers can use as a component in their Web applications. It's an innovative technology that also enables Web authors to use the languages they already know to create powerful cross-platform Web components.

Scriptlets are all this, but with the introduction of Active Desktop and with the upcoming Windows 98, they can also be employed to arrange small desktop and Intranet-based goodies and utilities, as we demonstrate in Chapter 8. For example, you can customize a shared folder writing a DHTML layer that hides the underlying data.

Overview of the Scriptlets Architecture

Scripting components (from which the name Scriptlet comes) provide you with an easy but powerful way to create controls from Web pages that use Microsoft DHTML. Web pages are actually HTML files. You can use scriptlets as you would use ordinary controls in pages viewed with IE4, and in development environments such as Visual Basic or Visual InterDev as well.

A scriptlet is composed of one or more HTML pages and may include anything you can embed: mostly images, but also controls, other Web pages, marquees, sounds, and applets. It is based on DHTML and you can use it anywhere that accepts ActiveX controls.

Basically, a scriptlet is an HTML-compliant document with the usual **.htm** extension, which may also be viewed as a stand-alone page with enabled Web browsers. The screenshot below shows IE4 putting one of Microsoft's demo scriptlets through its paces. The file is **calendar.htm**. You can download this file from the Microsoft Web site (**http://www.microsoft.com/scripting**) or from our site, at the usual address.

In the next figure, however, you can see the same `calendar.htm` file treated as a real scriptlet—that is, hosted in another HTML page which is acting as a container.

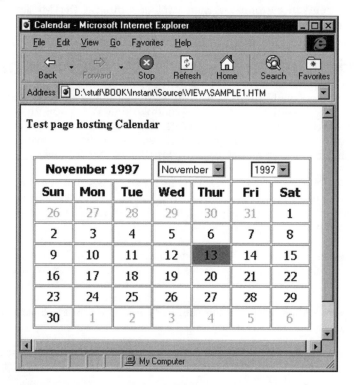

The scriptlet is a complete Web-ready HTML document, including some additional information that allows you to work with it as a control. This means, for instance, that it exposes properties you can get and set, methods you can call, events you can hook to, and so on.

Scriptlets and automation

Scriptlets are based on the DHTML object model in the sense that they are capable of exploiting the features of this model. Nobody prevents you from writing scriptlets that do something else. Anything that can be packaged into a Web component could be packaged as a scriptlet, because the DHTML object model lends itself to being driven from external objects. Such objects might be WebBrowser-based executables (written using Visual Basic or C++) as well as other HTML pages.

Actually, the key point of scriptlets is not to let you drive the DHTML elements from another page. The point is to let developers provide an abstraction layer over some DHTML implementation.

Basically, the idea behind scriptlets is to abstract away DHTML functionality and expose a public interface for the component you are building with DHTML. So the final goal is to let you provide a self–contained component based on

DHTML features. This component can then be automated in the usual object-oriented manner through its public interface made of properties and methods.

After all, DHTML is like a low-level but object-oriented Application Programming Interface (API) while scriptlets are software components built on top of it. This is a very important distinction and the heart of how scriptlets work.

Viewing Scriptlets as stand-alone files

Since scriptlets are pure HTML (and even ASP) files you might think they are immediately visible, although not functional, through any browser. Alas, this is not altogether true.

As you probably know, making pages display properly on a variety of browsers is an endless struggle, and may be an intractable problem not so different from some famous ones from combinatorial analysis.

Yes, scriptlets are Web pages, but if you don't take any reasonable precautions, even IE4 fails to display them as stand-alone documents without errors.

Furthermore, a scriptlet often needs to be initialized via scripting to become significant and start working as you would expect. If you ask Internet Explorer to show it, it's likely you will get an empty page.

Safe-display Scriptlets

The problem lies in the fact that scriptlets exploit a specific property of the **window** object, which is the root of the IE4 Scripting Object Model. IE4 only initializes this property properly if the page contains a scriptlet. Consequently, when the scriptlet is displayed as a normal Web page, sooner or later it will attempt to access an inconsistent or undefined object causing the browser to complain.

The message box doesn't reveal which is the missing property or method. It is **window.external** which makes the difference between the scriptlets and the traditional HTML pages.

Such an error only occurs with scriptlets that are not safe for display. And, of course, if you attempt to view them with browsers other than IE4.

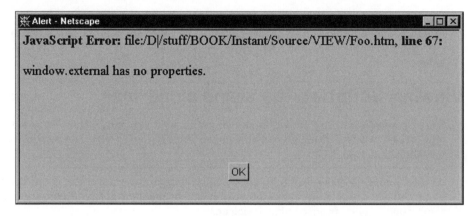

To avoid these error messages you should be careful while accessing objects in your scriptlets code. We'll be covering this aspect in more detail later.

Scriptlet Pros and Cons

As with everything, scriptlets have pros and cons. There are good reasons to take them into careful account, and as many excellent reasons to avoid them. It's up to you to decide time after time what to do. We can't hope to give an exhaustive coverage: our only goal is to provide you with some of the most evident features, whatever they are.

Undoubtedly, scriptlets are simple, and easy to write and maintain. The prerequisites are limited to a basic knowledge of the DHTML object model, and familiarity with a scripting language. This is not a strong constraint, and the same requirements hold true for any HTML developer. You have no need to learn complex, though powerful, programming languages. Above all, if you're already an expert scripter you have no need for further knowledge. You're already up and running!

Scriptlets may be used wherever ActiveX controls are accepted and also provide an efficient way to embed DHTML documents in your desktop applications. They're certainly small, often less than half the smallest ActiveX controls, but not as fast as binary executables. Scriptlets, however, are an excellent way to help you in transferring the graphical capabilities and metaphor of Web page metaphor to your applications, giving them a new, and richer, user interface.

Finally, due to the extreme simplicity of the scripts, you can also use scriptlets to prototype controls that you intend to develop further with other, more specific, tools, like the Microsoft Active Template Library (ATL). Assembling a scriptlet never takes long, so you can test ideas with the same ease you draft forms and dialogs with Visual Basic.

Because scriptlets allow you to define properties, methods and events exactly as ordinary ActiveX controls, it's easy for you to define and tune their public interface. Then, when you have finished, you certainly have a better understanding of the design required, and can start working in other environments that ensure better performance, or give you any other benefit you may need.

On the other hand, scriptlets are made of pure text and don't support code protection or licensing. They easily lend themselves to undesired code inspection and modifications. More, development tools that really make programming scriptlets a snap are still to come.

Why You Should Use Scriptlets

In the previous paragraph we've given an overview of the main advantages and disadvantages of scriptlets. Now we'd like to go on in a bit more detail, trying to answer the questions that a developer might reasonably ask. The first one is certainly: "OK, I'm a Web developer used to writing JavaScript and/or VBScript code. Why do I need scriptlets?"

Not all developers really need scriptlets. However, it's not just Web developers that may need to take a closer look at them. Scriptlets may also be of some use to Visual C++ and Visual Basic programmers. This is because of the features of the Active Desktop-enhanced shell of Windows 95 and the upcoming Windows 98. Both the new Windows desktop and the system folders have a WebBrowser control in the background. The WebBrowser itself has been improved to support PIDLs, that is, identifiers for the shell's namespace objects, files and folders included. Because of this, you can have HTML pages inside the desktop and the folders. The WebBrowser control, though, is the same as that used by IE4 and supports both DHTML and scriptlets.

This might not sound exciting at first, but it means you can write traditional applications much more easily and seamlessly by adopting and exploiting the Web interface. Your desktop program can be composed of DHTML pages, scripts, images, ActiveX controls, even without an executable module to put it all together. Not to mention what you could do in terms of Intranet facilities.

On the other hand, if you're developing Assembly code and are used to spending all your time squeezing even the last byte from the machine, well, it's quite unlikely you need to learn about scriptlets.

Before deciding, consider the following points.

Simplicity and Ease

You write scriptlets using script languages and have no need to know any other programming language. This is a really good thing if you aren't an expert programmer, but it is not even a primary and decisive reason for adopting or not adopting scriptlets. In fact, to give scriptlets a good and useful design you need to be a bit familiar with the basic concepts of object-oriented programming and hold some notions of software components internals. However, don't get this wrong: simplicity and ease are an advantage.

35

In addition, your entire cycle of editing, compiling and debugging takes a really short time to complete. Furthermore, in most cases it is all reduced to saving and refreshing the page by pressing F5. You have a text editor opened in a window and IE4 in the background. Edit the code, save, switch to another window, press F5, and *voilà, les jeux son faits*! Easier and faster than Visual Basic and Delphi too. Because of this, you can also seriously consider scriptlets for prototyping ActiveX controls.

Expressiveness

For the very first time it is possible to write reusable HTML code. This is an aspect of primary importance in any large-scale Web-oriented project. Furthermore, this reusability is obtained in the best and most understandable way: by means of components. With scriptlets, you take advantage of all the power and the richness of the DHTML object model and shape components that logically extend the standard collection of objects offered. Scriptlets are a layer of code that hides the details of HTML and DHTML making it easier for you to develop your Web code.

Maintenance and Usability

Scriptlets can be used everywhere, both on Web pages and Windows folders. They are pure ASCII text, so you don't need sophisticated tools to maintain them. The intrinsic simplicity of the script code decreases the level of maintenance. Outside HTML documents, scriptlets require a specialized ActiveX control to be inserted, say, in Visual Basic forms.

Why You Shouldn't Use Scriptlets

What constitutes a certain advantage—that is, being composed of text and not binary code—is also a drawback, for at least a couple of reasons. First and foremost, performance! The browser needs to interpret them and this tends to slow down the execution time. Second, clear source code is dangerous from the perspective of reusable and distributable components. Anyone can spy on your code, be they authorized or not. But, putting aside this aspect of security, human readable code means that anyone can attempt to read the code and modify it, sometimes introducing errors.

Another key point is the accessibility of scriptlets from different browsers. This is a factor that might prejudice their wide market's acceptance.

Code protection and distribution

Scriptlets have a double role: they are not only HTML pages but also software components. These two roles are a bit antithetical. While a Web document is made of pure text and must be coded as simply as possible, a software component is unreadable by construction. While a page is written to be duplicated, a software component is not! Being clear and readable means that someone can modify it too. Sometimes such updates might be unauthorized and even harmful to the code's robustness.

If scriptlets become a standard, then it will open up an entirely new market for developers. This scenario, however, poses a serious problem. How to safely license and distribute scriptlets while protecting and safeguarding both the users and the developers? When it comes to this, I think, something will have to change. What about compiled and digitally signed scriptlets?

In addition, a scriptlet may contain references to a collection of files (video, images, sounds, controls, other scriptlets or HTML pages). At the moment, though, you have to rely on your own memory to keep track of the file names the scriptlet requires, and call a generic utility to create cabinets or ZIP files.

We will come back to all these topics later in the book. In particular, we'll be discussing packaging and distributing scriptlets in Chapter 14.

Browser Compatibility

At the time of writing, another great point against scriptlets is their lack of transferability between different browsers. Unlike DHTML—which will become an accepted standard worldwide—for the moment scriptlets are Microsoft's technology and a feature specific to IE4. If you're writing Web-based software today, and want to take advantage of scriptlets, then you should be ready to renounce all the users that haven't upgraded yet to IE4. Netscape Navigator, Internet Explorer 3.x and even the preliminary versions of IE4, don't support scriptlets. Depending on how you write your scriptlets and the pages that actually host them, this may result in error messages. More often, however, scriptlets are simply ignored.

Developing multi-browser Web pages is not at all a trivial task. Scriptlets and DHTML are certainly the future—maybe the mid-term future—but I don't think they should be the immediate choice for everyone. This personal anecdote pretty well demonstrates what I'm saying.

I received an e-mail from a guy who attended one of the classes I regularly teach. He was asking me about the JavaScript's Image object which Internet Explorer's JScript didn't support until JScript 3.0, in the final release of IE4. I unsuccessfully suggested that he use DHTML and scriptlets to work around the specific problem, which was obtaining an animated button, not so different from the bitmapped anchor we've discussed above. To all my suggestions, he always replied "Yes, maybe you're right. But I want an audience as wide as possible, and want it now."

Authoring tools

At the time of writing, there are no authoring tools that provide you with full support for scriptlets. You can use normal text editors and type in all the HTML code manually or rely on more specialized tools such as ActiveX Control Pad. Microsoft FrontPage 97 and FrontPad Express are of course insufficient to support DHTML and scriptlets. Microsoft FrontPage 98—the first product that supports DHTML— has been released recently, and the new Visual InterDev product provides something closer to the Visual Studios that C++ and VB programmers have access to.

Make up your mind

We dedicated this paragraph to presenting and discuss the advantages and disadvantages of scriptlets. Perhaps, at this point, you're expecting a definite answer. Should we or should we not use scriptlets? Well, you ought to become familiar with scriptlets as soon as possible. However, this does not necessarily mean that you have to start writing them tomorrow. Scriptlets are a good solution and response to a precise requirement. They can grow and even eventually replace ActiveX controls, at least on Web pages. At the moment, there some points that need to be fixed, or improved, or simply fine-tuned. This will change and, judging from what we can see today, the answer to scriptlets is certainly positive.

Scriptlets versus ActiveX Controls

Apart from being made up of script and DHTML code, scriptlets can seem to be similar to ordinary ActiveX controls. To be honest, there are a number of substantial differences if you look at the implementation level. Nevertheless, ActiveX controls and scriptlets share a common idea and a common baseline. This makes them nearly identical to the users' eyes. In fact, the way you program them and the way you embed them in HTML pages is similar. It seems that scriptlets have been designed to become, sooner or later, a Web counterpart of ordinary ActiveX controls.

In this paragraph, we're going to examine and compare them. We aren't aiming to find and proclaim a winner. Our goal is simpler: just to let you know about differences and similarities.
Four areas are under examination:

 Implementation

 Compatibility

 Security

 Deployment

Compatibility and Security are also discussed in more detail, and from a wider viewpoint, later in the chapter. Deployment will be the subject of a chapter in our Advanced Topics section, at the end of the book and implementing scriptlets is of course the subject of the book!

Here, we'll focus on the impact these topics may have on scriptlets, especially in comparison with ActiveX controls.

Design, Structure and Implementation

When comparing scriptlets and ActiveX controls, the first, great, difference that strikes you is the languages you can use to develop them. ActiveX controls can be written in a variety of programming languages, including Visual Basic, C/C++, Delphi, and Visual J++. In addition, you can use specialized frameworks or class libraries such as MFC or ATL. Put another way, to develop ActiveX controls, you have a wide range of heterogeneous tools to rely on.

With scriptlets, things are slightly different. While you have the same facilities as regards languages, there aren't yet any powerful tools available for developing code. Of course, this is perfectly natural and comprehensible at the moment, since scriptlets are a new entry in the software components market.

To write your own scriptlets, you can use any scripting (not programming) languages that you know. From this point of view, therefore, scriptlets and ActiveX controls offer a similar degree of flexibility.

Furthermore, scriptlets aren't binary and don't require compiling and linking. Anyone can look at the underlying code without restrictions.

Designing a scriptlet is much the same process as designing a control. The interface they expose to the user is identical, as is the make up of properties, methods and events. So you concentrate on the functionality to provide and try to express it through a public interface. The nature and the structure of this programming interface is deliberately analogous.

To a Web developer, it isn't really significant whether the component he or she's using is an ActiveX control or a scriptlet.

Internal Structure

ActiveX controls are far more complex and require the implementation of some basic functions to handle aspects like embedding, licensing, in-place activation, and so on. Often, however, many of these aspects are hidden by the frameworks and the classes a programmer might be using.

With scriptlets you don't necessarily have to see all this stuff. Writing a scriptlet is somewhat akin writing an ActiveX control with a high-level tool such as Visual Basic 5. What you really need to take care of is the set of properties and methods to be exposed.

Usually, a scriptlet has a user interface given by the elements listed in the **<BODY>** section. Visual Basic controls, instead, are commonly formed by constituent controls that lie in the **UserControl** object. The activity of both the scriptlets and the Visual Basic-based ActiveX controls consists mostly in coordinating the functionality provided by the internal components.

Event implementation

One difference between controls and scriptlets comes in the notification of events. In both cases, the programmer calls a **RaiseEvent** function, but the results are different. All the custom events fired by scriptlets are routed to their respective recipients via a unique channel. That is, scriptlets always trigger the same event whose specific name is carried with the data associated with it. Ordinary ActiveX controls, instead, have a set of different events, each one with its own data. A user application that sinks scriptlets events should define a unique handler and distinguish between the various events with a multiple **if** or a **Select Case** statement.

On the other hand, a program that needs to reply to an ActiveX control's notifications will define a number of different handlers.

Object's Identification and Registration

As well as their internal structure, ActiveX controls have an external layer of code to provide identification, registration, and licensing. Nothing of the kind is supported by scriptlets. ActiveX controls are supposed to be uniquely identified throughout the whole world. Each control is identified with a 128-bit value, familiarly known as CLSID, which is guaranteed to be unique for a zillion of years to come. (Of course, CLSIDs are unique if, and only if, you have special routines and utilities to generate them!)

ActiveX controls need to be copied on to a computer and correctly registered. Again, the best way to do this is using proper functions or utilities, provided with all the development tools.

Scriptlets, instead, are identified by name and have no need of registry manipulation. If you want to uninstall a scriptlet from your computer, then just delete its file. (A scriptlet, in fact, can be made of more files, be they other nested scriptlets, GIF images, ActiveX controls or anything else you can include in a DHTML page.) If you want it to work on your machine, then just make a copy. No further tasks are required.

This may be seen as an advantage as well as a disadvantage. It makes dealing with scriptlets a lot easier and quicker, but also limits their commercial application.

Size and performance

Compiled code offers, on average, better performance and doesn't require runtime interpreters. However, ActiveX controls are rarely slim. Let's consider a control developed with Visual Basic. Its apparent size is about 20 or 30 KB, so you could say it's a really small and light component. A Visual Basic control, however, to work properly requires the Visual Basic virtual machine—which is the file **msvbvm50.dll** with a size of over 1.3 MB! In most cases, this file is unnecessary, since it is a widespread module you can find in almost every **Windows\System** directory as the result of previous downloads or other program installations.

The same holds true for controls developed with MFC, whose shared library requires over 1 MB of memory and disk space. Sometimes you can specify to avoid calls to dynamic libraries, but encompassing the runtime modules considerably increases the size of the controls.

If you need the slimmest and fastest controls, then you should check out the Active Template Library (ATL) which enables you to create components of about 30 or 40 KB without additional heavy modules.

Scriptlets are composed of pure HTML source code and are much smaller than the corresponding ActiveX controls. The most complex and sophisticated of them can reach 30 KB like the aforementioned calendar scriptlet. More often, scriptlets occupy very few kilobytes. For example, the clock scriptlet that can be downloaded or run from our site (**http://rapid.wrox.co.uk/books/138X**) is about 5 KB.

Signatures and Licensing

Scriptlets have a simple ASCII layout and their code is available to anyone who wants to look at it. This makes code tampering, unauthorized duplication, and all kinds of violation possible. Consider that the source code you're seeing is exactly what makes that module run. If you modify it, changes will apply immediately (although it won't affect the server-held original).

Scriptlets inherit the characteristics of Web pages, which are intended to be public documents. If you don't mind your scriptlets being public software components, then it's alright—just write them and don't worry!

Technically speaking, scriptlets are HTML pages. However, DHTML is just the system API you're using to write them, and VBScript or JavaScript is just your programming language. What you produce is essentially a software component.

It's quite reasonable to expect support for some specific features like digital signatures and licensing in the future. If Microsoft wants scriptlets to become cross-platform Web components, then the next step is mandatory: find out a safe and efficient way to compile and certify scriptlets.

Outside the Windows platform

Scriptlets have two advantages over ordinary ActiveX controls. The first one is their innate structural simplicity. The second point is a little more subtle. The HTML language is a Web standard worldwide. DHTML is supposed to replace it by the end of 1998, when the W3C consortium will hopefully approve that standard.

From then on, DHTML (maybe with slight differences from the current version supported by IE4) will become a new worldwide standard and all the browsers will agree and align to it. Having the DHTML object model available will quickly increase the demand for reusability. And scriptlets will be there, already up and running.

While this isn't a current scenario, it is a reasonable prediction. In this way, scriptlets may well become really cross-platform and cross-browser components, maybe at the expense of ActiveX.

Microsoft is working hard on transferring COM/DCOM over to non-Windows platforms, such as Unix. This will take a lot of effort, and will be very complex. On the other hand, programmers need interoperable, integrated, and possibly cross-platform components. Above all, they need them today, not in the remote future. Furthermore, these components should be portable and exploitable across the Internet, through the widest possible range of browsers. Specific technologies like ActiveX or JavaBeans all have pros and cons. Moreover, be practical. Are you really sure that there will ever come a time when Microsoft, Sun, Netscape, and other vendors, will agree on a unique and general standard for components? We don't think so.

41

Instead, HTML (followed by DHTML) is the standard. And the scriptlet proposal offers reusability and componentware inside the DHTML standard. Do you have a better idea?

Scriptlets Compatibility

We've just introduced the theme of scriptlet compatibility, and realized that, in a possible upcoming scenario, scriptlets might be eligible for the accolade of the best cross-platform and cross-browser Web components.

At the moment, however, scriptlets are supported only by IE4 and are commonly associated with the Windows 9x operating systems. So what about other platforms? This could give us an idea of the audience such a technology could gain.

We all agree that making COM/DCOM compatible with Unix, or wherever, is a huge task. Instead, it sounds much more doable to make an application run outside the Windows platforms.

This is exactly what's going on with IE4. IE4, in fact, is expected to support DHTML and scriptlets on Windows 9x, Windows NT, Windows 3.1, Unix, Macintosh, and even Windows CE. So scriptlets and DHTML are not tied to Windows in any way.

On the other hand, at the moment (repeat, at the moment) scriptlets and DHTML are strictly tied to IE4 as the browser. However, it's quite likely that this will change soon.

Security Considerations

A software component is marked safe for scripting and initialization if the author ensures that there's no way to use it to cause damage. A software component, like an ActiveX control, can be activated in two ways when viewed through a browser:

 Via scripting

 Via initialization parameters

Safe for scripting means that the control isn't exposing automation methods and properties that can harm the end user's computer. So when IE4 displays a page containing that component, it feels free to execute scripts. Another way of using components is through initialization. By the means of the **<PARAM VALUE>** tags you can set some of the component's properties upon loading. This may result in some damage for the end user. To avoid this, you should declare your component safe for initialization on having IE4 load it properly.

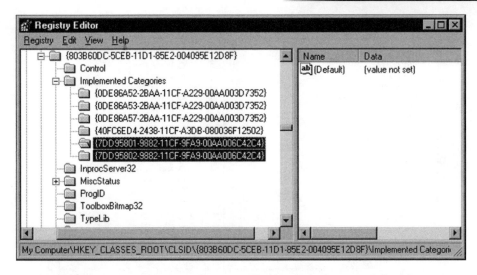

As the above picture shows, marking a control safe is a matter of adding a couple of entries to the registry. The two highlighted lines are those responsible for making any ActiveX control safe.

Scriptlet security

Scriptlets are HTML pages with script code that automatically downloads to your computer and executes. Therefore, they pose security problems, like any other ActiveX control. To prevent this, IE4 allows you to define different levels of security. They are:

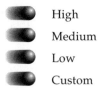

- High
- Medium
- Low
- Custom

Each of these levels has some default settings for potentially risky actions, such as downloading files or executing scripts. What IE4 actually does depends upon these settings.

The security features built into IE4 divide the Web into four zones. You can assign a security level to each one. Scriptlets will be downloaded to your computer only if they're coming from a server that you consider trustworthy. To enable scriptlets, set the security level for the specific server they reside on to Medium or Low. Unless you change something in the default settings, any Web server has a medium level of protection.

Furthermore, be sure to accept ActiveX controls marked safe for scripting and to prompt the user on controls that may be unsafe for scripting as well as initialization. The next two screenshots show just this.

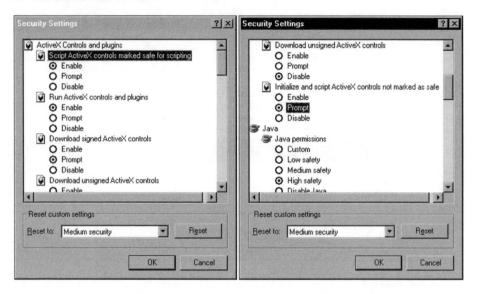

These settings ensure that scriptlets will work properly. A level of Medium or Low is also required for all the child components of a scriptlet.

Security issues are strictly tied to the security zones, which are a new feature of IE4.

Internet Security Zones

Security zones may be seen as a partition of the entire Web. There are sites that you feel can be trusted, and others that you evaluate as unreliable. You would therefore apply different security settings to them. The policy one-setting-fits-all is not so flexible and smart. Security zones have been introduced to fill this gap.

All the files you can receive and access belong to one of the four main areas:

Local Intranet

Trusted Sites

Internet Zone

Restricted Site

For the sake of generality, you can add the local files (My Computer) to these. Different security settings can apply to any of these four areas. Local Intranet includes all the documents that aren't local to the machine but accessible through a local network. Trusted and Restricted Sites enumerate a number of Web sites addresses. You can add or remove sites from these lists with IE4, using the menu command View| Internet Options| Security or by right-clicking the IE4 shortcut on the desktop and selecting Properties| Security. All the Internet addresses that don't belong to both Trusted and Restricted zone are by default part of the generic Internet Zone.

While talking of medium, high or low security level, we're addressing a collection of specific actions for which you have three options:

⬤ Enable

⬤ Prompt

⬤ Disable

Enable means that the action executes silently. Prompt requires a confirmation, while Disable silently ignores it. This is clear if you look at the previous figures.

Each predefined level has a bunch of settings for specific risky actions. You can also choose to define your own set of options.

Applying settings to zones

Each Internet zone has a different level of security that you can adapt to your own needs. By default, they are:

Zones	Security Level
Local Intranet	Medium
Trusted Sites	Low
Internet Zone	Medium
Restricted Sites	High
My Computer	------

IE4 shows the zone from which the document you're currently viewing is coming on the status bar. In the table above, we've added also a fifth zone, called My Computer, which encompasses all the local files.

Local files are considered inherently safe by IE4, and security checks never apply to them. Furthermore, you can't add local files or folders to any of the Internet security zones.

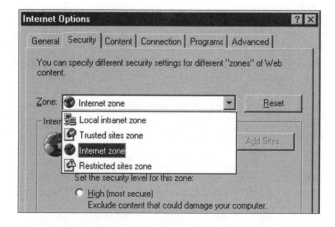

Scriptlets are downloaded to your computer only if their original Web server belongs to a zone whose security setting is Medium or Low. If you maintain the IE4 default settings, and put a Web site in the black list of the Restricted Zone, then you won't be able to get scriptlets from there. In fact, the default security level is High for Restricted sites. No matter the zone to which the site belongs, what really matters is its security level.

For instance, if you turn the level for Restricted Sites to Medium then you always get scriptlets from everywhere. Of course, the opposite is also true. If you turn the security level of your local Intranet to High, then IE4 never accesses scriptlets on any of the connected machines.

Using Custom Settings

If you're using standard security levels (High, Medium, Low) then you just have to make sure that the level of the desired site is Medium or Low. What if you're using custom settings for any of the zones? In this case, to have scriptlets working properly just enable IE4 to accept ActiveX controls marked safe and to prompt or accept those marked as unsafe.

Why don't scriptlets execute if you have a High level of protection? Because then, by default, IE4 ignores controls not marked safe for scripting. From IE4's point of view, scriptlets are just unmarked controls.

Development Tools

Today, scriptlets are simply an innovative technology and no tools available offer adequate support for them. This is quite reasonable, given the youth of scriptlets. However, the lack of dedicated authoring tools is a shortcoming that should disappear very shortly. But what kind of tools do you need to use them easily right now? And what kind of tools might you need in the future? The latter question might also be rephrased this way: what are the future development guidelines for scriptlets? And how will they evolve?

Let's start by seeing what you need to work with scriptlets today.

Tools You Need today

Since scriptlets are ASCII files, first of all you need a text editor. Notepad is fine, but perhaps we need a more sophisticated tool. ActiveX Control Pad might be a good choice. It is not a visual editor but helps in writing HTML code. It provides you with some facilities like Script Wizard and the ActiveX control dialog. Unfortunately, it doesn't support syntax highlighting.

However, using ActiveX Control Pad with scriptlets isn't of much help because you still have to insert any reference to them manually and also the script code can't be written down via ScriptWizard.

FrontPage 97 and FrontPage Express are both visual tools, but with some important drawbacks. First, they are heavily intrusive and each time you save they rewrite your source code completely. Second, and more important, they don't support DHTML. At first sight, this is not a deficiency. However, if you put together the two characteristics, then you have a great limit. FrontPage modifies the text you typed in, removing unknown and unsupported tag attributes. For example, consider the following simple HTML page

```
<HTML>
<BODY>
Some <B ID=text>text</B>.
</BODY>
</HTML>
```

Type this code into a new document created, say, with Notepad and save it with the **.htm** extension. Then open the same file with FrontPage Express or FrontPage 97 and ask the program to show its HTML source code. What you will see is this:

```
<html>

<head>
<meta http-equiv="Content-Type"
content="text/html; charset=iso-8859-1">
<meta name="GENERATOR" content="Microsoft FrontPage Express 2.0">
<title></title>
</head>

<body>

<p>Some <B ID=text>text</B>.</p>
</body>
</html>
```

Apart from the **<META>** tag and the added empty title, what's really important is that the body changed silently from

```
Some <B ID=text>text</B>.
```

to

```
Some <b>text</b>.
```

You can verify it also by switching between the Original and the Current view.

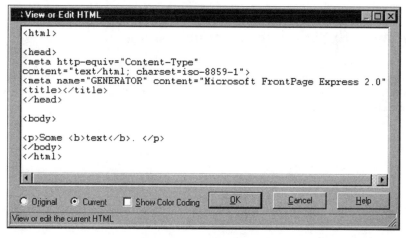

If you view this page with IE4 there are no differences at all. But just enhancing it with some script poses the first problem. For example, try the following

```
<HTML>
<SCRIPT language=VBScript for=text event=onmouseover>
text.style.color="blue"
</SCRIPT>
<SCRIPT language=VBScript for=text event=onmouseout>
text.style.color=""
</SCRIPT>
<BODY>
Some <B ID=text> text</B>.
</BODY>
</HTML>
```

We added two scripts just to change the style of the element identified by **text** when the mouse enters or exits over its area. If you save it with Notepad (or any other editor) and view it with IE4 then the result is what you expect.

Instead, save it with FrontPage and run IE4. Moving the mouse over the text won't produce any effect. What's going on? It's simple. With the best intentions in the world, FrontPage attempts to edit your text, removing what it doesn't understand or finds unusual. The ID attribute isn't supported in FrontPage 97. Consider, also, that the ID story we've just told you is not an exception. What can you do? Frankly, not much. Perhaps using another editor or perhaps upgrading to FrontPage 98—which has corrected this problem.

Writing Scriptlets with Developer Studio

If syntax highlighting is a must for you, then an easy way to get it, together with a non-intrusive save, is using the text editor integrated in the Developer Studio 97 environment. In this way, you can exploit the advanced features of a professional text editor produced just for developers.

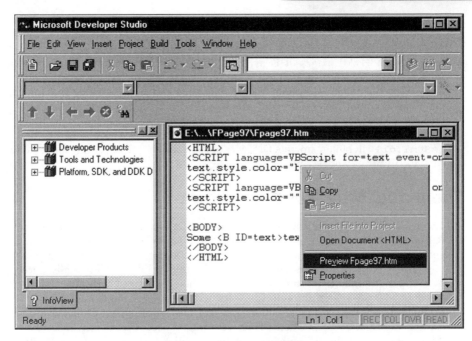

Moreover, since Developer Studio uses a WebBrowser control, you can also have a preview of your page just by switching a window. Another advantage of using DevStudio is the possibility of extending and fully customizing the IDE with add-ins, macros and wizards. You can find a first example of a wizard for creating skeleton scriptlets in the source code that accompanies an article of mine, which appeared in the January 98 issue of Microsoft Interactive Developer (MIND).

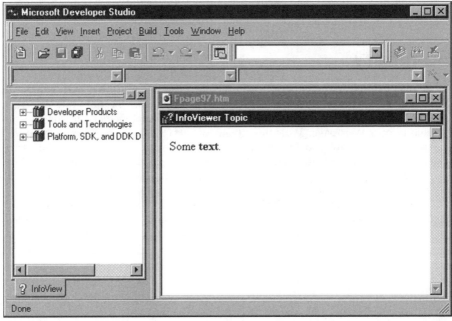

The WebBrowser control

The WebBrowser component is the part of IE4 that allows you to view and interact with HTML pages. It is available as an ActiveX control you might want to include in your Visual Basic or C++ project. It allows you to easily implement document browsing, URL navigation, and hyperlinking. The control maintains its own history list and offers functions to move back and forth through previously visited documents and local or remote folders.

The parsing and rendering of the HTML documents is accomplished by the `MsHtml.dll`. It builds up the DHTML object model, and arranges for hosting ActiveX Controls and scripts.

Tools You May Need in Future

The tools that will help you to work on scriptlets in the future are those that will shape the evolution of scriptlets. In our opinion, topics such as licensing and protection might become a central issue, if scriptlets are to succeed in populating both Web pages and Windows 9x folders. If scriptlets really succeed in becoming standard reusable components, then they must be safely and easily distributable. So a first absolute necessity will be for a compiler in order to produce non-human readable code. This will also allow you to hide licensing or signing information somewhere. Then you might need a packager, able to inform you of all the dependencies of the scriptlet and write down a setup cabinet file. Finally, you might want an editor with some facilities such as a few wizards and toolbars for specific tasks such as inserting certain tags. More, you might expect the IntelliSense support, encompassing all the features of VB5 such as word auto-completion, properties and methods suggestions, tooltips and more—all of which will be available in Visual InterDev 2.0.

As for authoring tools that use scriptlets, what is needed is just an enhanced version of FrontPage's and ActiveX Control Pad's ScriptWizard and a dialog that allows you to pick up and insert scriptlets inside DHTML documents.

Summary

In this chapter, we have shown samples of DHTML code that may evolve into scriptlets. We talked about HTML code reusability and the new role of scripting. Originally, it was nothing more than the glue to put together the constituent objects of a Web page. With the advent of DHTML a Web page has been enriched, and now you can see that it is formed by two basic components: the content and the code to change it. Scripting, therefore, gains another level of importance and becomes more like a programming language, in the sense that it is now capable of producing output that modifies the content and the user interface. The union of DHTML object model and scripts brings scriptlets to light. A second name for scriptlets might have been ActiveX Script Controls, that is ActiveX controls made up purely of VBScript and JavaScript code.

We've gone through the similarities and the differences that feature ActiveX and script components, and provided an overview of what scriptlets actually are. Our goal, in this chapter, was to help you understand the background, rather than the details—which will be covered in the rest of the book. We addressed important topics such as cross-platform and cross-browser compatibility, security and performance. Finally, we outlined some possible guidelines for further enhancements of this technology.

In particular, this chapter covered

- HTML code reusability.
- ActiveX and scriptlets comparison.
- Compatibility and Security.
- The development tools you may use today and may need tomorrow.

Further Reading

Since this is a book whose main topic is scriptlets, it should be quite unlikely to find related topics for which you may need further reading. In fact, we're supposed to give you a complete programmer's reference for scriptlet programming.

However, in this section we'd like to point you in the direction of a couple of references that can constitute a quick tutorial on the subject. While this book is going to cover the same topics in more detail, you may need a brief but complete overview of scriptlet programming, too.

If this is the case, then check out the Cutting Edge column in the January 98 issue of MIND, (Microsoft Internet Developer) where you can read a complete presentation of scriptlets. In particular, it also provides a DevStudio 97 wizard for generating simple scriptlets. Another source of quick-but-complete information is "*Professional IE4 Programming*", written by various authors and published by WROX Press, ISBN 1-861000-70-7. The book includes a chapter dedicated to scriptlets.

Again, if you need to focus on the specific features of the DHTML object model, then what's better than picking up "*Instant IE4 DHTML Programmer's Reference*" ISBN 1-861000-68-5 by Alex Homer and Chris Ullman, also published by WROX Press?

ActiveX controls and categories are well covered by David Chappell in his "*Understanding ActiveX and OLE*" from Microsoft Press. ISBN 1-57231-216-5.

Do you want to know more about the customization features of Developer Studio 97? Then, be sure to check out Steve Zimmerman's "*Extend Developer Studio 97 with Your Own Add-ins, Macros, and Wizards*" in Microsoft Systems Journal (MSJ), September 97.

51

Writing the First Scriptlets

Writing scriptlets is not a difficult task. It is easier, however, if you have the right tools and the right approach. First of all, you should think of scriptlets as normal Web pages hosted in another HTML document, which acts as a container. From this point of view, scriptlets can be considered as ordinary ActiveX controls and, therefore, handled in the same way.

As is explained later in the chapter, scriptlets and controls are inserted in Web pages via the same **<OBJECT>** tag. Some authoring tools—completely unaware of scriptlets—consider them pretty similar.

Like ActiveX controls, scriptlets may have a user interface and can expose an automation interface. In this way they can be driven and forced to serve your own purposes. When designing the host page you assign the scriptlet a client site. At run-time—that is when you view the page through a browser—the area you specified becomes the surface from which the scriptlet will draw some output.

The scriptlet sees this client site as the traditional **window** object defined by the Internet Explorer 4.0 Scripting Object Model.

In this chapter, we'll discuss scriptlet architecture and internal layout in detail. We will also discover how they are hosted and implemented by Internet Explorer 4.0. However, most of the chapter is devoted to understanding the scriptlet public interface—the key aspect that makes them so clean, elegant and generally pretty superb. More specifically, we'll aim to cover the following:

- The internal structure of a scriptlet.
- The scriptlet's public interface with both JavaScript and VBScript.
- How to host scriptlets in Web pages.
- How Internet Explorer 4.0 handles them.

In doing so we present the first, straightforward example of a scriptlet and also take advantage of the chance to discuss hosting and automation. In the next chapter, we will see a more advanced sample together with an automatic tool able to produce skeleton scriptlets.

The Scriptlet's Architecture

Up to this point, we've continually stressed that a scriptlet is nothing more than an HTML page (don't worry—this fact hasn't changed!). So the basic architecture of a scriptlet must follow the general template of a Web page.

```
<HTML>

<HEAD>
  <TITLE>Title of the Scriptlet Component</TITLE>
</HEAD>

<SCRIPT language=VBScript>
' Any scripts needed
</SCRIPT>

<BODY>
Constituent elements of the scriptlet's user interface
</BODY>
</HTML>
```

What is outlined above is the skeleton template of any HTML page. Scriptlets are no different. In the **<BODY>** section you can put anything that can be placed inside a Web page, even nothing at all! The body of a scriptlet will display through the client site at run-time. (Of course, when talking about a Web browser and Web pages, the expression "at run-time" always means "when the page is viewed through the browser".)

So, basically, a scriptlet is a page embedded inside another page. The container works as if it includes an ActiveX control able to display HTML pages. This viewer actually shows the scriptlet page. The script code defined in the container page can refer to the scriptlet by name and can control it via the exposed public interface.

From the scriptlet side, each exposed property or method corresponds to an internal subroutine that executes when the property or the method gets called. The internal procedures are usually written in JavaScript or VBScript and work just like ordinary scripts in an ordinary HTML page. That is, by modifying the state and the style of the constituent objects, firing and receiving events and performing specific tasks.

Now, let's see all this in more detail, starting with the internal layout of a scriptlet.

The Internal Layout of a Scriptlet

If you want to give a very simple description of DHTML documents, then you might say that they are HTML pages that have both content and the code to change it. The content is what is commonly perceived as the page content: text, images, controls, applets, marquees, lines, scripts and so forth. In short, everything that has a visual counterpart on the screen and that you can see and realize the presence of.

Scriptlets conform to this idea extremely well. They have both content and a layer of additional code that satisfies the following requirements:

Being the glue that binds together the constituent elements.

 Making the capabilities of the constituent elements available to the external world.

Inside the scriptlet's code we can distinguish two logically different types of script code. The first is the usual code used to respond to events: clicking, mouse moving, loading and the like. The second is the script code. This encompasses and encapsulates all this into a self-contained wrapper with just a few points of contact to the outside world.

A normal Web page hosts another Web page (the scriptlet) and refers to it through an **<OBJECT>** tag with a couple of special attributes. These attributes allow the browser to distinguish between scriptlets and ActiveX controls. In fact, both are inserted using the same tag: **<OBJECT>**.

From the container's point of view, scriptlets are just like any other component. They have a predefined site with a given width and height. Their entire output never exceeds that space. The container page is completely indifferent as to whether the constituent element is another HTML page or simply a table or an animated GIF.

From the browser standpoint, however, a scriptlet is a special object that needs special treatment. In practice, therefore, a scriptlet needs another instance of the Internet Explorer 4.0 viewer engine that parses the original HTML code, builds the Dynamic HTML object model and makes it available to the scriptlet's internal code. At least under Win32 a scriptlet is actually hosted through the same container object used to view any HTML page throughout Internet Explorer 4.0 (the scriptlet's host page included).

Interacting with the Container

If you want to use a scriptlet in a Web page, it's quite likely that you will want to use it again later. So you need to assign it a name or an ID.

```
<HTML>
<BODY>
<OBJECT ID=MyScriptlet data=myScriptlet.htm type="text/x-scriptlet">
</OBJECT>
</BODY>
</HTML>
```

By using such an ID, you can call it when needed. From now on, the scriptlet is completely and perhaps uniquely identified by this name. Using the usual object-oriented syntax, you can ask the scriptlet to execute some code, accordingly, to its public interface.

Before going on, let's take time out to clarify the previous statement about the possible uniqueness of an object's ID. There are no syntax contraindications if you identify more elements with the same ID throughout a Dynamic HTML page. In this case, of course, you can't pretend that code like the following works well.

```
<script language="VBScript">
Sub SetColorItemByID( sID )
   set obj=document.all.item( sID )      ' obj now may be a collection!
   obj.style.color = "yellow"            ' use obj.item(i).style.color, instead.
End Sub
</script>
```

In fact, if you attempt to get all the items with a given ID, then you could obtain a bit of a collection as well! The DHTML **all** collection can be asked for all the items with a given ID. If this ID is unique, then you are returned a reference to that object. If there are multiple objects with that ID, however, you are returned the collection of the objects. Having a single object or a collection of objects is quite different, of course! Thus, you must handle it with different syntaxes. You could use:

```
obj.style.color
```

to refer a given style property of a single object, while you need to resort to:

```
obj.item(i).style.color
```

to get the same over an object which belongs to a collection.

Having explained this, let's turn back to scriptlets. A scriptlet's public interface is the set of properties, methods and events it declares public and makes available to the callers.

This programming interface basically amounts to the only way to access the scriptlet's internals.

Any call that you make through the scriptlet's programming interface ends up calling an internal script procedure.

The Scriptlet's Public Interface

The body of a scriptlet might be defined at design time, or created dynamically at run-time through the properties and methods publicly exposed to external callers. If a scriptlet has a predefined body, then it will display if you attempt to see it as a stand-alone page (that is opening the scriptlet's HTML file). Sometimes, however, the user interface must be decided at run-time. For example, an animated button will only know at the last moment which image should be displayed. The scriptlet's body contains an empty **<IMG>** tag and if you try to see it as a stand-alone file you'll get a window like the one shown below:

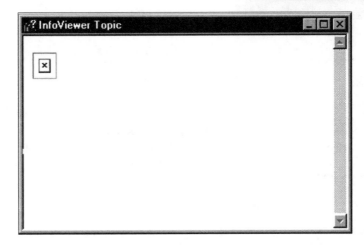

The script code contained in a scriptlet provides the functionality that you require, plus a number of private helper routines that help to give the code a better and more understandable structure.

If you don't need, or don't want, to provide automation capabilities, then a scriptlet is just one page hosted in another. However, this is a short-sighted vision of scriptlets which doesn't really make sense. So finally, we've reached the point and provided a public interface for automation.

When someone examines a scriptlet's property or method the browser passes the control to the scriptlet. Such a call is interpreted and then dispatched to the right internal procedure that does the job.

What, however, does "dispatched to the right procedure" actually mean? Simply, each scriptlet holds a public interface structure, which is, in effect, a sort of table of connections. For each externally callable name there is an internal procedure that gets executed. This is quite similar to what occurs with ActiveX controls. The following is the complete source code for a bare-bones scriptlet. The function **CreateMyScriptlet** defines the public interface of the component. All the methods and the properties listed there are callable outside the scriptlet.

```html
<html>

<head>
<title>Bare-bones Scriptlet</title>
</head>

<script language="JavaScript">
public_description = new CreateMyScriptlet();

function CreateMyScriptlet () {
  this.DoSomething = DoSomething;
  this.get_Title = DoGetTitle;
}

function DoSomething () {
  alert( "I'm a scriptlet's method." );
  return 1;
}
```

```
function DoGetTitle () {
  return document.title;
}

</script>

<body>
</body>
</html>
```

The scriptlet exposes a method called **DoSomething** and a read-only property called **Title**. This read-only property returns the title of the scriptlet's HTML page (that is 'Bare-bones scriptlet'). This file is available on our site as **barebone.htm**.

The next page is an example of how to use it.

```
<html>

<head>
<title>Using a Bare-bones Scriptlet</title>
</head>

<script language=JScript for=document event=onclick>
  alert( Scriptlet1.Title );
</script>

<body>
<object id=Scriptlet1 data=barebone.htm width=1 height=1
  type="text/x-scriptlet">
</object>
</body>
</html>
```

This page (available as **usebare.htm**) includes the previous scriptlet and assigns it an ID of **scriptlet1**. By clicking on the page you cause the **onclick** event to be raised and a message box with the title of the scriptlet's page to appear.

Actually, there are two possible approaches that can be taken to define the public interface of a scriptlet. The first one requires the use of JavaScript, while the second is a bit more flexible and allows you to use virtually any scripting language you may know.

In this chapter we will discuss both these solutions. However, as you'll learn later, there are a number of reasons for preferring the pure JavaScript method to the alternative.

Using JavaScript

With JavaScript you can create a new object called **public_description** and assign it the result of a function. This function works as the constructor of the scriptlet object. In one sense, the **public_description** variable is like a header file for a C++ class. It defines all the properties and methods that the scriptlet exposes. Here's an example:

```
<script language="Javascript">
  public_description = new CreateOurFirstScriptlet();
</script>
```

CreateOurFirstScriptlet is the constructor of the scriptlet. It doesn't matter what name you give it, since it is not a system routine. What's important is what this function actually does. Feel free to consider **CreateOurFirstScriptlet** as a placeholder for your own constructor. Inside its body you add properties and methods to the object itself. To identify the object (the scriptlet) you can use the JavaScript keyword **this**. What follows is a typical content for a constructor.

```
function CreateOurFirstScriptlet() {
   this.get_ImageName = DoGetImage;
   this.put_ImageName = DoPutImage;
   this.get_Text = DoGetText;
   this.put_Text = DoPutText;
   this.Paint = DoPaint;
   this.Refresh = DoRefresh;
}
```

The above function defines a new JavaScript object with two read/write properties—**ImageName** and **Text**—and two methods—**Paint** and **Refresh**. This object is assigned to the **public_description** variable.

Let's consider a line such as:

```
this.get_ImageName = DoGetImage;
```

On the left side we have a **get_ImageName** field belonging to the **this** object. On the right, however, there's a name that evaluates to a scriptlet's internal procedure. This means that the object's attribute specified on the left is actually implemented with the procedure, whose name appears on the right side of the assignment. Therefore, the body of the scriptlet's constructor looks like a dispatch table. It is composed of a series of assignments. The values on the left are references to the externally callable names. The values on the right, however, are the names of the internal procedures that actually provide such behaviors.

Naming Conventions

Unlike a C++ class, a COM object can only have methods. Sometimes, however, in development environments, using properties instead of methods is easier and much more natural. This leads to the definition of a public interface made up of methods, properties and events, plus a private table of functions that always implements them in terms of methods. Consequently, any attribute an object can have—a property or a method—has both a public and a private name. This is a convention that also applies to ActiveX components.

For example, when we call the **Title** property of the DHTML document object, we're actually calling one of two different functions exposed by the underlying COM object. Also, none of them are named **Title**! Instead, we have two different routines that read the current value and set a new one. This approach makes it much easier to expose read-only or write-only attributes.

To define properties and methods correctly for a scriptlet, we need to take a closer look at the commonly used naming conventions.

Identifying Properties

Let's now examine the code that forms the body of the **CreateOurFirstScriptlet** function more thoroughly.

```
this.get_ImageName = DoGetImage;
this.put_ImageName = DoPutImage;
```

The two lines above define a property whose public name is **ImageName**. Usually a property is implemented through a pair of **Get**/**Put** functions. The **Get** function takes care of returning the current value of the property, while its **Put** counterpart changes it. Scripting languages and Visual Basic shield you from this kind of low-level detail and allow you to call the external name directly. Thus,

```
Scriptlet1.ImageName = "myImage.gif"
MsgBox Scriptlet1.ImageName
```

are both legitimate expressions, that evaluate respectively to:

```
put_Image( "myImage.gif" )
```

and:

```
MsgBox get_Image()
```

Let's consider the following code again:

```
this.get_ImageName = DoGetImage;
this.put_ImageName = DoPutImage;
```

The names on the left side of the assignment ought to follow a precise convention. What the scriptlet exposes publicly is what you assign to the **this** keyword. If you want to expose a property that can be read and written, then you need to assign the object a couple of functions whose names begin with **get_** and **put_**, followed by the actual external name of the property.

```
this.get_Image = <name of the function that actually reads this property>;
this.put_Image = <name of the function that actually writes this property>;
```

What you assign to the **get_ImageName** property will be the name of the internal function that actually returns the current value of the property. What you assign to the **put_Image** property will be the name of the procedure that sets a new value for it.

The above code shows how to declare a read/write property called **ImageName**. This property is required to handle the file name of an image needed for the scriptlet behavior. If you want read-only or write-only properties then just omit the unnecessary declaration. For example, if we want **ImageName** to be read-only we need the following kind of declaration:

```
function CreateOurFirstScriptlet() {
   this.get_ImageName = DoGetImage;
// this.put_ImageName = DoPutImage;
   this.get_Text = DoGetText;
   this.put_Text = DoPutText;
```

```
    this.Paint = DoPaint;
    this.Refresh = DoRefresh;
}
```

Note that we commented out the Put function. Similarly, to have a write-only property we must avoid the Get function.

```
function CreateOurFirstScriptlet() {
//   this.get_ImageName = DoGetImage;
    this.put_ImageName = DoPutImage;
    this.get_Text = DoGetText;
    this.put_Text = DoPutText;
    this.Paint = DoPaint;
    this.Refresh = DoRefresh;
}
```

What appears on the right side of the assignments is just an internal function name—invisible outside the scriptlet. You can give them any name you like as long as you make sure that the scriptlet actually includes such functions.

A common notation assigns them the same name as the object's functions. In this case they would have been *get_ImageName* and *put_ImageName*. If you call them **DoGetImage** and **DoPutImage** everything will still work fine.

Identifying Methods

As for methods, there are no particular conventions to follow. You provide the **this** object with the external name of the method and assign it the name of the internal function that will implement such a behavior. For example, the following code defines two methods called **Paint** and **Refresh** that the scriptlet implements through the internal **DoPaint** and **DoRefresh** procedures.

```
    this.Paint = DoPaint;
    this.Refresh = DoRefresh;
```

You can give these procedures whatever names you prefer without having to follow any rules, as were seen for properties.

A Few Words About Events

Events have deliberately been left out of this discussion of the scriptlet's public interface. Later in the book there will be an entire chapter dedicated to them. In Chapter 6—Events Handling—we'll be explaining all the details. For now, just a few points to consider and a little advice.

From the syntax's point of view you aren't strictly required to declare events for scriptlets, even if they are regularly fired and handled by the container. A scriptlet can detect and fire two types of events: stock and custom. The first ones are the standard events broadcast by the DHTML event model, such as **onclick**, **onmouseover**, **onmouseout** and so on.

Custom events are non-standard events that the scriptlet triggers during its execution under particular circumstances. Whatever the type of event a scriptlet wants to fire, there's no code that gets executed within the scriptlet itself. Thus, you can raise events when needed without the hassle of declaring them in advance.

The reasons for this will be explained in greater detail in Chapter 6.

Even if you can avoid declaring events, for completeness and the documentation's sake, we suggest you do it anyway—provided your scriptlet makes use of them. In this case, all you have to do is extend the constructor by adding a line for each event fired.

```
function CreateOurFirstScriptlet() {
    this.get_Image = DoGetImage;
    this.put_Image = DoPutImage;
    this.get_Text = DoGetText;
    this.put_Text = DoPutText;
    this.Paint = DoPaint;
    this.Refresh = DoRefresh;
    this.event_OnEraseBkGnd = ""
    this.event_OnPaint = ""
}
```

The suggested syntax is **event_** followed by the name of the event you want to raise. In the example above, we've declared two events: **OnEraseBkGnd** and **OnPaint**. Of course, the right side of the assignment is the empty string, since the events—by design—require no implementation from the server object (in this case, the scriptlet). If you never fire such events, or if you fire other events, the scriptlet will continue to work as before.

So why do we suggest that you declare events anyway? Basically, in fact, for the sake of clarity and completeness. In this way, the whole public interface of the scriptlet will be well defined and consistent.

The public_description Object

The first sign of life for a scriptlet is the initialization of the **public_description** object. While the constructor can have any name, the object variable that stores that instance must have a fixed one; namely **public_description**. If you make an error while typing it, or deliberately use another name, then all that the constructor does will be ignored.

```
<script language="Javascript">
myScriptlet = new CreateScriptlet();
</script>
```

```
<script language="Javascript">
public_Description = new CreateScriptlet();
</script>
```

For instance, both the above fragments will give you a static scriptlet: unable to respond to any automation call. In other words, your scriptlet will work fine, except that you have no way of invoking its properties or methods. If you do, however, try to call methods and access properties, this is what you will see.

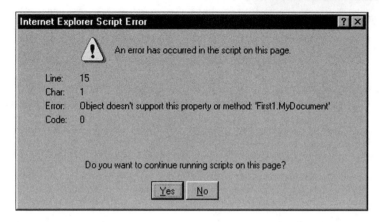

What's going on? Internet Explorer 4.0 expects to find a JavaScript object called **public_description** and, through it, access the scriptlet's automation interface. If it fails to find such an object, then the entire public interface remains inaccessible and this causes the message seen above.

*Note that when working with the public_description object the case is **very** important. The object absolutely requires lowercase to work as expected.*

The Scriptlet's Constructor

The **public_description** approach to defining the programming interface of a scriptlet requires you to write some JavaScript code. When you set up the constructor you're ultimately storing in the **public_description** the names of the functions to be executed correspondingly. You need such functions to be written in JavaScript. Otherwise you'll get an error message like the one shown above.

This is true only if you're following the public_description approach to defining a scriptlet's public interface.

The JavaScript requirement holds true for at least the outer layer of code. In fact, what really matters is that the name specified in the constructor belongs to a JavaScript procedure. Internally, it might also call directly a VBScript procedure and things will work properly anyway.

For instance, the following code will give you problems:

```
<script language="JavaScript">
public_description = new CreateMyScriptlet();

function CreateMyScriptlet() {
  this.put_Image = DoPutImage;    // DoPutImage is a VBScript procedure
  this.put_Text = put_Text;       // put_Text is a Javascript procedure
}
function put_Text() {
 // do something
}
</script>
```

63

```
<script language="VBScript">
Sub DoPutImage
  ' do something
End Sub
</script>
```

because the **DoPutImage** procedure is a VBScript procedure. If you really want the **put_Image** code to be written in VBScript, then you need to do the following:

```
<script language="JavaScript">
public_description = new CreateMyScriptlet();

function CreateMyScriptlet() {
  this.put_Image = put_Image;     // Javascript procedure
  this.put_Text = put_Text;       // Javascript procedure
}
function put_Text() {
  // do something
}

function put_Image() {
  DoPutImage();                   // VBScript procedure
  return;
}
</script>

<script language="VBScript">
Sub DoPutImage
  ' do something
End Sub
</script>
```

This works because the constructor maintains only references to JavaScript procedures, while you can call VBScript procedures seamlessly from within JavaScript code.

The Default Interface Description

The JavaScript **public_description** approach is not the only one you can take to define the public interface of a scriptlet. Alternatively, you can choose to follow a special naming convention that automatically exports all the functions whose name begins with **public_**. In doing so you don't need to use JavaScript, but can use VBScript instead.

If you don't create a valid **public_description** object, then all the functions exported are those with a name prefixed by the word **public**. For example, to export a read/write property called **ImageName** you need to define functions with the following, mandatory, names: **public_get_ImageName** and **public_put_ImageName**.

```
<script language="JavaScript">
function public_get_ImageName() {
  return mImage;    // it is supposed to be the current value of the property
}
function public_put_ImageName( sImage ) {
  mImage = sImage;
  // probably you need to do something else here…
  return;
}
</script>
```

64

It's the same for methods. A given **Paint** function must be declared as follows:

```
<script language="JavaScript">
function public_Paint() {
  // do something
  return;
}
</script>
```

What about events? Since the default interface description approach requires a function to be self-exportable, events simply don't need to be declared! In fact, as stated before, events are implemented on the container side by design. You can never have a procedure representing an event handler within a scriptlet. Instead, you can have a line of code raising an event. Note that a hypothetical **public_event_OnEraseBkGnd** function will be considered as a public method called **event_OnEraseBkGnd**.

Using VBScript

Let's see for completeness how the previously examined declarations will fit into the default interface description. To make things a bit more open, we'll be using VBScript. Above we outlined a scriptlet with the following JavaScript public interface:

```
function CreateOurFirstScriptlet() {
  this.get_ImageName = DoGetImage;
  this.put_ImageName = DoPutImage;
  this.get_Text = DoGetText;
  this.put_Text = DoPutText;
  this.Paint = DoPaint;
  this.Refresh = DoRefresh;
  this.event_OnEraseBkGnd = ""
  this.event_OnPaint = ""
}
```

Now let's try to express it using VBScript and the default interface description approach. Properties still need a pair of **Get/Put** functions.

```
<script language=VBScript>
Function public_get_ImageName()
  public_get_ImageName = mImage    ' it is supposed to be the current value
End Function
Sub public_put_ImageName( sImage )
  mImage = sImage
  ' do something else if needed
End Sub

Function public_get_Text()
  public_get_Text = mText    ' mText is supposed to be the current value
End Function
Sub public_put_Text( sText )
  mText = sText
  ' do something else if needed
End Sub
</script>
```

Methods just have their names prefixed with **public_**.

```
<script language=VBScript>
Sub public_Paint()
  ' do something
```

```
End Sub
</script>
```

Furthermore, no declaration is required for events.

If you choose to follow the default interface description then the language you're using isn't important. You may have methods written in JavaScript and properties in VBScript, but the scriptlet will still make them regularly available to any external caller.

Whatever the topic, each time you have two or more choices, they are rarely exact equivalents. So, at this point, you might be wondering which is the best approach to follow when it comes to defining a scriptlet's public interface. Stay tuned! That's just what we're going to approach next.

Little Games With public_description

After all **public_description** is not a keyword—though it is not just an object variable name either. Suppose, for example, you want to use a variable called **public_description** in your scriptlet's code and suppose you want to expose the automation interface through the default interface description. In the following code we've declared a generic variable with that name, but never initialized it.

```
<script language="JavaScript">
var public_description;
function public_DoSomething() {
  alert( "I'm a function" );
  return 1;
}
```

Nevertheless, Internet Explorer 4.0 recognizes the presence of a **public_description** object and handles it as if it really stores the automation interface of the scriptlet! Thus, it discards the next public method and presumes that the **public_description** object is correctly initialized. Since this is not the case (we've just declared the variable) it crashes! The same occurs if you initialize the **public_description** variable with a non-object type; say a string. It crashes yet again!

Once you have experienced all this, why not risk a third crash by trying to assign the **public_description** a standard object like the Javascript Date?

```
<script language="JavaScript">
public_description = new Date();
function public_DoSomething() {
  alert( "I'm a function" );
  return 1;
}
```

Surprisingly, there are no crashes, but the **DoSomething** method still remains inaccessible. Any attempt to call it produces the same error message seen above. What's this all about then? Why doesn't it crash now?

If it doesn't crash, maybe Internet Explorer 4.0 (or rather the component it uses to embed scriptlets in Dynamic HTML pages—more on this later) finds that **public_description** now holds a suitable object—a Date object!

66

Let's try to execute the following code from within a host HTML page and see what happens.

```html
<html>

<head>
<title>Use Date</title>
</head>

<body bgcolor="#C0C0C0">
Test page.
<hr>

<p>
<object id="Date1" data="Date.htm"
width="200" height="100" type="text/x-scriptlet">
</object>
</p>

<SCRIPT language=VBScript for=document event=onclick>
MsgBox Date1.getDate() & "/" & (1+Date1.getMonth()) & "/" & Date1.getYear()
</SCRIPT>

</body>
</html>
```

We have a scriptlet called **Date1,** which is implemented in a little file called **date.htm**. The full source code for the scriptlet is reproduced below.

```html
<html >

<script language="JavaScript">
public_description = new Date();
</script>

<body>
</body>
</html>
```

By clicking in the client area of the page (and outside the scriptlet's area) we generate an **onclick** event. What happens then is rendered in the picture on the right.

Our experiment gives an amazing result—we succeeded in cloning the JavaScript Date object.

```
<script language="JavaScript">
public_description = new Date();
</script>
```

The few lines above will suffice to make the scriptlet inherit all the methods of the Date object. More cleverly, this technique can be used to obtain real scriptlet inheritance. We will return to this in Chapter 12—Dynamic Methods and Inheritance.

What's the Best Approach?

Using JavaScript's public description, or the generic default interface description approach, doesn't limit your power in any way. In both cases, you'll be able to make your properties and methods callable outside the scriptlet. However, there are a few points to consider carefully before deciding which way to go.

To explain the difference between the two possibilities it is helpful to compare them with the usual ways of exporting functions from Windows DLLs. Since you might not be an expert Windows programmer, we'll briefly recall the key facts.

There are two ways to export functions from within Windows DLLs and make them visible to external callers, such as Visual Basic or other C/C++ programs. The first one requires you to create the so-called Definition Module File: a text file with a standard **.def** extension. DEF files list by name, and sometimes by number, all the functions that the DLL wishes to export. What you have to do is just write your functions and link the appropriate DEF file to the project. At any time you can consult the list of exported functions just by opening that given file.

The other way avoids using additional files. By adding a special keyword to the function's prototype you can make it self-exportable. That is, the compiler somehow signals those symbols to the linker, which will automatically put them into the appropriate export section of the final executable. If you want to know about the functions your DLL actually exports then you need to inspect all the source files that form the project.

Why You Should Use public description

JavaScript's **public_description** is quite similar to a DEF file. It allows you to have a single place in your code where the entire automation interface is described. If you need to add a new property or method, just drop a new line in the scriptlet constructor and write the function. At any moment in time you can find out, easily and quickly, how many, and above all what, attributes your scriptlet is exposing.

But there is much more. JavaScript's **public_description** is far more flexible.

In fact, it allows you to distinguish between internal and external names. You can have a **Paint** method implemented internally with a function called

GiveItTheNameYouWant(). This is an important feature. I dare say it is a bit more important than the possibility of giving your dog's name to a poor innocent function. This feature makes it easier to maintain your scriptlet's code. Suppose that, at a certain point, you want to enhance the behavior of a method; say **Paint**. You write your new function, assign it a name that makes sense to you (say, **DoPaintEx**) and just modify the reference which the **this.Paint** attribute points to. To comment it out, just revert your changes in the constructor. There's no need to change even a single byte in any of the two internal versions of the same method.

Why You Should Use the Default Description

The default description approach looks like using the keyword **_export**, or rather **_declspec(dllexport)**, to export functions from within a Windows DLL. You must have a perfect match between the externally callable name of your properties and methods, and the name by which they're implemented.

If you want to expose a method called **Paint**, then you absolutely must define a **public_Paint** subroutine and have it implement the desired behavior. You cannot choose a different name. However, you could maintain **public_Paint** as an outer wrapper of code and internally invoke another function.

```
<script language=VBScript>
Sub public_Paint()
  DoPaint
End Sub
</script>
```

If you organize your code this way, you can easily obtain almost the same flexibility as the previous approach. In fact, the above code is logically equivalent to the following:

```
<script language=Javascript>
function CreateOurFirstScriptlet() {
  this.Paint = DoPaint;
}
</script>
```

Of course, in this case we've obtained manually what is offered for free by JavaScript's **public_description**.

The default interface description does allow you to save some lines of code, but there does not exist a single place where all the interface attributes are gathered together.

Overall, What's Better?

Taking such a decision is pretty similar to picking good dishes from a restaurant menu. First you consider what the chef recommends—possibly consulting the waiter for more details—and then you make up your mind. In this case, the chef (that is, Microsoft) recommends JavaScript's **public_description** approach. The waiter (us) attempts to explain some details about the choices. The rest is up to you. Overall, however, JavaScript's **public_description** approach seems superior.

What If I'm Using Both?

What happens in the remote case in which you attempt to use both the approaches? Simply, the JavaScript approach takes precedence over the other. Suppose, for example, you're writing the following code:

```
<script language="JavaScript">
public_description = new CreateOurFirstScriptlet;
function CreateOurFirstScriptlet() {
  this.get_Image = DoGetImage;
  this.put_Image = DoPutImage;
  this.Paint = DoPaint;
}
function public_DoSomething() {
  // do something, possibly useful!
  return 1;
}
</script>
```

We have a public constructor that exposes the well-known **Image** property and **Paint** method. In addition, there's also a **public_DoSomething** method. What happens if you insert this scriptlet in an HTML page, and from there (or from a Visual Basic form) attempt to call **Image** or **Paint**? Everything works fine. And what happens if you call **DoSomething**? Then a nice error message will inform you that Internet Explorer 4.0 is unable to find the property or the method with that name.

If a **public_description** object is present, then Internet Explorer 4.0 ignores all the other functions that might have been declared public via the default interface description. Consequently, if you choose the latter approach, make sure you remove from your code any object called **public_description**.

Creating Scriptlets

So far we've seen some code snippets that demonstrated scriptlets in action. Now it's time to see what's really needed to write them. The core of any scriptlet is its **public_description** object (or equivalent) in which you define the programming interface. A scriptlet can have public properties, methods and events and can access virtually any of the features that DHTML introduced. So a valid prerequisite is a good understanding of the DHTML object model.

While writing scriptlets you can use and mix any script language you want. However, don't forget that Internet Explorer 4.0 natively supports only JScript (Microsoft's implementation of JavaScript) and VBScript.

A Very Simple Scriptlet

A scriptlet preserves the same structure as an HTML page, has an **<HTML>** signature, a **<HEAD>** section for the title, a **<BODY>** for the user interface and the actual content, and—above all—one, or more, **<SCRIPT>** tags. As explained earlier, at the moment there are no tools available to offer a predefined infrastructure, so you need to write them manually—tag after tag.

In the next chapter, however, we will build a special stand-alone wizard that lets you specify a few options and produce a perfectly functional scriptlet in a mere moment. A first example of such a wizard is available from:

`http://www.microsoft.com/mind`

with the source code for the January 1998 issue of the Microsoft Interactive Developer magazine. I wrote that wizard as a companion application for the Cutting Edge column, which was dedicated to scriptlets that month.

The wizard we'll see next is a big improvement on that one and, since it's a stand-alone executable module, you can use it outside the Developer Studio 97 environment.

In the rest of this section, you will learn about setting up a bare-bones scriptlet and hosting it in an HTML page. From then on all our efforts will address every possible way of writing smart and commercially sound scriptlets.

Skeleton of a Scriptlet

The first tag you meet is **<HTML>**. Usually, there is no need to add any attributes to it. For scriptlets, however, we recommend you always add an **ID** property so that you can refer to the entire page if necessary.

A skeleton scriptlet looks like this:

```
<html id=MyPage>

<head>
<title>Our First Scriptlet</title>
</head>

<script language="JavaScript">
public_description = new CreateFirstScriptlet;

function CreateFirstScriptlet() {
  this.TellMeSomething = HelloWorld;
}

function HelloWorld() {
  alert( "Hello, World!" );
}
</script>
```

```
<body>
</body>
</html>
```

As you can see, the **<HEAD>** section includes a title string and at the bottom of the code there's an empty body. If you don't need them, feel free to remove them. Your scriptlet won't suffer as a result of this. The scriptlet outlined above has just one method called **TellMeSomething.** This method is implemented via a JavaScript function called **HelloWorld**.

That's all, at least for this very basic sample. To show some other features in action, a straightforward enhancement we could do consists of adding a property to set and retrieve the background color of the scriptlet's area. In this way, we'll make use of properties, global variables and one-time initialization. We've also added the simplest body in the world. Let's see now how our previous code changes.

```
<html id=MyPage>

<head>
<title>Our First Scriptlet</title>
</head>

<SCRIPT language=VBScript for=window event=onload>
  document.bgColor = mBackColor
</SCRIPT>

<script language="Javascript">
public_description = new CreateFirstScriptlet;

var mBackColor = "lightcyan";

function CreateFirstScriptlet() {
  this.get_BackColor = get_BackColor;
  this.put_BackColor = put_BackColor;
  this.TellMeSomething = HelloWorld;
}

function get_BackColor() {
  return mBackColor;
}
function put_BackColor( cBackColor ) {
  mBackColor = cBackColor;
  document.bgColor = mBackColor;
  return 1;
}
function HelloWorld() {
  alert( "Hello, World!" );
}
</script>

<body>
Hello, World!
</body>
</html>
```

mBackColor is a global variable we use to keep track of the corresponding **BackColor** property. Each property, in fact, needs a storage support that makes it persistent, at least through the current session. This is always true if the property is available for reading. It's not necessarily true if the property is write-only. **mBackColor** is initialized with an HTML color string, say **"lightcyan"**. Of course, global variables must be declared outside of any function's body. The **var** keyword is just good programming practice.

To make **BackColor** public and, therefore, callable outside the scriptlet, we need to add a couple of lines to the scriptlet's constructor.

```
function CreateFirstScriptlet() {
   this.get_BackColor = get_BackColor;
   this.put_BackColor = put_BackColor;
   this.TellMeSomething = HelloWorld;
}
```

As stated before, if you want a read-only property then you need only cut off the **Put** function.

```
this.put_BackColor = put_BackColor;
```

You can do the opposite if you, for example, want a write-only attribute.

Let's take a look at how those **Get**/**Put** functions are implemented. The code for **get_BackColor** is self-explanatory. **put_BackColor** is, however, worth a few words.

```
function put_BackColor( cBackColor ) {
   mBackColor = cBackColor;
   document.bgColor = mBackColor;
   return 1;
}
```

It saves the new color setting into the global variable **mBackColor** and applies the changes immediately.

```
document.bgColor = mBackColor;
```

The above line just sets the background color for the scriptlet, through the standard **bgColor** property of the scriptlet's **document** object.

A scriptlet almost always needs a one-time initialization—a series of tasks carried out while the scriptlet itself is loading. A reasonable way of doing this is via the **window.onload** event.

```
<SCRIPT language=VBScript for=window event=onload>
   document.bgColor = mBackColor
</SCRIPT>
```

In this way, we set the document background color from the beginning. At the time of this call, **mBackColor** already holds its value.

Completing Our First Example

What we've seen so far is a simple, and basically useless, scriptlet that does, however, involve almost all of the features you need to know about. In particular, it lends itself very well to demonstrating the ideal skeleton of any scriptlet. A few things are still missing. Among them, we can list the event handling and the ambient properties—that is the environment the container exposes to the scriptlets. Both of these topics will be the subject of detailed chapters to follow.

For now, let's consider a third missing topic: how a scriptlet can make its own DHTML object model public.

As mentioned earlier, a scriptlet is viewed through a special container. This container recreates a DHTML object model on top of the scriptlet's source code. This means that a scriptlet holds its own **document** object, which is different from the document object of the hosting page.

A scriptlet can expose custom properties and methods that relate to its specific activity. In addition, it may also expose the standard object model, or a portion of it.

For example, a scriptlet can make its document public through the following code:

```
function CreateFirstScriptlet() {
    this.get_BackColor = get_BackColor;
    this.put_BackColor = put_BackColor;
    this.TellMeSomething = HelloWorld;
    this.MyDocument = window.document;
}
```

MyDocument is a read/write property that, in this case, evaluates to an object. Through it you can navigate the scriptlet's internal document object model and, say, change its title or its background color.

You can download or run this sample (first.zip) from our Web site:
http://rapid.wrox.uk.co/books/138X

Detecting when a Scriptlet is running

A scriptlet is an HTML or ASP page, and can also be displayed as stand-alone document. If you do this, then you might occasionally incur a system error due to a property or a method that Internet Explorer 4.0 doesn't find. This only happens if your scriptlet attempts to access its parent environment. (More on this in Chapter 5 – Container and Ambient Properties.) To work round this you should discover a way to detect whether a given page is viewed as a scriptlet or not. If the answer is yes, then you can safely access all the attributes you need. Otherwise, you'll need to avoid doing it.

The critical point is the **external** object exposed by the DHTML **window** object. Through this, you can access some of the properties and methods of the container's environment. Simply, you ought to skip over it if the scriptlet page is viewed as a stand-alone document.

To be more precise, the error occurs only from within VBScript code. The JScript's engine traps the exception and resumes the execution without any kind of warning. This behavior, however, might also cause undesirable side-effects in some circumstances. In conclusion, it's far better to provide a Boolean variable as a safeguard and access the **external** object only when absolutely safe.

One-time Access To the external Object

Since the **external** object gets initialized if, and only if, an HTML page is running as a scriptlet, to detect this circumstance we need to access it. Using JScript saves us from a message box in case of error. We just need to check it once and then store the result in a global variable for further use.

We can choose any of the properties exposed by **external** and check its type. The JScript's engine returns undefined if it fails to access the object. What we can do then is just:

```
var InScriptlet = (typeof(window.external.version)=="string")
```

The variable will contain True or False, according to the type of the property **external.version**. Usually this property contains a string, which denotes the current version of the scriptlet engine. At the moment this string is 4.0 Win32.

The complete source code for our first scriptlet becomes:

```
<html id=MyPage>

<head>
<title>Our First Scriptlet</title>
</head>

<SCRIPT language=VBScript for=window event=onload>
  document.bgColor = mBackColor
</SCRIPT>

<script language="Javascript">
public_description = new CreateFirstScriptlet;

var mBackColor = "lightcyan";
var InScriptlet = (typeof(window.external.version)=="string")

function CreateFirstScriptlet() {
  this.get_BackColor = get_BackColor;
  this.put_BackColor = put_BackColor;
  this.TellMeSomething = HelloWorld;
  this.MyDocument = window.document;
}

function DefaultTitle( s ) {
  DefaultTitle = s;
  return mBackColor;
}
function get_BackColor() {
  return mBackColor;
}
function put_BackColor( cBackColor ) {
  mBackColor = cBackColor;
  document.bgColor = mBackColor;
  return 1;
}
function HelloWorld() {
  alert( "Hello, World!" );
}
</script>

<body>
Hello, World!
</body>
</html>
```

Hosting Scriptlets in Web Pages

Once we have created our first functional scriptlet, it's time to discuss how to embed it in a host HTML page. At the moment there's just one way to do it: using the same tag—**<OBJECT>**—which is used for ActiveX controls. This is all a bit confusing for some non-updated tools, like FrontPage 97, that know how to treat ActiveX controls but remain baffled by scriptlets.

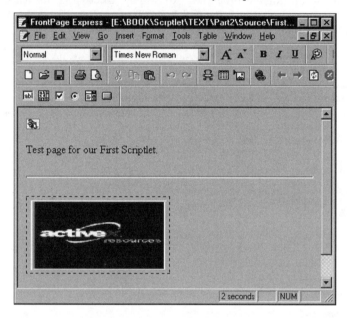

FrontPage Express and FrontPage 97 are deceived by the **<OBJECT>** tag. They attempt to read the control's properties as usual with ActiveX controls, but this time unsuccessfully.

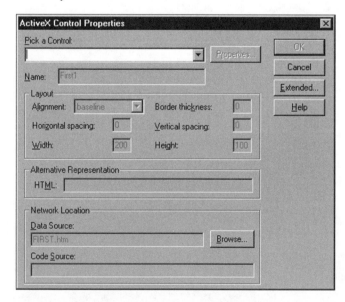

Thus, with these authoring tools you cannot edit properties at design-time and, instead, must resort to run-time script code to get the scriptlet to work the way you want. Fortunately, both are quite robust and no system errors appear. If you're using FrontPage 98, however, all this disappears.

A similar problem arises for script code to automate the scriptlet inside the page. ScriptWizard fails to detect scriptlets. ScriptWizard is the utility included both in FrontPage and ActiveX Control Pad to help you write script code.

In conclusion, if you want to embed a scriptlet in an HTML page, then do it manually!

The <OBJECT> tag

Since both ActiveX controls and scriptlets are inserted through the same tag, how does the browser distinguish between them? The following is a declaration for an ActiveX control.

```
<object
  id="Button1"
  classid="CLSID:D7053240-CE69-11CD-A777-00DD01143C57"
  width="70"
  height="32">
  <param name="Caption" value="Click Me!">
</object>
```

What makes the component uniquely identifiable, and constitutes an indirect reference to the actual file name, is the content of the **classid** attribute. It contains a 128-bit number: CLSID, which is used to retrieve the name of the executable module in the Windows registry.

A scriptlet is, instead, embedded through the following code:

```
<object
  id="First1"
  data="first.htm"
  width="100"
  height="100"
  type="text/x-scriptlet">
</object>
```

As you can see, there are a couple of key differences. The first one is the presence of **data** instead of **classid**; the second is the specific MIME type used. **data** refers to the straight file name that implements the component. Although we recommend that you put the container page and the scriptlet in the same directory, there is a way to specify an indirect path for the scriptlet file. For example, the following code:

```
<object
  id="First1"
  data="..\first.htm"
  width="100"
  height="100"
  type="text/x-scriptlet">
</object>
```

tells Internet Explorer 4.0 to search for the file **first.htm** in the folder immediately above the current one.

This is not the only way of inserting scriptlets into your pages. Here's an alternative method.

```
<object
  id="First1"
  width="100" height="100"
  type="text/x-scriptlet">
  <PARAM NAME="url" VALUE="http://www.server.com/first.htm">
</object>
```

Instead of **data**, it makes use of a **url** property. Behind the scenes, there's an ActiveX control that actually hosts the scriptlet. In this case, we're simply working directly with the properties of this Scriptlet Control. The property **url** is assigned the URL from which the code should be taken. Of course, the file can also reside locally.

Inserting a scriptlet this way gives you the opportunity to set some additional properties of the Scriptlet Control at design-time. For example, with this method you can decide whether a scrollbar should be used if the scriptlet is too big to fit in the client area, or whether the content should be made selectable.

```
<object
  id="First1"
  width="100" height="100"
  type="text/x-scriptlet">
  <PARAM NAME="url" VALUE="http://www.server.com/first.htm">
  <PARAM NAME="selectableContent" VALUE="1">
</object>
```

Aside from the URL, these properties are also available at run-time. Actually, they form the ambient properties a scriptlet can access through the aforementioned **external** object. All these topics, however, will be discussed in more detail in Chapter 5—Container and Ambient Properties.

Scriptlets' MIME Type

When inserting a scriptlet into an HTML page you also have to specify a particular MIME type. This helps Internet Explorer 4.0 to recognize it as a scriptlet and makes the distinction from ActiveX controls. When IE4 encounters an **<OBJECT>** tag with a MIME type of **text/x-scriptlet** then, among other things, it initializes the **external** object. This allows a scriptlet to work properly.

Internet Explorer 4.0 will support this MIME type on all platforms, from Win32 to Win16 and from Macintosh to Unix.

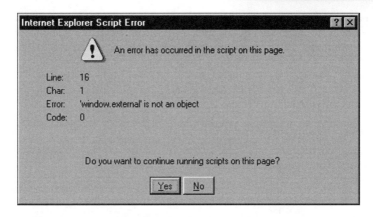

The above picture has been obtained by removing the **type** attribute from a declaration that correctly embeds a scriptlet into a host Web page.

Using Our First Scriptlet

At this point, we know how to create scriptlets and how to host them in HTML pages. At last, it's time to see them in action. The next illustration shows how the **first.htm** scriptlet we wrote earlier works.

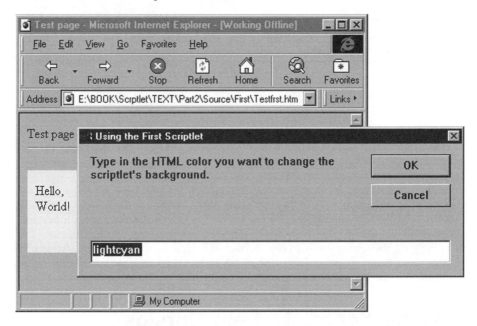

The scriptlet simply paints its client area and displays the string Hello, World. The initial color is **lightcyan**. It exposes a **BackColor** property, which represents just the background color of its site. In addition, the scriptlet makes available its **document** object through the property **MyDocument**.

The host page declares it and assign an **ID** of **First1**. We do this so we have another way to refer to the scriptlet itself. From now on, **First1** identifies the scriptlet and the usual object-oriented syntax allows us to call methods and properties.

The following listing presents the HTML page that produced the above screenshot after clicking on the document.

```
<html>

<head>
<title>Test page</title>
</head>

<SCRIPT language=VBScript for=document event=onclick>
  sColor = InputBox( _
       "Type in the HTML color you want to change the scriptlet's background.",
 _
       "Using the First Scriptlet", First1.BackColor  )
  First1.BackColor = sColor
  First1.MyDocument.title = First1.MyDocument.title + " [" + sColor + "]"
</SCRIPT>

<body bgcolor="#C0C0C0">
Test page for our First Scriptlet.

<hr>

<p>
<object
   id="First1" data="first.htm" width="100" height="100"
   type="text/x-scriptlet">
</object>
</p>

</body>
</html>
```

When the user clicks on the document area (not over the scriptlet's area), an **InputBox** will appear. Its edit field defaults to **First1.BackColor**, that is the current color of the scriptlet's background. Then, the color string entered by the user is stored back to the **First1.BackColor**. Because of the **put_BackColor**'s implementation, this has an immediate echo to the screen. As you should remember, **put_BackColor** is the name we assigned the procedure that actually implements the storage of the scriptlet's **BackColor** property.

Changing the background's color is also achieved by connecting a string with the color name to the current document title. To do this we use the **MyDocument** property, which mirrors the scriptlet's **document** object.

Viewing Scriptlets from Outside

You might be wondering what really happens under the hood when a scriptlet is running. Or rather, what does Internet Explorer 4.0 have to do to display a scriptlet? Before reading further, consider that this is a section that attempts to dig out some internal features of the IE4 implementation of scriptlets. You could skip it if you are not at all interested in such topics. Your understanding of the whole subject won't be affected if you do.

When the browser detects a scriptlet in the current HTML page, it embeds an instance of a specialized container that displays the content of the referenced scriptlet. As seen above, the **type** attribute plays a fundamental role.

But what's this specialized container IE4 embeds in the currently viewed page in order to display a scriptlet? It is just an ActiveX control that acts as the IE4 HTML viewer engine. In practice, it parses the HTML source code of the scriptlet's page and builds the DHTML object model. All of the rendering is done within the assigned site, just as with ordinary controls.

This ActiveX control is called Microsoft Scriptlet Component and it silently installs with the final release of Internet Explorer 4.0.

Internet Explorer 4.0 is supposed to ship for a number of different platforms. Win32 aside, of course, the implementation of the scriptlet's container won't be ActiveX-based.

The Microsoft Scriptlet Component

At the moment, this control is implemented through the file **msHtmlWb.dll**. This can be found in the **Windows\System** directory. The following figure shows how it is stored in the system registry.

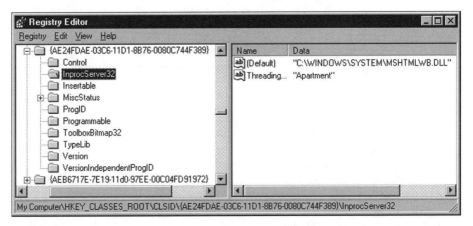

This control is the key that also allows you to make use of scriptlets within desktop applications, or generic ActiveX document containers. The Microsoft Scriptlet Component exposes a few fixed properties to let you customize the behavior and the appearance of the scriptlet's site. Of course, you cannot edit the scriptlet's properties at design-time with it.

Ultimately, the Microsoft Scriptlet Component is exactly what we said before—a specialized container! Actually, scriptlets are one of its properties.

In the rest of this chapter, we'll examine its internal structure and the logic that governs its activity. Then in later chapters we'll take into account its properties and see how to exploit them in our Visual Basic or C++ applications.

A View of Internals

Now let's see in a bit more detail how scriptlets are viewed—at least under Win32 platforms such as Windows 95 and Windows NT.

The Scriptlet Control encapsulates the HTML rendering engine of Internet Explorer 4.0 and uses it to load and run the scriptlet's page normally. This viewer is in the **msHtml.dll** and corresponds to the COM server whose identifier is CLSID_HTMLDocument. Once completely loaded, the scriptlet's page exposes its own DHTML object model and gets displayed.

From now on, the scriptlet component can interact with its container (for instance, Internet Explorer 4.0).

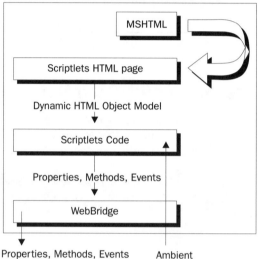

The outer box in the above diagram renders the scriptlet's site inside a host Web page. The scriptlet's DHTML object model, however, is available only to the script code that actually forms the scriptlet itself. Unless you export objects explicitly, the container won't ever be able to access the hierarchy, since the Scriptlet Component hides it. Though we have previously demonstrated how a scriptlet can export its own **document** object.

The script code built into the scriptlet defines its public interface, which is exposed to the host environment through a WebBridge object.

This bridge layer works as a broker. It interprets the external calls and passes them up to the scriptlet. The opposite occurs for the events fired by the scriptlet and notified out of it.

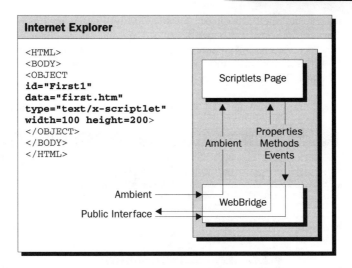

The WebBridge layer is always the same, whichever scriptlet it governs. It also negotiates with the container about the scriptlet's site and implements some general properties and methods inherent to the site's style and functionality. For instance, whether the site should display scrollbars or a context menu, or whether it should make its content selectable via drag-and-drop. These stock attributes are exposed to the scriptlet, but their actual implementation requires a negotiation with the container.

Snooping Among the Windows

Oversimplifying, we could say that inserting a scriptlet into an HTML page forces you to embed another WebBrowser's instance. This is untrue. What's really embedded is an instance of the IE4 viewer engine and, therefore, just a part of the WebBrowser component. Around it, the WebBridge layer takes care of hiding most of the details, presenting the page (that is, the scriptlet) as a real object component. Don't forget that while an ActiveX component is able to converse directly with its container, scriptlets are not. Scriptlets still need an intermediate layer that will host them and forward requests in and out.

Now let's take a look at the windows involved in such operations. The next figure shows the pile of windows created when Internet Explorer 4.0 is hosting a Web page—and a scriptlet is a Web page.

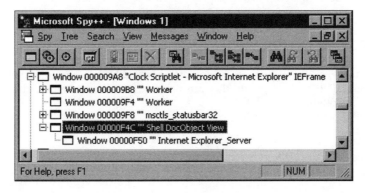

We can observe a "Shell DocObject View" window, which includes an "Internet Explorer_Server" window. Both windows occupy the entire client area of IE4. The drawing occurs inside the inner window. In fact, if the page hosts some windowed ActiveX controls, these windows would all be children of the server window of class "Internet Explorer_Server".

Let's see what happens when IE4 views a Web page with a scriptlet.

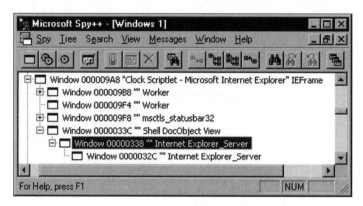

As you can see, there are two windows of the same "Internet Explorer_Server" class. The outer refers to the whole client area of the browser. The inner refers to the scriptlet. This demonstrates that the rendering engine of IE4 is duplicated when the browser opens a page which contains a scriptlet.

Summary

Our first trip into the world of scriptlets ends here. At this point, however, we have just scratched the surface and there's much more still to see and do. This chapter served the purpose of presenting an overview of the scriptlet creation process. Nevertheless, we have discussed a major portion of scriptlets-related topics.

In particular, you've learnt:

- How to define the scriptlet's public interface.
- How to detect when a page is viewed as a scriptlet.
- How to host scriptlets in Web pages.
- How Internet Explorer 4.0 implements scriptlets.

From now on, we'll go more and more thoroughly into programming details, covering all the other points that are required to write commercial-quality, real-world scriptlets.

Before this, however, we need to provide ourselves with a more powerful tool and a comfortable environment for working with the greatest ease. Therefore, in the next chapter we will build a wizard for automating the creation of scriptlets. This wizard will ask us for a few options and deliver, in an instant, ready-to-run source code.

In addition, we'll attempt to customize the Developer Studio environment— writing a few macros that will speed up our work.

Further Reading

In this chapter, we've presented quite new topics, so it's hard to give you suggestions for further reading. However, there's an article of mine that could be of help to those of you who want to know more about embedding the HTML viewer engine in a C++ application. The piece appears in the February 98 issue of Microsoft Interactive Developer (MIND) and is focused on how to write a namespace extension that extends the shell support for DHTML files. In practice, it shows you how to silently load an HTML file, have the engine build the DHTML object model and then use it for some analysis. It doesn't show, however, how to render a Web page. For this you can find appropriate examples in the Internet Client SDK. Both the article, and the afore mentioned samples should help you to form a more precise idea of what actually occurs behind the curtains when a scriptlet is up and running.

Facilities to Automate the Scriptlets' Creation

From now on this book will present several samples of scriptlets, both complex and simple. So it would be extremely helpful to have a tool to write them easily and quickly, or a series of facilities to save time and avoid the most boring coding tasks. Our opinion is that at the moment, and probably for a long time to come, the best development environment you can rely on for writing scriptlets is the Microsoft Developer Studio 97. It provides you with a cutting-edge text editor, syntax highlighting and a quick browser based on Internet Explorer 4.0's WebBrowser component. What could be better?

Also, Developer Studio 97—the version shipped with Visual Studio 97—allows you to fully customize its toolbars and menus. Add-ins and wizards complete the range of facilities you can exploit to adapt Developer Studio to suit all your needs. So, what then are our needs?

We want a wizard that can produce scriptlets and HTML test pages in an instant. Of course, we don't want a deaf and blind wizard, but a smart tool able to offer us some options and take these options carefully into account when producing code. However, such a wizard—even working perfectly—won't be enough.

Once we've finished with it, we're still far from having our scriptlet up and running. In fact, wizards are useful to start you off, but nothing more than that! We also need, therefore, some facilities to be available when editing HTML source code. Above all, we'd like to be able to test both the scriptlet and some sample pages in the same environment, and to do so as easily as clicking a toolbar button.

In this chapter, therefore, we're aiming to show you how to:

 Extend the Developer Studio 97 with macros.

 Create a custom toolbar with scriptlets facilities.

 Develop a stand-alone wizard to create scriptlets.

By the end of this chapter you will have a real and integrated development environment, where you can write your HTML components with the same ease as you're used to when writing C++ or Visual Basic code. For an explosive finish, we'll then be using the wizard (called, very imaginatively, Scriptlet Wizard) to rebuild as a scriptlet the bitmapped anchor component we touched on in a previous chapter.

Adapting DevStudio 97 to Our Needs

An ideal development environment would provide us with some facilities which aim to create scriptlets automatically and, therefore, to provide quick previews and some shortcuts for inserting standard blocks of code, such as the `<SCRIPT> </SCRIPT>` tag.

All this, and more, can be accomplished through the automation interface exposed by Microsoft Developer Studio 97.

Only the Developer Studio shipped with Visual Studio 97 offers adequate support for advanced user customization. Previous versions limit this feature to AppWizards and toolbar changes.

The newest product, however, also offers great support for macros and add-ins and exposes a comprehensive object model to let you literally build your own environment. Yes, this sounds exactly like the kind of support we're interested in.

Our goal is to have the following tools and utilities:

- A rich and powerful text-editor
- Syntax-highlighting
- A quick browser
- Shortcuts for the most commonly used pieces of code
- A wizard to build bare-bones scriptlets in just a few seconds

We can wait for the tools to arrive (if they ever do), or we can assemble our own using the WebBrowser control and some other specialized components. Both these solutions are fairly time-consuming and—above all—not immediately available. A better approach is exploiting what already exists, and has been designed to let you build your own extensions on top.

To start with, the following paragraph will offer a quick tour of the Developer Studio 97 facilities we're going to use next.

Macros, Wizards and Add-ins

There are basically three methods you can use in order to extend the Developer Studio environment. The simplest is to write some macros in an ActiveX Scripting language and make them available via toolbar buttons or menu commands. These macros run inside the DevStudio 97 IDE and can access the objects exposed. In this way, you can modify the active document, navigate the list of the opened windows, run any of the predefined commands and macros, and so on. A large number of macros are already built-in and you just have to know about them to use them.

Most of these macros refer to menu commands. More generally, let's say that most of these predefined macros execute programmatically a significant part of the usually entirely manual tasks To see the complete list, just open the Tools|Customize menu and choose the tab labeled Commands. From the Category combo, select the item All Commands.

To write your own macros, however, you need to open a different dialog. This is found under the Tools|Macro menu.

The picture shows how the dialog will appear once you've written some macros. Otherwise, it will show up blank. To add macros, just click on Edit. Notice that under the button Options >> you're given the possibility of associating your macro with a menu command or a toolbar. The screenshot on the right shows how it looks.

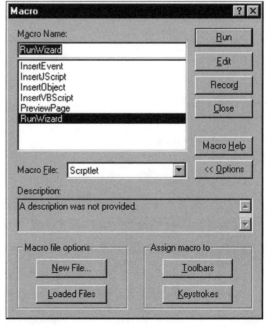

With macros you can do lots of things, but you are limited to the expressive power of a script language like VBScript. It is pretty easy to use, but sometimes there are tasks that you would accomplish better with more powerful tools.

Add-ins, for example, in-process COM servers—like ActiveX controls—are loaded when the IDE starts up. They can access the object model and modify it too. You can write them in C++, and even in Visual Basic. Since they are actually DLLs, you can create local or temporary files, perform any type of check, display your own dialogs, create windows, connect to other servers, read/write to the clipboard or the registry, and so on. In other words, you can exploit the power of a real programming language. Add-ins allow you to automatically respond to the Developer Studio's events. Receiving IDE events, however, is also possible with macros. This lets you hook for the build to start and finish, for the creation of new documents and for all the open/save activity. The environment also offers a wizard to help you to write bare-bones add-ins. To write and understand add-ins, it's recommended that you have a certain familiarity with simple COM programming.

The third way to program the Developer Studio environment is by using wizards. When you choose to create a new project, you're prompted with a dialog like this:

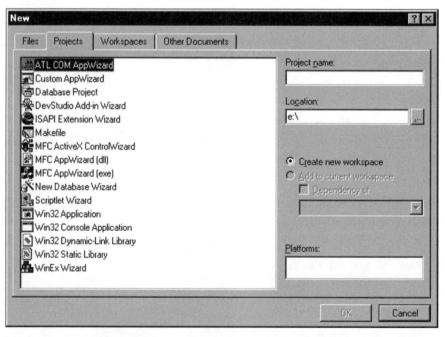

Once you've picked an item, an automatic procedure will guide you through the various steps of the process. The final result is a new opened project, whose files have the features you selected step-by-step. These wizards are mostly oriented to the building of applications. Hence their exact name; AppWizards. If we had an AppWizard for writing scriptlets, then we could allow the user to select options like the name of the pages, the standard events to support, the number and the name of properties and methods, stock properties and so on. However, such a wizard cannot work outside the Developer Studio environment.

What We Really Need?

For our purposes macros may certainly be an interesting choice. Due to their innate simplicity and the DevStudio 97 object model, you can easily write the shortcuts outlined above and automate the browsing of the pages you're currently writing. Add-ins aren't strictly required, though they could represent a more reliable and solid solution. However, writing an add-in is not as fast and easy as writing a macro.

Now for wizards—let's say we do need a wizard, but not an AppWizard. This happens for a number of reasons. First and foremost, we don't want to be tied to Developer Studio. It's much better for it to be a stand-alone (and portable) module. Furthermore, an AppWizard always sets up a project, which is not all that helpful in the case of scriptlets. A sample of an AppWizard for scriptlets is available from MIND and the Cutting-Edge column of January 98. It's an article of mine entitled simply "*Scriptlets*". Download the source code from:

> **http://www.microsoft.com/mind**

In conclusion, we're going to present a stand-alone wizard and some macros to make it far easier to write scriptlets from within DevStudio.

Writing Scriptlets-oriented Macros

Perhaps you don't know, but Developer Studio 97 has built-in support for HTML files. Since the DevStudio help system is based on the WebBrowser control, you can view both HTML pages and ActiveX documents inside it. In fact, when you attempt to install it, it checks for an updated version of Internet Explorer 3.0 or higher. This is an indirect demonstration of an instance where DevStudio really needs the WebBrowser component.

Notice that among the types of files you can add to any project there are also HTML pages. To verify this, just try to create a new file through the File|New menu. Once you've chosen the HTML format and saved the page, right-clicking on the active document allows you to see a Preview command. It lets the underlying WebBrowser component navigate up to the currently active file. So you can preview Web pages from within DevStudio 97.

Consider also that when you install Internet Explorer 4.0, it silently replaces the old WebBrowser control with a newer version that supports scriptlets and also DHTML.

Previewing Web pages

Since the IDE has the built-in capacity to preview Web pages, you could reasonably suppose that this feature is also available via a macro command. Fortunately, this is exactly the case. The macro name is **EditPreviewHTMLPage** and you can select it from the Tools|Customize menu listing all the commands from the Category combo on the File tab.

If you're like me, and prefer a straight toolbar button instead of a right-click context menu, then you can arrange a new toolbar, call it scriptlet (or whatever name you want), and drag-and-drop it over a reference to this macro.

While this may appear to be a very complex task, I can assure you that it's actually far more complex to explain than it is to do!
Briefly,

- Open the Tools|Customize dialog.
- Select the Toolbars tab.
- Create a new toolbar and give it the name you want.

At this point, you should have a tiny empty window floating around your screen. That window is a moveable toolbar you can dock anywhere in the DevStudio environment. To fill it, just use drag-and-drop. You can pick up macro commands, move existing buttons and even add new or existing menus. Again, this is harder to explain than to do since it all happens through drag-and-drop. For example, you could select the Commands tab on the Tools|Customize dialog, click on the All Commands category and pick up the **EditPreviewHTMLPage** item and drop it on to the toolbar. Once you add a button, the system asks you to choose a bitmap or to specify some text. You can choose a 16x16 icon from a variety of stock images. However, you can also define your own bitmaps using the following tricky process:

- Select any of the stock icons.
- Copy to the clipboard the 16x16 bitmap you want to use instead.
- Right-click on the button and choose Button Appearance.
- Press the Paste button.

What you obtain will look like this:

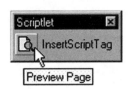

Clicking on the leftmost button is the same as right-clicking on an open HTML page and selecting the Preview command. Nothing more is needed for it to work.

In the picture above there's also a mysterious "InsertScriptTag" name. This is a macro we could have created before. To insert a macro in the toolbar, just select the Macros category in the usual Tools|Customize|Commands menu. Then, from the list of all the previously defined macros, drag-and-drop on the toolbar whatever you want.

Although the Preview button that has just been added works well, we can certainly do better. In fact, what happens if you click that button with a non-HTML document selected, or with no window opened? In that case, you will get an error!

A more elegant solution would be to write a custom macro that wraps this predefined command and runs it after verifying that the active document is an HTML page. To do this, we need to create a new macro file or add it to an existing file.

A macro file can be created through the dialog that appears when you choose the Tools|Macro menu and press the Options>> button. In particular, once you've chosen the Tools|Macro menu you have to:

- Enter the macro name
- Press Edit
- When prompted for a description, enter the necessary text (optional)
- Edit the macro VBScript code
- Save the work

DevStudio macros are stored in text files with a **.dsm** extension—a Developer Studio Macro. To add a macro to a custom toolbar, you should follow the steps mentioned before for "InsertScriptTag".

Here's an example of how to run the HTML viewer, but only if the active document really is a Web page.

```
Sub PreviewPage()
    if Not IsHTML() Then
        Exit Sub
    end if
    Application.ExecuteCommand "EditPreviewHTMLPage"
End Sub

Function IsHTML()
    if Application.Documents.Count = 0 Then
        IsHTML = False
        Exit Function
    end if

    if ActiveDocument.Type = "Text" Then
        if ActiveDocument.Language <> "HTML - IE 3.0" Then
            MsgBox "This macro can be used only with HTML files!", vbInformation, _
                "Scriptlet Toolbar"
            IsHTML = False
            Exit Function
        end if
    end if

    IsHTML = True
End Function
```

The macro **PreviewPage** first checks for the type of the active document and then executes the system command.

ActiveDocument is one of DevStudio 97's objects and represents the document window that currently holds the focus. Among its properties are **Type** and **Language**. These store information about the type of the file and the language it is written in. Feasible values for **Type** are:

- Text
- Resources
- Makefile
- Binary

Language allows a more precise control over the actual content of the document. The string HTML—IE 3.0 is what denotes a Web page. You might be wondering why this isn't IE4 instead of IE3. This is because when Microsoft released Visual Studio 97, IE4 was still to come. On the other hand, this is just a descriptive string for a type of document.

The rest of the above code is self-explanatory. The root of DevStudio 97's object model is an object called **Application.Documents**, which is the collection of all the document windows currently opened. Checking the **Count** property allows us to find out about their number.

If we attempt to run this macro when the top document isn't an HTML page, or when no document windows are open, we will receive the following warning:

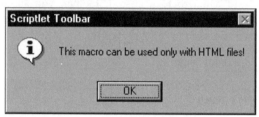

Shortcuts for Common Code Blocks

When writing code, be it an HTML page or a C++ procedure, there are always some blocks you use more often than others. Wouldn't it be nice to find a way of inserting them automatically into the document just by clicking somewhere? This is highly desirable, especially for structured commands such as **if..then**, **for..next** and more specific HTML tags.

Personally, I find it tedious, and even frustrating, to have to write **<SCRIPT> </SCRIPT>** each time I need to insert a block of script code. Not to mention all the many other frequently used attributes. Advanced authoring kits introduced ScriptWizard, or similar such tools, to meet this requirement. But now, we have no up-to-date tools (and moreover they wouldn't be free!) and so we need to edit the HTML code manually.

Let's see how easy it is to create and extend a drop-down menu of options for inserting predefined code blocks at the current cursor location.

```
Sub InsertVBScript()
    if Not IsHTML() Then
        Exit Sub
    end if

    Dim crlf
    crlf = Chr(13) + Chr(10)
    ActiveDocument.Selection = crlf + "<SCRIPT language=VBScript>" + crlf + _
            "Sub Proc" + crlf + "End Sub" + crlf+ "</SCRIPT> + crlf"
End Sub
```

Notice that the macro makes use of the **IsHTML** macro we've defined earlier. Into this sample, we add the following code block:

```
<SCRIPT language=VBScript>
Sub Proc
End Sub
</SCRIPT>
```

Note that at the line below the cursor position we exploit the property **Selection** of the aforementioned **ActiveDocument** object. **Selection** represents the text currently selected. If no text is selected, then it represents the current cursor position. By assigning it a string, you insert text wherever the cursor is—possibly replacing the selected text. To skip to the next line, a pair given by the characters carriage return (ASCII 13) and linefeed (ASCII 10), is sufficient. We do this through a variable called **crlf** defined as:

```
Dim crlf
crlf = Chr(13) + Chr(10)
```

Once we understand how to proceed, it's easy to duplicate this code and define several code blocks. For instance:

```
Sub InsertJScript()
  if Not IsHTML() Then
     Exit Sub
  end if

  Dim crlf
  crlf = Chr(13) + Chr(10)
  ActiveDocument.Selection = crlf + "<SCRIPT language=JScript>" + crlf +
"function Proc()  {" + crlf + "}" + crlf+ "</SCRIPT>"
End Sub

Sub InsertEvent()
  if Not IsHTML() Then
     Exit Sub
  end if

  Dim crlf
  crlf = Chr(13) + Chr(10)
  s1 = "<SCRIPT language=VBScript "
  s2 = "for=document event=onclick>"
  ActiveDocument.Selection = crlf + s1 + s2+ crlf + crlf + "</SCRIPT>"
End Sub

Sub InsertScriptlet ()
  if Not IsHTML() Then
     Exit Sub
  end if

  Dim crlf
  crlf = Chr(13) + Chr(10)

  s1 = "<OBJECT data=file.htm width=100 height=100 "
  s2 = "type=text/x-scriptlet>"
  ActiveDocument.Selection = crlf + s1 + s2+ crlf + crlf + "</OBJECT>"
End Sub
```

The **InsertVBScript** macro is almost identical to the **InsertJScript** one seen above. What changes is the name of language it inserts.

```
<SCRIPT language=VBScript>
Sub Proc
End Sub
</SCRIPT>
```

InsertEvent provides a skeleton of an event handler for free. In the above source, it does this just for VBScript, but it can easily be adapted to JScript too. The code inserted is:

```
<SCRIPT language=JScript for=document event=onclick>
</SCRIPT>
```

Of course, in most cases you need to change both the **for** and the **event** attributes. However, once you've got the idea you can rewrite them to suit your needs.

Finally, **InsertScriptlet** puts the structure needed to host a scriptlet inside your HTML code, that is:

```
OBJECT data=file.htm width=100 height=100 type=text/x-scriptlet>
</OBJECT>
```

Again, you will need to change both the file name and adapt the size of the site.

All these are single macros defined in a file called **scrptlet.dsm**. You can download this file from our Web site, which can be found at the following address:

http://rapid.wrox.co.uk/books/138X

Once you've downloaded it, just copy it to the **SHAREDIDE\MACROS** subdirectory of the Visual Studio 97 installation path, and make the IDE aware as shown below.

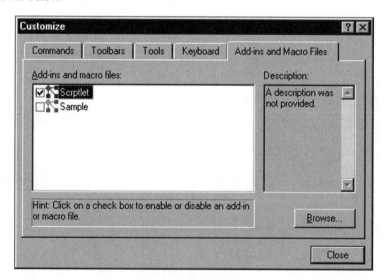

Putting It All Together

If we add these to the Scriptlet Toolbar as single macros, a large amount of screen space would be required to display them all. In addition, these blocks logically refer to a single insertion command. A good solution is to define a toolbar menu. A toolbar menu is a toolbar button that expands to show a menu. To create such an object just follow these instructions:

- Open the Tools|Customize dialog.
- Select the Commands tab and New Menu item from the Category combo.
- Define a name for it.
- Drag-and-drop the new menu on the scriptlet toolbar.
- Click on it to add new menu items

At this point you can open the Tools|Macro dialog and drag-and-drop the macros onto the toolbar menu. The final result is as follows:

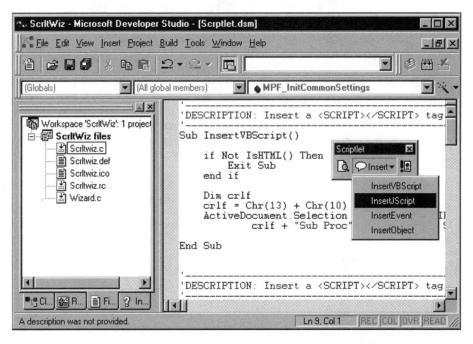

The menubar shown includes all the macros defined in the file **scrptlet.dsm**. All the insertion macros are grouped in a toolbar menu created as explained in the previous guide. The rightmost button, however, is a traditional button tied to another macro that will be discussed later.

Now that we have a number of useful accessories for editing the HTML source code from within an advanced and professional editor like DevStudio 97, we can start thinking about a wizard to automate the production of bare-bones scriptlets code.

97

The next goal will be defining its user interface. Then we'll implement it and attempt to integrate it (which is a stand-alone executable, not an AppWizard!) with our Scriptlet Toolbar.

What can a Wizard do for you?

The world is divided—there are people who love wizards and people who hate them. Wizards are the kind of software tool where there are just no half-measures. I don't know how you feel about them, but if you could try to love them then they really can save you a lot of work.

Usually, wizards aren't smart or clever. They offer a wide range of choices and work by combining them through a thread of if-then-elses. Wizards aren't CASE tools; they just save you from writing some code manually. That's all—but it really is significant.

As for scriptlets, a wizard can automatically do the following:

- Create a test page
- Create a file with a given name
- Assign the internal procedures names that follow a certain naming convention
- Add the default code for handling standard events
- Define some ambient features
- Include the declaration, for properties and methods
- Add a dummy implementation

Once you have generated the files, the wizard's job is finished and yours begins. Of course, you must put flesh on both the methods' and properties' body, as well as add the code that actually responds to the events. But you do now have a skeleton of clean code working perfectly to start with.

What's a Wizard?

A wizard is a series of dialogs that run, one by one, inside a frame window. The container window has a few buttons that allow you to move back and forth among the pages. Usually a wizard is composed of three or four different pages. A wizard is there to perform a precise task and to guide you, step by step, through the entire process.

From a programming point of view, a wizard is one of the Windows 95 common controls. To be precise, it's a specialized version of the **PropertySheet** control.

To run a wizard, you need to set up a call to the Win32 API function **PropertySheet**. While making such a call, you're required to specify a number of flags. If you include the constant **PSH_WIZARD**, then the dialogs that form the various sheets will be displayed sequentially, rather than all being available at the same time.

Both the Windows 95 and Windows NT 4.0 environments are full of wizards. An example is the procedure to create a new shortcut on the desktop.

How a Wizard Works

Basically, a wizard is asked to gather some information from various intermediate steps. That information is then made available to the final step, which will execute the ultimate goal of the wizard. For example, let's consider the creation of desktop shortcuts again.

The first page allows you to specify the name of the file you want the shortcut to represent. When you type in something and ask it for a new page, what you've just entered is validated. If it is consistent with the specific goals then the next page of the wizard is displayed. Otherwise an error message will inform you of what was wrong.

The second page of the wizard allows you to enter descriptive text for the item. This information will be added to the rest. At any stage you can choose to continue, or go back to the previous page and edit what you have already entered.

When the user clicks Finish, the wizard will start the decisive procedure, making available all the information the user specified at the various stages.

A wizard for creating scriptlets works in the same way. The first pages gather some of the user's preferences, while the Finish button actually writes a file with an **.htm** extension, according to the options set along the way.

Difference between Wizards and AppWizards

What's the difference, if any, between wizards and Developer Studio's AppWizards? First of all, both are indeed wizards; that is both are implemented as a series of dialogs among which the users can move back and forth. Developer Studio's AppWizards, however, are something special. They aim to build applications or, more generally, to handle projects supported by the IDE. In particular, AppWizards are DLLs that don't contain all the code they actually require. Instead, they contain only the code that serves the purposes of the Developer Studio environment. They are, in effect, simple extensions to the Developer Studio shell.

Traditionally, a wizard is a generic collection of the dialogs that guide the user to accomplish a given and, possibly complex, task. Creating particular source files is just an area to which a wizard can be applied well.

Wizard in Progress

Explaining the wizard internals is beyond the subject area of the book.
Consequently, you might want to read the next Further Reading section and
find out where to get more specific information on the subject. You can
download the full source code for the Scriptlet Wizard we're going to
demonstrate from the web site at the usual address:

    http://rapid.wrox.co.uk/books/138X

The wizard itself is a stand-alone executable module (called **scrltwiz.exe**)
that creates scriptlets in the current directory.

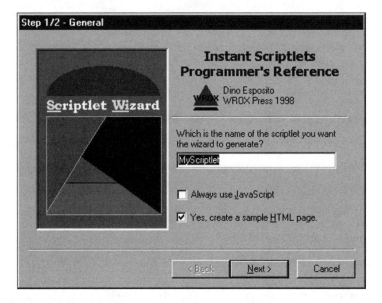

The options you can set are:

- 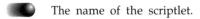 The name of the scriptlet.
- Whether or not you always want to use JavaScript as the script
  language.
- 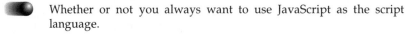 Whether or not you want the wizard to create a sample HTML page to
  test the scriptlet.

The name of the scriptlet is the name of the component (HotImage,
BitmapAnchor, ScrollablePicture, and the like). The file generated simply adds
the **.htm** extension to this name. Furthermore, you can also ask the wizard to
create a sample test page. In this case, the name is given by connecting Test
with the name of the scriptlet and adding the usual **.htm** extension. This
means that if you choose to create a scriptlet called HotImage you will end up
with two files called:

Hotimage.htm
TestHotimage.htm

By default, the wizard uses the VBScript language, except when it is declaring the public interface of the module. In this case, the code produced is always in JavaScript. However, you can stop the default behavior just by checking the option Always use JavaScript. In this case, all the script code generated will be JavaScript.

There's no way to force the wizard to follow the default interface description approach to defining the automation interface for the scriptlet, unless you want to modify its source code.

Specifying the Behavior of the Wizard

You can also choose to make the scriptlet's content selectable and to enable scrollbars if the content exceeds the client's area. In addition, you can add a default piece of code to catch some standard Dynamic HTML events such as **onclick**, **onmouseover**, **onmouseout**, **onmouseup**, **onmousedown**. The wizard will simply add a block like the following:

```
<script language=... for=document event=...>
</script>
```

Of course the wizard won't actually generate '...' but some real text. In fact, both the attributes **language** and **event** are determined dynamically, according to the user's preferences.

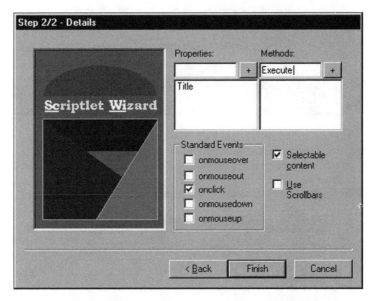

An important part of this wizard is the section that handles the declaration of properties and methods. The user interface shows two listboxes that will contain all the symbols defined. You just have to enter the name in the upper textbox and click the button whose caption is a plus sign +.

This works the same way for properties and methods. The screenshot above represents a scriptlet which will expose a property called **Title** and a method called **Execute**. If you type in the wrong name and want to remove it, just select the item and press delete.

When you click the Finish button, the wizard starts executing its real job; that is creating a couple of HTML files.

The wizard is an EXE file that you can run from anywhere and is composed of a single file which you can duplicate and move without problems.

The New DevStudio's Scriptlet Toolbar

Although the wizard is a stand-alone module, it can be integrated with the Developer Studio environment. You do this using the Tools menu. Start by clicking the Tools|Customize menu and select the Tools tab, as shown below.

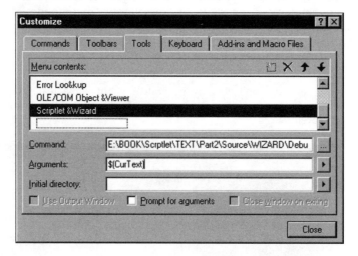

Add a new item and select the EXE file name that implements it. If necessary, you can choose a predefined argument to pass on its command line. Available choices include the currently selected text, the current directory and various others. From now on, a new item appears on the Tools menu. By clicking on it, we're able to run the Scriptlet Wizard from within Developer Studio.

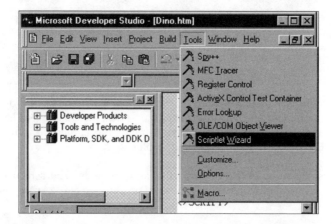

What's interesting in all this, is that any tool registered with the Developer Studio may be executed programmatically as a built-in macro. There's an upper limit, however, on the number of installable tools. Previously, we met the **Application.ExecuteCommand** method. Using it, we can start an external module too—provided that it is registered as a DevStudio tool. The number of default tools is six, so it's reasonable to assume that Scriptlet Wizard will be your seventh. This will be the case if you have installed only Visual C++. The Developer Studio environment is shared by a number of other products—like Visual J++ and Visual InterDev—and so the number of default tools will not be six. The following line of code, therefore, assumes that you have six tools installed and you should alter it accordingly.

```
Application.ExecuteCommand "UserTool7"
```

This allows you to run the wizard from within a macro file. This possibility opens up a new way to go. In fact, we can make our wizard interact more closely with the rest of the Developer Studio. For example, it would be nice to have the newly created scriptlet open as a new document in the DevStudio environment.

The best way to accomplish this is by creating an add-in module. However, we don't want to deprive you of the immeasurable pleasure of discovering, on your own, the best and the worst of add-in programming. So we're aiming to find another, equally powerful, approach entirely based on macros and VBScript code.

Make the Wizard interact with DevStudio

The final goal will be adding a new button to the Scriptlet Toolbar to run our wizard, and start editing the file when it has done.

The new macro: RunWizard, will begin asking for the name of the scriptlet.

```
Sub RunWizard
    s = InputBox( "Type in the name of the scriptlet you want the wizard to
                   generate.", "Scriptlet Wizard", "MyScriptlet" )
    ' more code follows
```

The string returned is passed to the wizard in such a way as to allow it to initialize and disable the name field. In practice, the wizard will only allow you to type in the name of the scriptlet if you don't pass it on the command line.

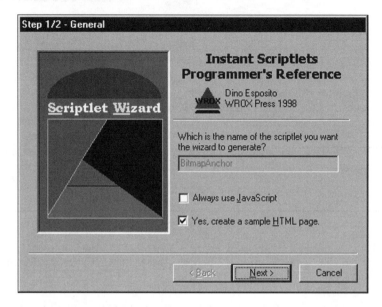

You cannot specify the argument to pass to any tool using indirection or variable. What we actually need to do is as follows:

- Get a string through a dialog.
- Pass it to the wizard and have it create a file with that name.
- Open that file in DevStudio.

Step 1 and Step 3 occur inside Developer Studio. While we can figure out a way to pass data to the wizard, the opposite is not so simple. Again, the ideal solution would be to put it all together in an add-in module.

A rudimentary technique—nevertheless perfectly adequate—for this kind of communication consists of:

- Using **InputBox** to get the desired scriptlet name.
- Opening a new HTML document and naming it.
- Saving the document in the desired path.
- Using a predefined argument (Current Text) to pass the name up to the wizard.

Using **InputBox** allows us to store the name of the file inside the VBScript code. Then we create a new HTML document, write this name to it and save it to a certain path. Notice that this is now the active document, and our string is the current text.

Furthermore, we need to modify our user-defined tool to get it to accept the current text on the command line. This is accomplished via the pseudo-command **$(CurText)**, as shown in the screenshot below.

104

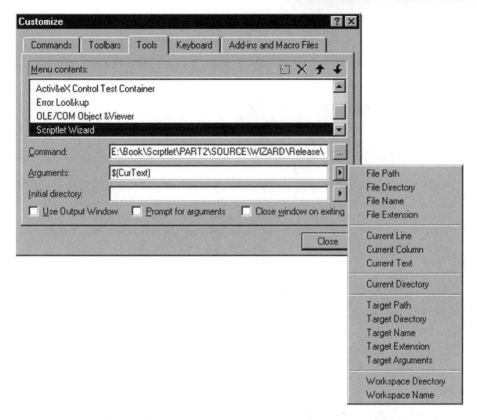

Applying this setting will run the wizard, passing the string entered through **InputBox** as the first command-line argument.

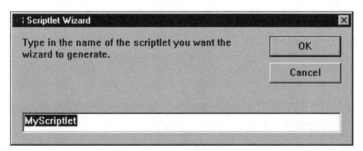

Before launching the wizard, we create a new HTML document with that name. This document will be rewritten by the wizard causing a nice side-effect when the control passes back to the Developer Studio.

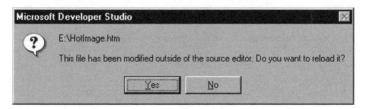

By clicking Yes, we have the scriptlet opened and ready for further editing! The whole source code for the macro is as follows:

```
Sub RunWizard()
    s = InputBox( "Type the name of the scriptlet you want the wizard to
generate.",
                "Scriptlet Wizard", "MyScriptlet" )
    Set NewDoc = Application.Documents.Add("Text")
    NewDoc.Language = "HTML - IE 3.0"
    NewDoc.Save ,True
    ActiveDocument.Selection = s
    Application.ExecuteCommand "UserTool7"
End Sub
```

The **Documents.Add** method creates and opens a new document window. The type of the document is one of the arguments. We also need to set the **Language** attribute to enable syntax-highlighting. The next step is saving the document. We avoid indicating a name so that the Developer Studio prompts us with the common Save dialog. This allows us to specify a path. The last step is writing something in the document. We need this in order to pass some data to the wizard. Because of the tool's setting, the wizard will receive the current text; that is the word at the current cursor location.

Do you remember the rightmost button of the scriptlet toolbar we mentioned earlier? Yes, it's a button that executes the **RunWizard** macro and, therefore, starts the process we discussed above.

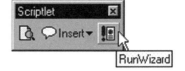

What You Have To Do

To access all these facilities, you first need to download the file **scrptlet.dsm** from our Web site

> **http://rapid.wrox.co.uk/books/138X**

This file includes all the macros described here. Alternatively, you could also retype it manually. The full source code is:

```
Sub InsertVBScript()
  if Not IsHTML() Then
 Exit Sub
  end if

  Dim crlf
  crlf = Chr(13) + Chr(10)
  ActiveDocument.Selection = crlf + "<SCRIPT language=VBScript>" + crlf + _
                    "Sub Proc" + crlf + "End Sub" + crlf+ "</SCRIPT>"
End Sub

Sub InsertJScript()
  if Not IsHTML() Then
 Exit Sub
  end if

  Dim crlf
  crlf = Chr(13) + Chr(10)
```

```
        ActiveDocument.Selection = crlf + "<SCRIPT language=JScript>" + crlf + _
                          "function Proc()  {" + crlf + "}" + crlf+ "</SCRIPT>"
  End Sub

  Sub InsertEvent()
    if Not IsHTML() Then
   Exit Sub
     end if

     Dim crlf
     crlf = Chr(13) + Chr(10)
     s1 = "<SCRIPT language=VBScript "
     s2 = "for=document event=onclick>"
     ActiveDocument.Selection = crlf + s1 + s2+ crlf + crlf + "</SCRIPT>"
  End Sub

  Sub InsertObject()
    if Not IsHTML() Then
   Exit Sub
     end if

     Dim crlf
     crlf = Chr(13) + Chr(10)
     s1 = "<OBJECT data=file.htm width=100 height=100 "
     s2 = "type=text/x-scriptlet>"
     ActiveDocument.Selection = crlf + s1 + s2+ crlf + crlf + "</OBJECT>"
  End Sub

  Sub PreviewPage()
    if Not IsHTML() Then
   Exit Sub
     end if

     Application.ExecuteCommand "EditPreviewHTMLPage"
  End Sub

  Sub RunWizard()
    s = InputBox( "Type the name of the scriptlet you want the wizard to
  generate.", _
                 "Scriptlet Wizard", "MyScriptlet" )
    Set NewDoc = Application.Documents.Add("Text")
    NewDoc.Language = "HTML - IE 3.0"
    NewDoc.Save ,True
    ActiveDocument.Selection = s
    Application.ExecuteCommand "UserTool7"
  End Sub

  Function IsHTML()
  On Error Resume Next
    if ActiveDocument.Type = "Text" Then
      if ActiveDocument.Language <> "HTML - IE 3.0" Then
          MsgBox "This macro can be used only with HTML files!", _
                 vbInformation, "Scriptlet Toolbar"
          IsHTML = False
          Exit Function
      end if
    end if

    IsHTML = True
  End Function
```

As well as the macro file, you also need the file **scrltwiz.zip**, which includes the wizard. Again, you can download it from our website.

Once you have it all, then:

- Copy the file **scrptlet.dsm** into the **SHAREDIDE\MACROS** directory of the Visual Studio installation path.

- Register the macros with Developer Studio. Open the Tools|Customize menu and select the Add-ins and Macro Files tab.

- Create your own toolbar and modify it as explained above.

- Unzip and copy the wizard somewhere on your hard-drive.

- Register a new user-defined tool within the Developer Studio. You can do this by opening the Tools|Customize menu and by selecting the Tools tab.

- Make sure you assign it the current text as the first argument. You can do this by specifying the macro command **$(CurText)**.

By this point, we have created a more comfortable environment in which to write and test scriptlets. However, even if you don't have Developer Studio you can still exploit the wizard.

In the next paragraph we'll show you how to use the wizard and how to create the skeleton for a complete scriptlet.

Scriptlets from the Wizard

A few chapters ago, we introduced the theme of HTML reusability. In doing so, we presented some capabilities of the DHTML object model and set up a bitmapped anchor—that is a bitmap which points to an internal or external link. In particular, that element was able to detect the mouse movements and changed its aspect accordingly. To be precise, it displays a raised frame when the mouse passes over and an embossed box when the mouse is pressed.

We stated then that this might have been a good example of a scriptlet. Now we're ready to put it into practice. This is also a good occasion to put the wizard through its paces.

A Bitmapped Anchor

In our previous implementation we relied on four mouse events and an **<IMG>** tag wrapped by an anchor **<A>**. These will also be the constituent elements of the scriptlet. Rewriting it as a scriptlet requires us to identify which attributes can be expressed as properties, and which as methods.

Basically, there are four possible states for a push image: normal, highlighted, pressed and disabled. The first three are affected by the mouse activity, which is always consistent. The last, instead, may be thought as the effect of a user's action. Hence, we could define the following properties and methods:

Name	Type	Description
Picture	Property	The file name of the image to be drawn in a normal state.
HotPicture	Property	The file name of the image to be drawn when the mouse is over the anchor.
DownPicture	Property	The file name of the image to be drawn when the anchor is clicked down.
Enable(bool)	Method	Toggles the state of the element from enabled to disabled

As the previous picture shows, the wizard allows us to insert both properties and methods, by typing their names in the proper textbox and by pressing the + button.

Once we've finished with it, the wizard writes a couple of files, called **BitmapAnchor.htm** (the scriptlet) and **TestBitmapAnchor.htm** (the test page), for us. Of course, we chose the name BitmapAnchor in the first page of the wizard. If you execute the wizard from the DevStudio's toolbar then you'll be asked to enter the name of the scriptlet before entering the wizard.
The next picture shows how the test page appears when viewed with Internet Explorer 4.0.

Editing the BitmapAnchor scriptlet

The source code generated by the wizard is as follows:

```
<HTML ID=MyPage>

<HEAD>
<TITLE>BitmapAnchor Scriptlet</TITLE>
</HEAD>

<SCRIPT language=VBScript for=window event=onload>
  InitBitmapAnchor
</SCRIPT>

<SCRIPT language=VBScript for=document event=onmouseover>
</SCRIPT>

<SCRIPT language=VBScript for=document event=onmousedown>
</SCRIPT>

<SCRIPT language=VBScript for=document event=onmouseup>
</SCRIPT>

<SCRIPT language=VBScript for=document event=onmouseout>
</SCRIPT>

<SCRIPT language=VBScript>
  Sub InitBitmapAnchor
  End Sub
</SCRIPT>


<SCRIPT language=JavaScript>
public_description = new CreateBitmapAnchor();
var InScriptlet = (typeof(window.external.version)=="string");

var mEnable="";
var mDownPicture="";
var mHotPicture="";
var mPicture="";

function CreateBitmapAnchor() {
  this.put_DownPicture = put_DownPicture;
```

```
      this.get_DownPicture = get_DownPicture;
      this.put_HotPicture = put_HotPicture;
      this.get_HotPicture = get_HotPicture;
      this.put_Picture = put_Picture;
      this.get_Picture = get_Picture;
      this.Enable = DoEnable;

      // Add here also the events declarations. Use the following notation:
      // this.event_OnXXXX = "";
   }


   /*-------------------------------------------------
   DownPicture property
   --------------------------------------------------*/
   function get_DownPicture()  {
     return mDownPicture;
   }
   function put_DownPicture( vDownPicture )  {
     mDownPicture = vDownPicture;
     // do something else
     return 1;
   }

   /*-------------------------------------------------
   HotPicture property
   --------------------------------------------------*/
   function get_HotPicture()  {
     return mHotPicture;
   }
   function put_HotPicture( vHotPicture )  {
     mHotPicture = vHotPicture;
     // do something else
     return 1;
   }

   /*-------------------------------------------------
   Picture property
   --------------------------------------------------*/
   function get_Picture()  {
     return mPicture;
   }
   function put_Picture( vPicture )  {
     mPicture = vPicture;
     // do something else
     return 1;
   }

   /*-------------------------------------------------
   Enable method
   --------------------------------------------------*/
   function DoEnable( bEnable )  {
     mEnable = bEnable;
     return 1;
   }

   </SCRIPT>

   <BODY bgcolor="cyan">
   Hello, I'm a scriptlet called BitmapAnchor!
   </BODY>
   </HTML>
```

The first changes we need to make are inherent to the scriptlet's user interface.
We need to insert at least an image. Look how we change the last four lines:

```
<BODY bgcolor="cyan">
<IMG src="" alt="" border=0>
</IMG>
</BODY>
```

This is the default body of the scriptlet. What is missing should be defined at run-time via script code. Here's how it appears now.

At this point, let's take a look at the test page too. The wizard produced the following code:

```
<HTML>
<HEAD>
<TITLE>BitmapAnchor Test Page</TITLE>
</HEAD>

<BODY>
<OBJECT id=bmp1 data="BitmapAnchor.htm" width=100 height=100 type="text/x-scriptlet">
</OBJECT>
</BODY>
</HTML>
```

We need to extend it in order to specify the images for the various states. This can be done in the **window.onload** event handler.

```
<HTML>
<HEAD>
<TITLE>BitmapAnchor Test Page</TITLE>
</HEAD>
<SCRIPT language=VBScript for=window event=onload>
  bmp1.Picture = "wrox_flat.gif"
  bmp1.HotPicture = "wrox_up.gif"
  bmp1.DownPicture = "wrox_down.gif"
</SCRIPT>
<BODY>
<OBJECT id=bmp1 data="BitmapAnchor.htm" width=100 height=100 type="text/x-scriptlet">
</OBJECT>
</BODY>
</HTML>
```

Of course, the scriptlet should take care of this information. Plus for the normal state it must draw the image. This is accomplished via the following code:

```
<SCRIPT language=JScript>
function put_Picture( vPicture )  {
  mPicture = vPicture;
  DoSetImage( mPicture );
  return 1;
}
</SCRIPT>
<SCRIPT language=VBScript>
  Sub DoSetImage( vImage )
    document.images.item(0).src = vImage
  End Sub
</SCRIPT>
```

Notice that a JScript procedure can make calls into a VBScript procedure. To set the image, we access the **document.images** collection and set the **src** attribute of the first item in the list. This is safe since the scriptlet, by design, includes just one **<IMG>** tag.

Once we have set the Picture property, the test page looks like the following.

Important changes have to be made to the scriptlet's event handlers. In particular, we need to specify the element for which the events must be caught. Whatever the size of the scriptlet, it is only the **<IMG>** element that detects the mouse movements. First we assign an ID string to the image in the Scriplet's body,

```
<BODY>
<IMG id="image" src="" alt="" border=0>
</IMG>
</BODY>
```

and then modify the event handlers like this:

```
<SCRIPT language=VBScript for=Image event=onmouseover>
  if mEnable Then
    DoSetImage mHotPicture
  end if
</SCRIPT>

<SCRIPT language=VBScript for=Image event=onmousedown>
  if mEnable Then
    DoSetImage mDownPicture
```

```
      end if
    </SCRIPT>

    <SCRIPT language=VBScript for=Image event=onmouseup>
      if mEnable Then
        DoSetImage mHotPicture
      end if
    </SCRIPT>

    <SCRIPT language=VBScript for=Image event=onmouseout>
      if mEnable Then
        DoSetImage mPicture
      end if
    </SCRIPT>
```

Running the test page now, we're able to see the image change while the mouse enters its area, exits its area or is clicked.

mEnable is a variable governed by the **Enable** method that determines the state of the anchor. It is initialized with 1 and is toggled by:

```
function DoEnable( bEnable )  {
  mEnable = bEnable;
  return 1;
}
```

Scriptlet's background

There are still a few problems to work around, mostly related to the scriptlet's background. In fact, if you look back at the last figure then you will realize that the scriptlet's area has a white frame around a colored background. This means that the image itself isn't drawn from the top left corner. In practice, there are margins that inflate the actual area by some pixels. To avoid this you have to do the following:

```
<SCRIPT language=VBScript>
  Sub InitBitmapAnchor
    document.body.style.marginTop = 0
    document.body.style.marginLeft = 0
    document.body.style.marginRight = 0
    document.body.style.marginBottom = 0
  End Sub
</SCRIPT>
```

This is accomplished when the scriptlet loads. Removing the padding around the scriptlet, however, doesn't remove the white background. The scriptlet, in fact, is a different window (and a different object) in relation to the **document** object of the host page. So it has its own **document** object and its own settings. If you don't want that white background, then define a new **BackColor** property and let the container set it via scripting. First you need to add some declaration lines:

```
var mBackColor="";

function CreateBitmapAnchor()  {
  this.put_DisabledPicture = put_DisabledPicture;
  this.get_DisabledPicture = get_DisabledPicture;
  this.put_DownPicture = put_DownPicture;
  this.get_DownPicture = get_DownPicture;
  this.put_HotPicture = put_HotPicture;
```

```
    this.get_HotPicture = get_HotPicture;
    this.put_Picture = put_Picture;
    this.get_Picture = get_Picture;
    this.get_BackColor = get_BackColor;
    this.put_BackColor = put_BackColor;
 this.Enable = DoEnable;

    // Add here also the events declarations. Use the following notation:
    // this.event_OnXXXX = "";
 }
```

Then you should add the following code for the new property.

```
function get_BackColor()  {
  return mBackColor;
}
function put_BackColor( vBackColor )  {
  mBackColor = vBackColor;
  document.bgColor = mBackColor;
  return 1;
}
```

The test page becomes:

```
<SCRIPT language=VBScript for=window event=onload>
  bmp1.Picture = "wrox1.gif"
  bmp1.HotPicture = "wrox2.gif"
  bmp1.DownPicture = "wrox3.gif"
  bmp1.BackColor = "silver"
</SCRIPT>
```

Of course, **BackColor** is assigned the current background color. As the next picture shows the scriptlet now works pretty well.

There is a better solution to solving the problem of background, but it requires you to know something about the container environment. Don't worry, however, as the next chapter is focused on just this very topic!

Oops, We Forgot the Anchor

In this example: called BitmapAnchor, we forgot the anchor! Let's try to remedy this right now. First of all, in the scriptlet's body we need to wrap the **<IMG>** tag with an anchor **<A>**.

```
<a id="anchor">
<img id="Image" src="" alt="" border=0>
</img>
</a>
```

Furthermore, we also assign it an ID. The location, to which the anchor points, should be determined at run-time via a new property **Href**.

```
var mHref="";

function CreateBitmapAnchor() {
  this.put_DisabledPicture = put_DisabledPicture;
  this.get_DisabledPicture = get_DisabledPicture;
  this.put_DownPicture = put_DownPicture;
  this.get_DownPicture = get_DownPicture;
  this.put_HotPicture = put_HotPicture;
  this.get_HotPicture = get_HotPicture;
  this.put_Picture = put_Picture;
  this.get_Picture = get_Picture;
  this.get_BackColor = get_BackColor;
  this.put_BackColor = put_BackColor;
  this.get_Href = get_Href;
  this.put_Href = put_Href;
  this.Enable = DoEnable;

  // Add here also the events declarations. Use the following notation:
  // this.event_OnXXXX = "";
}
function get_Href() {
  return mHref;
}
function put_Href( vHref ) {
  mHref = vHref;
  document.all("anchor").href = mHref;
  return 1;
}
```

When the scriptlet's **Href** is set, it gets a reference to the anchor using the ID as the search key. This is done through the document collection **all**. Then the anchor's **href** property is set with the value of the global variable **mHref**.

Finally, let's see how this changes the source code of the test page:

```
<SCRIPT language=VBScript for=window event=onload>
  bmp1.DisabledPicture = "wrox0.gif"
  bmp1.Picture = "wrox1.gif"
  bmp1.HotPicture = "wrox2.gif"
  bmp1.DownPicture = "wrox3.gif"
  bmp1.BackColor = "silver"
  bmp1.Href = "TestBitmapAnchor.htm"
</SCRIPT>
```

For simplicity, the test page makes the link point to itself.

To conclude, we've built a scriptlet starting from the code generated by the wizard and it certainly required less work than if we had had to write it all from scratch.

Summary

In this chapter, we have touched on a variety of very different topics and, on occasion, it seemed as if we were writing another book altogether We've covered wizards, Developer Studio customization and finally, and most importantly, scriptlets. We also provided more than an introductory sample. To summarize what has been presented here, let's start from the end—that is from the BitmapAnchor component.

It is not a simple Web object, since it exploits a large part of the DHTML functionality. It allows you to set the background color and different images for the various states of the element. If you observe it in action, you'll find it is very similar to the Windows flat toolbars. Such a component is not frequent on the Web, but it is quite simple to write with DHTML and the scriptlet's technology allows you to write it once and reuse it forever.

However, the major part of the chapter focused on other topics. Our purpose was to build a comfortable environment to write scriptlets. We outlined the main features of the ideal IDE for scriptlets and then tried to put them into practice within the Developer Studio IDE. Why DevStudio? Mainly because of its advanced features for text editing and browsing. While it is not a visual editor, it does provide you with some very specific characteristics which you won't find in most authoring tools.

In particular, we've shown you how to:

- Customize Developer Studio using VBScript macros.
- Exploit the Developer Studio's user interface.
- Make use of a wizard for writing scriptlets automatically.
- Extend the skeleton the wizard produces.
- Write a component to add visual effects to a normal anchor.

In the next chapter we'll turn back to scriptlets programming, specifically focusing on the parent environment a scriptlet can inherit.

Further Reading

There aren't many worthwhile things to read if you want to know more about Developer Studio customization. Your first option, of course, ought to be Microsoft's documentation which is available with DevStudio itself, and through the Microsoft Developer's network (MSDN) channels. There, you can find a full description of the object model, as well as a reference for VBScript—which is the only language supported at the moment.

However, the official documentation is often discursive and not enriched with insightful samples. A good support for it is an article which appeared in the September 97 issue of Microsoft Systems Journal (MSJ). Its title is *"Extend Developer Studio 97 with Your Own Macros, Add-ins and Wizards"* and the author is Steve Zimmermann. The article covers macros and add-ins very well, but admittedly discards the theme of wizards. If you want to read about Developer Studio custom AppWizards, then we can point you to a couple of other pieces. One appeared in the March 97 issue of MSJ and is *"Write Your Own C++ AppWizards"* by Walter Oney. In the same month, Windows Tech Journal published a similar piece—written by me—called *"A New Assistant"*.

The latter two articles, however, cover the Developer Studio custom AppWizards, but not how to write stand-alone wizards, like the one described in this chapter. As explained above the internal details of a wizard are a subject far beyond the scope of the book. Since wizards are nothing more than a Windows 95 common control, then you can check out *"Programming the Windows 95 User Interface"* by Nancy Winnick Cluts, which is published by Microsoft Press.

Late Breaking News!

Microsoft have brought out their own Scriptlet Wizard, downloadable with the new Server Scriptlet technology from **http://www.microsoft.com/scripting/**. We describe it and compare it with our wizard in Chapter 16.

Plus their site says that three firms do produce shippable products allowing the insertion of DHTML scriptlets onto a page. They are:

Pictorious iNetDeveloper and iNet solo found at
http://www.pictorius.com

SoftQuad HotMetal Pro at
http://www.sq.com/products/hotmetal/hmp-org.htm

and Powersoft Powersite at
http://www.sybase.com/products/powersite

Container and Ambient Properties

A scriptlet runs inside a host HTML page which acts as a container. Viewing a scriptlet's page as a stand-alone document or hosting it as Web component requires the browser to take slightly different approaches. In fact, there are a few properties that are just available to the scriptlet when it is running inside a client site. We've already come across this earlier when we explained how to detect whether a page is viewed as a scriptlet.

Each time you're considering concepts like client sites and the container environment, you need to address one key fact: the parent object provides the child with a collection of properties and inherited methods and events. This is true for ActiveX controls and also for scriptlets.

For example, an ActiveX control can access the parent's background color, its font and even the whole object model. The ActiveX Controls specification claims that each container ought to expose at least a common set of properties to the hosted elements.

The same occurs with scriptlets and IE4. The **window** object now exports a property called **external** that allows an internal object to access some attributes of the outer object. This reference, however, only gets initialized if an HTML page is viewed as a scriptlet, and holds a null value. As seen in Chapter 3, this fact may be exploited to figure out when an HTML page is running as a scriptlet.

In this chapter, we will examine the stock properties any scriptlet can access from its parent environment. A scriptlet doesn't deal with these stock properties directly and limits itself to invoking them through an interface provided by the WebBridge layer encountered in Chapter 3. We'll also discuss some practical circumstances where these stock properties become very handy.

After reading this chapter, you will have learnt about

- Scrolling the scriptlet's content.
- Implementing scriptlet's context menus.

Accessing style information from the parent.

 Using all this information to fuse the scriptlet with the host page.

All these features will be the starting point for discussing and building new, and more and more concrete, sample scriptlets.

The External Object

Personally, I started working with the IE4 object model from its first public beta release. Then I came across Platform Preview 2 and formed the idea that the final version of IE4 would probably only have changed the **document** object, provided that any other substantial changes were in order. Instead, the most significant difference between the last public beta version and the final product is, surprisingly, in the **window** object. In particular, there is a new object called **external,** which opens the door to HTML page embedding.

As explained earlier (see Chapter 3), scriptlets are hosted in HTML documents through a special container object. Under the Win32 platform this object is an ActiveX control. The content of the page, and its whole public interface, is made available to the outside world by means of a special software layer. This special software layer has the task of negotiating both the size and the position of the site with the actual container. Ultimately, this code wraps the viewer engine and can make its content selectable or scrollable. It can detect any right-click that occurs and also display a context menu.

In short, the **external** object is a code layer that places itself in the middle and works as a broker between the scriptlet and the container. In addition, it enriches the scriptlet capabilities with some environmental attributes such as the context menu, the scrollbars, and the possibility of raising custom events, as well as bubbling some standard notifications such as **onclick, onmousedown** and **onmouseover**.

To access these new features, you need to access the **external** object. For instance, you write the following code to allow users to select anything the scriptlet displays via drag-and-drop.

```
If InScriptlet Then
    window.external.selectableContent = True
End if
```

If you omit the **if** clause then the VBScript code above might produce a run-time error if the page is viewed outside as an ordinary Web page. **InScriptlet** is not a system function, but a simpler variable we initialized properly. More on this later.

The scrolling capability may be enabled in a similar fashion:

```
If InScriptlet Then
    window.external.scrollbar = True
End if
```

If this external property is set to True, then scrollbars will appear at the sides of the client site where the scriptlet's page is hosted. This allows you to move around the page's content, just as you usually do when using IE4, or any other browser. If you don't enable this feature then the output will be clipped to fit the actual size of the client site.

In conclusion, the **external** object is a read-only property exposed by the DHTML **window** object, and used and initialized only for those HTML pages embedded with the scriptlet's MIME type. The picture below shows this relationship through the Visual Basic 5 Object Browser.

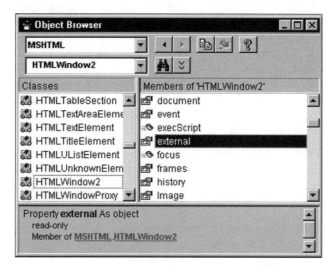

The **external** object gets initialized for each HTML page embedded via the **<OBJECT>** tag and declaring the right MIME type. No matter whether it is a real scriptlet or not. Consider the following example:

```
<HTML>
<SCRIPT for=document event=onclick>
window.external.scrollbar = 1
</SCRIPT>

<BODY bgcolor="cyan">
Embedded HTML page
</BODY>
</HTML>
```

It is a Web page that attempts to access the **external** object. It doesn't provide any of the typical scriptlet features, like methods, properties and so on. Suppose we call it **foo.htm**. Nevertheless, if you run such a host page

```
<HTML>
<BODY>
  <OBJECT id=foo1 data=foo.htm type="text/x-scriptlet">
  </OBJECT>
</BODY>
</HTML>
```

and click on the embedded page, then surprisingly a scrollbar appears. This demonstrates that once the **scrollbar** attribute is turned on, scrollbars are shown, regardless of the actual size of the site. If the content fits in the assigned area, the scrollbar is disabled but visible. Note also that while **external** is a read-only property, its descendants—such as **scrollbar**—aren't.

The **external** object is not the only way a scriptlet can access some of its parent's properties. In fact, a scriptlet can also get the parent's **style** object and therefore inherit all the CSS (Cascading Style Sheet) information.

In the rest of the chapter, we'll be examining both the stock attributes exposed via **external** and how to get a reference to the parent's **document** object.

Properties from the Parent

Basically, there are four properties that a scriptlet can inherit from the parent page. They are:

- **scrollbar**
- **selectableContent**
- **version**
- **frozen**

Of these, only two actually add some new functionality to the component itself. The last two simply denote the version string and the state of the host environment.

If you view an HTML document with IE4, or another browser, you can scroll the page content at your leisure if it exceeds the size of the screen. The program itself provides you with scrollbars and allows you to move around the content. Besides this, you can also select the text and copy it to the clipboard.

The container object, which embeds the scriptlet, is able to furnish the same functionality over the child page. Thus, using **selectableContent** and **scrollbar**, you can select the text of a scriptlet and have it scrolling both horizontally and vertically. The scrollbars apply to the specific client site where the component will be visible and available. For scriptlets, both of these features can be enabled from within a program or an HTML page.

The **version** string of the host environment is a read-only text set by the scriptlet's container. Finally, the last property; **frozen**, tells us whether the environment is ready to handle the events we want the scriptlet to generate.

The **external** object, which acts as a broker for this kind of information, only gets initialized in the presence of the scriptlet's MIME type, or when the Microsoft Scriptlet Component is used in Visual Basic applications.

In HTML code, any attempt to access **external** when it is uninitialized will result in a warning message if the script language is VBScript. Conversely, if you're writing JScript code then this kind of situation is handled automatically, and the error gets trapped. This feature is a great help in detecting whether a given HTML page is currently viewed like a scriptlet (that is, it is embedded in another one) or not.

The following table offers a summary of the stock properties a scriptlet can access.

Property	Type	Description
`scrollbar`	Boolean	If set to True it enables the use of scrollbars around the scriptlet's site. If the content of the page is too large for the actual size of the site, then this property will make horizontal and vertical scrollbars appear. Set to False by default.
`selectableContent`	Boolean	If set to True it enables the user to select the content of the page and copy it to the clipboard. Set to False by default.
`version`	String	Returns a string identifying the current version of the scriptlet's container object.
`frozen`	Boolean	If set to True it denotes that the page hosting the scriptlet is ready to receive and handle events. It's a read-only property.

The version Property

Undoubtedly, at this time, the **version** property is the least useful of the lot. In the future, however, it seems reasonable that you will need to check out some version information to detect the actual capability of the scriptlet's container. Imagine that the next update of IE4 changes something in the scriptlets management: how can you distinguish which engine you are talking to? Or how can your code detect which is the running platform? That's where the **version** property comes into play.

Such a property is also used a great deal to detect whether an HTML document is running as a scriptlet or as a stand-alone page. There is no particular reason to use **version** (in place of any other **external**-based attribute) to determine who's running the Web page and how, especially if our goal is simply to discover whether we're in a scriptlet or in an ordinary HTML page. We just need to check out whether the external object is a valid reference or is undefined. For example:

```
window.external.version
```

This is a good expression to test with. To improve it, we can wrap it in a more general expression, like the following JScript code fragment:

```
typeof(window.external.version)=="string"
```

We aren't interested in the actual content of the string; instead, we just want to know whether it is a valid object or not. So we should verify the type of the **external.version** property. We can exploit this feature to set up a safe and sound mechanism which determines whether a scriptlet is running as an ordinary Web page, or whether it is running as a scriptlet.

Back in Chapter 3 we demonstrated that the following piece of code detects this perfectly.

```
<SCRIPT language="JavaScript">
var InScriptlet = typeof(window.external.version)=="string";
</SCRIPT>
```

The **InScriptlet** variable is set with a boolean value reflecting the state of the **window.external** object.

What's version Intended for?

The **version** property is supposed to be an easy way to find out about the container object. At the moment its default value contains a number version and a string identifying the running platform. Of course, **version** is a read-only property and the following picture shows what happens if you attempt to modify it:

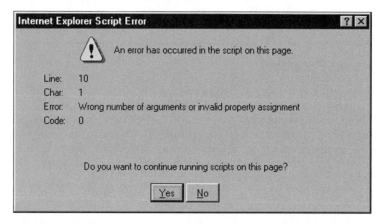

If you ask the scripting engine to display the content of the **version** property, at least under Win32 platforms, you are shown the string: 4.0 Win32.

Selecting the Scriptlet's Content

A scriptlet is an HTML page with its content made up of the usual tags, text and images. All these elements may be selectable—as through a browser. Any user may move the mouse over some HTML data and click to have it selected as text in an editor. Then it can be copied to the clipboard. When this happens, IE4 copies data in several different formats. To verify this, let's run the Clipboard Viewer which is one of the standard Windows accessories. You should have a shortcut to it in the Programs | Accessories folder. If not, you need to install it from the original Windows CD.

As shown below, the Clipboard Viewer displays the current content of the clipboard provided that it is in a supported and known format.

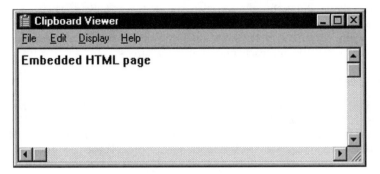

Data is copied as HTML text, Rich Text format, as well as pure ASCII text. What's new and interesting with IE4 is the possibility of copying data up to the clipboard in straight HTML format.

Scriptlets, however, offer a slightly different level of flexibility in relation to the standard HTML documents. By means of the **external** object you can decide whether or not the scriptlet's content may be selected and copied to the clipboard.

This feature is disabled by default and, unless we modify something in our scriptlet's code, users will be unable to select anything. To enable this we need to make a call to the **selectableContent** attribute. It is a boolean attribute that needs to be turned on.

```
<SCRIPT language="VBScript">
Sub InitScriptlet
  If InScriptlet then
    window.external.selectableContent = True
  End if
End Sub
</SCRIPT>
```

From now on, anything that appears in the scriptlet's user interface may be selected. The actual copying can only be done with the *Ctrl-C* key combination, or the browser's Edit|Copy menu.

Making a Scriptlet Scrollable

A scriptlet is given a site in the host container, be it a Visual Basic form or an HTML page. This site has a fixed width and height, which you are free to change. As you probably know, HTML page loading is faster if the **WIDTH** and **HEIGHT** tags are known in advance for the tags that support them.

As we discussed earlier, if necessary, you can make that area scrollable.

```
<SCRIPT language="VBScript">
Sub InitScriptlet
  If InScriptlet then
    window.external.scrollbar = True
  End if
```

127

```
End Sub
</SCRIPT>
```

The code above shows how a scriptlet can enable scrollbars. They effect the entire area assigned to the scriptlet. If you need to apply scrolling only to a region of the scriptlet's global area, then you can nest two or more scriptlets and enable scrollbars for each one at your leisure.

Scrolling Images

By exploiting this feature we can create scrollable images in a matter of seconds. GIF, JPEG or BMP images are a common presence on HTML pages. However, it's rare for an image to be scrolled separately from the whole page. The `<IMG>` tag allows you to insert images in any Web page. You can also specify the display size of the image, but can never force the appearance of scrollbars to navigate within the bitmap. To work around this, we can transform an `<IMG>` tag into a real scriptlet and enable the scrolling attribute.

> *If your goal is simply having scrollable images, you might want to consider an embedded frame with the scrolling attribute turned on. While this approach also works well outside IE4 it's far less object-oriented and reusable than this.*

Let's see how to write such a scroller component. The following code shows the first step of the process. The scriptlet looks like this:

```
<HTML>

<SCRIPT language=VBScript for="window" event="onload">
if InScriptlet Then
  window.external.scrollbar = True
end if
</SCRIPT>

<SCRIPT language=JavaScript>
public_description = new Init();
var InScriptlet = (typeof(window.external.version)=="string");
var mImage = "";

function Init() {
  this.get_Image = get_Image;
  this.put_Image = put_Image;
}

function get_Image() {
  return mImage;
}
function put_Image( vImage ) {
  mImage = vImage;
  document.images.item(0).src = mImage;
}
</SCRIPT>

<BODY>
<IMG id="image" src="">
</BODY>
</HTML>
```

The image is displayed with scrollbars and allows you to scroll the bitmap. Once you set the **scrollbar** property, both the bars are always shown.

128

However, the container is smart enough to automatically disable those not needed.

Let's see how to make use of such a scriptlet, called **scroller.htm**. Here's a page that hosts it and put it to work with an image called **setup.bmp**.

```
<HTML>

<SCRIPT language=VBScript for="window" event="onload">
Image1.Image = "setup.bmp"
</SCRIPT>

<BODY>
<OBJECT id=Image1 data="scroller.htm" type="text/x-scriptlet"
    width=450 height=250>
</OBJECT>

</BODY>
</HTML>
```

The code above shows how to host such a component in a Web page. If you run this sample, you'll certainly notice that a small, unused area still surrounds the image. Each time a browser, or a container object, displays a page it always assigns some default values to margins. This applies to HTML pages as well as scriptlets. However, when it occurs with scriptlets it sometimes produces nasty effects. In particular, when scrolling images, we don't want the margins to alter the scrolling process. So let's turn them off with the following lines of code.

```
<SCRIPT language=VBScript for="window" event="onload">
if InScriptlet Then
  window.external.scrollbar = True
end if
document.body.style.marginTop = 0
document.body.style.marginLeft = 0
document.body.style.marginBottom = 0
document.body.style.marginRight = 0
</SCRIPT>
```

The result is shown in this picture.

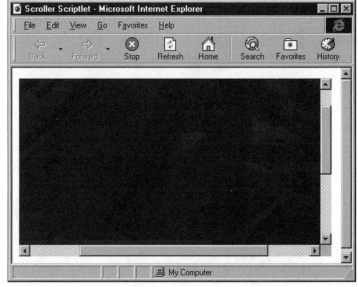

Now, we have something that closely resembles the **<IMG>** tag. In addition, it provides you with the ability to scroll an image inside the host Web page.

Of course, we can wrap the stock properties a scriptlet can access and make them available to users via a custom interface. Here's a complete example that also exposes the **scrollbar** property as if it were a scriptlet property.

```
<HTML>
<SCRIPT language=VBScript for="window" event="onload">
if InScriptlet Then
  if mScrollbar Then
    window.external.scrollbar = True
  end if
end if
document.body.style.marginTop = 0
document.body.style.marginLeft = 0
document.body.style.marginBottom = 0
document.body.style.marginRight = 0
</SCRIPT>

<SCRIPT language=JavaScript>
public_description = new Init();
var InScriptlet = (typeof(window.external.version)=="string");
var mImage = "";
var mScrollbar = 0;

function Init() {
  this.get_Image = get_Image;
  this.put_Image = put_Image;
  this.get_Scrollbar = get_Scrollbar;
  this.put_Scrollbar = put_Scrollbar;
}

function get_Image() {
  return mImage;
}
function put_Image( vImage ) {
  mImage = vImage;
  document.images.item(0).src = mImage;
}
function get_Scrollbar() {
  return mScrollbar;
}
function put_Scrollbar ( vScrollbar ) {
  mScrollbar = vScrollbar;
  if( InScriptlet )
    window.external.scrollbar = mScrollbar;
}
</SCRIPT>

<BODY>
<IMG id="image" src="">
</BODY>
</HTML>
```

Here's an example of a page that uses this new property

```
<HTML>
<HEAD>
<TITLE>Scroller Scriptlet</TITLE>
</HEAD>

<SCRIPT language=VBScript for="window" event=onload>
image1.Image = "setup.bmp"
```

130

```
        image1.Scrollbar = True
        </SCRIPT>

        <BODY>
        <OBJECT width=450 height=250 id=image1 data="scroll1.htm" type="text/x-
        scriptlet">
        </OBJECT>
        </BODY>

        </HTML>
```

Note that now the scrolling capability must be explicitly enabled to obtain the same result as the above figure.

Sending Events to the Host

Any scriptlet can notify events to its container. There are basically two types of events that a scriptlet can raise. Among these are standard events such as **onclick**, **onmouseup**, and the like, as well as custom events specific to the components internal state. Whether the scriptlet is bubbling up a standard event, or is firing one of its own events, it must make sure that the target object is in a consistent state and ready to receive such notifications. However, a scriptlet doesn't know anything about the container's state. For this reason, the container exposes an ambient property called **frozen** which a scriptlet must check before sending events in a safe way.

```
        <script language="VBscript" for="document" event="onclick">
          if (InScriptlet and (not window.external.frozen)) then
            window.external.bubbleEvent
          end if
        </script>
```

The code excerpt above shows what the scriptlet should do to take advantage of the **frozen** property and avoid run-time errors. The **frozen** property is updated by the container object, and sends a read-only attribute to the scriptlet's code. If the host environment freezes the events, a scriptlet shouldn't send anything.

Apart from checking to see if the scriptlet page is being run as a scriptlet (indicated by the **InScriptlet** variable) you must also check to make sure that the hosting container is ready to receive events. This is done by making sure the **window.external.frozen** property is false.

In the next chapter, we'll take a closer look at the events that a scriptlet can send to and receive from its external host.

Methods and Events

A scriptlet can also inherit methods from its host environment. In particular, the following table gives a complete list of the methods a scriptlet can exploit via the **external** interface.

Method	Description
bubbleEvent	This method passes the current event up to the host environment—be it an HTML page or in the form of a Visual Basic application.
raiseEvent	This method allows the scriptlet to raise a given event. Each custom event is identified by name and can carry any kind of data.
SetContextMenu	This method associates a popup menu with the client area of the scriptlet. The menu will be displayed each time a user right-clicks over the scriptlet window.

Basically, there are two kind of functionality to exploit: events and context menus. A scriptlet must rely on the host object to let it know about its internal state. In addition, the **container** object intercepts any right click events and takes care of displaying a context menu.

Bubbling and Raising Events

A scriptlet will be notified of all the standard Dynamic HTML events that occur for **window** objects, **document** objects, and any other elements that it contains. The **bubbleEvent** method is the method we would use to pass any trapped event to the container. This is referred to as **event bubbling**.

Scriptlets need to pass standard events explicitly to the host HTML page or the Visual Basic form, otherwise, they will never know about any **onmouseover**, **onmouseout** or **onclick** events that occur.

The correct code to handle any click the user makes on the scriptlet document area and make it available to the host environment is:

```
<script language="VBscript" for="document" event="onclick">
  if (InScriptlet and (not window.external.frozen)) then
    window.external.bubbleEvent
  end if
</script>
```

As you can see, **bubbleEvent** applies only to the standard events provided by the DHTML event model. If you want to know more about Dynamic HTML Event Bubbling, then check out "*Instant IE4 Dynamic HTML Programmer's Reference*" by Alex Homer and Chris Ullman, ISBN 1-861000-68-5 and "*Professional IE4 Programming*" ISBN 1-861000-70-7—both published by Wrox Press.

In the next chapter (entirely devoted to event handling) we will examine this topic in great detail, as it is crucial to using scriptlets. In the meantime, let's focus on the actual capability and role of the stock methods.

Bubbling Events up

Each time a scriptlet receives a message through the DHTML event engine it can reply by doing whatever is needed. However, a scriptlet is part of the

DHTML event architecture and could exploit the event bubbling mechanism. This means that a scriptlet has the power to pass the same message down to the host page or container. In fact, when you display an HTML page with say, an ActiveX control and click over it, then the control itself is given the chance to respond to the event first. Once it has done with it (or even before finishing), it can fire a similar event in the ambient host.

There is a similar logic behind the event bubbling of DHTML. The main difference is that now any DHTML element is considered as a separate object with the power of responding to standard events. Scriptlets are just HTML elements and so can also bubble events up. In particular, they will make use of the **window.external.bubbleEvent** method, which requires no further parameters. Of course, such a method is supposed to get called only within event handlers. More on this in the next chapter.

Firing Custom Events

A scriptlet can not only receive standard notifications, but can also raise specialized events. This is a point that highlights a key difference between scriptlets and ActiveX controls. To make things simpler, scriptlets support only one outgoing interface through which all the custom events are routed to their respective listeners (usually called sinks). The method used to serve this purpose is **window.external.raiseEvent**. This method takes two arguments. The first one is the name of the event that distinguishes between this event and all the other events the scriplet can fire. The second parameter is a reference to the actual data that must be carried out to the sink.

```
if( InScriptlet and (not window.external.frozen) ) {
   t = new Date();
   window.external.raiseEvent ("OnStopClock", t);
}
```

The fragment of JavaScript source code above shows how to send an **OnStopClock** event down to the host container. The host container will receive a common event and recognize it by name. The second argument is the data that the scriptlet needs to transmit with the event. In the code above, it is a **date** object that can be used to get the current time. This piece of code could be called from anywhere within the scriptlet's sources.

Give your Scriptlet a Context Menu

To add a context menu to a scriptlet, you need to write some code that requires a substantial use of arrays. At the time of writing, only VBScript, JavaScript and JScript are guaranteed to manage and create arrays compatible with the expectations of the **setContextMenu** stock method.

To define a context menu you initialize an array with **twice** the number of elements that you want for the menu. For each pair, the first item is the caption that will be drawn, while the second is the name of the function that gets called when the user clicks. To put a separator in the middle you just add a couple of empty items.

A scriptlet that supports a context menu could look like this.

133

```
<html >
<body>

<script language="VBScript" for="window" event="onload">
    InitMyScriptlet
</script>

<script language="VBScript">
dim menuItems(8)

Sub InitMyScriptlet
  if InScriptlet then
    menuItems(0) = "&Copy"
    menuItems(1) = "Copy"
    menuItems(2) = "&Paste"
    menuItems(3) = "Paste"
    menuItems(4) = ""
    menuItems(5) = ""
    menuItems(6) = "&Edit"
    menuItems(7) = "Edit"
    window.external.setContextMenu(menuItems)
  end if
End Sub

Sub Copy
  MsgBox "You selected Copy"
End Sub

Sub Paste
  MsgBox "You selected Paste"
End Sub

Sub Edit
  MsgBox "You selected Edit"
End Sub
</script>


<script language="Javascript ">
public_description = new CreateMyScriptlet();
var InScriptlet = (typeof(window.external.version) == "string");
function CreateMyScriptlet() {}
</script>

Right click here to show a context menu!
</body>
</html>
```

The syntax of **setContextMenu** requires you to specify an array previously filled in with the aforementioned pairs **<caption, function_name>.** A more formal description is the following:

menuItems(i) = caption for the i.th menu item
menuItems(i+1) = name of the function to be executed after the click

If we name the above scriptlet **menu1.htm**, then such a page hosts it successfully, as shown below.

```
<html>
<title>Test page using Scriptlets</title>
<body bgcolor="C0C0C0">
<b>Test page using Scriptlets</b>
```

```
<p>
<object id="Scriptlet1" data="Menu1.htm" align="bottom"
width="200" height="100" type="text/x-scriptlet">
</object>
</p>

<p> </p>
</body>
</html>
```

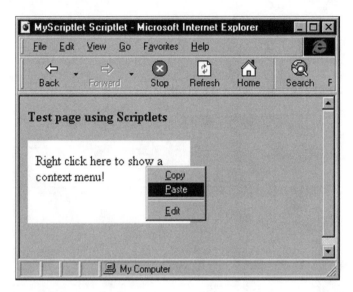

To be precise, **setContextMenu** just associates a popup menu with the
scriptlet. The container will then display the menu when the user right clicks.
Typically, such an association takes place during the **window.onload** event, but
we can change it dynamically. This means two things. Firstly, we can change
the context menu at a certain point. Secondly, the scriptlet has to do nothing in
particular to make the menu display.

Details About the Syntax

There are a couple of tricks to learn in order to deal with a scriptlet's context
menus more effectively. If you type the name of the procedure that executes
when the user clicks on the menu incorrectly, and turn it into the name of an
nonexistent function, then all the items that follow are cut off. For example, the
following code:

```
<script language="VBscript">
dim menuItems(8)

Sub InitMyScriptlet
  if InScriptlet then
    menuItems(0) = "&Copy"
    menuItems(1) = "Copy"
    menuItems(2) = "&Paste"
    menuItems(3) = "Past"
    menuItems(4) = ""
    menuItems(5) = ""
    menuItems(6) = "&Edit"
    menuItems(7) = "Edit"
```

135

```
      window.external.setContextMenu(menuItems)
   end if
End Sub

Sub Copy
  MsgBox "You selected Copy"
End Sub

Sub Paste
  MsgBox "You selected Paste"
End Sub

Sub Edit
  MsgBox "You selected Edit"
End Sub
</script>
```

will result in the following screenshot:

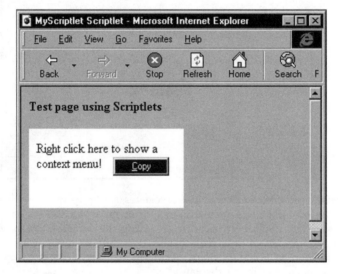

The structure of the menu can change at any moment in time. You can add new items or replace existing ones literally whenever you want. Sometimes you may need to declare an oversized array of items, whose last elements will become significant only from a certain moment. In this case, make sure that the placeholder items don't affect the correct behavior of the menu.

Using an item that points to a nonexistent function is a good way to get this effect. In doing so, you create a menu that can become larger after the page has been loaded. At least, this is what the user perceives. In practice, you declare more menu items than you really need at the beginning. The surplus items (placed at the bottom of the array) point to nonexistent functions and are initially cut off.

Then, by changing the function name they refer to, you could enable them and make them visible programmatically. If we were using empty strings instead of nonexistent function names, our menu would show lots of separators.

Since the array index is 0-based you should always have an odd number to denote the size of the menu item array. In the above code, however, we assigned it a size of 8. In this case the surplus item is ignored and the maximum number of allowed menu items is still 4.

Modifying the Menu

To dynamically modify a menu you just have to remember which was the last item appended, or which ones you want to replace the caption or the function of. Once we have modified the menu (adapting it to suit our needs) all that remains for us to do is reset it via **setContextMenu**. For example, let's modify the previous scriptlet by allowing it to extend its own context menu once you click on its area. We want it to display a maximum of 5 items, so we need to increase the size of the array to 9.

To make sure it initially displays only four items, we need to disable the last one. The code makes it point to a nonexistent **x** function.

```vbscript
<script language="VBscript">
dim menuItems(9)

Sub InitMyScriptlet
  if InScriptlet then
    menuItems(0) = "&Copy"
    menuItems(1) = "Copy"
    menuItems(2) = "&Paste"
    menuItems(3) = "Paste"
    menuItems(4) = ""
    menuItems(5) = ""
    menuItems(6) = "&Edit"
    menuItems(7) = "Edit"
    menuItems(8) = "Unused Item"
    menuItems(9) = "x"
    window.external.setContextMenu(menuItems)
  end if
End Sub

Sub Copy
  MsgBox "You selected Copy"
End Sub

Sub Paste
  MsgBox "You selected Paste"
End Sub

Sub Edit
  MsgBox "You selected Edit"
End Sub

Sub Another
  MsgBox "You selected Another Item"
End Sub
</script>

<script language=VBScript for=document event=onclick>
  menuItems(4) = "&Edit"
  menuItems(5) = "Edit"
  menuItems(6) = ""
  menuItems(7) = ""
  menuItems(8) = "&Another Item"
  menuItems(9) = "Another"
  window.external.setContextMenu(menuItems)
</script>
```

137

Initially, right-clicking on the scriptlet we still get what is shown two figures back. Instead, once we have clicked with the left button on the scriptlet's area the menu changes as illustrated above. In particular, the Edit item and the separator exchange their positions and a new item named "Another Item" is added. The next figure demonstrates it.

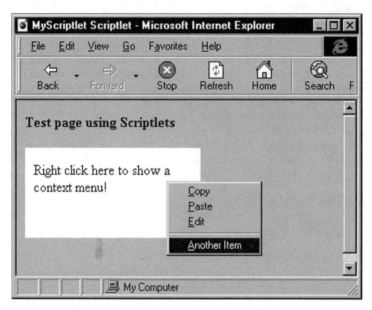

The interface exposed by the container for menus looks like the interface of the IE Popup Menu Control, which should be quite familiar. Anyway, from the scriptlet's perspective we can only add items at a given position using an array. There's no way to add bitmaps to the menu, or disable items under certain conditions.

Style Information from the Parent

Scriptlets are components hosted in a container page. Scriptlets, however, are also HTML pages with their own DHTML object model. The **document** object of the scriptlet is quite different from the **document** object of the host page. Above all, each one has different properties.

In some cases, it's impossible for a scriptlet to integrate smoothly into the parent's environment. For example, the scriptlet's background can't be transparent. This means that if the parent's background is textured then the scriptlet can't insert smoothly and appear as if it was a part of the whole page.

In other cases, however, this kind of graphic integration is perfectly possible. A scriptlet can inherit all the parent's style information and change its own look accordingly. Let's examine a quick and easy example.

As the picture shows, the scriptlet has a white area that contrasts with the colored background. The default color of the **document**'s background is white—unless you change it. We can get the component to expose a **bgcolor** property and modify it programmatically. This is an acceptable solution as long as you want to set it to a variant of color. Suppose, instead, that what you really need is something much simpler. For example, suppose you want the scriptlet to get the same background color as its parent. You might assign it explicitly from the host script code or, better yet, you can teach your own scriptlet to read and automatically set the parent's background color.

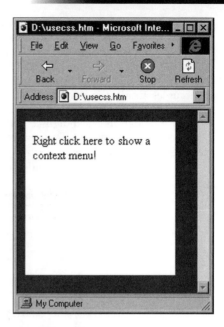

Getting the Parent's Background Color

The scriptlet background color is contained in the **document.bgColor** property. Each time you use DHTML properties, make sure you type in the right case to avoid sudden and hard-to-understand errors. The same is true for the host page. Thus, what is actually needed is a way to find out where the **document** object of the parent page is. The script necessary is just **window.parent.document**. The following code excerpt shows how a scriptlet can adopt the parent's **bgColor** as its own background color.

```
<script language="VBscript" for="window" event="onload">
  InitMyScriptlet
  document.bgColor = window.parent.document.bgColor
</script>
```

Of course, this technique doesn't end here and could be extended to import the parent's whole **style** object into the scriptlet.

```
<script language="VBscript" for="window" event="onload">
  InitMyScriptlet
  set parstyle = window.parent.document.body.style
  document.body.style.color = parstyle.color
  document.body.style.backgroundColor = parstyle.backgroundColor
</script>
```

The example above, in fact, assigns the **style** object of the parent page to a **parstyle** variable and uses it to map some of the parent styles to the corresponding properties of the scriptlet. In particular, the line

```
document.body.style.backgroundColor = parstyle.backgroundColor
```

assigns the scriptlet's body background the same body background color of the host page. Given this, any of the parent's style sheet properties can be inherited by a hosted scriptlet.

139

While this is not a technique that works in all cases, it is a good way to make the scriptlet as similar as possible to the parent. In particular, when there's a bitmap in the background this approach simply won't work. Even if you assign the same bitmap to the scriptlet it will be displayed from the client 0,0 pixel position, which is not compatible with the position the scriptlet actually occupies inside the parent area.

Let's consider the next figure. It illustrates how a scriptlet will draw over a bitmapped background. A scriptlet is an overlapped object with its own background area. Even if scriptlets are windowless objects, they behave as if they were really windows and hide the underlying portion of the document.

The following code shows how a scriptlet can acquire the background image of the parent. The background image is given by **document.body.background**.

```
<script language="VBscript" for="window" event="onload">
   InitMyScriptlet
   set parbody = window.parent.document.body
   set parstyle = parbody.style
   document.body.style.color = parstyle.color
   document.body.style.backgroundColor = parstyle.backgroundColor
   document.body.background = parbody.background
</script>
```

The following picture shows the end result. Note the misalignment of the image pixels around the scriptlet's area. To work round this limitation you should find out a way of drawing the background image with an offset or make the scriptlet's window transparent!

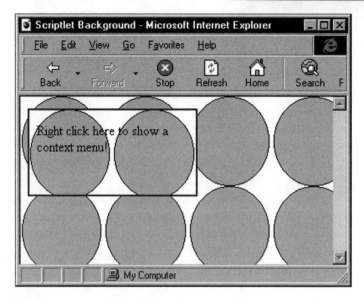

Summary

In this chapter, we've found out more about the relationship that binds a scriptlet to its container. We have walked through the various attributes a scriptlet can inherit from the outside world and we have shown how each of them could be exploited and used to enrich a script component.

We have discussed scrolling, selection, version information, and presented samples of context menus. All these features are the direct consequence of the scriptlet's architecture, made up of an HTML viewer and a bridge layer that takes care of the implementation of the container properties. A scriptlet is a page running inside another page and can be fused with it for graphic styles. Thus, we emphasized this aspect too and provided samples of how to access the **style** object of the container. In particular, we covered the following topics:

- Ambient properties and methods.
- Selecting the scriptlet's content.
- Scrolling the scriptlet's area.
- Sending and receiving events.
- Adding a context menu.
- Getting graphic styles from the parent.

There is, however, a topic that we just scratched the surface of here and which needs more thorough coverage. We're talking about events. A scriptlet can send custom events—as well as bubble up standard DHTML notifications. However, a scriptlet can receive only standard events, unless it hosts child scriptlets. The details of this, namely how to declare and handle events, will be the subject of the next chapter.

141

Chapter

6

Event Handling

Scriptlets are Web components built on top of the DHTML object model. Their internal structure, which closely resembles the ActiveX controls, offers good support for events. Scriptlets can raise events and are a basic part of the DHTML event bubbling mechanism.

There are two kinds of events a scriptlet must be aware of: custom and standard events. The custom events are raised when necessary and are under the full control of the component itself. On the other hand, the standard events are trapped through the common script procedures and may be passed up to the remaining elements of the page.

In this chapter, we're aiming to cover events in their widest possible sense. First of all, we'll discuss events declaration and implementation. Next, we'll learn why events don't need to be declared and yet why you should declare them anyway, plus how the routing engine that moves them works from the object down to the host. To complete the chapter we will concentrate on providing a detailed coverage of the syntax and some examples. In particular, you will find out how to

- Bubble standard DHTML events.
- Declare custom events.
- Pass data through events.
- Return values from events.

With this chapter our overview of scriptlets is about to end. After this, there will just be one more topic to cover: how to host scriptlets in desktop applications.

Event Bubbling

If you're already familiar with DHTML, then you should know about event bubbling. If not, we're now going to summarize its basic points.

IE4 sees any HTML page as a collection of objects. Every one of them may be identified with its own ID, and any formatting style that is globally defined may be applied to it. In addition to this, any page element also has the ability to catch standard events. Let's consider the following piece of DHTML code:

```
<HTML>
<SCRIPT language=VBScript for="elem1" event="onclick">
MsgBox "Clicked on the substring: HTML"
</SCRIPT>

<BODY>
This is a sample <SPAN id="elem1">HTML</SPAN> page.
</BODY>
</HTML>
```

The substring HTML is treated as if it was a stand-alone object, to which you can apply methods, properties and, therefore, why not events? While invoking methods and properties on a pseudo-object like the substring is quite reasonable, it's not so clear how it could ever receive events.

The syntax:

```
<SCRIPT language=VBScript for="elem1" event="onclick"
' code to execute when the specified element knows about the click
</SCRIPT>
```

means that the specified code executes when the user clicks over the portion of the page identified by the name **elem1**. The question is—how does the **elem1** element know about the event?

The Mechanism of Event Bubbling

The DHTML object model divides the page up into a collection of related elements. Any event that occurs on the document is progressively notified to every single element that forms the page content. If any of these has an ID, then you can handle the event at that level.

In the above example, if you click over the string HTML then you trigger a sequence of notifications.

IE4 starts searching for an object that can handle that event. It does this by going through the collection of all the page elements. Any one that has a handler procedure gets invoked. Once the first one has been found and has handled the event, IE4 keeps on searching until it reaches the topmost page element. Any of the previously visited elements can stop the process simply by turning on a given flag. This stepping through the page elements is known as **event bubbling**.

The search for all the valid objects proceeds through bottom-up logic—going from the smaller elements to those more general and comprehensive. The first one that can handle the event is the real target of the event. Then, the notification is bubbled up through the various parents of the element.

The default behavior, if any, occurs only after all the parent objects and the document object have been contacted.

At any of these levels, you can stop the back propagation by intervening in the new DHTML **event** object.

A Sample of Event Bubbling

Before going on, let's examine a more descriptive example. Consider the following code:

```
<HTML>
<SCRIPT language=VBScript for=elem1 event=onclick>
MsgBox "Clicked on the substring: HTML"
</SCRIPT>

<SCRIPT language=VBScript for="document" event="onclick">
MsgBox "Clicked on the page document"
</SCRIPT>

<BODY>
This is a sample <SPAN id="elem1">HTML</SPAN> page.
</BODY>
</HTML>
```

We have defined two different handlers for the same **onclick** event. If the user clicks over the string HTML—whose identifier is **elem1**—then the event will be processed, initially, by the **elem1** event handler and will result in a message box that reads:

Clicked on the substring: HTML

Next, the event bubbling continues and the same event is handled by the parent object—the **document** object. As a result, a new message box will appear showing the text:

Clicked on the page document

If the user clicks on the page area, but outside the string HTML, then only the second message will be shown.

The event Object

The **event** object is the code representation of any event that occurs inside a DHTML document. It is exposed by the **window** object, and is supposed to provide information about the event that is being processed. Among the properties that the object includes, we can list:

Property	Type	Description
button	Integer	The mouse button that caused the event (1=left).
cancelBubble	Boolean	If set to True causes the event bubbling to stop.
srcElement	Object	It represents the object that fired the event.
x	Integer	x coordinate of the mouse click.
y	Integer	y coordinate of the mouse click.

145

Property	Type	Description
shiftKey	Boolean	It is set to True if the Shift key is pressed.
ctrlKey	Boolean	It is set to True if the Ctrl key is pressed.
altKey	Boolean	It is set to True if the Alt key is pressed.
returnValue	Integer	It contains the value that we want to return back to the source element.

There are three basic properties: **srcElement**, **cancelBubble** and **returnValue**. The first one denotes the object that originally fired the event. The others allow you to implement two more interesting functions. By using those attributes, in fact, we can stop the event bubbling at any level and we can return values to the caller. The latter also gives the ability to cancel or modify the default behavior.

The following code snippets show how to use the **event.srcElement** object.

```
<HTML>
<SCRIPT language=VBScript for="elem1" event="onclick">
MsgBox "Processed by: " + window.event.srcElement.id
</SCRIPT>

<SCRIPT language=VBScript for="document" event="onclick">
MsgBox "Processed by the document"
</SCRIPT>

<BODY>
This is a sample <SPAN id="elem1">HTML</SPAN> page.
</BODY>
</HTML>
```

The expression **window.event.srcElement.id** returns the ID of the element that originates the event, whichever it is. Of course, if the element hasn't got an ID an empty string will be returned. Usually, however, the **document** object hasn't got an ID. To give an element an ID, you assign an ID to the **<BODY>** tag. Just make sure not to assign the string 'document' as this could cause a bit of recursion.

```
<HTML>
<SCRIPT language=VBScript for=elem1 event="onclick">
MsgBox "Processed by: " + window.event.srcElement.id
</SCRIPT>

<SCRIPT language=VBScript for=document event="onclick">
MsgBox "Processed at the document level. Source element is " +
window.event.srcElement.id
</SCRIPT>

<BODY id="document1">
This is a sample <SPAN id="elem1">HTML</SPAN> page.
</BODY>
</HTML>
```

If you run this code (**event2.htm**) from our Web site at **http://rapid.wrox.co.uk/books/138X** you'll notice that if you click outside the string HTML—that is, outside the object **elem1**—then IE4 will prompt the following message:

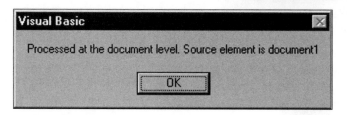

Instead, if you click over the string HTML, you'll get a couple of message boxes.

The above dialog notifies you that the event is being processed at the first level, that is, by the object that actually originates it. The next figure shows what happens next, when the event is processed at the document level.

Although the event is being processed at the document level, the source element is still the **elem1** object, which originally fired the event.

With event bubbling, you can also have a single point where all the code that responds to a given event is located. For example, instead of writing different handlers for processing the same event at different levels, you could write a unique function that processes it at the document level after distinguishing between the source elements. While this is not always the best thing you can do, nevertheless it sometimes gives you an opportunity to write more compact and equally readable code.

Canceling an Event

Event bubbling can also be interrupted quite easily. IE4 takes care of invoking the hierarchy of objects that can handle a given event. Any one of them can prevent the others from receiving notifications. To do this, just set the **cancelBubble** property.

```
<HTML>
<SCRIPT language=VBScript for="elem1" event="onclick">
i = MsgBox ("Processed by: " + window.event.srcElement.id +". Cancel
bubbling?",
     vbYesNo)
if i=vbYes Then
  window.event.cancelBubble = True
end if
</SCRIPT>
```

```
<SCRIPT language=VBScript for=document event="onclick">
MsgBox "Processed at the document level. Source element is " +
    window.event.srcElement.id
</SCRIPT>

<BODY id=document1>
This is a sample <SPAN id="elem1">HTML page</SPAN>.
</BODY>
</HTML>
```

If you run the file **event3.htm** from our Web site at:
http://rapid.wrox.co.uk/books/138X, you will see the following window:

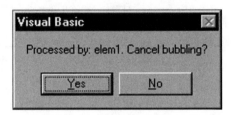

By clicking Yes, you can cause the **cancelBubble** property to become True and
stop the bubbling. This may be done by any element in the hierarchy.

Stopping the bubbling is not always enough if your goal is preventing the
events from being handled at any further level after yours. There are
circumstances in which a default behavior is associated with the event. Stopping
the bubbling simply stops it from being notified to the remaining page
elements, but the default behavior still occurs. To prevent anything from taking
place, we need to take a slightly different approach and make use of a slightly
more powerful attribute.

Modifying the Default Behavior

Suppose you're working with anchors. Once you click over them, the system
goes through the usual collection of possibly interested objects and gives you
the opportunity to process the event at various levels. This behavior is almost
identical to the previous case. However, an anchor includes a reference to a
different location. Once IE4 finishes bubbling up the events, it jumps to the
specified URL. This occurs whether or not you stop the bubbling. Try out the
following example. You can run **anchor.htm** from our Web site.

```
<HTML>
<SCRIPT language=VBScript for="elem1" event="onclick">
i = MsgBox ("Processed by: " + window.event.srcElement.id +". Cancel
bubbling?", vbYesNo)
if i=vbYes Then
  window.event.cancelBubble = True
end if
</SCRIPT>

<SCRIPT language=VBScript for="document" event="onclick">
MsgBox "Processed at the document level. Source element is " +
window.event.srcElement.id
</SCRIPT>
```

```
<BODY id=document1>
This is a sample <a href=anchor.htm id="elem1">HTML</a> page.
</BODY>
</HTML>
```

The page appears as shown in this screenshot:

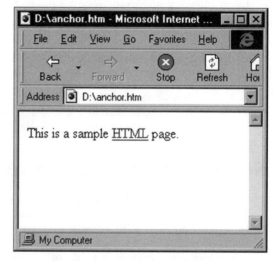

By clicking on the HTML string, you will be successively prompted to cancel bubbling and to process the event at the document level. This is exactly what occurred before. What's different is that at the end of the process, IE4 jumps to the referenced URL (in the sample above, for simplicity, the **href** attribute points to the same page **anchor.htm**) and, thus, regardless of what is clicked, the browser still tries to go to the new page.

To change the default behavior you need to follow a two-step process. Firstly, do something instead of the default; secondly, cancel the standard event. The next example, called **anchor2.htm**, does just this.

```
<HTML>
<SCRIPT language=VBScript for="elem1" event="onclick">
i = MsgBox ("Going to: " + window.event.srcElement.href + ". Cancel event?",
vbYesNo)
if i=vbYes Then
  window.event.cancelBubble = True
  window.event.returnValue = False
end if
</SCRIPT>

<SCRIPT language=VBScript for="document" event="onclick">
MsgBox "Processed at the document level"
</SCRIPT>

<BODY id=document1>
This is a sample <a href=anchor.htm id="elem1">HTML</a> page.
</BODY>
</HTML>
```

In this page, you detect when the user clicks over the **elem1** object (the anchor) and ask for confirmation before jumping to the **href** location. Notice how the **srcElement** property allows you to access the target URL indirectly. To prevent the standard behavior taking place you need to set **returnValue** to False.

149

In this way, you've, basically, told IE4 not to perform its usual tasks.

Bubbling and Return Values

Event bubbling and event return values are different and independent things. If you want to stop both of them, you should do it separately by means of two distinct calls.

```
window.event.cancelBubble = True
window.event.returnValue = False
```

In fact, if you don't stop the bubbling the event will be processed at all levels. The only difference is that in the end the default behavior isn't executed because the **returnValue** is set to False.

Scriptlet's Standard Events

Up to this point, we have only discussed how events are managed by the DHTML object model. A scriptlet is a high-level portion of this model and is, therefore, endowed with slightly different tools.

A scriptlet can handle two kinds of events: standard events, just like any other DHTML component, and custom events, just like any other software object component. A scriptlet receives notification of basic events—like those related to keyboard and mouse activity—and can bubble them up to the rest of the container environment.

There is nothing a scriptlet can do to alter an event. Scriptlets hook on the events via script code, the same way an ordinary HTML page does. They are free to process the event. The host doesn't know of such events, unless the scriptlet itself lets it know through a bubbling mechanism.

A scriptlet that wants to pass standard events up to its container needs to do so via the **external** object.

Bubbled Events

Since a scriptlet is nothing more than a Web page, it can hook on events in the same way as any other HTML page. The necessary script code looks the same.

```
<SCRIPT language=VBScript for="elem" event="onclick">
...
</SCRIPT>
```

Code like this gives the scriptlet the opportunity of catching and processing any standard event, that is, any event that the DHTML engine intercepts and broadcasts. All the events that can be trapped by the standard objects can be trapped within a scriptlet. For example, those inherent in the keyboard and mouse are:

 onkeydown

- onkeypress
- onkeyup
- onmousedown
- onmouseup
- onmousemove
- onmouseover
- onmouseout
- onclick
- ondblclick

The events caught by the **document** object can be handled as well.

All these events—when occurring inside a scriptlet—are invisible to the container environment. However, a scriptlet can reflect them (all or in part) and make the host page aware of them. This means, for example, that a scriptlet can notify the host each time it is clicked, or each time the mouse passes over its area. The host page then has the opportunity to respond by executing script code.

This is a subject where an insightful example is worth much more than a hundred carefully chosen words. Suppose we have a scriptlet that represents a clickable object. The component has a given behavior, but its main code executes when it is clicked. In addition, this code is almost entirely customizable by the end user. So a reasonable architecture requires the host page to process the click event too. The question now is—how can a scriptlet reflect its own DHTML events up to the host environment?

Reflecting Events

In order to discuss event reflection, let's consider the following sample. You can run it (**usebmp.htm**) from **http://rapid.wrox.co.uk/books/138X**.

```
<HTML>

<SCRIPT language=VBScript for="window" event="onload">
  document.body.style.marginLeft = 0
  document.body.style.marginRight = 0
  document.body.style.marginTop = 0
  document.body.style.marginBottom = 0
  document.bgColor = window.parent.document.bgColor
</SCRIPT>

<SCRIPT language=VBScript for="image" event="onmouseover">
  document.images.item(0).src = mHotImage
</SCRIPT>

<SCRIPT language=VBScript for="image" event="onmouseout">
  document.images.item(0).src = mNormalImage
</SCRIPT>

<SCRIPT language=JavaScript>
public_description = new Init();
var InScriptlet = (typeof(window.external.version)=="string");
var mNormalImage = "";
```

```
    var mHotImage = "";

    function Init() {
      this.get_NormalImage = get_NormalImage;
      this.put_NormalImage = put_NormalImage;
      this.get_HotImage = get_HotImage;
      this.put_HotImage = put_HotImage;
    }

    function get_NormalImage() {
      return mNormalImage;
    }
    function put_NormalImage( vImage ) {
      mNormalImage= vImage;
      document.images.item(0).src = mNormalImage;
    }

    function get_HotImage() {
      return mHotImage;
    }
    function put_HotImage( vImage ) {
      mHotImage= vImage;
    }

    </SCRIPT>

    <BODY>
    <IMG id="image" src="">
    </BODY>
    </HTML>
```

The code above is the scriptlet itself, called **bmpbtn.htm**, which is contained by
usebmp.htm the page you actually load:

```
    <HTML>

    <SCRIPT language=VBScript for="window" event=onload>
    Image1.NormalImage = "normal.gif"
    Image1.HotImage = "hot.gif"
    </SCRIPT>

    <BODY bgcolor="#C0C0C0">
    <OBJECT id=Image1 data="bmpbtn.htm" type="text/x-scriptlet" width=100
    height=100>
    </OBJECT>

    </BODY>
    </HTML>
```

The next two figures show what
happens when you run it:

The scriptlet is intended to act as a button; adding a bit of support for animation. When the mouse enters its client area, in fact, the scriptlet changes the underlying bitmap.

This example gathers together some of the topics discussed in this and recent chapters. In order, they are:

- Ambient properties, such as the margins.
- Style information from the host page.
- Accessing the external object.
- Processing standard events.

Now we have a scriptlet that reduces the surrounding margins to zero, uses the same background color as the parent's and responds to **onmouseover** and **onmouseout** events.

```
<SCRIPT language=VBScript for="image" event="onmouseover">
  document.images.item(0).src = mHotImage
</SCRIPT>
```

The code snippet above shows how a scriptlet can trap any event that occurs inside the DHTML object model. Let's see how a scriptlet can notify its container of a standard DHTML event.

Notifying a Click Event

Our component (resembling a button) needs to trigger a precise event when the user clicks over its area. This event must be notified to the host page—as if the scriptlet was an ordinary ActiveX control. Such behavior is guaranteed by the **window.external.bubbleEvent** method. We met this in the previous chapter when dealing with the stock methods.

bubbleEvent is a method that takes no parameters and limits itself to bubbling the current event outside the scriptlet's boundaries. To expose, say, an **onclick** event, a scriptlet needs to:

- Trap the event.
- Check the state of the host regarding events.

Bubble the event.

For our example, the event handler translates into a piece of code like this:

```
<SCRIPT language=VBScript for="image" event="onclick">
  if InScriptlet And (not window.external.frozen) Then
    window.external.bubbleEvent
  end if
</SCRIPT>
```

Once the event is raised it is trapped by the host page through code like the following:

```
<HTML>
<SCRIPT language=VBScript for="window" event=onload>
Image1.NormalImage = "normal.gif"
Image1.HotImage = "hot.gif"
</SCRIPT>
```

```
<SCRIPT language=VBScript for="Image1" event=onclick>
MsgBox "Clicked"
</SCRIPT>
```

```
<BODY bgcolor="#C0C0C0">
<OBJECT id=Image1 data="bmpbtn.htm" type="text/x-scriptlet" width=100
height=100>
</OBJECT>
</BODY>
</HTML>
```

The **event** object isn't defined for DHTML events raised by a scriptlet. In fact, if you attempt to write something like this:

```
MsgBox "Clicked on " + window.event.srcElement.id
```

inside a scriptlet page, you'll get an error.

Scriptlet's Custom Events

Within the COM model, events require quite complex management. However, to keep it simple, let's say that firing an event means that a server object makes a call to its client, giving it the chance to execute some code.

Events are little more than calls that the server object (in this case, the scriptlet) makes to some pieces of code (the event handlers) specified by the container. However, all this is accomplished behind the scenes.

As a scriptlet writer, there's nothing you have to do to implement events. Or rather, you can raise an event, but can't say anything about its actual implementation. From the scriptlet's side, an event is just like sending a message with a given name and some parameters.

A scriptlet can define a number of custom events, the names and data of which may be decided as late as at run-time.

ActiveX Controls and Events

Normally, an ActiveX component, which is the closest point of comparison for a scriptlet, must declare all the events it can fire somewhere in its source code. In particular, if you develop your controls with Visual Basic 5 scriptlet you need to declare the events prototypes and use the statement **RaiseEvent** to actually trigger them. Specifying the events prototypes means assigning a name and a series of arguments to the events. The declaration is used by the IDE to set up a proper type library, which will expose the right event set. By using it, host applications will catch events when using the component.

Things are a great deal simpler for scriptlets. In fact, you don't need to declare events but you should still fire them via an explicit command.

Event Declaration

In a previous chapter, we recommended that, when defining the scriptlet's public interface, you declare events along with properties and methods. The suggested syntax is:

```
<SCRIPT language=JavaScript>
public_description = new Init();
var InScriptlet = (typeof(window.external.version)=="string");

function Init() {
  ...
  this.event_onInitialize = "";
  this.event_onRefresh = "";
}
</SCRIPT>
```

However, **event_onInitialize** and **event_onRefresh** don't affect the working of the scriptlet at all, and from this point of view they are completely useless expressions. However, they're good for documentation purposes. As an indirect confirmation of this, take the fact that if you're following the default interface description approach to expose the scriptlet's attributes, you really have no way of declaring events!

Whether you declare them or not, you can always raise the corresponding events and—above all—the host page will always receive them. What's going on?

A declaration like the one above is present for the sake of clarity. There are no syntax implications behind it. If you add those lines, then you can have a full idea of the interface exposed by the scriptlet by looking at the **public_description** object—just as for properties, methods, and events.

Notice that the part to the right of the = sign is the empty string. In fact, events have no server-side implementation and raising an event may be considered quite similar to invoking an external piece of code.

Why doesn't a scriptlet need custom events declaration? Because all the specific events are always routed to the container through the same comprehensive standard event, called **onscriptletevent**.

155

This subject is expanded upon later in the chapter.

Raising Custom Events

So we have learnt that a scriptlet can raise custom events and that it has no need to declare them in advance. However, we have also recommended that you insert the event declaration in the **public_description** object anyway.

To raise an event a scriptlet must again use the **external** object and the **raiseEvent** method. The syntax is the following:

```
window.external.raiseEvent event_name, event_data
```

event_name is a string denoting the actual name of the event. **event_data** is anything that a scriptlet wants to pass down to its container with the event.

Above, we mentioned two custom events: **onInitialize** and **onRefresh**. Well, suppose our scriptlet really has such events to fire at a certain moment. In order to discuss a complete sample, let's say that the Web component will trigger **onInitialize** during its **window.onLoad** event, and **onRefresh** each time it is clicked.

The code you have to write looks like this:

```
<SCRIPT language=VBScript for="window" event="onload">
  if InScriptlet and (not window.external.frozen) Then
    window.external.raiseEvent "onInitialize", window.document
  end if
</SCRIPT>
<SCRIPT language=VBScript for="document" event="onclick">
  if InScriptlet and (not window.external.frozen) Then
    window.external.raiseEvent "onRefresh", 1
  end if
</SCRIPT>
```

Naturally, a custom event can be raised from anywhere in the scriptlet's source code, not necessarily from the code that processes an event. For example, you might also want to raise events when some properties get updated, or some special methods are invoked.

Through the **event_data** slot you can pass any kind of data from the scriptlet to the container. If you need to pass more than one variable, you should pack them into a single object, say an array. Furthermore, all the syntax details of the custom events a scriptlet can raise must be clearly and publicly documented to allow other programmers to use them in container pages.

Event Routing

When a container hosts an ActiveX control and needs to process one of its events, just define a specific procedure that maps the prototype of the given event. For example, if you want to catch the **onclick** event from a component, you can use the syntax seen so far

```
<SCRIPT language=VBScript for="document" event="onclick">
...
</SCRIPT>
```

or you can exploit a standard naming convention to define your handler code.

```
<SCRIPT language=VBScript>
Sub document_onClick
  :
End Sub
</SCRIPT>
```

However, if a host page needs to trap the above **onInitialize** event, then the following code:

```
<SCRIPT language=VBScript>
Sub Scriptlet1_onInitialize(...)
  :
Ensd Sub
</SCRIPT>
```

simply won't work. Under the hood, such a piece of code ends up calling an **onInitialize** entry in the component's outgoing interface. While this is perfectly legitimate with ActiveX controls, it is unacceptable and unsupported for scriptlets.

At least under Win32, scriptlets are implemented through a lightweight ActiveX control with some functionality taken from the WebBrowser control. This control can host any scriptlet and should expose the interface of the inside server—not its own! To work around this, the custom events have been exposed through a common and unique interface.

In practice, the container that wraps the scriptlet (see Chapter 3 for details) inside an HTML page or a desktop application exposes all the scriptlet's custom events as if they were a single and generic **onscriptletevent**, and not a variety of specialized notifications.

To put it another way, the WebBridge layer (see Chapter 3 again), that works under any scriptlet, has the task of negotiating between the scriptlet and the actual container. So it arranges things in such a way that the scriptlet raises different events, but the host sees them as the same event fired with different parameters.

A Common Interface

Whatever event is actually raised by the scriptlet, the client is always notified of a fixed **onscriptletevent** custom event. It can distinguish between them through a multiple **if**, or a **Select/Case** statement based on the **event_name** argument.

For example:

```
<script language="Javascript" for="Scriptlet1"
        event="onscriptletevent(name,data)">
if( eventname=="OnInitialize" ) {
   alert("Initializing");
```

```
    }
    else {
      if( eventname=="OnRefresh" ) {
        alert("Refreshing");
      }
    }
    </script>
```

On the scriptlet side, the corresponding code would be

```
window.external.raiseEvent "OnInitialize",
window.external.raiseEvent "OnRefresh", window.document
```

In the example, the empty string and the **window.document** represent the data that has just been passed in. This parameter, of course, is expected to change according to the real goal of the event. Also, as previously discussed, the **window.external.frozen** property should be checked before firing events.

Since all the events a scriptlet raises are perceived by the container as occurrences of the same event (**onscriptletevent**—with different parameters) then you can define events at any time, and qualify them with a string.

Passing Data

Through the second argument of **window.external.raiseEvent** you can pass any kind of data. In the following example:

```
<script language="Javascript" for="Image1"
event="onscriptletevent(n,imageName)">
   if( n=="OnHotState" )
   alert( "The image is: " + imageName );
</script>
```

the container receives a string with the name of the image used to render the button in its hot state. At different moments in time, you can pass different types of data for the same event. The source code that originates the event might be:

```
if InScriptlet And (not window.external.frozen) Then
    window.external.raiseEvent "OnHotState", mHotImage
end if
```

You can find a full example that shows how to deal with custom events on our Web site. Download or run the file **usebmp3.htm**.

Returning Values from Events

If you attempt to access the **window.event** object from within a bubbled event, you'll get a system error that reminds you that object is undefined. For example, the following code on the host side:

```
<script language="Javascript" for="Image1" event="onclick">
  alert( window.event.srcElement.id );
</script>
```

will produce the following error:

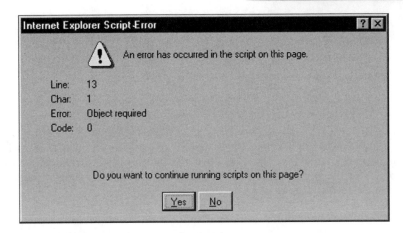

However, sometimes you really need to return values from an event. Moreover, this kind of requirement can arise for both bubbled and custom events. Is there then a way to work around this apparent limitation and get events to return regular values? The answer is clearly yes. In fact, the DHTML object model allows you to return values from events by the means of the **returnValue** property we've already discussed above, while discussing techniques to prevent the default behavior taking place.

When you're about to respond to an event in the host environment, it's natural for you to try to access the **window.event** object to find out more about who originated the event, plus the state of the mouse and the keyboard. You might also think you can set back a value too. However, as the above picture shows, accessing **window.event** from a bubbled or custom event results in an error message. If you think it over a bit, you'll understand and agree.

When you call **window.event** from within a host page, you're really addressing the **window** object of the container page, not the scriptlet's. And, in fact, the **window** object of the host is undefined and produces an error.

This does not mean, however, that we can't return values from an event, nor that we can't know about the element which raised the event. Both bubbled and raised events cause the scriptlet to set a valid **event** slot, which is available to the container. The only tricky aspect is that you do not have to call **window.event** but, instead, the scriptlet's **event** object. Look at the next example, called **usebmp4.htm** and available on our Web site.

```
<HTML>
<SCRIPT language=VBScript for="window" event="onload">
Image1.NormalImage = "normal.gif"
Image1.HotImage = "hot.gif"
</SCRIPT>
```

```
<script language="Javascript" for="Image1" event="onclick">
    alert("OnClick originated by <"+Image1.event.srcElement.id+">")
    Image1.event.returnValue = 12;
</script>

<script language="Javascript" for="Image1" event="onscriptletevent(n,o)">
    if( n=="OnHotState" ) {
        alert(n + " originated by <"+Image1.event.srcElement.id+">")
```

159

```
        Image1.event.returnValue = 42
    }
    </script>
```

```
<BODY bgcolor="#C0C0C0">
<OBJECT id=Image1 data="bmpbtn4.htm" type="text/x-scriptlet"
        width=100 height=100>
</OBJECT>
</BODY>
</HTML>
```

The scriptlet is a slightly enhanced version of the one we looked at earlier. It is a bitmapped button that changes when the mouse passes over its area and responds to the users clicking. The scriptlet also raises a custom event when its internal state turns from normal to hot.

In the sample, the scriptlet is known through an ID of **Image1**. An HTML page that needs to access the event information for a scriptlet's event must call the event property of **Image1** instead of **window**. So to get the name of the element that notified the event, just call:

```
alert( Image1.event.srcElement.id );
```

At this point it is clear that **event** is a perfectly valid object, so that you can use its **returnValue** buffer to return any value to the caller.

```
Image1.event.returnValue = 12;
```

From the scriptlet's perspective, this is the code that allows you to handle the host's return value.

```
if InScriptlet And (not window.external.frozen) Then
    window.external.raiseEvent "OnHotState", 0
    MsgBox "return value is " + CStr(window.event.returnValue)
end if
```

Notice that the scriptlet can safely handle the event data returned via the usual **window.event** object.

Putting it all together

To conclude the chapter, let's see a complete sample of a reasonably complex scriptlet that need some event handling. The idea is to build a component that resembles the traditional checkbox elements. That is, a component that has two possible states: checked and unchecked. Usually such controls have some explanatory text associated, and notify that their state has changed. So, let's design a Checkbox scriptlet that exposes two properties like **Text** and **Value** and two methods such as **Pressed** and **Released**.

Text will indicate the text we find near the button, whereas **Value** evaluates to 0 or 1 according to the button is being released or pressed. Of course, **Pressed** and **Released** change the component state as their names suggest.

The component is given by an **<IMG>** tag that renders the button and a text. Both have a specific ID. Each time the user clicks on the bitmap or the text the component's internal state changes and a proper event is raised.

The following file, you can run from our site, is the scriptlet. Its name is **checkbox.htm**.

```
<HTML>
<HEAD>
<TITLE>CheckBox Scriptlet</TITLE>
</HEAD>

<SCRIPT language=VBScript for=window event=onload>
  InitCheckBox
</SCRIPT>

<SCRIPT language=VBScript for=check event=onclick>
  if mChecked = 0 Then
    DoDown
  else
    DoUp
  end if
</SCRIPT>

<SCRIPT language=VBScript for=text event=onclick>
  if mChecked = 0 Then
    DoDown
  else
    DoUp
  end if
</SCRIPT>

<SCRIPT language=VBScript>
  Sub InitCheckBox
    document.bgcolor = window.parent.document.bgcolor
    document.body.style.margin = 0
  End Sub
</SCRIPT>


<SCRIPT language=JavaScript>
public_description = new CreateCheckBox();
var InScriptlet = (typeof(window.external.version)=="string");

var mChecked=0;
var mText="";

function CreateCheckBox() {
  this.Pressed = DoDown;
  this.Released = DoUp;
  this.get_Value = get_Value;
  this.put_Value = put_Value;
  this.get_Text = get_Text;
  this.put_Text = put_Text;

  this.event_OnPress = "";
  this.event_OnRelease = "";
}

function DoDown() {
  mChecked = 1;
  check.src = "dn.bmp";
  document.all("text").style.fontWeight = 700;
  if( InScriptlet && !window.external.frozen )
    window.external.raiseEvent( "OnPress", "" );
```

```
        return 1;
    }

    function DoUp() {
        mChecked = 0;
        check.src = "up.bmp";
        document.all("text").style.fontWeight = 400;
        if( InScriptlet && !window.external.frozen )
            window.external.raiseEvent( "OnRelease", "" );
        return 1;
    }

    function get_Value() {
        return mChecked;
    }
    function put_Value( v ) {
        mChecked = v;
        if( mChecked == 0 )
            DoUp();
        else
            DoDown();
        return;
    }

    function get_Text() {
        return mText;
    }
    function put_Text( s ) {
        mText = s;
        o = document.all( "text" );
        o.innerHTML = mText;
        return;
    }
</SCRIPT>

<BODY>
<img id=check src=up.bmp align=absbottom> <SPAN id=text></SPAN>
</BODY>
</HTML>
```

While loading, the scriptlet grabs the parent's background color and removes any margin. It is made up of an image identified by **check** and a string whose ID is **text**. All that the scriptlet does is detect the **onclick** event on both the constituent elements, and behave as we've instructed. It calls **DoUp** and **DoDown** according to the current state. Both of these routines have similar behaviors. Each modifies the content of a global variable **mChecked**, replace the bitmap to reflect the user action, update the weight of the text font passing from bold (a value of 700) to normal (a value of 400) and vice versa. Finally, they raise the proper event.

Let's see now how to write a host page. The following is called **testchkb.htm**.

```
<HTML>
<HEAD>
<TITLE>Checkbox Test Page</TITLE>
</HEAD>

<SCRIPT for="window" event="onload">
    Check1.Text = "Click Me!";
    if( Check1.Value == 1 )
        document.all("text").innerText = "checked";
</SCRIPT>
```

```
<SCRIPT for="Check1" event="onscriptletevent(n,o)">
  if( n=="OnPress" )
     document.all("text").innerText = "checked";
  else
  if( n=="OnRelease" )
     document.all("text").innerText = "unchecked";
</SCRIPT>

<SCRIPT for="text" event="onclick">
  if( text.innerText == "checked" )
     Check1.Released();
  else
     Check1.Pressed();
</SCRIPT>

<BODY bgcolor=C0C0C0>
This is a demo page that hosts a CheckBox scriptlet. <hr>
<OBJECT id=Check1 data="Checkbox.htm" height=20 type="text/x-scriptlet">
</OBJECT>
<hr>
Now the checkbox is: <b><SPAN id=text>unchecked</SPAN></b>.
</BODY>
</HTML>
```

Initially, this page looks like the next figure.

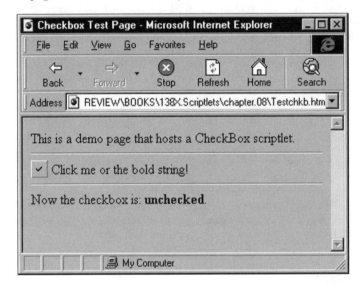

The page detects the **onscriptletevent** event and handles it this way:

```
<SCRIPT for="Check1" event="onscriptletevent(n,o)">
  if( n=="OnPress" )
     document.all("text").innerText = "checked";
  else
  if( n=="OnRelease" )
     document.all("text").innerText = "unchecked";
</SCRIPT>
```

It updates the text ("checked" or "unchecked") displayed by a **<SPAN>** tag at the bottom of the page. In this case, no arguments are passed from the scriptlet. The following picture shows how things go when you check the component. Remember that you can get this result by clicking on the bitmap as well as the text.

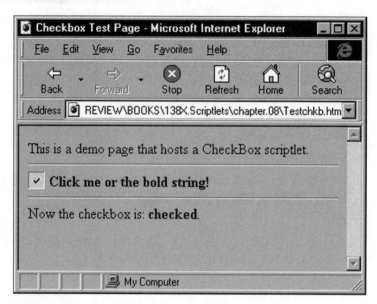

But there is more. We've added a third opportunity to change the components's state. Clicking on the 'state' string on the host page (the one drawn in bold). This element is identified by an ID of **text**. When the user clicks over it, we toggle the state of the checkbox using the **innerText** property to decide what to do.

```
<SCRIPT for="text" event="onclick">
  if( text.innerText == "checked" )
     Check1.Released();
  else
     Check1.Pressed();
</SCRIPT>
```

Note an interesting side-effect that takes place here. You might expect to must change the text explicitly, passing from "checked" to "unchecked" and vice versa. Instead, it suffices to issue a call to the proper method. By design, when the method executes it fires an **onscriptletevent** event. The host page traps it and updates the text denoting the component's state.

Summary

Events are one of the most characteristic aspects of components programming. Scriptlets are, essentially, components made of script code and HTML. Because scriptlets are a means to reuse Web scripting, they are subject to the DHTML object model and can receive and send standard events, most of which are bound to keyboard and mouse activity. A scriptlet is a part of the DHTML event bubbling hierarchy and can continue or break the chain. All the events a scriptlet detects are invisible to the external world, unless the scriptlet itself bubbles them up.

In addition to this, a scriptlet can raise custom events and through them communicate with the host page. In this chapter, we've covered all the programming aspects of the events. In particular:

- What is DHTML event bubbling?
- How to alter the default behavior for standard events.
- Why you might not want to declare custom events in the code.
- How a host page can receive a scriptlet's custom event.
- Passing and returning data through bubbled and custom events.

In the following chapters we're going to examine some features of the scriptlet's user interface and also examine how to host them in desktop applications, as well as in HTML pages.

Scriptlets' User Interface

The user interface of a scriptlet is simply the content of the **<BODY>** tag in the HTML page that contains it. The scriptlets are hosted by a certain kind of container object. In most cases this container object is another HTML page. In other cases, as we will be discussing in the next chapter, it could be a Visual Basic form.

We would all agree that HTML is changing the way people present information and software applications. And DHTML furthers this cause. What's really important is that HTML is changing the metaphor through which people use the computer and interact with the operating system.

We think that applications that access the Web are successful for two basic reasons: firstly, the Internet is a real breakthrough which allows people and software designers to pose and satisfy requirements that a few years ago were simply impractical. Secondly, since Web applications are based on the HTML language they present a more accurate and attractive interface to users that appears to be easier to use and understand. Maybe it's not even a matter of being easier or more impressive. HTML just introduces a different approach and a new metaphor; one which is quite different from the traditional desktop software.

This chapter is devoted to a scriptlet's user interface. We will be discussing the typical structure of a body, the initialization process required and some more advanced topics; such as the dynamic resizing of the scriptlet's area. More precisely,

- One-Time scriptlets initialization
- Visibility problems
- How to dynamically enlarge the scriptlet's site
- Working with invisible components

Anything that you can see in a **<BODY>** tag, you can see in the scriptlet output window, even complex HTML structures such as frames, tables, controls and other scriptlets too. This is a general rule to keep in mind when working with these new Web components.

A Few Rules for the User Interface

So far we have constantly repeated that a scriptlet is just an HTML page hosted in another HTML page, which acts as a container. Thus, what rules can we recommend for the user interface that aren't already known to existing Web developers? None what so ever.

Conceptually, writing scriptlets is a task that places itself in the middle of two other important tasks. It is almost identical to writing Web pages and quite similar to designing ActiveX controls. The similarity to HTML stems from the inner structure of a scriptlet and from the object model that lies underneath. The similarity to ActiveX controls is entirely based on the public interface they expose. In both cases, this public interface is made up of properties, events and methods. When writing scriptlets you face most of the problems you're used to facing when designing ActiveX controls.

Next, we'll examine a few points that can help you to design better scriptlets. What follows is a list of my top ten tips for great DHTML programming.

Is Script Initialization Required?

If you take a look at Microsoft's scripting Web site, that is:

`http://www.microsoft.com/scripting`

you should come across the Calendar scriptlet sample. To help you recognize it, here's a preview:

This scriptlet is self-initializing; that is it doesn't need any script code to make it work properly and show output data that makes sense. It's generally accepted that any significant piece of code needs some kind of initialization. However, this starting information needn't always be provided by either the programmer or the end user. In some cases, in fact, the scriptlet is perfectly capable of getting all the required data by itself. For instance, a calendar or a clock just needs the current date, or the current time, to begin to work properly.

Thus, they don't require any other kind of initialization and even if you attempt to use them as stand-alone pages, you will have a valid display. The Clock example is available on our Web site, from the samples for the Wrox book, Professional IE4 Programming.

In other cases, however, you definitely need to specify some data before the Web component will start to work as expected. Consider one of the examples we built in a previous chapter. A scriptlet that represents a bitmapped button must show an image as its own user interface. The name of the actual GIF or JPEG file is entered via script and only when the scriptlet's page is loaded by a container. This means that if you attempt to display the scriptlet's page as an ordinary document, then you'll run into an uninteresting effect—like the following:

Of course, which path the scriptlet follows depends solely upon the role it plays. But the programmer ought to always try to give it a decent user interface, even if the scriptlet needs initialization via script. Something like the picture shown above is just about acceptable, but if possible do it better!

Fusing the Scriptlet to the Host User Interface

A scriptlet is a page element at the same level as an ActiveX control or a Java applet. It is a part of the page but occupies its own site; another HTML page. The scriptlet's page is a nested document where Internet Explorer 4.0 builds another instance of the standard DHTML object model.

When Internet Explorer 4.0 instantiates a scriptlet inside a page, it calls the parsing and viewing engine. This creates a new copy of the DHTML hierarchy specific to the inner page. Wouldn't it, however, be nice if these objects were automatically assigned the same values as the parent's environment? For example, the scriptlet **document** object could assume the same background color, the same font, the same margins and the same foreground text color as that set in the parent.

In Chapter 5, we saw how to get this result by exploiting the **window.parent** object. Given the current implementation of scriptlets this is only way you are able to get it. However, when fusing the user interface of a scriptlet as closely as possible to its host environment there are a number of aspects to take into account. We'll talk about this right away.

After all, Scriptlets Are HTML Pages

Never forget that scriptlets are HTML pages and so you can apply any of the formatting rules and any of the predefined tags you would use for ordinary pages. The previous section recommended that you let the component inherit all the interface features of its parent. However, there is one that seems like it should be left out. Namely: Transparency.

Consider that a scriptlet is a completely new and independent page embedded within another page. It's quite similar to overlapping windows. And just like overlapping windows, you have two distinct objects each with its own background, mouse cursor and window-procedure. If the parent window has a textured background, then the child could duplicate it. However, this doesn't mean that the two windows' backgrounds are perfectly aligned. Each window background is obtained by tiling a given bitmap, but each window starts doing so from its own 0,0 relative position. As a result, you don't have a common background for the windows. We illustrated this in Chapter 5. Even if you assign the scriptlet the same bitmap as the parent, it is not likely you'll ever have a perfect alignment. In Win32 we can work around this through specific styles of windows, but the same isn't possible in a cross-platform environment such as the Web.

Getting transparency inside a single Dynamic HTML page is much easier than getting it from within a scriptlet, in relation to a host page.

In conclusion, don't forget that scriptlets are really new pages created with their own default styles and placed on top of the parent page.

The Scriptlet's Right Size

A golden rule to optimize page performance on the major browsers is to always assign a precise width and height to any HTML element that supports it. In fact, if the browser knows in advance the space needed by a certain element it can reserve the space and go on to load the rest of the page. Scriptlets are no exception. They are inserted through the **<OBJECT>** tag, which recognizes the **WIDTH** and the **HEIGHT** attributes. If you don't specify a size for a scriptlet then it is assigned a default one. When the browser knows the width and height of a component in advance, it speeds up the drawing process since it can leave enough space and go on.

However, there might be scriptlets for which the right size is an issue that can affect the user interface. Think of components that are enhancements of an image. In this case the scriptlet can't have any pre-defined size, but should have exactly the same dimensions as the image it is using.

The problem is how can you know the size of the actual image when you're inserting the scriptlet in the host page? You first define a scriptlet inside a page and then you program it through script code. The answer is that the scriptlet itself should be able to change its width and height dynamically to adapt to the parameters it receives.

Make a Scriptlet as Configurable as You Can

A scriptlet is a piece of reusable code. No matter whether it is written in DHTML, VBScript, or JScript. It is—and must be—reusable. So before you put it down in source code, stop for a while and reflect over all the properties it could expose and all the operations that lend themselves to becoming public methods.

Scriptlets have been introduced to promote the DHTML object model up to the role of a development platform. Therefore, as a programmer, you ought to follow this path and write components which are really useful and reusable.

A couple of points on scriptlet user interface design. The first option is to make it as similar as possible to the parent. This means that you have to access the style information from the host environment. A second option is to expose all the user interface standard properties, such as: font, colors, margins, borders, and the like and make them programmable. As a general word of advice—try to avoid fixed-style attributes.

Be Careful with Default Settings

This point stems directly from the previous one. Any programmable properties you define must also be assigned default values. Think of a clock scriptlet, which exposes attributes for the background and the foreground colors, the font and the borders. All of these might be set at run-time, but very few of them will actually be changed. So it's very important that you give them the best predefined settings you can for the sake of your component's look and feel.

Limit the Number of External References

Although we are all used to thinking of an HTML page as a whole, it is actually made up of a variety of different files. In most cases, we have only GIF or JPEG images, or other nested HTML documents. Whatever it is, packaging an HTML file for distribution is a process that can create surprises. This scenario is mirrored in scriptlets and is even more important. If you add ActiveX controls to a scriptlet, then you need to make them available along

171

with the page. If you use lots of GIFs to give it a colorful user interface, then you need to package them up together. Even if you use script languages other than IE's standard scripting languages (JScript and VBScript), you must also distribute the specific DLL for the language. Overall, try to limit the number of elements referenced outside the document itself as much as possible. We'll talk about this in more detail in Chapter 14.

Encompass Complex Functionality

Scriptlets should guarantee reusability, that is, you should be able to write it once and reuse it forever. The first time you approach the DHTML object model, it's easy to be dazzled by the potential it has to make your pages dynamic and more attractive. So it's natural that you start writing code, even complex code, without thinking about its reusability. Sometimes you are a victim of a special syndrome. Everything seems to be so quick and easy to produce that encompassing code in reusable structures, which will make it even quicker and easier to call, doesn't even seem to be a significant issue.

Don't make this mistake. Always try to put complex DHTML functionality into a flexible and reusable structure such as a scriptlet.

Encompass and Simplify Complex Functionality

Simply considering putting complex functionality—like frames synchronization or data-binding—into scriptlets isn't enough. Before proceeding it is also important that you consider making it reusable in a really simple way. scriptlets give you the chance to isolate some repetitive and standard code. For example, you might want to encapsulate some of the advanced DHTML features like filter transitions or data-bound tables into scriptlets and get them to take place with the simpler invocation of a method.

Although the DHTML object model provides a high-level way of working, you could write a further layer of code on top of it to better encompass some of the more complex functionality. Scriptlets are a great way to do this.

Did you know that Scriptlets could be nested?

The scriptlet's user interface can contain anything that can be part of an HTML page—even other scriptlets! Nesting scriptlets is a powerful technique that doesn't require particular shrewdness, and is easy and flexible too. The best analogy we can find to explain both the inner meaning of the **<BODY>** tag in a scriptlet, and nesting, is with the ActiveX controls you can write with Visual Basic 5. Almost any component developed with Visual Basic 5 is composed of other child or constituent controls. Among them are other ActiveX controls realized in pure Visual Basic.

When writing such components you are really just assembling various pieces of code, each one with its own properties. By nesting scriptlets you can obtain effects which are otherwise unattainable. In the next paragraph, we'll show you a composed scriptlet in detail and illustrate some of the opportunities you can exploit.

Nested Scriptlets

If you add scrollbar support to a scriptlet then it applies to its entire area. There is no way to limit it to a given section. The same holds true for selectable content. If needed, you can include one scriptlet in another, exactly as you would do with other HTML elements. The following is a piece of code taken from one of the samples available on our Web site at: **http://rapid.wrox.co.uk/books/138X**.

```
<BODY bgcolor="C0C0C0">
FlexText! <img id=sizer src=dn.gif align=absbottom>
<br>
<OBJECT id=Text1 data="Text.htm" width=100 height=40 type="text/x-scriptlet">
</OBJECT>
</BODY>
```

It comes from a scriptlet and shows how to nest two or more of them. The scriptlet, called **Text1** and implemented in the file **text.htm**, is part of a larger scriptlet called **flextext.htm**. The snippet above shows the **<BODY>** tag of the main component. Look at the next screenshot to see how it appears at run-time.

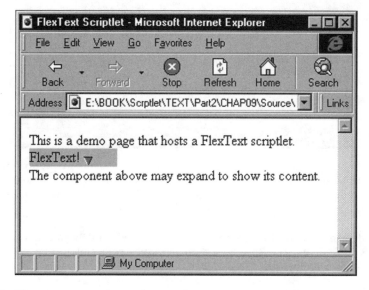

The FlexText component is made up of text, an image, and an inner scriptlet. By clicking on the image—which represents an up/down arrow—you cause the child scriptlet to appear and disappear. The final behavior is somewhat akin to the Windows comboboxes.

The following source code comes from the file **testflex.htm** and is the test page for the component. All this HTML code has been generated by the scriptlet Wizard we encountered in Chapter 4.

```
<HTML>
<HEAD>
<TITLE>FlexText Test Page</TITLE>
</HEAD>
```

```
<BODY>
This is a demo page that hosts a FlexText scriptlet.<br>
<OBJECT align="absbottom" id=FlexText1 data="FlexText.htm" width=100 height=20
    type="text/x-scriptlet">
</OBJECT><br>
The component above may expand to show its content just like a Windows
combobox.
</BODY>
</HTML>
```

Normally, the inner scriptlet is hidden. When you click on the arrow button it becomes visible and causes the rest of the page to shift down. The next screenshot shows what really happens.

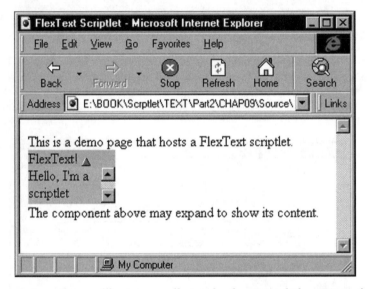

As you can see, the scrollbars now affect only the expanded portion of the component, that is the internal scriptlet—the one with an ID of **Text1**. Having two or more scriptlets allows you to apply global settings (like scrolling and selecting capabilities) to single parts of the component.

We will turn back to this example later in the book. In the meantime, let's take a quick look at its source code, just to introduce some interesting user interface issues, like visibility and dynamic resize.

The body of the scriptlet is composed of two distinct objects: a little image called **sizer** and another scriptlet called **Text1**. The idea is that the main component appears as text followed by a tiny triangle to denote it could be expanded or collapsed.

When the user clicks over it, the following code executes:

```
<SCRIPT language=VBScript for=sizer event="onclick">
    Set o = document.all("Text1")
    if o.style.pixelHeight = 1 Then
        o.style.pixelWidth = 100
        o.style.pixelHeight = 40
        sizer.src = "up.gif"
        MyPage.style.pixelHeight = MyPage.style.pixelHeight + 40
```

174

```
     else
        o.style.pixelWidth = 1
        o.style.pixelHeight = 1
        sizer.src = "dn.gif"
        MyPage.style.pixelHeight = MyPage.style.pixelHeight - 40
     end if
</SCRIPT>
```

The main scriptlet changes the image displayed to reflect whether it is being expanded or not. This is accomplished through the lines:

```
sizer.src = "up.gif"
sizer.src = "dn.gif"
```

During the scriptlet loading, the internal **Text1** is resized to 1x1 pixels. This actually makes it invisible.

```
Set o = document.all("Text1")
o.style.pixelHeight = 1
o.style.pixelWidth = 1
```

So, to show its content we need to enlarge its dimensions. However, this won't be sufficient since the scriptlet is included in another one. Or rather, if we change the size of the internal scriptlet, we only half succeed. The internal component now holds the right size, but it is clipped out by the smaller size of its container.

In conclusion, what remains to be done is to enlarge the main scriptlet in the same way.

The source code shown above makes use of two different approaches for the same task. We will be discussing it in greater detail in the section that follows.

We resized the component to 1x1 pixels to make it invisible. If you assign it a size of 0x0 pixels, then it is discarded and you can't restore it on the page.

Visibility Options

It's easy and also natural to associate scriptlets with something you can see and interact with. However, this doesn't mean that you cannot have invisible components. Among all the addressable style tags there are a couple that can be used to modify the visibility options of any DHTML element—scriptlets included.

Basically there are three ways that you can affect the size and the visibility of scriptlets. In fact, you can:

- Turn the visibility flag off
- Turn the display flag off
- Resize the component to make it invisible

In the previous example we demonstrated how to change the dimensions of a scriptlet's site dynamically. Now it's time to go a bit deeper and to become familiar with the **visibility** and **display** styles that reflect two different ways of writing hidden scriptlets.

Differences between Visibility and Display

Both **visibility** and **display** are two attributes of the **style** object that apply to every element that can appear in HTML pages. Technically speaking, both of them are capable of making any component of a DHTML page appear and disappear. What's different is the way they act and the syntax they require.

After all, **visibility** and **display** are very different properties and you should make sure you understand when to make use of one or the other. Basically, they both hide or restore an element, but they don't have the same impact on the underlying page. Furthermore, they need special keywords to be enabled.

What does Visibility do?

To make an element visible, assign the word **Visible** to the property. The other option is **Hidden**. You can do it in an ordinary HTML page, as well as in a scriptlet.

```
<SCRIPT language=VBScript>
  Image1.style.setAttribute "visibility", "Visible"
</SCRIPT>
```

The above code shows how an element called **Image1** can be made visible programmatically. Of course, exchanging the word **Visible** for the word **Hidden** results in hiding the same element. Better yet, you can write down a small procedure like the following.

```
<SCRIPT language=VBScript>
Sub SetVisibility( obj, status )
  If status = True Then
    obj.style.setAttribute "visibility", "Visible"
  Else
    obj.style.setAttribute "visibility", "Hidden"
  End if
End Sub
</SCRIPT>
```

The function gets the **style** object of the element and changes the value of the **visibility** attribute according to the boolean parameter. We can use it this way:

```
<HTML>
<HEAD>
<TITLE>Element Visibility</TITLE>
</HEAD>

<SCRIPT language=VBScript>
mVisible = True
</SCRIPT>
```

```
<SCRIPT language=VBScript for="document" event="onclick">
  mVisible = not mVisible
  SetVisibility Button1, mVisible
</SCRIPT>

<SCRIPT language=VBScript>
Sub SetVisibility( obj, status )
  If status = True Then
    obj.style.setAttribute "visibility", "Visible"
  Else
    obj.style.setAttribute "visibility", "Hidden"
  End if
End Sub
</SCRIPT>

<BODY>
Click on the page to have the button to appear and disappear.<br>
<INPUT TYPE=button NAME="Button1" VALUE="I'm a button.">
</OBJECT>
</BODY>
</HTML>
```

The next picture shows the above file (called **elemvis.htm**) in action.

In an HTML page, modifying the value of the **visibility** property results in a different way of drawing the element. That is—the element always preserves its own space on the page, whether it is visible or hidden. What actually changes is how it is drawn. If **visibility** is set to the string **Visible**, then the element displays as usual and as expected. If **visibility** is set to the string **Hidden** instead, then the Dynamic HTML viewer avoids painting it, although the space occupied is not freed up.

The previous example only works well with DHTML elements since it accesses the **style** object. If you attempt to pass the **SetVisibility** routine a scriptlet, then you'll get an error unless the scriptlet exposes its own **style** object.

Let's now see another example that shows how to toggle the visibility flag of a scriptlet. The following code is taken from a demo called **Visible.htm** which you can run or download from our Web site.

```
<HTML>
<HEAD>
<TITLE>Visible Test Page</TITLE>
</HEAD>
```

```
<SCRIPT language=VBScript>
  mVisible = True
</SCRIPT>

<SCRIPT language=VBScript for=document event="onclick">
  mVisible = not mVisible
  Visible1.SetVisibility mVisible
</SCRIPT>

<BODY>
<OBJECT id=Visible1 data="Visible.htm" width=100 height=100 type="text/x-
scriptlet">
</OBJECT>
</BODY>
</HTML>
```

The code above is the page that includes the Visible scriptlet. By clicking on the page area you cause the **visibility** flag of some of the scriptlet's elements to switch between **visible** and **hidden**. The first time you run the page, it looks like this:

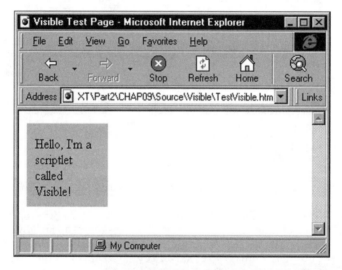

By clicking on the document area, you cause the **SetVisibility** method to be invoked with a value of False. What happens is the following:

The scriptlet source code includes a component that encompasses the substring "**called Visible**". This substring is then followed by an exclamation mark. The visibility setting affects only this string, making it invisible, but not moving anything else. Let's see the scriptlet source code. (Note that this has also been generated in an instant by using our scriptlet Wizard.)

```
<HTML ID=MyPage>
<HEAD>
<TITLE>Visible scriptlet</TITLE>
</HEAD>

<SCRIPT language=JavaScript>
public_description = new CreateVisible();
var InScriptlet = (typeof(window.external.version)=="string");

function CreateVisible()  {
  this.SetVisibility = DoSetVisibility;
}

function DoSetVisibility( bStyle )  {
  if( bStyle != 0 )
    text.style.setAttribute( "visibility", "visible" );
  else
    text.style.setAttribute( "visibility", "hidden" );
  return 1;
}
</SCRIPT>

<BODY bgcolor="cyan">
Hello, I'm a scriptlet <SPAN id=text>called Visible</SPAN>!
</BODY>
</HTML>
```

Notice how the **visibility** attribute is changed according to the boolean value passed in. Also pay attention to the use of the **<SPAN>** tag, which, in this case, has the sole purpose of assigning an ID to a given substring.

What does Display do?

A similar role is played by the **display** attribute. The biggest difference is in the final effect: **display** allows the rest of the page to shift up after a piece of HTML code has been cut off from the screen. Let's set up a similar example and see the differences. Again, our Scriptlet Wizard helps considerably in quickly producing a perfect working scriptlet and its test page.

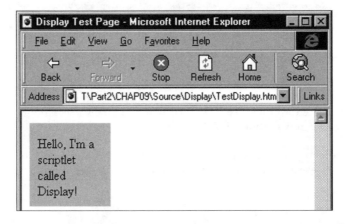

```
<HTML>
<HEAD>
<TITLE>Display Test Page</TITLE>
</HEAD>

<SCRIPT language=VBScript>
  mDisplay = True
</SCRIPT>

<SCRIPT language=VBScript for=document event="onclick">
  mDisplay = not mDisplay
  Display1.SetDisplay mDisplay
</SCRIPT>

<BODY>
<OBJECT id=Display1 data="Display.htm" width=100 height=100 type="text/x-
scriptlet">
</OBJECT>
</BODY>
</HTML>
```

The test page that produces the output is almost identical to the previous one. By clicking on the document area you can toggle the boolean value that gets passed to the **SetDisplay** method which has been exposed by the scriptlet.

```
<HTML ID=MyPage>
<HEAD>
<TITLE>Display Scriptlet</TITLE>
</HEAD>

<SCRIPT language=JavaScript>
public_description = new CreateDisplay();
var InScriptlet = (typeof(window.external.version)=="string");

function CreateDisplay() {
  this.SetDisplay = DoSetDisplay;
}

function DoSetDisplay( bStyle )  {
  if( bStyle != 0 )
    text.style.setAttribute( "display", "" );
  else
    text.style.setAttribute( "display", "none" );
  return 1;
}
</SCRIPT>

<BODY bgcolor="cyan">
Hello, I'm a scriptlet <SPAN id=text>called Display</SPAN>!
</BODY>
</HTML>
```

The scriptlet source code shows off a similar template to the one in the visibility sample. What's new is the syntax required by the **display** attribute. It is not **visible** or **hidden** any more, but an empty string or **none**. By assigning the empty string to **display** you tell Internet Explorer 4.0 that the drawing procedure must execute normally. **none** tells the browser that it must skip drawing the specified HTML element.

As in the above example, the element identified by **text** may be painted or not. If it is assigned the string **none,** the effect is slightly different from before:

180

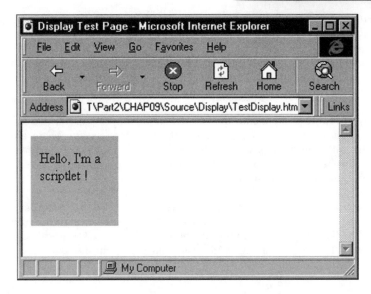

As you can see, the missing string now causes the later text (the exclamation mark) to shift up. The browser behaves as if that string wasn't part of the actual page.

Scriptlets and Dynamic HTML Pages

If you modify the **visibility** and **display** attributes inside a straight HTML document then you're working on a single level of source code. To put it another way, if you aren't using scriptlets there's only one **document** object to work with. Everything you do will affect the current page.

However, if you're changing some visibility attributes within a scriptlet, then all the modifications will apply to the scriptlet's **document** object and not the page's. This is what happens in the examples shown above. The scriptlet is inside an HTML page. All the changes occur within its boundaries and don't affect the outside world. To reflect this on the hosting page you also need to resize the scriptlet's area dynamically.

There is more to say on this subject but we will postpone this discussion until we have covered some features of the hidden scriptlets.

Hidden Scriptlets

There might be situations in which you would use a scriptlet as a silent and invisible server. While having a rich user interface is a much appreciated characteristic for a visual component, not all components will be for the user!

When someone attempts to explain this concept to Visual Basic programmers the natural example that comes to mind is the timer control. Before version 5 got shipped, there was only one straightforward way to use timers in Visual Basic—drop an invisible timer control somewhere in the form. Such a component simply exposes methods and events that allow the programmer to be notified of expired intervals on a regular basis. This control is visible only at design-time, that is, when we're designing the form. When we run it, in fact, the control works in the background and there's no footprint of it on the screen. We want to have a scriptlet that can do the same. In other words, we're interested in scriptlets that work without a user interface and without taking up space on the hosting page.

Usually, invisible components maintain their display status for the full lifetime of the application. However, you can intervene if necessary. There are two ways of doing this. The first is getting the scriptlet itself to resize properly. We will discuss this technique in a short while. A second approach requires the page to hide or show the component.

Again, you can choose to modify the **visibility** or the **display** attribute as best suits your own needs. The following is the page **testdisp.htm** adapted to modify the scriptlet's visibility attributes. This new page is called **testdsp2.htm** and is available as usual on our Web site.

```
<HTML>
<HEAD>
<TITLE>Display Test Page</TITLE>
</HEAD>

<SCRIPT language=VBScript>
  mDisplay = True
</SCRIPT>

<SCRIPT language=VBScript for="document" event="onclick">
  mDisplay = not mDisplay
  if mDisplay Then
    Display1.style.setAttribute "display", ""
  else
    Display1.style.setAttribute "display", "none"
  end if
</SCRIPT>

<BODY>
<OBJECT id=Display1 data="Display.htm" width=100 height=100 type="text/x-
scriptlet">
</OBJECT>
Other text...
</BODY>
</HTML>
```

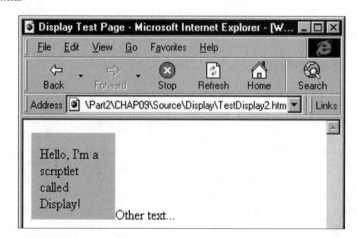

The picture shows the page of the source code listed above. If you click anywhere on the document's area, then you cause the new code (that with an opaque background) to execute. It will toggle the **display** attribute for the scriptlet from empty to **none** and vice versa. When it is set to **none** the entire scriptlet will disappear from the page. For an example see the next screenshot.

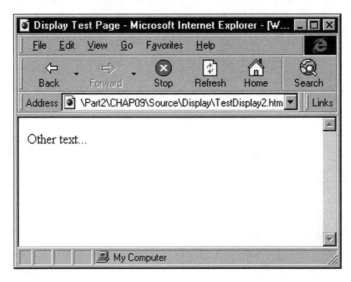

Note how the rest of the page moves up after the scriptlet gets hidden. Be careful to always bracket the strings **display** and **visibility** in quotes, as well as their values.

Define Hidden Scriptlets

Now we know how to toggle between the various visibility states. But what about if—more simply—we just need to have an invisible scriptlet in our pages? What we have done so far programmatically, we could do while declaring the scriptlet in the host page.

```
<object id=Scriptlet1 width=1 height=1 type="text/x-scriptlet"
data="scriptlet.htm"
    style="visibility:hidden">
</object>
```

The code snippet above shows a possible declaration for an invisible scriptlet. There we used the **visibility** attribute and had to specify a 1x1 pixels size to avoid wasting space. An alternative solution is the following:

```
<object id=Scriptlet1 type="text/x-scriptlet" data="scriptlet.htm"
    style="display:none">
</object>
```

This is based on the **display** attribute.

183

Changing the Size Dynamically

You often need to change the size of a scriptlet dynamically. If it isn't a problem to do it from within the host page, then just modify the value of the **width** and **height** attributes. The following code is an enhancement of a previous sample. The file is available on our Web site and is called **testdsp3.htm**.

```
<HTML>
<HEAD>
<TITLE>Display Test Page</TITLE>
</HEAD>

<SCRIPT language=VBScript>
  mDisplay = True
</SCRIPT>
```

```
<SCRIPT language=VBScript for="document" event="onclick">
  mDisplay = not mDisplay
  if mDisplay Then
    Display1.width = 100
  else
    Display1.width = 50
  end if
</SCRIPT>
```

```
<BODY>
<OBJECT id=Display1 data="Display.htm" width=100 height=100 type="text/x-
scriptlet">
</OBJECT>
Other text...
</BODY>
</HTML>
```

The demo reduces the width of the scriptlet by half. The code, however, is executed by the host page.

Now it's getting a bit trickier to get the scriptlet to resize itself automatically. After all, the problem is getting the right object to modify. For this role, as usual, there are many competitors but just one winner. The first thought that comes to mind is to use the scriptlet's **window** object.

```
<SCRIPT language=VBScript for="document" event="onclick">
  window.resizeto 100, 100
</SCRIPT>
```

Rather surprisingly, such code has the effect of resizing the Internet Explorer 4.0 main window. Other possible competitors are the various settable styles of the **document.body** object. For example, you could try the following:

```
<SCRIPT language=VBScript for="document" event="onclick">
  document.body.style.pixelHeight = 50
</SCRIPT>
```

The result is somewhat ambivalent: neither error nor success.

So, what's the right way for a scriptlet to self-resize? What you have to do is amazing. First and foremost you need to assign an ID to the HTML page that implements the scriptlet.

Sometimes, in the code excerpts shown so far, we used syntax like this for scriptlets:

```
<HTML id=MyPage>
...
</HTML>
```

Making use of that ID is not necessary, but helps a lot if you want your scriptlet to resize itself. So suppose you have a scriptlet like this one:

```
<HTML ID=MyPage>
<HEAD>
<TITLE>Resize Scriptlet</TITLE>
</HEAD>

<SCRIPT language=VBScript for="document" event="onclick">
  mResize = not mResize
  if mResize <> 0 Then
    MyPage.style.pixelHeight = MyPage.style.pixelHeight*2
    MyPage.style.pixelWidth = MyPage.style.pixelWidth*2
  else
    MyPage.style.pixelHeight = MyPage.style.pixelHeight/2
    MyPage.style.pixelWidth = MyPage.style.pixelWidth/2
  end if
</SCRIPT>

<SCRIPT language=JavaScript>
public_description = new CreateResize();
var InScriptlet = (typeof(window.external.version)=="string");
mResize = -1
function CreateResize()  {
}
</SCRIPT>

<BODY bgcolor="cyan">
Hello, I'm a scriptlet called Resize!
</BODY>
</HTML>
```

185

When we click on its document's area (in the Scriplet) we cause the browser to toggle the boolean value of the global variable **mResize**. Note that the variable is declared in a JavaScript script section and is also used in VBScript.

Since in VBScript the value of True corresponds to the number -1, we need to assign it this way to ensure it all works properly. The key to resizing scriptlets is in the following expressions:

```
MyPage.style.pixelWidth = …
MyPage.style.pixelHeight = …
```

where **MyPage** is the ID of the HTML tag and represents the scriptlet's page. Once we know this, all that remains to be done is to invoke the **style** object and its **pixelWidth** and **pixelHeight** properties. The numeric values you pass in must be expressed in pixels.

This is the right way to resize scriptlets dynamically. Furthermore, this is the only way provided.

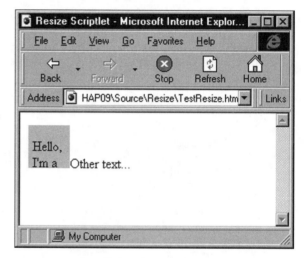

Summary

Being able to manipulate the user interface elements is an important issue and allows you to create interesting visual effects. In this chapter, we've run into scriptlet's visibility and dynamic layout calculations and discovered how to get them to work properly. In addition, we have provided a few golden rules to keep in mind when designing and writing scriptlets.

Web components for Web developers have the same power as ActiveX controls, but are far less painful. In fact, as long as the page is viewed through Internet Explorer 4.0, you have full support for them. This isn't true for ActiveX technology. Scriptlets are available for all the platforms and operating systems for which Internet Explorer 4.0 is available. Aside from the Win32 world, Internet Explorer 4.0 is supposed to ship for Windows 3.x, Windows CE, Mac and Unix. By comparison, the porting of the ActiveX technology to Mac, Win16 or Unix is a recent process.

Designing powerful, elegant, and flexible components is as important as making them really appealing and attractive.

A second point to consider is that scriptlets are a way to carry code reusability into the rapidly changing world of scripting and HTML. So use scriptlets not only to exploit the features of DHTML, but for structuring complex functionality too. Mix tables and data binding, for instance, and create your own tables with sorting capabilities. Use the basic timing properties to set up compelling timers and so on.

The user interface of a scriptlet is important and fundamental even when the component is not visible. Why? Because for HTML and scripting, the boundary between end users and programmers is purely indicative and changes from day to day, and according to the project's specifications.

In this chapter, we covered:

- Advice for great scriptlets programming
- Scriptlet's visibility topics
- Hidden servers
- Nested scriptlets
- How to resize the scriptlet's area

In the next chapter we will examine the issues you face when trying to move scriptlets outside HTML pages and host them in desktop applications.

Further Reading

Once more it's very hard to point you toward other books or articles that can explain better, or in more detail, the topics discussed here.

Nevertheless, I'd like to point out a column by Michael Hyman, which you can find monthly in Microsoft Interactive Developer. It is called "How It's Done", and often offers great insights on how to make your Web pages more and more lively and lovely. Michael usually presents pure DHTML solutions, but we have found inspiration there for some of the real-world scriptlets you'll see in the chapters to come.

Hosting Scriptlets in Desktop Applications

Considering the architecture of scriptlets, you can't avoid comparing them with ActiveX controls. They offer a quite similar programming interface to the users and are hosted in HTML pages in almost the same way.

Under Win32, scriptlets are supported by Internet Explorer 4.0 and resort to a hidden ActiveX control, which is smaller than WebBrowser and more specific. This same component may also be used to host scriptlets in desktop applications. A scriptlet can be hosted in HTML pages as well as in Visual Basic forms and in Visual InterDev.

This sort of language-independence has two causes. First, the Microsoft Scriptlet Control—installed as part of Internet Explorer 4.0. Secondly, the ActiveX awareness of many of today's development environments.

Why should you use scriptlets in Windows-based programs? Well, there are a number of reasons. The most obvious is the ease with which you can embed HTML documents in desktop applications. As a result, you can import the HTML browsing metaphor into the boundaries of the Windows shell. Don't forget that the Active Desktop brings some of the Web world features straight to the shell folders, through the Customize this folder... wizard.

Scriptlets are part of DHTML architecture and can be used (and exploited) without limitation wherever HTML is accepted. Moreover, using DHTML and scriptlets in desktop applications, or in the Windows 9x shell, poses fewer problems for the portability and backward compatibility of your next applications. In this chapter, we'll discuss:

- How to host HTML documents in real-world applications
- The Microsoft Scriptlet Control
- Scriptlets in Visual Basic applications
- Using scriptlets in other development environments

You will also discover that Visual Basic is the development tool that offers the best support for DHTML and scriptlets.

This whole chapter is somewhat advanced and requires you to be familiar with development tools like Visual Basic and Visual C++. On the other hand, we are aiming to show how to use scriptlets in desktop applications and if this is not your specific goal then you might want to skip the chapter.

How Can I Host HTML Pages?

A frequent problem that is arising more and more often in the programmers' community is—'How can I host HTML documents in my desktop applications?' Although HTML files are simply ASCII files, writing your own parser module is neither reasonable nor doable. In this section we're going to outline three possible solutions to this problem. The first one is the most well known approach and is based on the WebBrowser control. This component is an ActiveX control which is installed by IE40 (and even IE30) that provides you with the same browsing capability as IE. Actually, IE itself is using this component. The next figure shows it in the Visual Basic controls list.

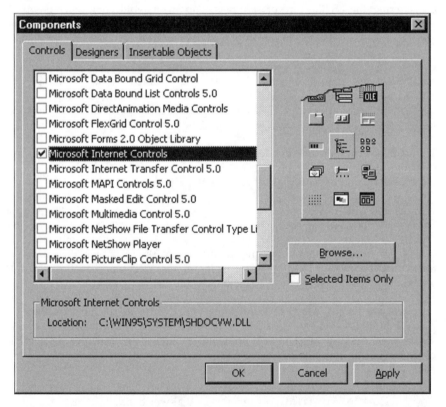

While this is a satisfying solution, it does force you to distribute a large quantity of bytes. For example, you need to distribute the WebBrowser's file **shdocvw.dll**, which is almost 2 MB. In addition, you can't forget **msHtml.dll** for the DHTML support and that increases the bulk by another 2 MB or so. And the list goes on.

A lighter solution is based on scriptlets. You still need **msHtml.dll,** but you can avoid **shdocvw.dll** in favor of the smaller **msHtmlwb.dll**. The WebBrowser control is implemented inside **shdocvw.dll**, while the Microsoft Scriptlet Control is in the latter library.

If this all sounds a bit confusing just consider that—as we've repeated on many occasions—scriptlets are nothing more than HTML documents. This means that a component capable of displaying scriptlets can support ordinary Web pages in the same way.

Finally, we are going to address a possible third approach, which allows you to bring a bit of the Web into your next applications. The latest version of the Microsoft Internet Client SDK comes with an interesting example. It shows you how to call a semi-undocumented function from the **msHtml.dll** library, to implement HTML-based dialogs.

In the following paragraphs, we'll look at these approaches in more detail, emphasizing their advantages as well as their drawbacks.

The WebBrowser Control

The WebBrowser control can now be considered fully documented. It's been around for a while—since the first beta versions of Internet Explorer 3.0. Basically, it has a navigational method that allows you to go to a specified URL. Not to mention the fact that that URL might be a shell folder, a remote or local HTML page, or even a document for which an application that works as an ActiveX server exists on the current machine. Most of the Office applications (Word, Excel, PowerPoint) are ActiveX servers and, provided that you have Office installed, you can see the document through your own WebBrowser-based application too.

Using such a control from within an MFC or Visual Basic application is quite easy. What follows is a quick tutorial on this very subject.

First of all, you might want to include the component in your project. You can pick it up from the list of available controls that any development environment that supports ActiveX contains. For example, in Visual Basic it is given by the *Ctrl-T* key combination. In an MFC you can right-click on the resource editor panel and select the Insert Active<u>X</u> Control... item. The next screenshot shows what you can do with Visual C++.

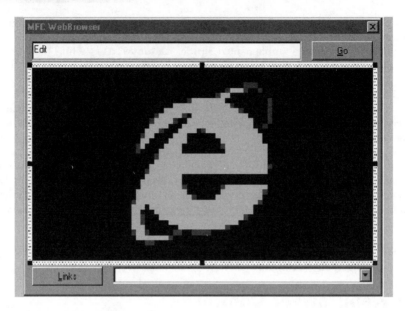

To display a given page what you need, in most cases, is some code like this:

```
CHAR pszUrl[MAX_PATH];
CEdit* pEdit = (CEdit*) GetDlgItem(IDC_EDIT1);
pEdit->GetWindowText( pszUrl, MAX_PATH );
m_WebBrowser.Navigate( pszUrl, 0, NULL, NULL, NULL);
```

If you're using Visual Basic, it changes to the following:

```
Dim url As String
url = Trim$(Text1.Text)
WebBrowser1.Navigate url
```

In both cases, you assign the WebBrowser control a site on your dialog or form and get the HTML document to display there.

This component also shows off a number of methods and events. For instance, it lets you know when the document has completed its download and is safe for you to access the DHTML object model. WebBrowser includes a variety of advanced functions (history list and hyperlinking, to name a few) and is tightly linked to the Internet Explorer 4.0 automation server.

Of all the approaches you can follow to host HTML documents in your own applications, the WebBrowser's is the most powerful. If you are interested in finding out more then take a closer look at the Microsoft Internet Client SDK documentation and read the Further Reading section at the end of the chapter. In particular, we recommend that you check out the Drill samples in the **SAMPLES\DRILL** subdirectory of the Internet Client SDK.

For an updated version of the Internet Client SDK you can check the following address:

```
http://www.microsoft.com/msdn/sdk/inetsdk/help/
outline.htm#outline
```

Scriptlets: A Better Approach?

After all, the WebBrowser object is an ActiveX control, which takes the name of the document to be opened as input. The Microsoft Scriptlet Control works much the same. However, there's an important difference between them. The Microsoft scriptlet component is a sort of placeholder for the actual scriptlet's file. That is, the control has been designed to host scriptlets and not just HTML documents. This means that if you attempt to use it as a simpler HTML viewer you run into nasty side effects.

To keep it brief, you can't change the HTML file to be viewed through the Scriptlet Control. The link between the control and the scriptlet is established at design-time. Since the control actually hosts scriptlets then the HTML file is displayed as a particular case.

For example, suppose your goal is to write a full-fledged HTML viewer that lets you choose which file to open and then loads and displays it. You just can't do this by using the scriptlet control. In fact, when you drop the component onto a form you're required to specify which is the referenced URL. Furthermore, once you have done it, you can't change it when the program is running.

There is a reason for this. The Scriptlet Control is intended to be an almost invisible and transparent layer of code that wraps a given, and one-time fixed, Web component. The underlying idea is that you drop in a scriptlet in the same way as an ActiveX control. That's why the scriptlet container and the actual component are so tightly bound—they must look as if they are a single object!

A Scriptlet-based HTML Viewer

If you're happy to decide at design-time which HTML file is to be viewed, then not only can you exploit the scriptlet Component as a viewer, but you can do better than that with the WebBrowser.

Once you have added a reference to the control into your project in Visual Basic, then you just have to set its URL property directly in the property box.

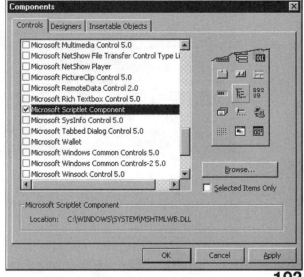

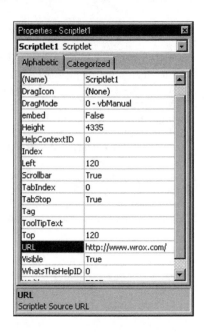

Of course, you have to specify an absolute path to the actual document or a remote URL (the control's **URL** property), add scrollbar support (the **Scrollbar** property), if needed, and have a complete and scrollable HTML window in a matter of seconds. The figure shows a screenshot with most of the properties that the Scriptlet Control makes available to programmers when hosted in a Visual Basic form.

A Built-in Function

The latest version of the Microsoft Internet Client SDK offers an interesting example that constitutes a further proposal on this subject. The project may be found in the **SAMPLES\HTMLDLG** path or listed with the other SDK samples online at **http://www.microsoft.com/msdn/sdk/inetsdk/help/c-frame.htm#outline.htm**. It shows that the **msHtml.dll** library exports a function called **ShowHTMLDialog**. This function is capable of hosting any HTML page in a window. This function doesn't seem to be fully documented, though the example mentioned above does show you how to use it. The next screenshot illustrates the demo program that ships with the SDK in action.

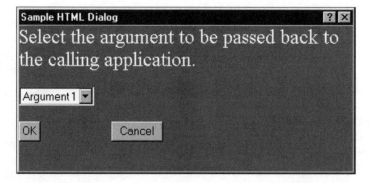

The full prototype of the routine can be found in the header file **mshtmhst.htm**. The function doesn't accept a string that points to a file name. Instead, it requires a pointer to a URL moniker.

Personally, I was surprised by such a function and only discovered it through the aforementioned sample. However, consider that to exchange parameters with the rest of the calling application you must write specific script code in the page viewed. To my knowledge, the only way to get more information about this is to take a closer look at the source code available.

Whether your goal is simply displaying HTML pages, or specifically using scriptlets in your application's dialogs, then the best way to do it is by the means of the Microsoft Scriptlet Control. We're going to say more on it starting with the next section.

The Microsoft Scriptlet Control

If you're thinking of using scriptlets in desktop applications, then you must consider the Microsoft Scriptlet Control. It is a redistributable small dynamic library that works as the container object for a scriptlet. If you look at its programming interface, then you come across all the stock properties and methods we have discussed so far for objects that host scriptlets.

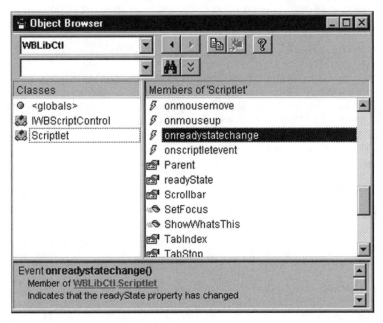

The picture above shows how the control appears in the Visual Basic Object Browser. To get to the screen illustrated above, you need to create a Visual Basic project, then add the Scriptlet Control to it, and finally press *F2* and select the module **WBLibCtl** from the topmost combobox that renders all the libraries referenced in the current project.

As you can see, the Object Browser exposes all the properties and methods of a scriptlet container. Once you've linked a given HTML file name that refers to a scriptlet to its **url** property, then the control and the scriptlet become a single component. This allows you to start invoking the methods and attributes as if you were working with a server module. However, even once you've linked to a specific URL, methods and properties of the scriptlet don't show up in the object browser because they aren't part of the scriptlet control but only exposed by the HTML page it hosts. Actually you're talking to the Scriptlet control that passes your requests down to the Web component it includes.

The screenshot above shows how the control appears in the Visual Basic development environment. You can set and read all the properties and invoke all the methods of the scriptlet as if they were exposed directly by the control. In addition, you can call those explicitly made available by the component. For example, you can add the scrollbars setting

```
Scriptlet1.Scrollbar = True
```

However, this **Scrollbar** is different from the **scrollbar** stock property we met in Chapter 5. They're different because (apart from the different case) if they weren't you should be able to invoke **selectableContent** or **version** in the same way. However, if you do so you get an error message box. The **Scrollbar** with the upper case is a property of the scriptlet ActiveX control while the other is a property exposed by the environment that hosts the scriptlet. Then, very likely, the control's **Scrollbar** property is a wrapper around the scriptlet's **scrollbar** property.

Key Facts to Remember

To take advantage of the Microsoft Scriptlet Component in desktop applications, you need to do the following:

- Include the control in your current project.
- Set the scriptlet name at design-time.
- Initialize it when its state is consistent and ready.
- Invoke the properties and methods provided by the scriptlet.
- Invoke the properties and methods provided by the host IDE.

Invoking any of the scriptlet's properties and methods is safe only when the state of the component is ready. This state of readiness is not notified until the Internet Explorer 4.0 Dynamic HTML engine finishes building the object model. The component receives an event called **onreadystatechange**. It also exposes a read-only property called **readyState**. By combining these two attributes, you are made aware when it's the right time to initialize the scriptlet. To be exact, you should wait for the **readyState** property to assume a value of 4. This means that the component is completely loaded, and is ready to work.

Initializing the Component

There are five possible ready states. They are expressed by the enumerate type just called **READYSTATE**. Here's it's a C/C++ declaration.

```
enum tagREADYSTATE {
  READYSTATE_UNINITIALIZED = 0,
  READYSTATE_LOADING = 1,
  READYSTATE_LOADED = 2,
  READYSTATE_INTERACTIVE = 3,
  READYSTATE_COMPLETE = 4
} READYSTATE
```

The best way to hook for the component to become ready is to handle the **onreadystatechange** event, and check the value of the **readyState** property against 4.

Once you have specified the name of the scriptlet file, stored it in the **url** property, and waited for the state to become ready, you can finally access all the attributes of the scriptlet. In addition, you can manipulate, through the scriptlet itself, all the accessory properties that the container (be it Visual Basic or any other ActiveX based development environment) makes available.

For instance, if you're using Visual Basic you can dynamically resize your scriptlet in a much simpler way than the ones we examined in the previous chapter. The next code snippet shows how you can move and resize the Scriptlet control and place it at the center of the form leaving only a border of 100 pixels all around.

```
Sub Form_Resize()
  Offset = 100
  Scriptlet1.Move Offset, Offset, Form1.ScaleWidth-2*Offset, _
                 Form1.ScaleHeight-2*Offset
End Sub
```

Analogously, if your goal is to hide and restore the scriptlet, then in Visual Basic you can do it smoothly through the **Visible** property instead of Dynamic HTML elements.

```
Sub Scriptlet1_onreadystatechange()
  If readyState = 4 Then
    Scriptlet1.Visible = False
  End if
End Sub
```

Both **Move** and **Visible**, though, are methods and properties that apply to the external scriptlet control layer and not to the HTML scriptlet itself.

However, when it comes to using scriptlets in desktop applications the concept of scriptlet and the concept of scriptlet control really coincide. The key to this is the design-time only **url** property. More on this later.

197

Scriptlets in Visual Basic

Using scriptlets in Visual Basic applications is quick and easy, if you respect the few rules listed above. For any scriptlet you want to add, insert a copy of the Scriptlet Control. Place and resize it as needed. So far you've worked only with a generic scriptlet container. Once you've finished, then it's time to assign it a specific file name which implements an HTML component. This association necessarily occurs at design-time. Give the **url** property the name of the scriptlet's file. This name is the same one you would have assigned to the **data** attribute if you were using it in an HTML host page.

Specifying the URL

There's a significant drawback when assigning the URL from which you are downloading the scriptlet's file. However, while this results in a bit of uneventful behavior, it's both understandable and reasonable. Let's see why.

You must specify the full path from which the control can access the HTML file with the scriptlet's public interface. By full path, we really mean that you should indicate the drive, the directories, and the file name. This is an absolute path, which is maintained when you distribute your application!

This is a big drawback. However, this stems from the logical correspondence between ActiveX controls and scriptlets. An ActiveX control is referenced through its 128-bit long CLSID. Each computer that hosts that application may or may not have a given control installed. If it is installed, the control is found through its CLSID stored in the local machine's registry.

Conceptually, scriptlets should be treated the same way. They don't have a CLSID, you just identify them by name. However, if you avoid drive and path, programs usually search for files in the public system directories. This doesn't happen with scriptlets. Even if you copy the files into the Windows directory, the Scriptlet Component fails.

So what else can you do? Use a semi-relative path. Even this way, however, things don't go seamlessly.

```
Scriptlet1.url = file://\script\hotbtn.htm
```

The above assignment forces the component to look for the **hotbtn.htm** scriptlet in a directory called **script**. This folder is placed immediately under the root of the current drive. Of course, you need to locate such a file in that path, whatever the current drive.

Absolute Paths

The requirement for absolute paths makes it a bit harder to use scriptlets in local applications, but is perfectly reasonable in Web-based projects. In fact, if you assume you download scriptlets from a URL, then absolute paths aren't a problem at all.

As mentioned earlier, **url** is a design-time property. This characteristic binds together an instance of the container and the scriptlet itself. In this way, the user perceives the scriptlet as a whole. The next screenshot shows a Visual Basic form that hosts a couple of scriptlets.

The two white areas (including the one selected) are the sites of a couple of scriptlets. The scriptlet we're using needs to be initialized through scripting before showing something significant. We're using a hot button scriptlet, that is a component that works as a button and shows different images according to the mouse movements.

Initializing the scriptlet

The **url** property must be set at design-time. The first moment at which you can access the public interface of the scriptlet isn't the **Form_Load** procedure as expected, but the scriptlet's **onreadystatechange** event. The following code snippet shows the details of how to initialize a Web component.

```
Private Sub Scriptlet2_onreadystatechange()
    If Scriptlet2.readyState = 4 Then
        Scriptlet2.Picture = "go1.bmp"
        Scriptlet2.HotPicture = "go2.bmp"
        Scriptlet2.DownPicture = "go3.bmp"
        Scriptlet2.BackColor = "#C0C0C0"
    End If
End Sub
```

Place anything you need to initialize the scriptlet here. As shown above, you can use the common object-oriented syntax to access the scriptlet's programming interface.

If you think it over, you'll realize that it's a bit unusual. We stated that we're using scriptlets through an ActiveX control. In fact, **Scriptlet2** seen above is the name of an instance of the Microsoft Scriptlet Control. This component is a simple host for the actual scriptlet we reference through the **url** property. Despite this, we're mixing **Scriptlet2**, which is an ActiveX control, with properties that are specific to the hosted HTML Scriptlet. In other words, we're calling properties like **Picture** or **HotPicture** as if they were part of the type library of the Microsoft Scriptlet Control, and not properties of the hosted scriptlet.

199

Accessing the Scriptlet's Programming Interface

Before going on, let's summarize what we've learnt so far. First, if you want to use scriptlets in a desktop application, then you need the Microsoft Scriptlet Control. It is an ordinary ActiveX control that hosts a scriptlet and works as a broker for its properties and methods.

In Visual Basic, you drop such a control into the form and assign its **url** property to make it refer to the correct scriptlet. The actual name of the scriptlet is given by **Scriptlet1.url**. This means that **Scriptlet1** is the name of the ActiveX control that is wrapping the scriptlet. Therefore, it is not the scriptlet's object. Nevertheless, you can add any of the scriptlet's attributes after the dot. That is:

```
Scriptlet1.BackColor
Scriptlet1.Picture
Scriptlet1.Enable
```

The above expressions are all legitimate (if we are using a scriptlet that supports these properties). It implies that **BackColor** and the others are all properties of the **Scriptlet1** object—that is the container object. In fact, they are attributes of the scriptlet, which is, in turn, a property of the **Scriptlet1** object!

Provided that you specify the correct case for the names, Visual Basic allows you to call them as if they were real and native properties of the object.

A Visual Basic Sample

The next screenshot presents a little Visual Basic applet hosting a couple of scriptlets that implement hot-tracking and bitmapped buttons. Each time you move the mouse over the Go or the New area, the bitmap changes and shows itself as if it's a 3-D button. The final effect is almost identical to the flat toolbars we find in Office 97 and the most recent Microsoft applications.

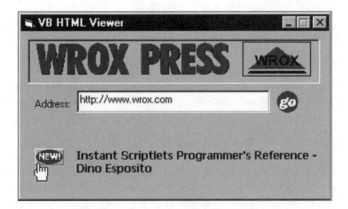

The scriptlet used in the above sample is called **hotbtn.htm**. Let's look at its source code.

```
<HTML ID=MyPage>
<HEAD>
<TITLE>BitmapButton Scriptlet</TITLE>
</HEAD>

<SCRIPT language=VBScript for="window" event="onload">
  InitBitmapButton
</SCRIPT>

<SCRIPT language=VBScript for="Image" event="onmouseover">
if mEnable Then
  document.images.item(0).style.cursor = "hand"
  DoSetImage mHotPicture
end if
</SCRIPT>

<SCRIPT language=VBScript for="Image" event="onmousedown">
if mEnable Then
  DoSetImage mDownPicture
end if
</SCRIPT>

<SCRIPT language=VBScript for="Image" event="onmouseup">
if mEnable Then
  DoSetImage mHotPicture
end if
</SCRIPT>

<SCRIPT language=VBScript for="Image" event="onmouseout">
if mEnable Then
  document.images.item(0).style.cursor = ""
  DoSetImage mPicture
end if
</SCRIPT>

<SCRIPT language=VBScript for="Image" event="onclick">
if InScriptlet Then
  window.external.bubbleEvent
end if
</SCRIPT>

<SCRIPT language=VBScript>
  Sub InitBitmapButton
    document.body.style.marginTop = 0
    document.body.style.marginLeft = 0
    document.body.style.marginRight = 0
    document.body.style.marginBottom = 0
  End Sub
</SCRIPT>

<SCRIPT language=VBScript>
  Sub DoSetImage( vImage )
    document.images.item(0).src = vImage
  End Sub
</SCRIPT>

<SCRIPT language=JavaScript>
public_description = new CreateBitmapButton();
var InScriptlet = (typeof(window.external.version)=="string");

var mEnable=1;
var mDownPicture="";
var mHotPicture="";
var mPicture="";
var mBackColor="";
var mHref="";
```

```
function CreateBitmapButton()  {
  this.put_DownPicture = put_DownPicture;
  this.get_DownPicture = get_DownPicture;
  this.put_HotPicture = put_HotPicture;
  this.get_HotPicture = get_HotPicture;
  this.put_Picture = put_Picture;
  this.get_Picture = get_Picture;
  this.get_BackColor = get_BackColor;
  this.put_BackColor = put_BackColor;
}

function get_DownPicture()  {
  return mDownPicture;
}
function put_DownPicture( vDownPicture )  {
  mDownPicture = vDownPicture;
  return 1;
}

function get_HotPicture()  {
  return mHotPicture;
}
function put_HotPicture( vHotPicture )  {
  mHotPicture = vHotPicture;
  return 1;
}

function get_Picture()  {
  return mPicture;
}
function put_Picture( vPicture )  {
  mPicture = vPicture;
  DoSetImage( mPicture );
  return 1;
}

function get_BackColor()  {
  return mBackColor;
}
function put_BackColor( vBackColor )  {
  mBackColor = vBackColor;
  document.bgColor = mBackColor;
  return 1;
}
</SCRIPT>
<BODY>
<img id="Image" src="" alt="" border=0>
</img>
</BODY>
</HTML>
```

The scriptlet is composed of an image that changes according to the movements
of the mouse. **Picture**, **HotPicture** and **DownPicture** are the names of the
properties that keep track of the various images for the normal, hot and pressed
states. In addition, **BackColor** allows you to set the background color. Notice
that here you're unable to grasp the background color of the Visual Basic form,
at least through the approach seen in Chapter 5. For this reason, we have
exposed the **BackColor** property, to let you gain some transparency.
The scriptlet behaves as expected when the mouse is clicked down, gets
released, or moves over a hot site. The mouse cursor is changed by the line:

```
document.images.item(0).style.cursor = "hand"
```

when we're moving over the scriptlet's **<IMG>** tag.

202

Furthermore, the scriptlet bubbles up the **onclick** event, which is caught and handled in Visual Basic code like this:

```
Private Sub Scriptlet2_onclick()
   MsgBox "Visit the WROX's Web site.", , "VB Scriptlets"
End Sub
```

Of course feel free to replace **Scriptlet2** with the actual name you give to your Scriptlet Control.

By default, Visual Basic adds a lot of stock properties to any control that it hosts. Amongst others, there's the **TooltipText** property. This property denotes the string to be displayed every time the mouse pauses over the control's area. By simply assigning:

```
Scriptlet1.TooltipText = "New cool book!"
```

you can have a tooltip on the scriptlet. In this particular case, there is another way to obtain the same effect. Since our **hotbtn.htm** scriptlet is based on an **<IMG>** tag, the tooltip text can be defined through the **alt** attribute. Such a property represents the alternative text to be displayed in place of the image— under Win32, Internet Explorer 4.0 also uses it for tooltips.

The following piece of script shows how to assign tooltip text to an image in pure HTML code. Of course this only works for **<IMG>** tags.

```
<SCRIPT language=VBScript>
   Sub DoSetTooltip( vText )
      document.images.item(0).alt = vText
   End Sub
</SCRIPT>
```

You can download this application **vbscrlet.zip** from our Web site at:

http://rapid.wrox.co.uk/books/138X.

The zip file contains a handy Readme.txt to help you set the project up.

That's all on Visual Basic. The next section is a bit more straightforward. This is mostly due to some internal features of the language run-time engine that allow you to access the scriptlet's programming interface through the straight container object. As we're going to see right now, other development environments don't offer the same kind of facility.

Scriptlets in Other Environments

Scriptlets were publicly announced just a few days before Internet Explorer 4.0 shipped. The timing suggests that the development team must have had to work hard (and to tight deadlines) to deliver a suitable product in such a short time.

Due to this—and this is not officially well-known—at present scriptlets are supported only in Visual Basic and Visual InterDev. This means that what we hinted at earlier—namely that you could use scriptlets even in Visual C++ or Delphi applications—was not altogether true.

It's quite likely and reasonable to suggest that this will change with the next release of Internet Explorer 4.0—perhaps before the already rumored Internet Explorer 5.0.

However, if you intend to develop or just experiment with scriptlets applications today, you must turn your attention to Visual Basic only.

What Can We Do Ourselves?

At this point you might be wondering what is wrong with Delphi or MFC applications and why Visual Basic has been privileged. If you think this through then you may identify the following fundamental point—although we're using an ActiveX control (like the Microsoft Scriptlet Control) we're unable to import or correctly use scriptlets in Delphi or Visual C++.

The problems you can easily experiment with and reproduce are slightly different for Delphi and MFC. In principle, an expert and seasoned COM programmer could succeed in working around them. But what is the price to pay? Is it really worth such time and effort? Certainly, it would be nice if Microsoft provided a more usable programming interface for scriptlets even outside the Web documents world. On the other hand, a more general hosting of scriptlets in ActiveX-aware development environments is in order.

In the next sections, we'll examine, in a bit more detail, why it's very difficult to use scriptlets with Delphi, Visual C++ and MFC. Hopefully, this will be of help in finding working solutions.

Scriptlets in Delphi

At a first sight, using scriptlets in Delphi (we have tested only the latest Delphi 3 version) does not seem to pose any kind of problem. You can successfully register the Microsoft Scriptlet Control with the Component Palette and then insert a copy of the control in any form. During the installation process, Delphi creates a component that wraps the functionality of the ActiveX control reading directly from the type library. This file—usually called **WBlib.pas**—is created in the VCL directory. It is the source for the suggestions the editor can provide when you are editing the application's files.

The following listing shows a little Delphi program that attempts to use a scriptlet through the ActiveX control. Note that the scriptlet control is rendered through a **TScriptlet** object.

```
unit D3Scriptlet;

interface

uses
    Windows, Messages, SysUtils, Classes, Graphics, Controls, Forms, Dialogs,
    OleCtrls, WBLib_TLB;

type
    TForm1 = class(TForm)
      Scriptlet1: TScriptlet;
      procedure FormCreate(Sender: TObject);
      procedure Scriptlet1onreadystatechange(Sender: TObject);
    private
      { Private declarations }
    public
      { Public declarations }
    end;

var
    Form1: TForm1;

implementation

{$R *.DFM}

procedure TForm1.FormCreate(Sender: TObject);
begin
ShowMessage( 'Now creating the form' );
end;

procedure TForm1.Scriptlet1onreadystatechange(Sender: TObject);
begin
if Scriptlet1.readyState = 4 then
begin
  ShowMessage (Scriptlet1.url);
end;
end;

end.
```

The source code works well, but it has a significant limitation. Once you have set the URL through the object inspector, there's nothing more you can do. To understand why, let's turn back to some previous sections in this same chapter and focus on a key point. The point that Visual Basic allows us to use the scriptlet's properties as if they were part of the scriptlet's ActiveX control interface.

Programming the Scriptlet

Often a scriptlet hasn't any predefined behavior and, therefore, needs scripting to do anything significant. This means that you must access the scriptlet's programming interface. As mentioned earlier, scriptlets are hosted in desktop applications through an ActiveX control. From such a programming environment we see this control and not the scriptlet itself. Visual Basic allows us to call the properties and methods of the scriptlet directly through this control. This is a shortcut that brings your calls to the proper engine.

Consider the above sample, and suppose we have assigned the **Scriptlet1.url** the file **mycomp.htm** exposing a method called **DoSomething**. Well, Visual Basic allows us to call:

```
Scriptlet1.DoSomething
```

but Delphi and MFC do not. To be honest, both Delphi and MFC are in the right, since Visual Basic accepts that syntax because of some of its internal and less well-known features. In Visual Basic programming, in fact, you could take such a shortcut in the presence of some default method or property, which is silently invoked if needed. Maybe this is exactly what occurs under the hood. If you know more about this then here would be a good starting point for further investigations.

In conclusion, with Delphi it's easy to use scriptlets provided that you don't need to program them!

Scriptlets in Visual C++

This same problem would also certainly arise with Visual C++ and with any other environment that supports the COM model in the standard way—that is without special shortcuts or additional features.

So it is reasonable to expect to find the same situation when attempting to use scriptlets with Visual C++. In this case, however, there's more.

The screenshot above shows the menu that allows you to insert an ActiveX control into a Visual C++ dialog. You can get such a menu by right-clicking on the resource editor window. By selecting Insert OLE Control... we obtain a listbox with all the insertable controls registered on the specific machine. The screenshot is taken from Visual C++ 4.2, but it looks identical in the more recent 5.0 version.

Once you've picked up the Microsoft Scriptlet Control from the popup list, you will come across the following strange message box.

The Microsoft Scriptlet Control is certainly a lightweight ActiveX control and if you compare it to the oldest OCX controls it is missing a great number of interfaces. The first time I got such a message, I concluded that it was time to install a newer version of Visual C++. In fact, it seems that the control is a real ActiveX Control and implements a reduced number of interfaces. Consequently, it is not surprising that a development tool released a few weeks after the official presentation of ActiveX technology has only limited support for ActiveX controls.

However—and this is a bit less understandable—the same occurs with Visual C++ 5.0 too.

If you compare, using tools like OLE Viewer (a tool that ships i.e. with Visual C++), the interfaces exposed by the Microsoft Scriptlet Control and any other control accepted by Visual C++, you will note a few differences. However, the fact that the message is really due to a missing interface (and, in that case, which one) is still to be proved.

Summary

I must confess that when I first heard of scriptlet technology (September 97)—just a couple of weeks before the final release of Internet Explorer 4.0—such components were neither supported nor documented in all the public platform previews of IE 4. In addition, the first draft papers appeared on the Web only about a week before September 30, when Internet Explorer 4.0 shipped. All this means that Scriptlet Technology is too young, even in a world where the word "young" is such a short lived term. Technologies follow one after another and are rarely given enough time to become adult, mature and well established.

Scriptlets have been thought up and developed in too short a time to make them well supported over all the available hosting platforms. So the development team focused on a couple of environments—Visual Basic and IE4—and made sure that things worked fine there.

What remains to be done—including enhancements, optimization, testing, and more—has been postponed until the next releases of Internet Explorer.

If you're using scriptlets through HTML pages it's quite likely that you won't see this. The coverage of desktop applications is one of the shortcomings of the current implementation. In this chapter, we have seen:

- How to make use of scriptlets in Visual Basic applications
- The features of the Microsoft Scriptlet Control
- Why scriptlets aren't supported well in Delphi
- What happens with Visual C++

Further Reading

Web browsing objects are—or rather have been—a hot topic for cutting-edge programmers. The first article on the subject that I can remember is by Joshua Trupin and appeared in MSJ in June 1996. The title was "*The Visual Programmer Puts ActiveX Documents Objects Through Their Paces*". While the piece is mainly focused on the concept of ActiveX Documents, it succeeds in showing the potential of such a component. A more comprehensive tutorial on WebBrowser may be found in Microsoft Interactive Developer, October 1997. The author is Aaron Skonnard and the piece is entitled: "*Boning up on the Internet Client SDK: Web Browsing Objects*" and, among other things, presents examples in both Visual Basic and MFC. Aside from the official documentation this could be a good starting point for experimenting with WebBrowser.

Making Callbacks with Scriptlets

The callback mechanism is a standard part of the Windows operating system. Basically, it allows an application module to pass a piece of its own code down to another module and then have it call this code back. In other words, a module can receive a reference to an external piece of code (say, a function), which has been defined by another module, and execute it—passing some arguments if necessary.

A typical example of this is the enumeration functions we can find in the Win32 SDK. Routines like **EnumWindows** or **EnumFonts** go through the entire list of the active windows or the registered fonts and call user-defined procedures for each item. When we call such functions we specify, as an argument, the code we want them to execute for each window or font that is found.

An interesting application of this allows the programmers to indicate a set of operations to be accomplished indirectly on all the members of a certain collection.

Making callbacks from a program means that you should invoke a given method or function with a fixed prototype and a standard and well-documented behavior. You pass in a reference to some of your code and get it called when appropriate. The callback mechanism gives us a way to intervene inside the code that another module executes.

The entire Windows world is heavily based on this principle so, when you create an object, you're actually just creating a procedure that the system will call back for every event in the object's life cycle.

The callback mechanism applies mostly to low-level Windows programming. So what about scriptlets? Since scriptlets are pieces of code built on top of the DHTML object model, you may need to perform the same operations on a collection of elements. To do so you might want to simply search through the collection's items for a **for...next** statement. You could also do the same in the page itself. However, this is a routine task and is probably better left to a specialized component. In HTML some of these components are scriptlets.

In this chapter we'll be covering two ways to implement callbacks with scriptlets. You will learn:

- How to take advantage of the window's **execScript** method.

- How to use custom events to invoke callback code.

- How a scriptlet can access and modify the parent's script code.

The examples we're about to discuss present a simple timer and a generic object enumerator, which provides a higher-level interface for searching through a DHTML collection.

What a Timer Can Do for You?

Timers are an important feature that can't be left out of any programming environment. Basically, they are software interfaces for a clock-based mechanism that let you know when a given interval of time expires. The way you code this, or rather the way you're allowed to code this, may vary quite a bit according to the actual features of the language, or the development environment, you're working with.

If you're using a timer then you probably need to be informed when a given interval ends. It's also likely that, at this point, you might want to execute some code. Sometimes, this code only runs once. In other cases it runs repeatedly, each time that amount of time expires. For example, if you need an answer from the user within, say, ten seconds, then you set a timer and reset it at the end. On the other hand, if you're coding a slide-show then you need to ensure that a certain operation (say, displaying an image) executes every fixed number of seconds continuously, unless you stop it.

There's always something to say and experience with timers. They are an endless source of inspiration for programmers. Timers are used much more than you might suspect in the Windows operating system.

Timers are the typical field of application for callbacks. Didn't we say, a few lines above, that timers often need to run a piece of code? Didn't we also say that timers are software objects? So you need to figure out how to get in touch with the timer to get it to execute the code you specify, or to get notified about the time expiration.

Typical Interfaces for Timers

There are two basic ways in which a timer can communicate with its clients. It can notify them that the interval has expired, or it can silently execute the specified code. To put it another way, a client/server relationship is established between a timer and an application—with the timer playing the role of the server. The client needs to connect to the server and set it up to work as desired. In doing so, the client receives and stores an identifier for the timer. When this is complete the client must stop the timer and release it. The set/ reset operations are an absolute necessity. When initializing the timer in your

Windows code, you can ask it to raise an event (or send a message), or to execute a specified procedure. When using timers with script code, however, you can only execute a given piece of code.

The timer receives the interval length and detects when it expires. At this point it can follow two different paths:

 Notify the circumstance to the client and have it execute its own code.

 Execute the client's code directly, provided a reference is held

What a timer can actually do is decided by the software interface it's wrapped in. In the Win16 and Win32 SDK, timers are handled through a function called **SetTimer**. This function can take a pointer to the actual code to execute it. If no pointer is given, then it just sends a message when the interval expires.

This is for traditional programming languages, but what about scriptlets?

Fortunately, the DHTML object model provides some basic services for setting up timers. They are easy to use and powerful, but offer only one way of working. In fact, DHTML timers require you to specify the script code to be executed, besides the number of milliseconds to wait between two successive calls.

In the following paragraphs we'll be examining the built-in DHTML services for timers and we will also start investigating how to extend and exploit them. Along the way you'll discover that nesting timers into other objects—such as scriptlets—poses a number of new problems that have to be addressed.

Dynamic HTML Basic Services

The **window** object exposes a method called **setInterval** that actually works as a timer. To be precise, the **window** object also defines a **setTimeout** method whose semantics are a little different. We'll talk about this later in the chapter.

The **setInterval**'s precise syntax is:

```
TimerID = window.setInterval( expression, timeInterval [, language] )
```

The parameter **expression** denotes the code to be executed every specified number of milliseconds. It may be a string like:

```
"d=new Date();alert(d.getDate());"
```

or

```
"s=\"Any text\";alert(s);"
```

or a function name as well:

```
"DoSomething();"
```

What matters is that it refers to executable code. If the expression includes a function's name, then the function itself must be within reach and part of the same HTML page.

The `timeInterval` argument specifies the length of the time interval. It must be expressed in milliseconds. The expression gets evaluated repeatedly—every time such an interval expires in fact. Finally, `language` is an optional string parameter that refers to the script language in which the code to be executed is expressed. In all the above cases it would have been `JScript`.

Choosing a Language for Code Expressions

By default the code is assumed to be in the same language as the `<SCRIPT>` where it is declared. For example, consider the following code snippet:

```
<script language="VBScript">
Sub InitClock
    mTimer = window.setInterval( "DoUpdateClock", 1000 )
End Sub
</script>
```

It is written in VBScript and includes a call to `window.setInterval`. Unless you state explicitly that the expression must be passed to a specific parser, then it is evaluated by the same script parser that interprets the parent expression. In this case—VBScript. If you use a line like this instead:

```
mTimer = window.setInterval( "DoUpdateClock();", 1000 )
```

you'll get an error since the expression is in JScript while the default language parser is VBScript. If you want to specify a JScript expression from within a VBScript-based `<SCRIPT>` tag, you ought to resort to:

```
mTimer = window.setInterval( "DoUpdateClock();", 1000, "JScript" )
```

Setting and Clearing a Time Interval

The `window.setInterval` method creates a timer and runs the specified code every given number of milliseconds. The method returns a numeric value that renders the internal identifier of the timer object. You'll need it when you want to stop the timer.

```
window.clearInterval( mTimer );
```

The line above follows on from the previous blocks of code and shows how to stop a timer executing.

What you do during the timer activity, and how often you get it called, is completely up to you.

If you look at the `window` object's documentation you'll notice the presence of a similar method: `setTimeout`. It exhibits an almost identical prototype, but behaves quite differently. In fact, `setTimeout` accepts a script expression, but executes it only once and only the specified number of milliseconds after the page has completed loading.

214

The Clock Sample

If you have read a previous Wrox publication: *"Professional IE4 Programming"*
(ISBN 1-861000-70-7), then you will know how to insert a running clock into an
HTML page viewed through Internet Explorer 4.0. In case you don't, the next
screenshot gives you an idea of how it looks.

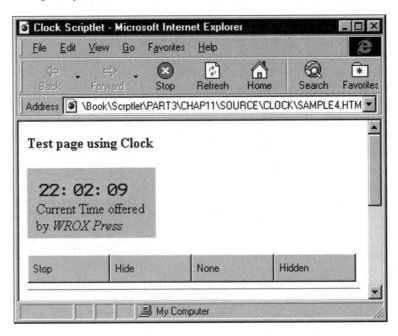

The source code for this is available on our Web site at:
http://rapid.wrox.co.uk/books/138X. The file is called **useclock.htm**.

As you can see, we've been able to put a clock in an HTML page without it
being an ActiveX control. A clock is naturally implemented through a timer and
the clock scriptlet is no exception.

The code snippet seen above is taken from the file **clock.htm** that helps to
produce the output shown above. The clock is produced by an HTML table.
The three fields of this table get updated every second with the current time.

A clock doesn't require complex semantics or any sophisticated design work.
Other components, however, might need to include a timer and pass it to the
code specified by the host environment. This means that you have—in order—
the HTML page, the scriptlet and the timer inside the scriptlet. If the code that
must be run is contained in the HTML page, the scriptlet must be able to
access it. More importantly, this occurs outside the scriptlet's boundaries.

The clock sample is a stepping stone towards the construction of a more generic
timer object that fulfills the following constraints:

 It must be a self-contained script component.

It must be able to pulse every specified number of seconds.

 It must support a dual-interface and execute code-expressions or raise events.

And above all, this component must be able to access the code wherever it is located, whether it's local code or that belonging to the parent.

Accessing Code Expressions

If you use DHTML code directly, then you have the timer and the code it executes all gathered in a single page (host page or scriptlets page—it's all the same). This means that there is a unique namespace for all the objects referred to in the code expressions you might pass to the timer. In other words, you can safely issue calls like these,

```
mTimer = window.setInterval( "DoUpdateClock();", 1000, "JScript" )
```

Safe in the knowledge that the parser will always find **DoUpdateClock**.

However, suppose you have a scriptlet which encompasses a timer. And suppose the code expressions depend upon the parent page routines. A possible scenario is the following:

```
Timer1.Start "DoSomething", 3000
```

where **Timer1** is a scriptlet that wraps the DHTML's timer object. It should end up calling the function **DoSomething** every three seconds. **DoSomething** is a client piece of code you can find in the document hosting the scriptlet.

You may want the scriptlet to regularly execute a function defined in the host pageas if you were using the traditional callback model of Windows programming. Unfortunately, however, if **DoSomething** is defined outside the scriptlet file there's no way to access the function's code. What we really need is a way to pass an indirect reference to a piece of code across different modules.

DHTML does a good job on its own, allowing you to execute explicit instructions such as **alert** or **MsgBox**, but it can't immediately run a structured piece of code by procedure name.

The rest of this chapter is devoted to building a consistent solution for this kind of problem. To start with, we'll attempt to design a more generic timer object, building it on top of the **window**'s timer methods.

A More Generic Timer Object

Using timers through the methods of the **window** object is easy and doesn't involve many parameters being sent or received. So why do we want another object? There are a number of reasons and you can judge for yourself whether they are all worthy of consideration.

The first that comes to mind is that the **setInterval** method you use is just a method. Plus, it always requires you to pass in a code expression. This is not a drawback, since you usually need to do something on a regular basis if you set up a timer. However, if we encapsulate a timer in a new object—a scriptlet—then we'll be able to:

- Accept a code expression.
- Fire an event instead of running a procedure.
- Use seconds instead of milliseconds.

Furthermore, we have an even simpler and more readable syntax to face.

Instead of:

```
mTimer = window.setInterval( "DoSomething();", 1000, "JScript" )
...
window.clearInterval( mTimer )
```

wouldn't it be better to use:

```
Timer1.Start "DoSomething ();", 1
...
Timer1.Stop
```

Of course, we need to write a scriptlet for this. Thus, in doing so, we start to move towards a scriptlet-based callback mechanism.

A Bare-bone Timer Scriptlet

A bare-bone timer scriptlet would expose a couple of methods to start and stop the activity. In addition, it must define and use internally a variable to store the identifier of the timer. The skeleton of such a component might look like this:

```
<HTML ID=MyPage>
<HEAD>
<TITLE>Timer Scriptlet</TITLE>
</HEAD>

<SCRIPT language=JavaScript>
public_description = new CreateTimer();
var InScriptlet = (typeof(window.external.version)=="string");
var mTimer = "";

function CreateTimer()  {
   this.Start = DoStart;
   this.Stop = DoStop;
   this.event_OnTimer = "";
}

function DoStart(proc, secs )  {
   window.setInterval( proc, secs*1000 );
   return 1;
}

function DoStop()  {
   window.clearInterval( mTimer );
```

```
    }
    </SCRIPT>

    <BODY>
    </BODY>
    </HTML>
```

As you can see, we've arranged it to accept the amount of time in seconds instead of milliseconds. While the latter solution is clearly more flexible, in most cases seconds suffice and are far easier to deal with and understand.

The code snippet shown above is a simple wrapper built around the **window.setInterval** method. It passes the code expression down to the parsing engine as it is—without checking or requesting any kind of verification.

This has an obvious drawback: if you attempt to specify a procedure name when setting the timer, then it never gets executed and you're prompted with an error box. Consider, in fact, that the procedure you're passing to the scriptlet is defined in the host page. Consequently, it is not viewable from within the scriptlet's page.

On the other hand, if you're defining a timer object, you need to run some code. In addition, this code may vary from time to time. So it must be considered as a parameter and can't be hard-coded inside the scriptlet itself.

This means that we definitely need to make some enhancements to this code.

Implementing it Through Events

The easiest way to work around the above problem is by using events to notify the parent page that the given interval has expired. In this way, you can associate a fixed piece of code with the internal timer and get it to dynamically execute any more specific code. When you fire events, you actually cause the parent to run code. This is exactly the result we're aiming to achieve.

The scriptlet's code seen above becomes:

```
<HTML ID=MyPage>
<HEAD>
<TITLE>Timer Scriptlet</TITLE>
</HEAD>

<SCRIPT language=JavaScript>
public_description = new CreateTimer();
var InScriptlet = (typeof(window.external.version)=="string");
var mTimer = "";

function CreateTimer()  {
  this.Start = DoStart;
  this.Stop = DoStop;
  this.event_OnTimer = "";
}

function DoStart( secs )  {
  mTimer = window.setInterval( "DoFireEvent();", secs*1000 );
  return 1;
}
```

```
function DoFireEvent() {
  if( InScriptlet && !(window.external.frozen) ) {
    window.external.raiseEvent( "OnTimer", 0 );
  }
}
```

```
function DoStop() {
  window.clearInterval( mTimer );
}
</SCRIPT>
<BODY>
</BODY>
</HTML>
```

Let's call this scriptlet **timer1.htm**. The major change is that now you can limit the interval passed to the **Start** method. The code to be executed (if any), which responds to the event, is specified in the container page.

Now the timer regularly invokes a JScript procedure called **DoFireEvent**. This function simply raises a custom **OnTimer** event, allowing the host page to handle it as necessary. Notice that in this way we also avoid the problem of specifying the script language for the code expression. Or rather, the users of our scriptlet don't need to worry about it. They just write the code for an event and can proceed using whichever script language they prefer. This won't affect the scriptlet.

We have isolated the timer from the rest of the hosting page. When we call **setInterval** we now specify a code that resides inside the scriptlet.

```
window.setInterval( "DoFireEvent();", secs*1000 );
```

In fact, **DoFireEvent** is a scriptlet's internal procedure that raises an event. It can be hooked on the host page and handled with code written in any valid script language.

Using a Timer Scriptlet

Now, let's see how to use the previous scriptlet. The following page is called **testtim1.htm**.

```
<html>
<head>
<title>Timer Test Page</title>
</head>

<body">
<script language="JScript" for=Timer1 event="onscriptletevent(n,0)">
  alert( "Interval Expired (event)." );
</script>

Clicking on the "Set Timer" button you'll set up a timer that triggers an event
every 3 seconds. The code used is like this:
<hr>
<code>Timer1.Start 3</code>
<hr>

<object id=Timer1 data="Timer1.htm"
        width=20 height=20 type="text/x-scriptlet">
</object>
```

```
<input type="button" name="Method" value="Set Timer"
       language="VBScript"
       onclick="Timer1.Start 3">
<input type="button" name="Stop" value="Stop Timer"
       language="VBScript"
       onclick="Timer1.Stop">
</body>
</html>
```

All that we need to set the timer up is a line like:

```
Timer1.Start 3
```

The only parameter needed is the interval range in seconds. Any notification arrives through the **onscriptletevent** event. As usual, its first argument is the name of the specific event raised. In this case: **OnTimer**. Check out Chapter 6—*Event Handling*, to find out more about events.

In the above sample, the second argument **onscriptletevent** is unused and set to zero. However, you can take advantage of it, if necessary, and have the host page know everything that suits your needs.

Since such a scriptlet isn't supposed to have any user interface, you might want it to be invisible. You can do this via:

```
style="display:none"
```

added directly to the **<OBJECT>** tag.

```
<object id=Timer1 data="Timer1.htm" width=1 height=1 type="text/x-scriptlet"
        style:"display:none">
</object>
```

See Chapter 7 for more details about displaying scriptlets.

Scriptlet Callbacks

If we limit ourselves to timers, this would be it. Our not-so-secret plans, however, require us to take callbacks into account. This means that we would like to insert a scriptlet into an HTML page and have it go through any collection of elements and execute a piece of code for each of them.

Again, we can follow the same event-driven approach seen just now for timers. Alternatively, we could set up a generic mechanism to make the scriptlet execute a generic piece of code—even if it's declared in its parent page.

On the road to achieving this result, we'll stop for a few moments and examine a slightly simpler sample. Let's implement a scriptlet timer that also accepts a piece of code from its host page and tries to execute it for every interval.

We'll build this example using the previous scriptlet code as a base. There are very few changes that need to be made to the public interface.

```
<HTML ID=MyPage>
<HEAD>
```

```
<TITLE>Timer Scriptlet</TITLE>
</HEAD>

<SCRIPT language=JavaScript>
public_description = new CreateTimer();
var InScriptlet = (typeof(window.external.version)=="string");
var mTimer = "";

function CreateTimer()  {
   this.Start = DoStart;
   this.Stop = DoStop;
   this.event_OnTimer = "";
}

function DoStart( secs, procName )  {
   if( procName.length==0 )
     mTimer = window.setInterval( "DoFireEvent();", secs*1000 );
   else {
     parDoc = window.parent.document;
     scr = parDoc.all(procName);
     origCode = ExtractJScriptCode( scr);
     mTimer = window.setInterval( origCode, 1000*secs );
   }
   return 1;
}

function DoFireEvent()  {
   if( InScriptlet && !(window.external.frozen) )  {
     window.external.raiseEvent( "OnTimer", 0 );
   }
}

function DoStop()  {
   window.clearInterval( mTimer );
}

function ExtractJScriptCode( scrObj )  {
   ...
}
</SCRIPT>
<BODY>
</BODY>
</HTML>
```

The scriptlet code still needs to be completed. For now, let's notice that the **Start** method has the following prototype:

```
object.Start( secs, procName )
```

We've added a second argument that may denote the code expression should be executed time after time. If this argument is missing then the behavior is the same as in the previous example. That is—the scriptlet raises an event. However, if the command line holds a significant expression then it executes when the interval has expired.

*The argument **procName** could be defined optional because in the code we introduced a test like **if(procName.length==0)** that provides a default behavior if the parameter is empty.*

Accessing the Parent's Script Code

When writing a line like this:

```
mTimer = window.setInterval( codeExpr, 1000*secs );
```

the string **codeExpr** denotes a series of executable expressions that follow the JScript or the VBScript syntax. However, in almost all cases it will refer to a subroutine defined—of course—in the parent's script sections.

window.setInterval internally uses **window.execScript** to run DHTML code indirectly. However, the **execScript** sees all the procedures defined in its scope, that is, in the current page.

So there is no chance that, in the host page, code such as:

```
Timer1.Start "DoSomething();", 3
...
<script language=JScript>
function DoSomething()   {
  alert( "Hello" );
}
</script>
```

will work without some kind of arrangement in the Timer object. That's because the **DoSomething** method is defined outside the scriptlet's scope (to be precise—in a completely different file).

What we need is a way to identify a piece of script code throughout the hierarchy of pages that form a given document.

This is akin to callbacks in Win32 programming. In Win32 we have a way of identifying a function throughout the modules that actually form a running process. The entire callback mechanism in Windows relies on function addresses. Do we have a similar mechanism present here? Yes, indeed we do.

In terms of DHTML, element IDs are the equivalent of function addresses.

Element IDs Identify Parent's Code

So instead of passing a code expression to the scriptlet, let's limit ourselves to sending in the ID string of a **<SCRIPT>** section. In practice, the above snippet should be rewritten like this:

```
Timer1.Start "DoSomething", 3
...
<script id="DoSomething" language=JScript>
function DoSomethingOrAnyOtherName()   {
  alert( "Hello!" );
}
</script>
```

where we assigned an ID to the **<SCRIPT>** tag.

Now the scriptlet receives a string that it explicitly knows to be a reference to a piece of parent's script code. Yes, it's a reference—or the HTML counterpart of a Win32 function address.

At this point, what happens inside the scriptlet is the same as what occurs inside the Windows system when a program issues a callback instruction. The system needs to jump to the specified address and run the code it finds there.

```
parDoc = window.parent.document;
scrObj = parDoc.all( procName );
origCode = ExtractJScriptCode( scrObj );
mTimer = window.setInterval( origCode, 1000*secs );
```

This is exactly what is done in the above code fragment. We have, however, still to address the **ExtractJScriptCode**'s internals.

Extracting Source Code

Now that the scriptlet holds an ID, it can recover the associated code and assign it to the **window.setInterval** method. First of all, we need to access the parent's document object. This is done via:

```
parDoc = window.parent.document;
```

Next, we need a reference to the specified script object. We get at this through an ID-based search through the **all** collection.

```
scrObj = parDoc.all(procName);
```

At this point, assuming that the ID is unique, we have an **HTMLScriptElement** object. After all, the body of this script is an executable script expression. So all that remains is to extract it and use it, as you would do with an ordinary code expression.

```
function ExtractJScriptCode( scrObj ) {
    s = scrObj.text;
    i = s.indexOf( "{" );
    code = s.substring( i, s.length );
    return code;
}
```

In this example, we're using JScript as our script language. In addition, we expect the code to have the following template:

```
<SCRIPT language=JScript>
function Name()  {
}
</SCRIPT>
```

As you can see, it's not an unreasonable requirement.

The function **ExtractJScriptCode** listed above gets the inner text of the tag by means of:

```
s = scrObj.text
i = s.indexOf( "{" );
```

223

and then takes it up to the first curly bracket. Finally, it picks up the remaining string. In relation to the above sample, the string returned by **ExtractJScriptCode** is:

```
{
  alert( "Hello!" );
}
```

This is a perfectly regular code expression and can be passed to **setInterval**.

While this is a good solution, it doesn't work if your JScript code calls into other user-defined functions. Since we want to keep the required assumptions as limited as possible, we have avoided going into more detail on this. Consider that any user-defined procedure must be seen as a reference to its code and executed through **execScript**. *The actual code will be obtained with the process seen above.*

Putting it all together

Let's see now how to use such a scriptlet. Its full source code is in the file **timer.htm** while the host page is **testtimr.htm**. Both are available at: **http://rapid.wrox.co.uk/books/138X**.

The final version of the scriptlet is as follows:

```
<HTML ID=MyPage>
<HEAD>
<TITLE>Timer Scriptlet</TITLE>
</HEAD>

<SCRIPT language=JavaScript>
public_description = new CreateTimer();
var InScriptlet = (typeof(window.external.version)=="string");
var mTimer = "";

function CreateTimer()  {
  this.Start = DoStart;
  this.Stop = DoStop;
  this.event_OnTimer = "";
}

function DoStart( proc, secs )  {
  if( proc.length==0 )
    mTimer = window.setInterval( "DoFireEvent();", secs*1000 );
  else  {
    parDoc = window.parent.document;
    scr = parDoc.all(proc);
    origCode = ExtractJScriptCode( scr );
    mTimer = window.setInterval( origCode, 1000*secs );
  }
  return 1;
}

function DoStop()  {
  window.clearInterval( mTimer );
}

//////////////////////////////////////////////////////
//
//   Internal routines
//
```

```
function ExtractJScriptCode( scr ) {
    s = scr.text;
    i = s.indexOf( "{" );
    code = s.substring( i, s.length );
    return code;
}

function DoFireEvent() {
    if( InScriptlet && (!window.external.frozen) ) {
        window.external.raiseEvent( "OnTimer", "" );
    }
}
</SCRIPT>

<BODY>
</BODY>
</HTML>
```

The next figure shows how to take advantage of this scriptlet.

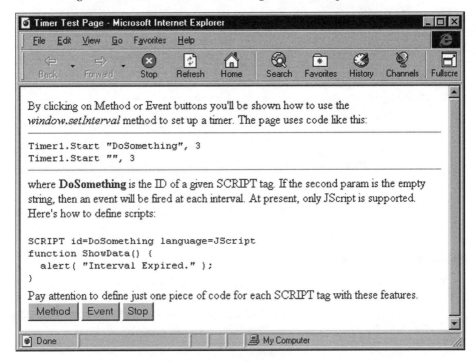

The source code that produces it is the following:

```
<html>
<head>
<title>Timer Test Page</title>
</head>

<body">
<script language="JScript" for=Timer1 event="onscriptletevent(n,o)">
  alert( "Interval Expired (event)." );
</script>

<script language="JScript" id="DoSomething">
function Notify() {
```

```
      alert( "Interval Expired." );
}
</script>

By clicking on Method or Event buttons you'll be shown how to use the
<i>window.setInterval</i> method to set up a timer. The page uses code like
this:
<hr>
<code>Timer1.Start &quot;DoSomething&quot;, 3 <br>
Timer1.Start &quot;&quot;, 3 </code>
<hr>

where <b>DoSomething</b> is the ID of a given SCRIPT tag. If
the second param is the empty string, then an event will be fired
at each interval. At present, only JScript is supported. Here's
how to define scripts:<br>
<br>
<code>SCRIPT id=DoSomething language=JScript<br>
function ShowData() {<br>
  alert( &quot;Interval Expired.&quot; );<br>
}<br>
</code>Pay attention to define just one piece of code for each
SCRIPT tag with these features.

<object id=Timer1 data="Timer.htm"
        width=1 height=1 type="text/x-scriptlet">
</object>

<input type="button" name="Method" value="Method"
        language="VBScript"
        onclick="Timer1.Start &quot;DoSomething&quot;, 3">

<input type="button" name="Event" value="Event"
        language="VBScript"
        onclick="Timer1.Start &quot;&quot;, 3">

<input type="button" name="Stop" value="Stop"
        language="VBScript"
        onclick="Timer1.Stop">
</body>
</html>
```

So What Assumptions Have We Made?

We have made a number of assumptions so far. First of all in terms of
language. We've always used JScript. So if you download the Timer sample seen
above from our Web site and want to reuse it, then make sure you always pass
it JScript code. The key instructions are:

```
origCode = ExtractJScriptCode( scr );
mTimer = window.setInterval( origCode, 1000*secs );
```

Here we assume that the **<SCRIPT>** tag we passed in through its ID is written
in JScript and, therefore, inform the **setInterval**.

To make it support VBScript, you need some enhancements and possibly other
assumptions on the script template. In particular, you need to make the routine
that extracts the source code a bit smarter and have it detect VBScript code too.

Another assumption we've made so far is that we need the JScript code to have
a given prototype. The final assumption is that you need to pass the timer a
string denoting a unique **<SCRIPT>** identifier on the parent's page.

Now we've reached the first important result. We've figured out a way to force a scriptlet to call a piece of script code defined in the host page. However, we want more. We also want the scriptlet to be able to invoke an external piece of code exchanging parameters.

In the rest of the chapter, we're aiming to build a generic enumerator scriptlet. That is, a scriptlet with a method that takes in collection input and a procedure ID and then calls that routine for each item.

Walking through a DHTML Collection

The classic way to take advantage of callbacks is to scan lists of homogeneous objects on which you want to perform the same actions. For example, in Win32 programming you might want to enumerate all the fonts available on a machine and display them in a combobox.

In this case, the lists are the sequence of registered fonts, and the actions are the code necessary to extract a descriptive name and add an item to a given combobox.

The DHTML object model has plenty of collections and sometimes you might want to apply the same procedure to each element. To walk through a collection, of course, you don't necessarily need to work with scriptlets. You can apply a given procedure to any element of a collection in the following way:

```
<SCRIPT language=JScript for="document" event="onclick">
  coll = document.images;
  for( i=0; i<coll.length; i++ )
    DoSomething( coll.item(i) );
</SCRIPT>
```

Compare this code to the following one:

```
Enum1.Walk document.images, "DoSomething"
```

Here, we have a possible scriptlet called **Enum1**. This scriptlet is supposed to be able to walk through any kind of DHTML collection. For each item found it invokes the specified procedure.

You will notice that there are a lot of similarities to what was experienced earlier with timers. How many times would you rewrite that **for** loop, if you didn't wrap it in a reusable component?

With timers we were a bit more fortunate since there was a method— **setInterval**—that automatically provided indirect code execution.

Now, however, our goal is setting up a generic mechanism for callbacks. To start off we need something that works the same way as **setInterval** and is capable of indirect code execution. We must, therefore, exploit all the facilities the object model has to offer. Fortunately, among them are methods for executing script code.

Let's turn to the original problem: walking a DHTML collection. There are two ways to approach the problem: raising events to let the client page do what is needed, or executing the code referenced in the call itself.

As for the latter, the solution previously described still works well, but a generic engine for scriptlet callbacks also needs to take parameters into careful account. In fact, in all the previous examples the invoked procedure never took arguments. While this might be acceptable for timers, it's obviously no good for generic callbacks.

In the rest of the chapter, we're going to see the details of indirect code execution and how a scriptlet can pass parameters back to a client procedure. We will show this with and without events. As you can imagine, the latter is a bit trickier.

Walking the Easiest Way

To begin with, let's see how we can write a generic object enumerator that is used to fire events for each element it finds. This scriptlet's interface should expose a method called **Walk** and an event called, say, **OnItemFound**. We can discuss endlessly the possibilities of **Walk**'s command line. However, there's not enough space here for all that. So we've chosen to define it this way:

```
object.Walk( tagName )
```

tagName is a string denoting the type of the object we want to walk. Possible values are: **OBJECT**, **SCRIPT**, **A**, **IMG**, **BR**, **TABLE**, **TD**, and any other tag supported by DHTML. In practice, you can ask this enumerator scriptlet to list (and process) all the elements with the given tag one by one. Of course, the elements are supposed to be part of the host page.

```
<HTML ID=MyPage>
<HEAD>
<TITLE>Enum Scriptlet</TITLE>
</HEAD>

<SCRIPT language=JavaScript>
public_description = new CreateEnum();
var InScriptlet = (typeof(window.external.version)=="string");

function CreateEnum()  {
  this.Walk = DoWalk;
  this.event_OnItemFound = "";
}

function DoWalk( objType )  {
  var i=0;
  parDoc = window.parent.document;
  coll = parDoc.all.tags(objType);

  for( i=0; i<coll.length; i++ )  {
    if( InScriptlet && (!window.external.frozen) )
       window.external.raiseEvent("OnItemFound", coll.item(i));
  }
  return 1;
}
</SCRIPT>

<BODY>
```

```
</BODY>
</HTML>
```

The source code for the **Walk** method first grasps the document object of the parent page

```
parDoc = window.parent.document;
```

and then extracts the collection of all the given tags.

```
coll = parDoc.all.tags( objType );
```

This list is obtained by the means of the generic **all** collection. At this point, the list is scanned item by item. If the list is empty, then **coll.length** evaluates to 0 and the **for** loop never starts. For each element in the list, the scriptlet fires a custom event and passes a reference to it as the second argument of **raiseEvent**.

```
window.external.raiseEvent("OnItemFound", coll.item(i));
```

The above scriptlet is available on **http://rapid.wrox.co.uk/books/138X** as **enumev.htm**.

Using an Enumerator Scriptlet

Let's see now how to exploit this component in a real HTML page. This scriptlet doesn't even need a meaningful user interface—so we make it invisible by assigning the string **none** to the **display** style's attribute.

```
<HTML>
<HEAD>
<TITLE>Enum Test Page</TITLE>
</HEAD>

<SCRIPT language=VBScript for="Enum1" event="onscriptletevent(n,o)">
  if n="OnItemFound" then
    ShowData o
  end if
</SCRIPT>

<SCRIPT language=VBScript for="document" event="onclick">
  Enum1.Walk "object"
</SCRIPT>

<SCRIPT language=JScript>
function ShowData( obj ) {
  alert( "OBJECT DATA = "+obj.data );
  alert( "OBJECT CLASSID = "+obj.classid );
}
</SCRIPT>

<BODY>
This page shows how to use a scriptlet that enumerates all the
elements of a given collection and fires an event for any it finds. <hr>
Click everywhere, and see what happens!
<OBJECT id=Enum1 data="EnumEv.htm" type="text/x-scriptlet"
style="display:none">
</OBJECT>
</BODY>
</HTML>
```

You can download or run this page called **testenev.htm** from our Web site at the usual address of **http://rapid.wrox.co.uk/books/138X**.

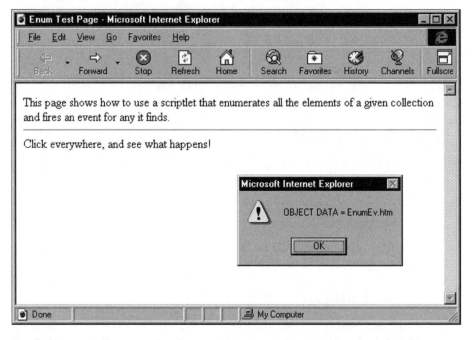

By clicking anywhere on the document you run the **Walk** method for the enumerator scriptlet and ask it to collect all the objects that the current page (the host page) includes.

```
Enum1.Walk "object"
```

The tag **<OBJECT>** is used for inserting both scriptlets and ActiveX controls. For each case, however, it has different attributes. The source code that handles the event passes the argument received down to a helper function called **ShowData**. Note that we're using both VBScript and JScript as our script language.

The **ShowData** function is what we want to execute for any **<OBJECT>** tag in the page. In particular, it displays both the **data** and the **classid** attribute for the object. Of course, they are mutually exclusive, so only one of them will have a non-null value.

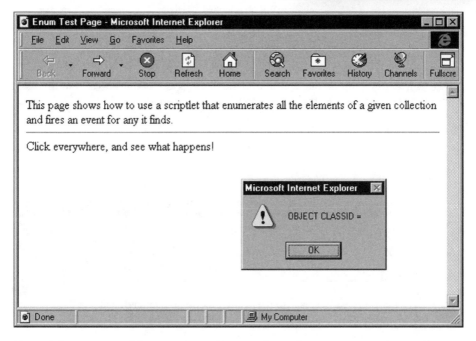

You might want to add some ActiveX controls to the test page and see what happens.

To demonstrate the flexibility of the enumerator scriptlet, let's try to modify the previous page this way (the new file is available as **tstenev1.htm**).

```
<HTML>
<HEAD>
<TITLE>Enum Test Page</TITLE>
</HEAD>

<SCRIPT language=VBScript for="Enum1" event="onscriptletevent(n,o)">
  if n="OnItemFound" then
    ShowData o
  end if
</SCRIPT>

<SCRIPT language=VBScript for="document" event="onclick">
  Enum1.Walk "b"
</SCRIPT>

<SCRIPT language=JScript>
function ShowData( obj ) {
  alert( "Text found = "+obj.innerText );
}
</SCRIPT>

<BODY>
<B>This page</B> shows how to use a <B>scriptlet</B> that enumerates all the
elements drawn in <B>bold</B> in the page and fires an <B>event</B>
for any it finds. <hr>
<B>Click</B> everywhere, and <B>see</B> what happens!
<OBJECT id=Enum1 data="EnumEv.htm" type="text/x-scriptlet"
style="display:none">
</OBJECT>
</BODY>
</HTML>
```

Now we've defined several substrings in bold through the **<B>** tag. By using the instruction:

```
Enum1.Walk "b"
```

we can enumerate all the words and the strings defined in bold throughout the host page, and handle them separately by the means of:

```
function ShowData( obj ) {
  alert( "Text found = "+obj.innerText );
}
```

This is shown in the next figure.

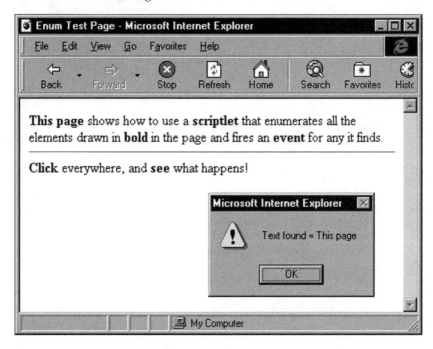

Enumerating the Scriptlets in a Page

The DHTML object model provides you with several built-in collections. Many others, however, can be created dynamically using a matching string. For example:

```
coll = document.all.tags("OBJECT")
```

returns the list of all the elements inserted through an **<OBJECT>** tag. Among them there are both ActiveX controls and scriptlets. If you want to apply some code just to the scriptlets in a page, then you can use the **data**, or better yet the **type**, attribute to distinguish between controls and scriptlets. As repeatedly mentioned, for scriptlets (and only for them) the **type** attribute must be set to *"text/x-scriptlet"*.

So far we've shown how to enumerate the content of a collection using events. Now let's see how to specify the code to be executed in a callback fashion.

Indirect Code Execution

The **window** object exposes a method called **execScript** whose declaration is the following:

```
Sub execScript(code As String, language As String)
```

As its first argument **code**, the method takes a string representing a procedure name, or more generally a code expression, and executes it. The **language** parameter, by contrast, is a string denoting the script the previous argument uses.

Let's see a first and very simple way of using it. Consider the code:

```
Function Quote( s )
   s = Chr(34) + s + Chr(34)
   Quote = s
End Function

Sub Button1_Click()
   sCode = "ImgScrl1.Image=" + Quote("image2.gif")
   window.execscript sCode, "VBScript"
end sub
```

This formats a string and passes it to the parser module of the specified language. In the above sample, we're preparing a string given by "**ImgScrl1.Image=**" plus "**image2.gif**" enclosed in quotes. The string obtained is then passed to **window.execScript** for evaluation.

The code shown above produces the same result as:

```
ImgScrl1.Image = "image2.gif"
```

This is just a demonstration and we certainly do not encourage you to follow this approach to issue any script commands.

On the other hand, **execScript** is a really helpful method since it allows you to execute code specified in an indirect way. You can handle script code the same way you handle strings or other types of variables. This works because of the interpreted nature of the script languages.

We can take advantage of this for implementing our callback mechanism. Again, there are a couple of key aspects to remember:

 We need a way to reference script code across HTML pages.

 We need to call script code on a page passing data from a different HTML page.

Since an example is often more useful than thousands of words, let's address exactly what we're aiming to demonstrate. Our goal is to reproduce the Walk example, as seen earlier, but to do this while avoiding events. In practice, we want to get code like this:

```
Enum1.Walk "object", "ShowData"
```

where the scriptlet is passed both the collection and a reference to the code to be invoked for each item. This code is defined in the host HTML page and gets called from within the scriptlet's page. In addition, when this code runs it needs some arguments.

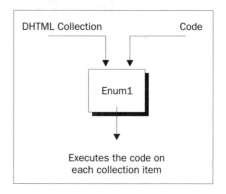

The diagram above gives a high-level description of how the host and the scriptlet work together. The code to be executed passes from the host to the scriptlet page along with a DHTML collection. Then the scriptlet invokes the specified code, passing the various items as an argument.

Comparison with Win32 Callbacks

Sometimes, when you pass a function address to a Win32 service you need to specify two items of information:

 The function address

The module where the function resides

A similar situation occurs with scriptlets. In this case, the function address is the **<SCRIPT>** identifier. The module that contains it is the **document** object to which that ID refers.

Another similarity comes from the fact that in Win32, callback functions often have a fixed prototype. This means that whoever issues the indirect call can assume that the function, or the method it is calling, works exactly as expected.

The most efficient way to allow the scriptlet to access script code on the parent page is by referring to it through an ID and getting the scriptlet to read the source code. A DHTML **ID** plays the same role as a Win32 address. When it's time to jump to the specified address, the system needs to arrange the stack properly. In the same way, we need to properly format the string to pass to **execScript**. This means that the function whose **ID** has been passed must have a fixed and well-known prototype.

Passing Parameters

To complete our scriptlet—so that it will automatically enumerate and process all the items of a collection—we need to slightly enhance the code discussed earlier for timers. The specific problem to solve is how to pass parameters back to a client procedure.

```
<HTML ID=MyPage>
<HEAD>
<TITLE>Enum Scriptlet</TITLE>
</HEAD>

<SCRIPT language=JavaScript>
public_description = new CreateEnum();
var InScriptlet = (typeof(window.external.version)=="string");

function CreateEnum()  {
  this.Walk = DoWalk;
}

function DoWalk( objType, proc )  {
  var i=0;
  parDoc = window.parent.document;
  scr = parDoc.all(proc);
  origCode = ExtractJScriptCode( scr );

  coll = parDoc.all.tags(objType);

  for( i=0; i<coll.length; i++ )  {
    window.execScript( origCode, "JScript");
  }
  return 1;
}

function ExtractJScriptCode( scr )  {
  s = scr.text;
  i = s.indexOf( "{" );
  code = s.substring( i, s.length );
  return code;
}
</SCRIPT>

<BODY>
</BODY>
</HTML>
```

The code above looks like what we've seen for timers. The only difference lies in the **window.execScript** method, which is called instead of **window.setInterval**. Let's take a closer look at this source:

```
window.execScript( origCode, "JScript");
```

The variable **origCode** is the body of the procedure whose **ID** the scriptlet received through the **Walk** method. We passed that **ID** with the clear intention of processing any element of a given collection. This means that **origCode** is a code expression that expects to work on a certain object. The next code snippet illustrates what is done on the host side.

```
<SCRIPT language=VBScript for=document event=onclick>
  Enum1.Walk "object", "DoSomething"
</SCRIPT>
```

```
<SCRIPT id=DoSomething language=JScript>
function ShowData( obj ) {
  alert( "OBJECT DATA = "+obj.data );
  alert( "OBJECT CLASSID = "+obj.classid );
}
</SCRIPT>
```

ShowData is the actual procedure the scriptlet will call back, passing a reference to the *i.th* element of the collection of the "**OBJECT**" tags through **obj**. This also means that the callback function we want to use with this enumerator scriptlet must have the following prototype:

```
FuncName( obj )
```

Once the scriptlet's got the original source code for the callback procedure, it holds a string like:

```
{
  alert( "OBJECT DATA = "+obj.data );
  alert( "OBJECT CLASSID = "+obj.classid );
}
```

It is this string that **execScript** will try to execute. As you can see, there's no initialization for **obj** (the actual object to process) in that string! Thus, we need to do something to work it out.

Script Modifications

At this point we're working on the scriptlet's side and need to dynamically modify the script code it is going to execute. In practice, all that remains to be done is to merely insert one or two lines of code that assign **obj** a valid value. But what is a valid value for **obj**?

It should be assigned the *i.th* object of the specified collection. This collection is taken from the parent's document. From the scriptlet's side, the *i.th* object is given by:

```
window.parent.document.all.tags(objType).item(i)
```

objType is a string that contains the name of the tag to enumerate, for example, "**OBJECT**". The above expression needs to be rendered as a string and inserted in the body to execute through the following assignment:

```
s = expression
obj = s
```

The body to execute must become:

```
{
  obj = expression
  alert( "OBJECT DATA = "+obj.data );
  alert( "OBJECT CLASSID = "+obj.classid );
}
```

The highlighted portion of code is added at run-time. The **Walk** method changes to this:

```
function DoWalk( objType, proc )  {
  var i=0;
  parDoc = window.parent.document;
  scr = parDoc.all(proc);
  origCode = ExtractJScriptCode( scr );

  coll = parDoc.all.tags(objType);

  for( i=0; i<coll.length; i++ )  {
    s = "window.parent.document.all.tags("+"\""+objType+"\""+").item(" + i +
")";
    code = ParamCode( origCode, s );
    window.execScript( code, "JScript");
  }
  return 1;
}
```

The helper function **ParamCode** just adds a line to the original code.

```
function ParamCode( code, argVal )  {
  s = code;
  i = s.indexOf( "{" );
  suffix = s.substring( i+1, s.length );
  prefix = "{\nobj = "+argVal+";\n";
  return prefix + suffix;
}
```

The routine receives a string denoting a piece of script code and a string to insert immediately after the beginning of it. The function finds the first occurrence of an opened curly bracket and extracts the remaining text. Then it adds a prefix in the form of:

```
"{" + argVal
```

and concatenates everything.

Now we're ready to consider a full example. Remember the two enumerator pages seen earlier that used events? We will now try to rewrite these pages.

The Full Example

To summarize, we have a scriptlet that works as an enumerator object. It accepts a reference to a DHTML collection and goes through it processing the various elements found. The scriptlet source code is **enum.htm** and is the following:

```
<HTML>
<HEAD>
<TITLE>Enum Scriptlet</TITLE>
</HEAD>

<SCRIPT language=JavaScript>
public_description = new CreateEnum();
var InScriptlet = (typeof(window.external.version)=="string");

function CreateEnum()  {
  this.Walk = DoWalk;
}
```

```
function DoWalk( objType, proc )  {
  var i=0;
  parDoc = window.parent.document;
  scr = parDoc.all(proc);
  origCode = ExtractJScriptCode( scr );

  coll = parDoc.all.tags(objType);

  for( i=0; i<coll.length; i++ )  {
    s = "window.parent.document.all.tags("+"\""+objType+"\""+").item(" + i +
")";
    code = ParamCode( origCode, s );
    alert( code );  // for debug purpose only
    window.execScript( code, "JScript");
  }
  return 1;
}


/////////////////////////////////////////////////
//
//   Internal routines
//

function ExtractJScriptCode( scr )  {
  s = scr.text;
  i = s.indexOf( "{" );
  code = s.substring( i, s.length );
  return code;
}

function ParamCode( code, argVal )  {
  s = code;
  i = s.indexOf( "{" );
  suffix = s.substring( i+1, s.length );
  prefix = "{\nobj = "+argVal+";\n";
  return prefix + suffix;
}
</SCRIPT>

<BODY>
</BODY>
</HTML>
```

The next page, however, shows how to make use of it. If you download or run
testenum.htm from our Web site at **http://rapid.wrox.co.uk/books/
138X** you will come across the following code:

```
<HTML>
<HEAD>
<TITLE>Enum Test Page</TITLE>
</HEAD>

<SCRIPT language=VBScript for="document" event="onclick">
  Enum1.Walk "object", "DoSomething"
</SCRIPT>

<SCRIPT id="DoSomething" language=JScript>
function ShowData( obj )  {
  alert( "OBJECT DATA = "+obj.data );
  alert( "OBJECT CLASSID = "+obj.classid );
}
</SCRIPT>

<BODY>
This page shows how to use a scriptlet that enumerates all the
```

```
elements of a given collection and executes some code for any it finds. <hr>
Click everywhere, and see what happens!

<OBJECT id=Enum1 data="Enum.htm" type="text/x-scriptlet" style="display:none">
</OBJECT>
</BODY>
</HTML>
```

This sample lists the **<OBJECT>** tags in the current page and displays some information. As explained above, the sample page includes only one **<OBJECT>** tag – that is the Scriptlet itself. So for a more exhaustive test you might want to add other ActiveX controls to the page.

The next screenshot shows the final results.

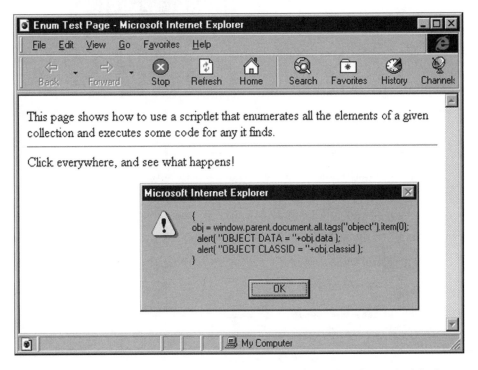

The message box in the foreground shows how the code has been modified because of the script modifications explained above. Note that the **obj** variable now gets initialized properly and the successive calls to it make perfect sense.

```
alert( obj.data );
alert( obj.classid );
```

The screenshot refers to the first item in the object collection and shows an index of 0. The next figure illustrates the execution of the code on the item.

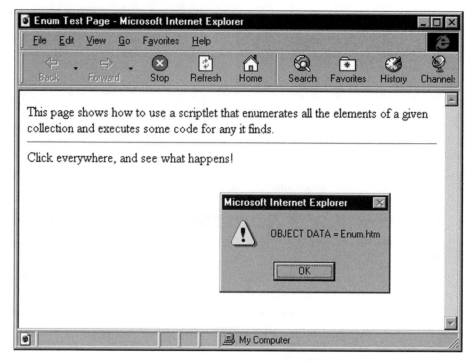

Again, the implementation chosen forces us to always use JScript for specifying the behavior of the enumerator.

For completeness, let's consider the case of another collection. The source code of the host page is **testenm1.htm** (available on our Web site as usual).

```
<HTML>
<HEAD>
<TITLE>Enum Test Page</TITLE>
</HEAD>

<SCRIPT language=VBScript for="document" event="onclick">
  Enum1.Walk "b", "DoSomething"
</SCRIPT>

<SCRIPT id="DoSomething" language=JScript>
function ShowData( obj ) {
    alert( "Text found = "+obj.innerText );
}
</SCRIPT>

<BODY>
<B>This page</B> shows how to use a <B>scriptlet</B> that enumerates all the
elements drawn in <B>bold</B> in the page and fires an <B>event</B> for any it
finds. <hr>
<B>Click</B> everywhere, and <B>see</B> what happens!
<OBJECT id=Enum1 data="Enum.htm" type="text/x-scriptlet" style="display:none">
</OBJECT>

</BODY>
</HTML>
```

The next picture illustrates the case of a collection of bold text (the tag is `<B>`). The message box shows the code that is going to be executed for the second (index of 1) item of the collection—namely the string "scriptlet".

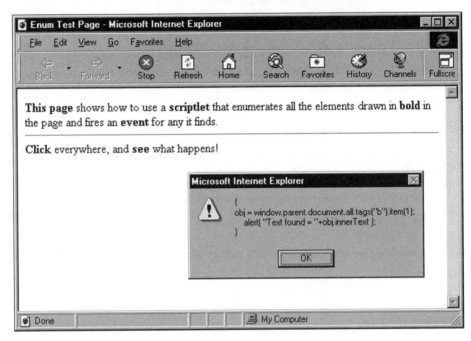

And, as expected, executing the code will produce a message box with that text.

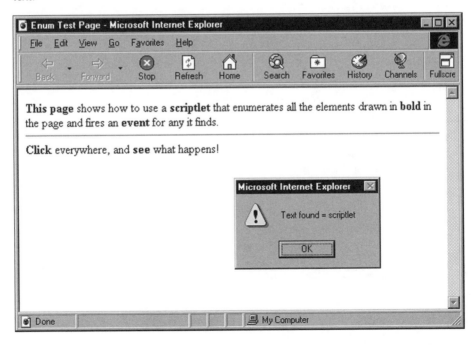

Summary

This chapter was basically concerned with callbacks—that is a programming technique that might be very useful in real applications. Even if you never make use of them by reading this you have learned about run-time code modifications, cross-page referencing and DHTML timers.

We have analyzed two interesting methods of the **window** object: **execScript** and **setInterval**, plus their consequences and applications. To be precise, we covered:

- Dynamic HTML timers.
- Getting timers to raise events.
- Scriptlets executing code in the parent's environment.
- Indirect code execution.
- Dynamic updates of the script code.

We have also built a couple of scriptlets that hide several details of the collections enumeration from the users and which offer a dual approach to invoking script code indirectly.

In the following chapters we will continue presenting real-world examples of scriptlets. In the next chapter, for instance, it's time to talk about resizable tables.

Grids and Resizable Tables

When it comes to using HTML documents, developers, in most cases, need to display tables containing some kind of data. They might be records from a remote database, or perhaps memory arrays. What matters is that you need an advanced, and pretty smart, object to deal with this amount of structured data.

The HTML language has introduced some tags that help with the presentation of tabular data. These constructs are tables and frames.

In addition, DHTML offers support for data-binding. Data-binding can be seen as an automatic way of associating a source of data with HTML tags. The logic behind this is not so different from those data-aware controls we find in RAD tools like Visual Basic or Delphi. Such controls expose a small set of properties that let you bind the component to a data-source and a certain field. Once you load the control, it automatically fills in its user-interface with the content of the data-source. Data-binding works in much the same way, but instead of data-aware controls we have data-aware tags.

For example, a table element can be filled out with the content of a SQL query issued through RDS (Remote Data Service) or by the content of a flat file like the ones Access exports. To find out more about data-binding consult the Further Reading section at the end of the chapter for relevant literature.

These paragraphs dedicated to data-binding demonstrate that, sooner or later, any HTML developer needs a way to display structured data in the very widest sense of the word. Structured data means arrays, query results and—more generally—any information that can be displayed in grids or tables.

The goal of this chapter is to provide a reusable component that works as a grid control—accepting and displaying data in separate and, possibly, resizable columns. By reading this chapter, you will able to use and rewrite a scriptlet that can:

- Display data in a tabular manner.
- Update its content dynamically.
- Allow index-based access to the data.

● Resize its columns.

● Be completely customizable for colors and fonts.

Using such a component will be easier than ever. Just assign it a site on the parent page and start populating through the proper methods.

We'll build it progressively. The final result is shown below:

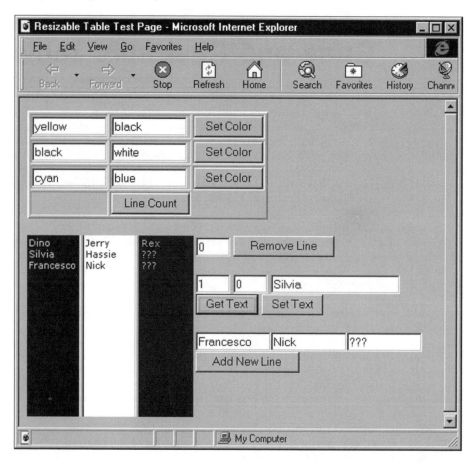

The 3-column table is the scriptlet we're talking about here. To fill and empty it we create a few simple and intuitive methods, as the buttons shown above suggest.

Designing the Framework

An HTML **<TABLE>** tag offers the natural way to implement tables of data. So why write this scriptlet? The main reason is that tables are powerful constructs, but they require you to write a lot of code. We need something more abstract which provides a way to access any element with a natural syntax based on row and column indexes.

Of course, we want the component to be highly reusable and it is this desired feature that suggests the use of scriptlets. Additionally, scriptlets are HTML pages. So tables and any other services may be used seamlessly.

An HTML table is a collection of cells, each of which has its own HTML text. We could state that a table is a collection of nested HTML pages. Any cell (in a row or in a column) can output anything that is HTML-compliant: images, ActiveX controls, marquees and the like.

An HTML table allows the developer to customize fonts, colors and borders. But a table doesn't support the dynamic resizing of the columns.

What we've got in mind is something that closely resembles the Windows 95 report views. In Windows 95 you can change the width of any column on-the-fly (via drag-and-drop) to fit its content.

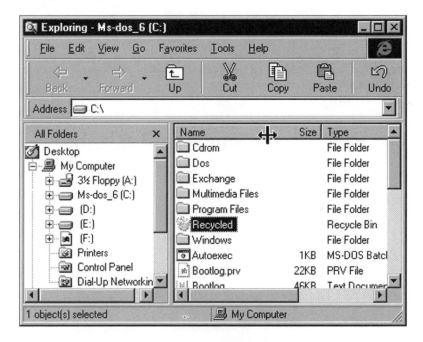

Wouldn't it be nice if we could do the same in our HTML pages? We could insert a component, give it the right size, fill it with data and then dynamically resize its columns to fit the actual data better. A typical page has a layout like this.

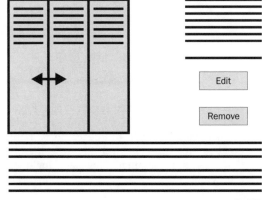

What HTML Components We Need?

To create a grid component with resizable columns we have two choices:

 Use tables and implement the drag-and-drop on our own.

 Use frames and assign different pages for each column.

While DHTML does allow rudimentary forms of drag-and-drop—even firing off a couple of events to notify the start of such operations—you don't have many tools available for complete control. So to support resizable columns it's better to check out alternative approaches.

Frames divide the page into a variety of separate components that are actually other Web pages. The browser offers built-in support for resize and you can vary the size of a single frame whenever you feel like it.

Using frames, however, presents some minor drawbacks. One of these is the fact that not all browsers recognize them. The answer to this is easy since we're going to use frames inside scriptlets. Scriptlets—as you are now completely aware—are only supported by IE4 and this is a browser that provides great support for frames.

Using Frames to Make it Resizable

Given this, creating a grid component means creating a framed page. The body of our scriptlet will be composed of a **<FRAMESET>** tag, and a series of child **<FRAME>** elements. A page with frames is, in fact, a multi-document page; a page composed of a different page for every frame.

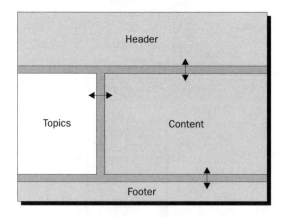

The diagram shows a typical HTML page with frames. Every section displays a different Web page. In fact, Content, Footer, Header and Topics are all implemented through **content.htm**, **footer.htm**, **header.htm**, and **topics.htm** files. Behind all these files, however, there's the main document that acts as a container. This page includes a **<FRAMESET>** tag like the following:

```
<frameset rows="20%,*,10%">
    <frame src="header.htm" name="frameHeader">
    <frameset cols="25%,75%">
        <frame src="topics.htm" name="frameTopics">
        <frame src="content.htm" name="frameContent">
    </frameset>
    <frame src="footer.htm" name="frameFooter">
</frameset>
```

This code produces a template like the one in the diagram. All the sections are resizable. The browser provides this feature by default. The programmer can choose, however, to disable it through the **noresize** attribute.

What Frames Can Do For You

If you want to add frames to your scriptlets or HTML pages, start by getting to know the **<FRAMESET>** tag. Framesets can contain both multiple frames and nested framesets. This is well illustrated by the lines shown above. What follows are some of the attributes that feature a frameset:

Attributes	Description
border	Thickness of the border that separates the various frames. It requires a number.
borderColor	A string that evaluates to an HTML color.
cols	A string that identifies the width of the columns.
rows	A string that identifies the height of the rows.
frameBorder	A Yes/No string specifying whether you want a surrounding frame.
title	The title of the frameset page.

A frameset is composed of single frames. A frame is identified by a tag called **<FRAME>** which has all the following properties:

Attributes	Description
marginHeight	A number specifying the height of the surrounding margin.
marginWidth	A number specifying the width of the surrounding margin.
name	A name for the frame. It's used to identify it as a target for HTML output.
noresize	It accepts Yes or No and makes the frame resizable.
scrolling	A Yes/No string to specify whether you want the frame to be scrollable or not.
src	The name of the page whose content appears in the frame.

A frameset is composed of multiple frames placed horizontally or vertically. To fix their respective dimensions we need to set the **cols** or **rows** properties of the **frameset** object. These properties follow a special syntax. You can set

249

width or height using pixels (an absolute measurement) or percentages. In the latter case, you can tell the frameset that a given horizontal frame must initially occupy 25% of the available space. For example, to divide a frameset into three equal parts would require use of the following code:

```
<frameset cols="33%,33%,33%">
  <frame src="page.htm" name="column1" noresize>
  <frame src="page.htm" name="column2" scrolling=no>
  <frame src="page.htm" name="column3" noresize>
</frameset>
```

By omitting the % symbol you ask the browser to consider the values as pixels. You can also use a * symbol to denote any size. The **noresize** attribute makes the size of the frame fixed, while:

```
scrolling=no
```

cuts off the exceeding text by neglecting to give the page a scrollbar.

You've probably guessed that we'll be using frames to implement our grid component with resizable columns. If you've guessed this, then you might be wondering about some of the drawbacks.

Drawbacks of Frames

Adopting the frame-based approach over the one based on **<TABLE>** and hand-finished drag-and-drop, makes it far easier and quicker to develop but does, however, introduces some little snags. For example, it's very hard to add new frames dynamically. Even if you resort to tricks—like hiding undesired columns or sizing them to 0—you won't be able to make the implementation perfect. The grid component has a fixed number of frames and you need to modify its source code if you want to add or subtract columns.

In addition, the frameset code (like that seen above) must be outside the body of the page. This is a topic which will be expanded upon later.

Another disadvantage is that with frames you need to maintain and distribute at least two pages. One is the outline page where you define the framesets you intend to use. The other is the specific page you want to display in any frame. In the case of a grid, however, you can always use the same content page for all the columns. In fact, you might want to generate the text to be displayed in each frame dynamically. In the next example, we'll use a blank HTML page called **pane.htm**, with this code:

```
<html>
<body bgcolor="#C0C0C0">
</body>
</html>
```

Framesets in Internet Explorer 4.0

Note that in IE4 **<BODY>** and **<FRAMESET>** elements are mutually exclusive. This means that if you try to use both in the same document it will result in the first one being treated correctly while the other is ignored. For example:

```html
<html>
<body bgcolor="#C0C0C0" font=Tahoma>
<frameset cols="33%,33%,33%">
   <frame src="page.htm" name="column1" noresize>
   <frame src="page.htm" name="column2" scrolling=no>
   <frame src="page.htm" name="column3" noresize>
</frameset>
</body>
</html>
```

This will display a gray page with no trace of frames because there is both a
<BODY> and a **<FRAMESET>** in the page. IE4 assigns precedence to the first one
it meets.

The picture on the left shows what
happens when **<BODY>** takes precedence
over **<FRAMESET>**. The picture below
shows exactly the reverse.

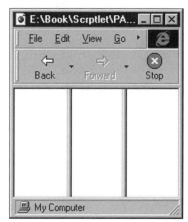

Designing the Scriptlet's Interface

So far, we've made several points about the best way to code a grid scriptlet
and we have decided to use frames. The user interface of the component is
provided by three resizable frames. All the host frames are produced by the
same bare-bone HTML page that we saw earlier.

If you want to modify this scriptlet to make it support a different number of
columns, you just need to adapt its source code. The following is the frame
declaration we're using for our scriptlet.

```html
<HTML ID=MyPage>
<HEAD>
<TITLE>Resizable Table Scriptlet</TITLE>
</HEAD>

<FRAMESET id="fset" COLS="33%,33%,33%">
   <FRAME src="pane.htm">
   <FRAME src="pane.htm">
   <FRAME src="pane.htm">
</FRAMESET>
</HTML>
```

In particular, you might want to add or remove the **<FRAME>** tag and change the **COLS** attribute of the **<FRAMESET>**. To add a fourth column, you need to change it by using the following code:

```
<HTML ID=MyPage>
<HEAD>
<TITLE>Resizable Table Scriptlet</TITLE>
</HEAD>

<FRAMESET id="fset" COLS="25%,25%,25%,25%">
  <FRAME src="pane.htm">
  <FRAME src="pane.htm">
  <FRAME src="pane.htm">
  <FRAME src="pane.htm">
</FRAMESET>
</HTML>
```

The code above shows some basic snippets from the scriptlet. As for the public interface that other components can use to automate it, we need methods for the following:

- Adding a new line.
- Reading and writing a specified cell.
- Getting the total number of lines.
- Changing the background and the foreground colors.
- Removing a line.

By "line" we mean a line of text split into as many parts as there are columns. A cell is a text identified by two indexes—one for the row and one for the column. Each column is actually a different HTML page. Although the physical source file stored in the **src** attribute of the frame is always the same, the Dynamic HTML object model allows us to modify it at leisure. In this way, we finally have three completely different pages. All the differences between them are stored in memory.

A component like this looks like a matrix and, therefore, completely hides the fact it is actually composed of three (or any number of) different pages.

Structure of a Single Page

Any page is assigned a continuous string of text. This string is displayed line by line. Adding a new line or updating an existing one ends up modifying a specific substring of the page content. In particular, we need to ensure that the text for a certain row is always on the same line. To separate the text for the items on the *i.th* and *i+1.th* rows, we use the **
** tag. Examine the screenshot below:

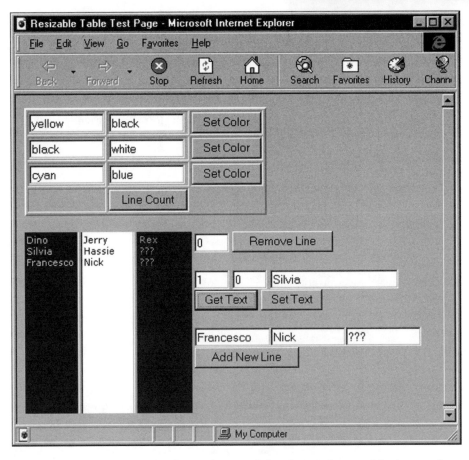

The text that appears in the first column, of the three column table, is stored as:

```
Dino<br>Silvia<br>Francesco
```

Of course, this is true for all the columns. Whatever the action we want to execute on this grid we need a way to quickly access a specified element. The most natural way to achieve this is by way of the row and column index. For example, to get back the string "Silvia" we would issue a command like this:

```
s = Grid1.GetText 1,0
```

where 1 is the 0-based index of the row and 0 denotes the first column. But how do we reach such a result? All will be revealed later in this chapter.

Furthermore, we can't forget that we're working in a frameset page containing three different frames. The actual content of each one is stored in a different file. That is, in a quite different document object model. How can we access the content of the second column? Accessing the **window.document** object of the scriptlet simply won't work.

Accessing the Content of the Frames

The document object of an HTML page exposes a collection called **frames**. For example:

```
alert( document.frames.length );
```

displays the total number of frames that actually form the currently viewed page. You can access the *i.th* frame through an expression like:

```
document.frames(i)
```

From now on, you're in the frame context and can modify its attributes such as **src** or **scrolling**. You could radically modify the content of a frame page simply by having it point to a different HTML file.

```
document.frames(i).src = "another.htm";
document.frames(i).scrolling = "no";
```

In particular, you can access the content of the page through the **document** property. Here's an example of how to modify the style of the various frame pages.

```
<SCRIPT language=VBScript for=window event=onload>
  InitResTable
</SCRIPT>

<SCRIPT language=VBScript>
  Sub InitResTable
    document.frames(0).document.body.style.fontFamily = "Verdana"
    document.frames(1).document.body.style.fontFamily = "Verdana"
    document.frames(2).document.body.style.fontFamily = "Verdana"
    document.frames(0).document.body.style.fontSize = "8pt"
    document.frames(1).document.body.style.fontSize = "8pt"
    document.frames(2).document.body.style.fontSize = "8pt"
    document.frames(0).document.body.style.margin = "2px"
    document.frames(1).document.body.style.margin = "2px"
    document.frames(2).document.body.style.margin = "2px"
  End Sub
</SCRIPT>
```

In the sample above, we have set fonts and margins for all the frames that form the grid component. The suffix **px** means pixel and **pt** stands for point. If you want to know the HTML source code of a given frame just do the following:

```
alert( document.frames(i).document.body.innerHTML );
```

A First Version of the Scriptlet

Now we've gathered enough information to compile a rudimentary and simple version of the grid scriptlet. In the next listing there's still no implementation for the methods of the scriptlet's public interface. However, we will discuss this in due course.

```
<HTML ID=MyPage>
<HEAD>
<TITLE>Resizable Table Scriptlet</TITLE>
</HEAD>

<SCRIPT language=VBScript for=window event=onload>
  InitResTable
</SCRIPT>

<SCRIPT language=VBScript>
  Sub InitResTable
      document.frames(0).document.body.style.fontFamily = "Verdana"
      document.frames(1).document.body.style.fontFamily = "Verdana"
      document.frames(2).document.body.style.fontFamily = "Verdana"
      document.frames(0).document.body.style.fontSize = "8pt"
      document.frames(1).document.body.style.fontSize = "8pt"
      document.frames(2).document.body.style.fontSize = "8pt"
      document.frames(0).document.body.style.margin = "2px"
      document.frames(1).document.body.style.margin = "2px"
      document.frames(2).document.body.style.margin = "2px"
  End Sub
</SCRIPT>

<SCRIPT language=JavaScript>
public_description = new CreateResTable();
var InScriptlet = (typeof(window.external.version)=="string");
var mLineCount = 0;

function CreateResTable()  {
   this.AddLine = AddLine;
   this.GetText = GetText;
   this.SetText = SetText;
   this.RemoveLine = RemoveLine;
   this.GetLineCount = GetLineCount;
   this.SetColor = SetColor;
}
</SCRIPT>

<FRAMESET COLS=33%,33%,33%>
   <FRAME src="pane.htm">
   <FRAME src="pane.htm">
   <FRAME src="pane.htm">
</FRAMESET>
</HTML>
```

During the scriptlet loading stage we slightly modify the **style** object of all the frames. In particular, we change the font to, for example, Verdana 8 and the margins to 2 pixels. This means that the text will be 2 pixels away from the borders of the frame in all directions.

If we comment the body of the **CreateResTable** function (otherwise we get a run-time error) and run the scriptlet, what we'll see is what renders the next picture.

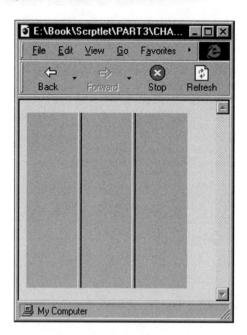

The output is caused by the host page that follows:

```
<html>
<body bgcolor=gainsboro>

<object id="ResTable1" data="ResTab3.htm" align="left" type="text/x-scriptlet"
        width=200 height=211>
</object>

</body>
</html>
```

To make the scriptlet attractive and, above all, useful there is one fundamental step that needs to be taken. We should figure out a way to identify a cell uniquely through its row and column position.

Indexing the Items

The first way to index grid items is by assigning a sort of previously calculated **ID** to any cell. The content of any cell will be enclosed in a **<SPAN>** or **<DIV>** tag in general or, in fact, any tag that doesn't have repercussions on what appears on the screen. This **ID** should contain both the row and the column index.

For example, the following JScript function might be used to add a new text **s** to a specified column **col**.

```
function AddTextLine(col, s)  {
  orig = document.frames(col).document.body.innerHTML;
  if( orig != "" )
      orig = orig + "<br>";

  temp = "<SPAN id=pos"+mLineCount+">" + s + "</SPAN>"
  document.frames(col).document.body.innerHTML = orig+temp;
}
```

First, we save the original **innerHTML** text of the given frame source's body and add a **
** separator if there's an existing cell—that is if the HTML text isn't empty. Next, we compose the new string to concatenate.

```
temp = "<SPAN id=pos"+mLineCount+">" + s + "</SPAN>"
```

mLineCount is a scriptlet's internal variable which returns the number of the rows. The final step consists of adding it to the rest.

```
document.frames(col).document.body.innerHTML = orig+temp;
```

Note that the string "**Any String**" is inserted through an HTML text of:

```
<SPAN id=posX>Any String</SPAN>
```

Actually, the **ID** is given by a standard prefix, for example, **pos**. It can be, however, any other standard prefix, even none. The column is not strictly necessary for an obvious reason. Columns are rendered by separate files and this results in separate object hierarchies. In practice, the 3rd element of column 3 can never be confused with the 3rd element of column 1. Compare the code to access both:

```
index = "pos"+row;
s = document.frames(col).document.all(index).innerHTML;
```

As you can see, the variable **index** is the same, namely **pos3**. However, we're searching for an element with that **ID** in two completely different object collections:

```
document.frames(1).document.all
```

and

```
document.frames(3).document.all
```

Once we have identified any unique cell, we should figure out how to get them. The solution to this is relatively straightforward and it has already been introduced above:

```
index = "pos"+row;
s = document.frames(col).document.all(index).innerHTML;
```

The code returns a string containing the HTML code of the given cell. **row** and **col** are the indexes of the row and the column we want. As mentioned earlier, a cell here is retrieved through an **ID** of **posX**, where **X** is the number of the row. If we just wanted the text displayed—without any formatting commands—then we'd be using **innerText** instead of **innerHTML**.

```
function GetLineCount()  {
  return mLineCount;
}

function GetText(row,col)  {
  if( row > mLineCount-1 )
     return 0;
  if( col > 2 )
     return 0;
```

```
    index = "pos"+row;
    s = document.frames(col).document.all(index).innerText;
    return s;
}
```

The code listed above is an excerpt from the scriptlet's source code. (We present the full source code later in the chapter).

In particular, note the function **GetText**. This returns the text of the cell on the specified row and column.

Updating the Content

Given the three frame layout of the scriptlet's page, adding a new line means adding three different strings or a single string with special formatting. To put it another way, each new line should cover the three columns, so we actually need to add three substrings. We can do this through three parameters and three different calls, or by passing in a single string whose items can be easily split. A possible approach for the latter is by separating the string items with a special character like the pipe |, the more common comma, semi-colon, or whichever you prefer.

A Method for Adding Lines

Our scriptlet exposes a way to add a new line that requires you to specify three different strings—one for each column. This is done for the sake of simplicity. A more flexible solution is to always pass in a single string whose internal items are separated by a special character. This alternate solution will be discussed later.

The method **AddLine** of the scriptlet looks like this:

```
function AddLine(s1,s2,s3)  {
  AddTextLine( 0, s1 );
  AddTextLine( 1, s2 );
  AddTextLine( 2, s3 );
  mLineCount ++;
  return 1;
}

// This is a helper routine invisible to external callers
function AddTextLine(col, s)  {
  orig = document.frames(col).document.body.innerHTML;
  if( orig != "" )
      orig = orig + "<br>";
  temp = "<SPAN id=pos"+mLineCount+">" + s + "</SPAN>"
  document.frames(col).document.body.innerHTML = orig+temp;
}
```

In this listing, you'll recognize the **AddTextLine** routine, which was examined a little earlier. **AddLine** requires no further comment. It just calls a helper routine while specifying the column and the row where the given text must be added. The text is in the HTML format.

A Better Method to Add Lines

The approach we've just seen works well enough, so we shouldn't have any reason to change it. However, this scriptlet has a fixed user interface (always three columns) and you might want to modify it to suit your needs. The method discussed for adding new lines requires that you know how many lines the table shows. Thus, if we modify the user interface of the component, then we need to modify this method too.

A better way to pass in the content of a new line is the following. Use a single string argument, but concatenate the various strings keeping them separated by a special character. We chose the pipe | for this. In terms of method, the number of columns is determined at run-time and it equals the number of pipe characters, plus one. Here's how we could rewrite **AddLine**:

```
function AddLine(s)   {
  var sep = "|";
  var temp = s;
  i = 0;
  col = 0;
  bExit = 0;

  while( bExit==0 )  {
    i = temp.indexOf( sep );
    if( i>0 ) {
       itemStr = temp.substring(0, i);
       AddTextLine(col, itemStr);
       col++;
       temp = temp.substring(i+1, temp.length);
    }
    else   {
       bExit = 1;
       AddTextLine(col, temp);
       col++;
    }
  }

  mLineCount ++;
  return 1;
}
```

The core of the function is in the loop governed by a **while** statement. First, we get the position of the first separator character and extract the relative substring.

```
i   = temp.indexOf( sep );
itemStr = temp.substring(0, i);
```

Note that the first character in a JScript string is at position 0. The **indexOf** method will return '–1' if there are no occurrences of the specified character in the string. In this case, we have reached the final item and all that remains is to add the remaining string to the current column.

```
AddTextLine(col, temp);
```

However,

```
if( i>0 ) {
  itemStr = temp.substring(0, i);
```

```
        AddTextLine(col, itemStr);
        col++;
        temp = temp.substring(i+1, temp.length);
    }
```

if we find a separator in the examined string, then we extract the substring that goes from the beginning up to there. This string is then added to the current column with the same helper routine seen above (**AddTextLine**).

To complete operations, we just increase the index of the current column by one and cut off the substring already added from the working buffer.

This method requires a bit more calculation, but it ensures that you don't have to change anything else—whatever the number of columns you want the scriptlet to support.

Getting and Setting the Text

We've now found how to index any element we put in the grid component. In this way, we're able to access the desired cell by exploiting the power of the DHTML **all** collection. Of course, the same approach must also be followed to modify the content of a cell. The grid component exposes a function **SetText** that does just this.

```
function SetText(s,row,col) {
    if( row > mLineCount-1 )
        return 0;
    if( col > document.frames.length-1 )
        return 0;

    index = "pos"+row;
    document.frames(col).document.all(index).innerHTML = s;
    return 1;
}
```

The main part of this source code is spent validating the parameters. The row must be between 0 and **mLineCount** minus one, while the column cannot exceed the actual number of frames (that is, our columns). We're using **document.frames.length** minus one since the first element of any DHTML collection always has an index of 0.

Changing the Colors

Since each column is produced by a different HTML page, then you are free to modify the graphic settings for each column. Let's now consider the fact that we have different pages for different columns. To be honest, we always use the same HTML file for all the frames.

```
<FRAMESET COLS=33%,33%,33%>
    <FRAME src="pane.htm">
    <FRAME src="pane.htm">
    <FRAME src="pane.htm">
</FRAMESET>
```

and the **pane.htm** file has an almost empty body.

```
<html>
<body bgcolor="#C0C0C0">
</body>
</html>
```

How can we assign different formatting settings to any column? This is the beauty of DHTML. In practice, the **FRAME**'s **src** attribute is just an initialization setting for the page. Then the browser builds up the whole DHTML object model on top of the page and gives us the chance to change the exposed properties.

Thus, we can easily change all the style properties for any of the columns. In particular, the grid component allows the users to set the foreground and background color.

```
function SetColor(col, fgcolor, bgcolor) {
  document.frames(col).document.bgColor = bgcolor;
  document.frames(col).document.fgColor = fgcolor;
  return 1;
}
```

As you can see, the source code for doing so is quite straightforward! Making other attributes—like fonts—customizable is easy too. If you want, you could also directly expose the **style** object of all the columns, thereby making the customization process really easy.

A working version of the grid component is displayed below. This sample is available on our Web site as **resTab3.htm**.

```
<HTML ID=MyPage>
<HEAD>
<TITLE>Resizable Table Scriptlet</TITLE>
</HEAD>

<SCRIPT language=VBScript for=window event=onload>
  InitResTable
</SCRIPT>

<SCRIPT language=VBScript>
  Sub InitResTable
    for i=0 to document.frames.length-1
      document.frames(i).document.body.style.fontFamily = "Verdana"
      document.frames(i).document.body.style.fontSize = "8pt"
      document.frames(i).document.body.style.margin = "2px"
    next
  End Sub
</SCRIPT>

<SCRIPT language=JavaScript>
public_description = new CreateResTable();
var InScriptlet = (typeof(window.external.version)=="string");
var mLineCount = 0;

function CreateResTable() {
  this.AddLine = AddLine;
  this.GetText = GetText;
  this.SetText = SetText;
  this.RemoveLine = RemoveLine;
  this.GetLineCount = GetLineCount;
  this.SetColor = SetColor;
}
```

```
function RemoveLine(row)  {
  alert( "Not implemented yet" );
  return 1;
}

function SetColor(col, fgcolor, bgcolor) {
  document.frames(col).document.bgColor = bgcolor;
  document.frames(col).document.fgColor = fgcolor;
  return 1;
}

function GetLineCount()  {
  return mLineCount;
}

function AddLine(s)  {
  var sep = "|";
  var temp = s;
  i = 0;
  col = 0;
  bExit = 0;

  while( bExit==0 )  {
    i = temp.indexOf( sep );
    if( i>0 )  {
       itemStr = temp.substring(0, i);
       AddTextLine(col, itemStr);
       col++;
       temp = temp.substring(i+1, temp.length);
    }
    else  {
       bExit = 1;
       AddTextLine(col, temp);
       col++;
    }
  }

  mLineCount ++;
  return 1;
}


function SetText(s,row,col)  {
  if( row > mLineCount-1 )
     return 0;
  if( col > document.frames.length-1 )
     return 0;

  index = "pos"+row;
  document.frames(col).document.all(index).innerHTML = s;
  return 1;
}

function GetText(row,col)  {
  if( row > mLineCount-1 )
     return 0;
  if( col > document.frames.length-1 )
     return 0;

  index = "pos"+row;
  s = document.frames(col).document.all(index).innerHTML;
  return s;
}


///////////////////////////////////////////
//
// Internal functions
```

```
//

function AddTextLine(col, s)  {
  orig = document.frames(col).document.body.innerHTML;
  if( orig != "" )
      orig = orig + "<br>";

  temp = "<SPAN id=pos"+mLineCount+">" + s + "</SPAN>"
  document.frames(col).document.body.innerHTML = orig+temp;
}
</SCRIPT>

<FRAMESET COLS=33%,33%,33%>
  <FRAME src="pane.htm">
  <FRAME src="pane.htm">
  <FRAME src="pane.htm">
</FRAMESET>
</HTML>
```

The page **usetab3.htm**, instead, shows how to test the component.

```
<HTML>
<HEAD>
<TITLE>Using the GRID Scriptlet</TITLE>
</HEAD>
<BODY bgcolor=gainsboro>
Fill in the Grid Scriptlet!<hr>

<OBJECT id=ResTable1 data="ResTab3.htm" type="text/x-scriptlet"
        width=300 height=100>
</OBJECT>
<p>
<input type="text" size="11" name="T1">
<input type="text" size="11" name="T2">
<input type="text" size="11" name="T3">
<input type="button" name="B1" value="Add New Line"
       language="VBScript"
       onclick="ResTable1.AddLine
T1.Value+Chr(124)+T2.Value+Chr(124)+T3.Value">
</BODY>
</HTML>
```

The output is in the next figure. In this we can observe three edit boxes whose
content is concatenated when we click on the button "Add New Line". The
separator character is the pipe—that is 124 of the ASCII table.

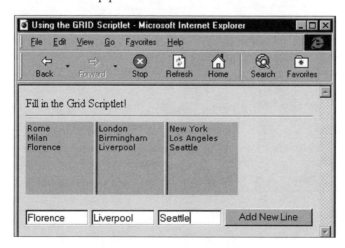

The source code for the scriptlet has been kept as straightforward as possible. Now if you need to change it to implement, for example, a 5 column table all that is required is an alteration of the frameset.

```
<FRAMESET COLS=20%,20%,20%,20%,20%>
  <FRAME src="pane.htm">
  <FRAME src="pane.htm">
  <FRAME src="pane.htm">
  <FRAME src="pane.htm">
  <FRAME src="pane.htm">
</FRAMESET>
```

The file **restab5.htm** (available on our Web site) is identical to the previous **restab3.htm** except for the slight changes in the frameset shown above. To use it properly, let's update the test page this way. The file is **usetab5.htm**.

```
<HTML>
<HEAD>
<TITLE>Using the GRID Scriptlet - 5 columns</TITLE>
</HEAD>
<BODY bgcolor=gainsboro>
Fill in the Grid Scriptlet!<hr>

<OBJECT id=ResTable1 data="ResTab5.htm" type="text/x-scriptlet"
        width=300 height=100>
</OBJECT>
<p>
<input type="text" size="11" name="T1">
<input type="text" size="11" name="T2">
<input type="text" size="11" name="T3">
<input type="text" size="11" name="T4">
<input type="text" size="11" name="T5">
<input type="button" name="B1" value="Add New Line"
        language="VBScript"
        onclick="ResTable1.AddLine T1.Value + Chr(124) + T2.Value + Chr(124) +
                 T3.Value + Chr(124)+ T4.Value + Chr(124) + T5.Value">
</BODY>
</HTML>
```

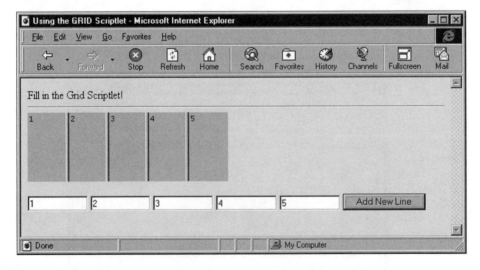

The picture shows how it looks.

If you look back to a previous paragraph in this chapter you'll realize that of all the declared functionality for this scriptlet, one is still missing. That is—how to remove items from our table.

Problems Removing Items

At first sight, there is no reason why this task should be any more complex than any other. Nevertheless, it is. There are a couple of issues to take care of:

 How to accomplish the deletion of a line?

 How to arrange the remaining items?

Because of the internal organization of the grid, deleting a line is a process that involves all the columns. Basically, it should consist of removing a substring and the following **
** tag, if there is one present (Note that the last item isn't followed by a break tag).

To identify a line we can use the usual index-based notation. A possible prototype for the method is:

```
function RemoveLine(row)
```

Starting from there, we can build the **ID** of the corresponding column's elements and empty their **outerHTML** property. When canceling the **outerHTML** property of an element we actually remove it from the page. In this case, however, we need to do a little more. In fact, to cause the rest of the text to shift up the break attribute must also disappear.

By combining these operations we actually manage to remove a line from the grid component. Unfortunately, however, this only works well the first time or so. The problem is that we identified the cell by the exact number of the row. So the first time we delete a line all the cells are arranged properly and the cell with an ID of 3 is really on the third row.

The situation changes when you start removing lines. Now the cell with an ID of 3 is not necessarily placed on the third row. That depends upon which lines you have removed. In fact, deleting row 2 causes the cell with a row index of 3 to shift to position 2.

An endless series of misalignments and errors—that could make us think about taking the remove capability away from our component—originate from this.

A Better Way to Index

As you've probably guessed, the problem is not in the remove action itself but in the incorrect and inadequate indexing technique we've chosen. A better way to do it is to avoid setting an explicit row position in the **ID**, relying instead on the power of the DHTML object model to keep track of all the cells.

If we assign the same ID to a certain set of HTML elements, what we really create is a new collection. Due to DHTML, we can search through this collection in the usual way by using the **item** collection. In this way we don't need to build a string ID in the form of **pos3** to access the third element, we just need to get a reference to the collection and address its third item.

```
coll = document.frames(col).document.all("item");
```

The line above returns a single object if the specified ID is unique throughout the document. Otherwise it returns a collection. Such a collection could be explored with a loop like this:

```
for( i=0; i<coll.length; i++ )  {
  alert( coll.item(i).innerText );
}
```

If we remove an item, we stop worrying about its ID. We just need to extract the collection again and get it perfectly aligned according to the last changes. All the problems seen above have completely disappeared.

A Slightly Better Approach

An even better approach that takes into account the specific layout of our example also allows us to avoid IDs. We can get the same result through:

```
coll = document.frames(col).document.all.tags("SPAN");
```

In this case, we ask for the collection formed by all the elements with a **<SPAN>** tag. This is a bit more efficient, because it doesn't require the DHTML engine to compare IDs.

The expressions:

```
coll = document.frames(col).document.all.tags("SPAN");
```

and

```
coll = document.frames(col).document.all("item");
```

are not functionally identical. Or rather, they aren't in all cases. However, each page of our grid component has no **<SPAN>** elements other than the ones we need to implement the cells. For this reason, and in this specific context, the two expressions above are identical.

Rearranging the Scriptlet

Given this, a certain rearrangement of the scriptlet's internal code is in order. Basically, we need to change the code to get and set text, and also to add the remove functions.

AddLine preserves the same features and an identical structure. However, the helper routine **AddTextLine** significantly changes.

```
function AddTextLine(col, s)  {
  orig = document.frames(col).document.body.innerHTML;
  if( orig != "" )
      orig = orig + "<br>";

  temp = "<SPAN>" + s + "</SPAN>"
  document.frames(col).document.body.innerHTML = orig+temp;
}
```

Quantitatively, the changes are limited to the highlighted line. This is a modification of great conceptual value.

From this change a number of others spring into action. For example, we now need a different way to identify the cell that we want to read from or write to. Here's a **GetItem** helper function that replaces the old:

```
index = "pos"+row;
obj = document.frames(col).document.all(index);
```

The **GetItem** function is used by the **GetText** and **SetText** methods.

```
function SetText(s,row,col)  {
  if( row > mLineCount-1 )
      return 0;
  if( col > document.frames.length )
      return 0;

  obj = GetItem(row,col);
  obj.innerHTML = s;
  return 1;
}

function GetText(row,col)  {
  if( row > mLineCount-1 )
      return 0;
  if( col > document.frames.length )
      return 0;

  obj = GetItem(row,col);
  s = obj.innerHTML;
  return s;
}

function GetItem(row, col)  {
  coll = document.frames(col).document.all.tags("SPAN");
  return coll.item(row);
}
```

Removing Items

The new organization of the grid greatly simplifies the deletion of a line. Now the operation is divided up into two different steps. Firstly, by getting a collection of all the **<SPAN>** elements and removing the *i.th* item. Secondly, by getting a collection of all the **
** tags and, again, removing the *i.th* item—if it is not the last item.

The collection of the **<SPAN>** elements denotes the strings that are displayed on the specified column, while the **
** list are the separators that cause them to appear on different lines. If we don't remove the breaks, then the remaining portion of the column will never shift up and the occupied space never gets freed up.

267

Adopting a DHTML collection saves us from re-indexing after a deletion and also provides us with a powerful and easy-to-use programming tool.

The **RemoveLine** method looks like this:

```
function RemoveLine(row)  {
  if( mLineCount==0 )
    return 0;
  if( row > mLineCount-1 )
    return 0;

  for( i=0; i<document.frames.length; i++ )  {
    coll = document.frames(i).document.all.tags("SPAN");
    if( coll.length != 0 )
      coll.item(row).outerHTML = "";

    coll = document.frames(i).document.all.tags("BR");
    if( coll.length != 0 )
      if( row+1 <= coll.length )
        coll.item(row).outerHTML = "";
  }

  mLineCount --;
  return 1;
}
```

The Full Example

You can download the final and complete source code for this scriptlet from our Web site. The file is **grid.htm** and the test page **testgrid.htm**.

The next screenshot shows how it looks when you work with it and how it behaves.

Of course, what you see rendered here is a bit different from what you get when you initially run the page. Try adding new lines and setting non-default colors. The buttons Get Text and Set Text return the content of a cell identified by the row and the column index entered in the near edit fields.

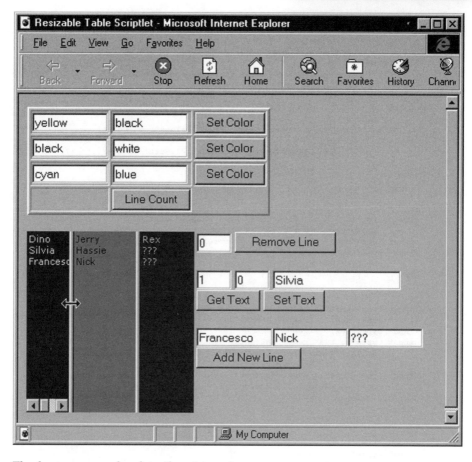

The host page rendered in the picture is:

```
<html>
<head>
<title>Grid Test Page</title>
</head>

<body background="tao.gif">
<div align="left">
<table border="2">
   <tr>
      <td><input type="text" size="11" name="ForeColor1" value="black"> </td>
      <td><input type="text" size="11" name="Color1" value="#C0C0C0"> </td>
      <td><input type="button" name="SetColor1" value="Set Color"
language="VBScript"
              onclick="ResTable1.SetColor 0,ForeColor1.Value,Color1.Value">
</td>
   </tr>
   <tr>
      <td><input type="text" size="11" name="ForeColor2" value="black"> </td>
      <td><input type="text" size="11" name="Color2" value="#C0C0C0"> </td>
      <td><input type="button" name="SetColor2" value="Set Color"
language="VBScript"
              onclick="ResTable1.SetColor 1,ForeColor2.Value,Color2.Value">
</td>
   </tr>
```

269

```
    <tr>
       <td><input type="text" size="11" name="ForeColor3" value="black"> </td>
       <td><input type="text" size="11" name="Color3" value="#C0C0C0"> </td>
       <td><input type="button" name="SetColor3" value="Set Color"
language="VBScript"
                  onclick="ResTable1.SetColor 2,ForeColor3.Value,Color3.Value"> 
</td>
    </tr>
    <tr>
       <td> </td>
       <td><input type="button" name="Lines" value="Line Count"
language="VBScript"
                  onclick="MsgBox CStr(ResTable1.GetLineCount())"> </td>
    </tr>
</table>
</div>

<p>
<object id="ResTable1" data="grid.htm" align="left" width="200" height="211"
        type="text/x-scriptlet"></object>
<input type="text" size="4" name="RemoveLine" value="0">
<input type="button" name="Remove" value="Remove Line" language="VBScript"
       onclick="ResTable1.RemoveLine(CInt(RemoveLine.Value))">
</p>

<p>
<input type="text" size="4" name="Row" value="0">
<input type="text" size="4" name="Col" value="0">
<input type="text" size="20" name="Text" value="Text">
<input type="button" name="GetText1" value="Get Text" language="VBScript"
       onclick="Text.Value = ResTable1.GetText(
CInt(Row.Value),CInt(Col.Value))">
<input type="button" name="SetText" value="Set Text" language="VBScript"
       onclick="ResTable1.SetText Text.Value, CInt(Row.Value),
CInt(Col.Value)">
<br></p>

<p>
<input type="text" size="11" name="T1">
<input type="text" size="11" name="T2">
<input type="text" size="11" name="T3">
<input type="button" name="B1" value="Add New Line" language="VBScript"
       onclick="ResTable1.AddLine
T1.Value+Chr(124)+T2.Value+Chr(124)+T3.Value">
</p>
</body>
</html>
```

The complete source code for the resizable table or grid component is the
following:

```
<HTML ID=MyPage>
<HEAD>
<TITLE>Grid Scriptlet</TITLE>
</HEAD>

<SCRIPT language=VBScript for=window event=onload>
  InitResTable
</SCRIPT>

<SCRIPT language=VBScript>
  Sub InitResTable
     for i=0 to document.frames.length-1
        document.frames(i).document.body.style.fontFamily = "Verdana"
        document.frames(i).document.body.style.fontSize = "8pt"
        document.frames(i).document.body.style.margin = "2px"
```

```
      next
   End Sub
</SCRIPT>


<SCRIPT language=JavaScript>
public_description = new CreateResTable();
var InScriptlet = (typeof(window.external.version)=="string");
var mLineCount = 0;

function CreateResTable()  {
   this.AddLine = AddLine;
   this.GetText = GetText;
   this.SetText = SetText;
   this.RemoveLine = RemoveLine;
   this.GetLineCount = GetLineCount;
   this.SetColor = SetColor;
}

function RemoveLine(row)  {
   if( mLineCount==0 )
     return 0;
   if( row > mLineCount-1 )
     return 0;

   for( i=0; i<document.frames.length; i++ )  {
     coll = document.frames(i).document.all.tags("SPAN");
     if( coll.length != 0 )
        coll.item(row).outerHTML = "";

     coll = document.frames(i).document.all.tags("BR");
     if( coll.length != 0 )
       if( row+1 <= coll.length )
         coll.item(row).outerHTML = "";
   }

   mLineCount --;
   return 1;
}

function SetColor(col, fgcolor, bgcolor)  {
   document.frames(col).document.bgColor = bgcolor;
   document.frames(col).document.fgColor = fgcolor;
   return 1;
}

function GetLineCount()  {
   return mLineCount;
}

function AddLine(s)  {
   var sep = "|";
   var temp = s;
   i = 0;
   var col = 0;
   bExit = 0;

   while( bExit==0 )  {
     i = temp.indexOf( sep );
     if( i>0 )  {
        itemStr = temp.substring(0, i);
        AddTextLine(col, itemStr);
        col++;
        temp = temp.substring(i+1, temp.length);
     }
     else  {
        bExit = 1;
```

271

```
            AddTextLine(col, temp);
            col++;
        }
    }

    // if the string has less items than needed...
    if( col < document.frames.length-1 ) {
        for( i=col; i<document.frames.length; i++ )
            AddTextLine( i, "" );
    }

    mLineCount ++;
    return 1;
}

function SetText(s,row,col) {
    if( row > mLineCount-1 )
        return 0;
    if( col > document.frames.length-1 )
        return 0;

    obj = GetItem(row,col);
    obj.innerHTML = s;
    return 1;
}

function GetText(row,col) {
    if( row > mLineCount-1 )
        return 0;
    if( col > document.frames.length-1 )
        return 0;

    obj = GetItem(row,col);
    s = obj.innerHTML;
    return s;
}


//////////////////////////////////////////////
//
// Internal functions
//

function AddTextLine(col, s) {
    orig = document.frames(col).document.body.innerHTML;
    if( orig != "" )
        orig = orig + "<br>";

    temp = "<SPAN>" + s + "</SPAN>"
    document.frames(col).document.body.innerHTML = orig+temp;
}

function GetItem(row, col) {
    coll = document.frames(col).document.all.tags("SPAN");
    return coll.item(row);
}
</SCRIPT>

<FRAMESET COLS=33%,33%,33%>
    <FRAME src="pane.htm">
    <FRAME src="pane.htm">
    <FRAME src="pane.htm">
</FRAMESET>
</HTML>
```

In our last implementation we made the scriptlet somewhat more robust. In fact, suppose you try to add an incomplete line, that is a line with fewer items than are actually needed. If this is the case then you could get problems when removing items because the collections of the different frames may have different lengths. Instead, the fragment below—added to the **AddLine** method—ensures that each add operation really adds something to all the defined frames. When this code is executed, the variable **col** is set with the number of columns that a substring was added to. What remains, therefore, is just to complete the loop by adding the empty string.

```
if( col < document.frames.length-1 )  {
   for( i=col; i<document.frames.length; i++ )
     AddTextLine( i, "" );
}
```

Summary

The grid component we presented here is an example of real-world programming with scriptlets. It combines the power of DHTML with some features of the standard HTML language, like frames. The result is a fully reusable component. To be honest, it is not completely flexible—but it shouldn't be too hard to adapt it to a variety of requirements.

In writing this scriptlet we took a closer look at collections and the run-time modifications of the text. In particular, we covered:

- Framesets in IE4.
- Dynamic creation of DHTML collections.
- Using frames with DHTML.
- Scripting for advanced manipulation of HTML content.

Further Reading

At the beginning of the chapter, we repeatedly mentioned data-binding. Data binding is a DHTML feature and is not specifically targeted at scriptlets. Because of this, we don't provide full coverage of it here but, instead, list some references where you can find useful and comprehensive information.

If you want a brief introduction to the subject to give yourself an idea about it, then your best choice is an article which appeared in the July 97 issue of MIND. The author is Rich Rollmann, and the piece is entitled *"Data-binding in Dynamic HTML"*.

In-depth coverage of data-binding, along with numerous real-world examples, can be found in our *"Professional IE4 Programming"*, ISBN 1-861000-70-7. There you can find examples that show you how to employ both flat files and remote databases through ODBC.

Frames are a nice feature of HTML. However, if you don't know in detail all the attributes they support we recommend you read *Instant HTML Programmer's Reference, ISBN 1-861001-56-8*.

Chapter

11

Splittable Windows

Many of the most advanced and up-to-date software packages support splittable windows. Technically speaking, a split-window is a window that lets you create more views of the same content. This is very useful if you have a lengthy document to read or browse. Usually, you're required to click somewhere and then have the available screen doubled. You can resize the two (or more) views via drag-and-drop. Any of the views can be scrolled and browsed separately. Therefore, in reality, split windows are a single window with two complementary views on the same content. What's important is that the views are all part of the same object and come from an internal partitioning of the parent component.

How can splittable windows apply to scriptlets? It's easy—we can write scriptlets that provide you with splittable views. If you really think about this then you can't avoid realizing that HTML files are good subjects for splitting. One of the golden rules of so-called "netiquette" says that any Web administrator should ensure that the pages available to the user never exceed a certain size or require more than a given scrolling. However, not all administrators follow this rule and you often find yourself moving back and forth through endless HTML pages.

Internet Explorer 4.0 doesn't offer this functionality natively, but it would be nice to extend it in this way. So, what we are actually aiming to do in this chapter is to show you how to:

- Take advantage of frames to implement splittable HTML windows.
- Write a splittable scriptlet.
- Have an auto-resizable scriptlet that fits into the parent's area.
- Extend Internet Explorer 4.0 to make its views splittable.

What you'll have after reading this chapter is a scriptlet you can use like an embeddable viewer inside other Web pages. This viewer shows off scrolling capabilities and is also splittable.

Implementing Splitting with Frames

As the previous chapter demonstrated, frames can often be a big help. In particular, they seem to be made to favor resizable views. Implementing resizable borders in pure DHTML code would be a huge job. On the other hand, the major browsers now support frames and we can take advantage of them without any major worries.

Using frames, however, always poses the same problem and the same drawbacks. HTML frames are embedded documents—that is documents hosted by a container page. In the case of scriptlets the host page is, of course, the scriptlet itself. But, you still have to distribute separate pages for each frame you want to use.

This isn't bad news, however, because it means we've found an immediate application for frame-based scriptlets. Since frames require separate HTML files, we can think of it as a generic component that hosts and displays another HTML page. In practice, we can put a component inside a document and ask it to show some HTML content. More cleverly, this technique brings us to splittable windows.

User Interface for Splittable windows

Microsoft Word was one of the first programs to provide support for split windows. To enable this feature you need to open the Window menu and pick the Split command, as shown below.

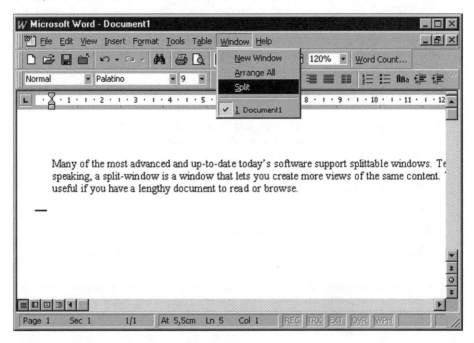

Once you've done this you can divide up the available screen of the current view as best suits your needs. To remove the splitting just use the **Window|Remove Split** menu option. Other programs allow splitting through double clicking in the upper portion of the window, just below the top border. Others (Microsoft Word included) require clicking on a small button placed over the scrollbar.

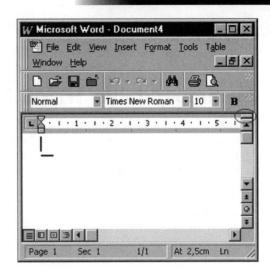

A User Interface for Splittable Scriptlets

Our goal in this chapter is to design and code a scriptlet that supports splitting through frames. In practice, the body of the scriptlet's page will include a frameset with two separate, horizontal frames. Here's a possible body content:

```
<FRAMESET id="fset" ROWS="100%">
  <FRAME id="first" src="">
  <FRAME id="secnd" src="">
</FRAMESET>
```

By combining the value of the frameset's rows attribute and the frames' properties, the scriptlet appears as if it was a regular, and not a framed, page. The second view, in fact, is completely hidden to the user. Both the frameset and the single frames have their own IDs.

The assignment:

```
ROWS="100%"
```

means that we want the first frame to occupy the whole available space (100%). Initially, the second frame is invisible (takes a 0-length space). However, if you use this code:

```
ROWS="100%,0"
```

then a resizable border will appear at the bottom of the window.

The scriptlet exposes a few properties through which callers can set the file to view and also enable or disable splitting.

In the previous chapter, we discovered that frames have a tricky layout, in other words, a layout that is hard to change dynamically. While this represented a small problem with grid or resizable tables, it is quite different here. Now we need exactly two frames. The first one is always visible to show the content of

277

the selected file. The second just serves the purpose of realizing a split window. Of course, we are limited—as usual—to a maximum of two views per document, but we will be free to modify our scriptlet if we desire.

An Embeddable HTML Viewer

Let's start to create a Web component that works as an embeddable DHTML viewer. This means that we want to obtain a component that will host any HTML page ready to display any other HTML data. In certain cases, the scriptlet could also replace the WebBrowser control in desktop applications.

We want the content of this object to be scrollable, selectable and, possibly, splittable into two or more views. Of course, the source of the content (the file name) should be modifiable at run-time.

As you will probably have noticed, all these constraints match typical scriptlets properties.

Let's examine the bare-bones code for this component.

```
<HTML ID=MyPage>
<HEAD>
<TITLE>Splitter Scriptlet</TITLE>
</HEAD>

<SCRIPT language=VBScript for=window event=onload>
  InitSplitter
</SCRIPT>

<SCRIPT language=VBScript>
  Sub InitSplitter
    document.all("first").document.body.style.margin = "1px"
    document.all("secnd").document.body.style.margin = "1px"
  End Sub
</SCRIPT>

<SCRIPT language=JavaScript>
public_description = new CreateSplitter();
var InScriptlet = (typeof(window.external.version)=="string");

function CreateSplitter()  {
}
</SCRIPT>

<FRAMESET id=fset ROWS=100%>
  <FRAME id=first src="">
  <FRAME id=second src="">
</FRAMESET>

</HTML>
```

The scriptlet page is made up of two frames, only the first of which is initially visible. This is the effect of the line:

```
<FRAMESET id=fset ROWS=100%>
```

This line of code ensures that IE4 gives the first frame 100% of the available space. During the initialization stage we also set some preferences for margins.

```
document.all("first").document.body.style.margin = "1px"
document.all("secnd").document.body.style.margin = "1px"
```

For graphic improvements alone we set the margins of the frame to one pixel. Such a basic component creates a page like this:

The code for the test page might the following:

```
<html>
<head>
<title>Splitter Test Page</title>
</head>

<body background="tao.gif">
Click on the document to split the view!<hr>

<object id=Splitter1 data="splitter.htm" type="text/x-scriptlet"
        width=350 height=200 align=left>
</object>

</body>
</html>
```

The second frame is hidden and the first one is uninitialized—that is, its **src** attribute doesn't refer to any HTML page.

Since we want this scriptlet to become an embeddable viewer, then it's clear that we need to expose at least a property that binds it to an HTML page. In addition, since we also want the scriptlet to be splittable, then the same HTML page will be assigned to both the frames.

This being said, let's now proceed to design the scriptlet's public interface.

The Public Interface

There are at least two essential properties:

 Enable

 File

Enable is a boolean variable that enables or disables the split capability. **File** is a read/write property that denotes the document that the frame is currently hosting. Besides this, the parent environment might be interested to know whether the scriptlet's window is split or in the normal state. This is easily accomplished through a couple of custom events.

In addition, we could also make a reference to the **document** object of the hosted page available. Given all this, the public interface of the scriptlet can be designed this way:

```
function CreateSplitter()  {
    this.put_Enable = put_Enable;
    this.get_Enable = get_Enable;
    this.put_File = put_File;
    this.get_File = get_File;
    this.get_innerDocument = get_innerDocument;
    this.event_OnSplit = "";
    this.event_OnReset = "";
}
```

Setting the Frame Content

As mentioned earlier, **File** is a read-write property that contains the name of the file to be viewed. Its implementation is quite straightforward:

```
var mFile = "";
...
function get_File()  {
   return mFile;
}

function put_File(src)  {
   document.all("first").src = src;
   document.all("second").src = src;
   return 1;
}
```

mFile is an internal variable used to store the name of the source file. When you set this property both the **src** attributes of the frames get updated.

```
document.all("first").src = src;
document.all("second").src = src;
```

This ensures that, when the window is split, both the views are synchronized and perfectly aligned on the same content.

Creating a Split View

Since the scriptlet is already a container window based on frames, what is actually needed to enable and disable split views is to show or hide the secondary frame. The next diagram explains how HTML split views work. In practice, the scriptlet includes a **<FRAMESET>** tag instead of a **<BODY>** tag. The frameset contains two frames, only one of which is initially displayed. This frame occupies 100% of the available space, that is the entire scriptlet's area.

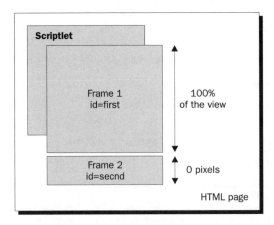

To the naked eye there are, at this point, no perceivable differences between a traditional scriptlet's window and a framed page. When the host page sets the **File** property, then the **src** attribute of both frames is set and this affects the content of the viewable scriptlet's screen. Now the scriptlet's screen displays the specified document.

What changes when the property **Enable** is modified? **Enable,** by design, makes the hidden frame visible and vice versa.

```
var mEnabled = "";
…

function get_Enable()  {
  return mEnabled;
}

function put_Enable( bYes )  {
  mEnabled = bYes;
  if( mEnabled )
    document.all("fset").rows = "0%,100%"
  else
    document.all("fset").rows = "100%"
  return mEnabled;
}
```

Enable works by modifying the content of the frameset's **rows** attribute. Its current value is stored in the **mEnable** internal variable. The splitter is enabled when we are given the opportunity to resize the views properly. That is, when the resizable bar is visible. This occurs when—as shown in the listing above—the **rows** attribute is set to:

```
document.all("fset").rows = "0%,100%"
```

Let's now consider how the size of the frames change after **rows**. When this attribute is set to "100%" then the upper frame occupies all the available scriptlet's screen and the other is invisible. By contrast, when it is set to "0%,100%" then the upper frame is still visible but its area is null. The lower frame, instead, takes the whole area. As a result, IE4 shows two frames (one of which is zero sized) and the split bar that allows resizing. There's a great difference between "100%" and "0%,100%" or even "100%,0%" when these values are assigned to **rows**. In the former case, in fact, IE4 ignores all the frames except the first one and never displays the split bar. In other cases, instead, it is explicitly required to show two frames, one with a null value. Added to this is the fact that having two frames means having them separated by a split bar.

Let's see now how the full scriptlet looks. The file is called **splitter.htm**.

```
<HTML ID=MyPage>
<HEAD>
<TITLE>Splitter Scriptlet</TITLE>
</HEAD>

<SCRIPT language=VBScript for=window event=onload>
  InitSplitter
</SCRIPT>

<SCRIPT language=VBScript>
  Sub InitSplitter
    document.all("first").document.body.style.margin = "1px"
    document.all("second").document.body.style.margin = "1px"
  End Sub
</SCRIPT>

<SCRIPT language=JavaScript>
public_description = new CreateSplitter();
var InScriptlet = (typeof(window.external.version)=="string");
var mEnabled = 0;
var mFile = "";

function CreateSplitter() {
  this.put_Enable = put_Enable;
  this.get_Enable = get_Enable;
  this.put_File = put_File;
  this.get_File = get_File;
  this.get_innerDocument = get_innerDocument;
  this.event_OnSplit = "";
  this.event_OnReset = "";
}

function get_innerDocument() {
  return document.frames(0).document;
}

function get_Enable() {
  return mEnabled;
}
function put_Enable(bYes) {
  mEnabled = bYes;
  if( mEnabled ) {
    document.all("fset").rows = "0%,100%"
    fireEvent( "OnSplit" );
  }
  else {
    document.all("fset").rows = "100%"
    fireEvent( "OnReset" );
  }
  return mEnabled;
```

```
}
function get_File()  {
  return mFile;
}
function put_File(src)  {
  document.all("first").src = src;
  document.all("second").src = src;
  return 1;
}

/////////////////////////////////
//
//  Internal Functions
//

function fireEvent( name )  {
  if( InScriptlet && (!window.external.frozen) )  {
    window.external.raiseEvent( name, 0 );
  }
}
</SCRIPT>

<FRAMESET id=fset ROWS="100%">
  <FRAME id=first src="">
  <FRAME id=second src="">
</FRAMESET>

</HTML>
```

A test page for this component might be the following. Note that we need an
external HTML file to display through the scriptlet. In this case, we call it
demo.htm, however, feel free to use any HTML file you want.

```
<html>
<head>
<title>Splitter Test Page</title>
</head>

<script language=VBscript for="window" event="onload">
  Splitter1.File = "demo.htm"
</script>

<script language=VBscript for="splitter1" event="onscriptletevent(n,o)">
  if n="OnSplit" Then
    document.all("split").innerText = "unsplit"
  end if

  if n="OnReset" Then
    document.all("split").innerText = "split"
  end if
</script>

<script language=VBscript for="document" event="onclick">
  Splitter1.Enable = Not Splitter1.Enable
</script>

<body background="tao.gif">
Click on the document to <span id=split>split</span> the view!<hr>

<object id=Splitter1 data=splitter.htm type="text/x-scriptlet"
        width=350 height=200 align=left>
</object>

</body>
</html>
```

If you run such page called
usesplit.htm you should
come across the next picture.

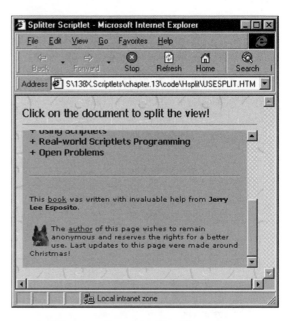

By clicking anywhere on the document (outside the scriptlet's area) you'll cause
the **Enable** property to be toggled. When we turn on the **Enable** property a
resizable bar appears at the top of the scriptlet's area. The next figure
demonstrates this.

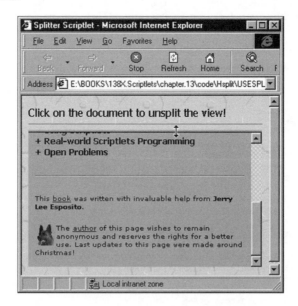

By looking closely at the topmost border of the scriptlet's area in the screenshot, we can see a raised line denoting a resizable window. By dragging it you can arrange the frames at your leisure.

Making the Inner Document Available

Through the scriptlet we can also make the **document** object of the currently viewed page available to external callers. This is done by accessing one of the frames (it doesn't matter which one). Here's how to do it:

```
function get_innerDocument() {
  return document.frames(0).document;
}
```

Exporting this property helps to further "hide" the frames that are used—under the hood—to implement the splitter. The user who makes calls to the scriptlet doesn't need to know about frames and can access the object model of the displayed page as if it was the only page displayed. When a frame hosts another page it makes its own object model visible and not the object model of the embedded page. To access the real page, you would think you have to pass through the **frames** collection, but this implies you have to know about frames. However, if the scriptlet exposes the inner **document** object directly, then the presence of frames becomes a mere implementation detail.

Raising Events

Once you insert this scriptlet into a Web page you just need to set the **Enable** property to enable the splitting capabilities. By doing this we are just letting the browser know that the second frame is also now visible. Undoubtedly, this is an important event in the scriptlet's life cycle and is worth publicizing.

Scriptlets can fire custom events whenever needed. The host page catches them and possibly replies. In this case it's reasonable to raise two events: one when the page is split and one when the view resets to normal.

It occurs inside the code that handles the **Enable** property. The source code seen above changes and becomes like this:

```
function get_Enable()  {
  return mEnabled;
}

function put_Enable( bYes )  {
  mEnabled = bYes;
  if( mEnabled )  {
    document.all("fset").rows = "0%,100%"
    fireEvent( "OnSplit" );
  }
  else  {
    document.all("fset").rows = "100%"
    fireEvent( "OnReset" );
  }
  return mEnabled;
}
```

The two new events are called **OnSplit** and **OnReset**. Their names are self-explanatory. We don't need to pass any data through them up to the host page. In the listing above there's a still to be defined function called **fireEvent**. It is a helper routine that evaluates to:

```
function fireEvent( name )  {
  if( InScriptlet && (!window.external.frozen) )  {
    window.external.raiseEvent( name, 0 );
  }
}
```

The Full Example

The test page seen above uses the **window.onload** event to set a fixed page to be displayed by the **Splitter** scriptlet component.

```
Splitter1.File = "demo.htm"
```

Of course you can use any predefined HTML page, but since the scriptlet works as an embeddable viewer you definitely need to specify which page it has to display. It is also important to note that the body of the test page presents a simple string of text with one peculiarity: an embedded **<SPAN>** tag. This just serves the purpose of identifying an element of the page, which we might need to change at run-time.

```
Click on the document to <span id=split>split</span> the view!
```

The string enclosed in the **<SPAN>** tag is "split". If you compare the next two figures, you'll notice that that word change according to the split state of the scriptlet.

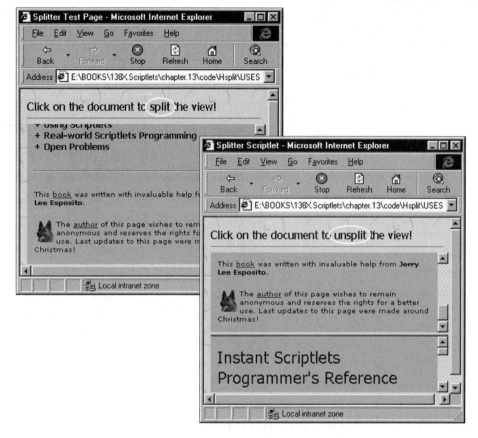

How does this occur? Put simply—the host pages catches and handles the
relative events fired by the scriptlet.

```
<script language=VBscript for="splitter1" event="onscriptletevent(n,o)">
  if n="OnSplit" Then
    document.all("split").innerText = "unsplit"
  end if

  if n="OnReset" Then
    document.all("split").innerText = "split"
  end if
</script>
```

When an event is detected for the scriptlet, the page searches for an element
whose ID is **split**. If it finds it, then it changes its **innerText** property
accordingly. That's all!

The state (split or not) is toggled by clicking anywhere on the host page client
area.

```
<script language=VBscript for="document" event="onclick">
  Splitter1.Enable = Not Splitter1.Enable
</script>
```

Split windows give different and independent views of the same content. As for HTML content—if you jump to another location, say through a hyperlink, the new page will be displayed instead of the original.

Vertical Splitting

We presented an example of horizontal splitting. However, nothing prevents us from doing the same vertically. From an implementation point of view there are really only a few changes to be made—most of which are connected to exchanging the frameset's **rows** and **cols** properties. The next screenshot shows an example.

Auto-resizable Scriptlets

Now that we have a scriptlet capable of providing splitting features, what about Internet Explorer 4.0? Wouldn't it be nice if the browser could offer such functionality? Unfortunately, we'll have to wait at least until the next major release for this useful addition.

However, is it possible to do something—even with today's software? The answer is—"Yes, we can". But we need to accept a few compromises and start off by studying how to make a scriptlet automatically resizable.

What are Resizable Scriptlets?

A scriptlet is an HTML page that supports the DHTML object model. A scriptlet has a site on the parent's page and can resize it dynamically. What matters is that a scriptlet can change its width and height at any moment in time. So what? The scriptlet knows everything about its parent since it is able to access its **document** object and its **body**. So any scriptlet could know what the width and the height of the hosting page is and could, therefore, resize it properly to cover the whole area.

```
h = window.Parent.document.body.clientHeight
w = window.Parent.document.body.clientWidth
```

The lines of code above show how to get the width and the height of the parent window document's area from within a scriptlet. At this point it's easy for a Web component to auto-modify its size to fit in.

What we call a resizable scriptlet is actually a normal scriptlet that implements such functionality.

Get Informed about Parent's Resize

Everything a scriptlet can do, however, is limited to the scriptlet activity. When loading, a scriptlet can adapt its size to cover the entire parent's client area. But what if the parent is resized by the user? Such a circumstance is regularly notified through an event, but it occurs at the level of the window's parent.

```
<script language=VBscript for="window" event="onresize">
   MsgBox "Parent Window is Resizing"
</script>
```

The same **onresize** event is trapped by both the scriptlet and the host page. Despite the name they are quite different events. The resizing that caused it to be sent relates to different windows. If you handle it within the scriptlet, then you'll only be informed about the resizing of the scriptlet's window. What you need instead is information about variations in the size of the parent window. In other words, we need to find out a way to forward the parent window resize events down to the scriptlet. First of all, we need to catch the event in the host page and then invoke some code in the scriptlet. For example:

```
<script language=VBscript for="window" event="onresize">
   Splitter1.Resize
</script>
```

The method **Resize**—a scriptlet method we'll define later—executes all the tasks necessary to ensure that the scriptlet occupies the entire client area of the parent.

Do we need the Scriptlet's onresize event?

Thus, for this purpose we don't need the scriptlet's **onresize** event. We only need to make sure that a scriptlet's defined piece of code executes in response to parent's resizing. This is exactly what the above fragment ensures.

The scriptlet's **onresize** event is detected only when the scriptlet itself is resized, not the parent! Instead, for our purposes the only event of interest is the parent resize.

To verify this try the following example:

```
<HTML ID=MyPage>

<SCRIPT language=VBScript for="window" event="onresize">
  MsgBox "Resizing Scriptlet window"
</SCRIPT>

<SCRIPT language=VBScript for="document" event="onclick">
  MyPage.style.pixelwidth = MyPage.style.pixelwidth/2
</SCRIPT>
```

```
<SCRIPT language=JavaScript>
public_description = new CreateResize();
var InScriptlet = (typeof(window.external.version)=="string");

function CreateResize()  {
}
</SCRIPT>

<BODY bgcolor="cyan">Click Me!</BODY>
</HTML>
```

This scriptlet (called **onres.htm**) pops out a message box each time an **onresize** event is raised for the scriptlet window. Furthermore, the scriptlet halves its width each time it gets clicked. A possible test page for this scriptlet is the following **testres.htm**.

```
<html>
<body>
<object data="onres.htm" type="text/x-scriptlet">
</object>
</body>
</html>
```

As you can see, if you click on the scriptlet area you force it to resize and, therefore, raise an event. Any changes in the parent window are completely ignored.

In conclusion, to get informed about the parent page resize we need it to tell us about itself. The easiest way to achieve this is by having the host page call a specific scriptlet method like, the already mentioned, **Resize**.

How to resize the Scriptlet

A good question now is—what's required for a method like **Resize**? Such a procedure must include the following lines:

```
Function Resize()  {
   h = window.Parent.document.body.clientHeight;
   w = window.Parent.document.body.clientWidth;
   MyPage.style.pixelHeight = h;
   MyPage.style.pixelWidth = w;
}
```

Remember that **MyPage** is the scriptlet's page ID. We set it as the ID of the initial **<HTML>** tag. As explained in Chapter 7—defining such an ID is necessary if you want to dynamically resize your scriptlets.

By using the above lines the scriptlet changes its own width and height using the same dimensions as those of the parent's client area. These lines should be part of a public procedure.

There are two extensions that need to be entered into our code to enable the scriptlet to resize properly and occupy the entire parent's area.

 Have the scriptlet expose a method—call it **Resize** or whatever you like—able to expand the scriptlet size to completely cover the host.

Have the host page call that method in response to any **onresize**
event.

```
<script language=VBscript for="window" event="onresize">
  Scriptlet1.Resize
</script>
```

Now that we know how to make a scriptlet auto-resizable, let's take a closer
look at IE4.

Extending Internet Explorer 4.0

Everything we have done so far has had a clear objective—to add splittable
document support to Internet Explorer 4.0. In practice, we would like to open
an HTML file in Internet Explorer 4.0 and split it into two or more views as
necessary. Of course, this kind of support can only be added by using a special
trick and not IE4's native code.

Let's now reiterate what we have and also address what we need. We have an
embeddable HTML viewer implemented as a scriptlet. We also can produce an
enhanced version which supports auto-resizing. This means that we can create a
host page that includes a scriptlet capable of automatically enlarging its size to
fit Internet Explorer 4.0's client area. Not only that, but it is also capable of
rearranging its width and height every time someone resizes the browser
window.

That's it for things we already have, but what about the features we still need?
What is required can be summarized as:

 Find a way to enable and disable splitting.

 Find a way to handle IE4 window's scrollbars.

In our previous example, we could click anywhere in the host page to enable
or disable the splitter. A similar, or equivalent, behavior needs to be retained
here. The adopted solution suggests leaving a certain number of unused pixels
at the top of the document. By clicking there we can set or reset the splitter.

The splitter, then, is the scriptlet we have already examined. In addition, it has
been enriched with the autosize capability.

Structure of the Page

To be honest, what we're about to demonstrate is not a way to extend Internet
Explorer 4.0 with splittable windows but, more precisely, a trick to make a
given HTML page splittable when it is viewed through Internet Explorer 4.0.

We make use of the splitter component—which is itself a container. Actually,
what we see through Internet Explorer 4.0 is not the file we selected on the
Address Bar or via the File|Open menu, but an HTML document, which is
assigned to the splitter's **File** property.

The following diagram illustrates what we mean:

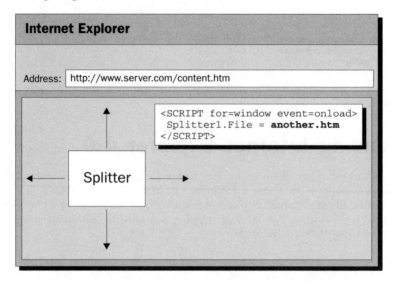

On the address bar (or in any other way) you tell Internet Explorer 4.0 to open and display a file, say **content.htm**. Furthermore, suppose this file includes a splitter scriptlet with auto-resize capabilities. The parent page also forwards all the messages related to changes in size to the scriptlet. Hence, the scriptlet covers the entire client area of Internet Explorer 4.0, minus a thin border at the top to allow splitting. The coverage is persistent—maintained even if the parent's size changes.

What's happened so far? Although we opened a file called **content.htm**, we're actually viewing the content of a file called **splitter.htm**—that is the default scriptlet's user interface.

The next step is obvious. The splitter scriptlet is frame-based and provides a property **File** whose only purpose in life is assigning a source to the scriptlet's frames. By setting **File** :

```
<script language=JScript for=window event=onload>
  Splitter1.File = "another.htm";
</script>
```

we can at last display the final document in IE's client area.

To summarize, we have:

- Opened **content.htm** through the Address bar.
- Made the embedded splitter cover the whole of the available area.
- Hosted **another.htm** inside the scriptlet and, consequently, inside IE4.

In practice, we have opened one file to see another one! What we have learned is that this document is now splittable when viewed through a browser that supports DHTML and scriptlets, as well as frames.

Structure of the Code

Let's take a look at this enhanced version of the splitter scriptlet. The file is called **splitex.htm**.

```
<HTML ID=MyPage>
<HEAD>
<TITLE>Splitter Scriptlet</TITLE>
</HEAD>

<SCRIPT language=VBScript for="window" event="onload">
  InitSplitter
</SCRIPT>

<SCRIPT language=VBScript>
  Sub InitSplitter
    document.all("first").document.body.style.margin = "0px"
    document.all("second").document.body.style.margin = "0px"
    DoResize
  End Sub

  Sub DoResize
    splitArea = 5
    window.Parent.document.body.style.margin = "0px"
    window.Parent.document.body.scroll = "no"
    window.Parent.document.body.scrollTop = 0
    window.Parent.document.body.scrollLeft = 0
    h = window.Parent.document.body.clientHeight-splitArea
    w = window.Parent.document.body.clientWidth
    MyPage.style.pixelHeight = h
    MyPage.style.pixelWidth = w
  End Sub
</SCRIPT>

<SCRIPT language=JavaScript>
public_description = new CreateSplitter();
var InScriptlet = (typeof(window.external.version)=="string");
var mEnabled = 0;
var mFile = "";

function CreateSplitter() {
  this.put_Enable = put_Enable;
  this.get_Enable = get_Enable;
  this.put_File = put_File;
  this.get_File = get_File;
  this.event_OnSplit = "";
  this.event_OnReset = "";
  this.Resize = Resize;
}

function Resize() {
  DoResize();
}

function get_Enable() {
  return mEnabled;
}
function put_Enable(bYes) {
  mEnabled = bYes;
  if( mEnabled ) {
    document.all("fset").rows = "0%,100%"
    fireEvent( "OnSplit" );
  }
  else {
    document.all("fset").rows = "100%"
    fireEvent( "OnReset" );
```

```
      }
      return mEnabled;
  }

  function get_File()  {
    return mFile;
  }
  function put_File(src)  {
    document.all("first").src = src;
    document.all("second").src = src;
    return 1;
  }

  //  Internal Functions
  function fireEvent( name )  {
    if( InScriptlet && (!window.external.frozen) )  {
      window.external.raiseEvent( name, 0 );
    }
  }
}
</SCRIPT>

<FRAMESET id=fset ROWS=100%>
  <FRAME id=first src="">
  <FRAME id=second src="">
</FRAMESET>
</HTML>
```

Notice that in the **DoResize** internal procedure we're using a variable called
splitArea. This serves the purpose of denoting the height of the topmost area
where the user can click to enable, or disable the splitter.

```
h = window.Parent.document.body.clientHeight - splitArea
```

With the line of code above we ensure that the upper margin of the embedded
document is set to a certain number of pixels. This space will separate
Explorer's address bar from the beginning of the viewed document. However,
we could make it clearer to understand where to click for splitting views if we
use the same Word convention—a little bitmap denoting a button placed at the
top of the views.

The source code for the host page might be:

```
<html>
<head>
<title>AutoSize Test Page</title>
</head>

<script language=VBscript for="window" event="onload">
  Splitter1.File = "demo.htm"
</script>

<script language=VBscript for="button" event="onclick">
  Splitter1.Enable = Not Splitter1.Enable
</script>

<script language=VBscript for="window" event="onresize">
  Splitter1.Resize
</script>

<body>
<IMG id=button src=splitter.bmp alt="Click to split/unsplit"></IMG>
<object id=Splitter1 data=splitex.htm type="text/x-scriptlet"
        width=1 height=1>
```

```
</object>
</body>
</html>
```

This file is available on our Web site and is called **testsplt.htm**. Note the following fundamental steps—forwarding the **onresize** event and manipulating the splitter scriptlet. Actually, the user can enable and disable the splitter by clicking on a small image placed at the top of the view. This image has an ID of **button**.

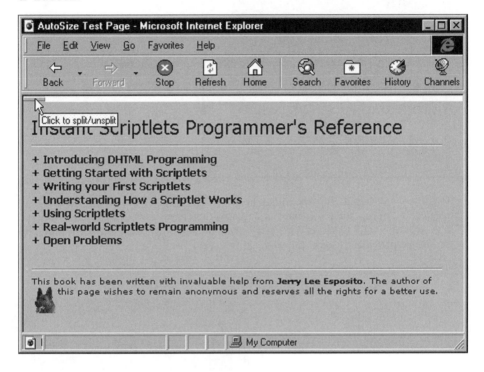

Don't Forget the Scrollbars

In the source code of **splitex.htm** there are a few lines entirely dedicated to scrollbars.

```
window.Parent.document.body.scroll = "no"
window.Parent.document.body.scrollTop = 0
window.Parent.document.body.scrollLeft = 0
```

Are they really useful? Look at the next figure, and judge for yourself.

295

Yes, they seem really useful!

Once we have split the document in two, the frames we're using behind the scenes are doing their job well and displaying their own scrollbars. However, has any one told Explorer we don't need its standard scrollbar anymore? Not if we don't provide at least this line.

```
window.Parent.document.body.scroll = "no"
```

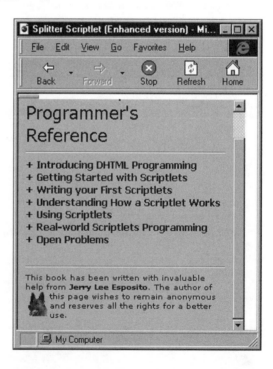

However, such a line simply hides IE4's scrollbar. Omitting the last two lines listed above creates what you can see in the screenshot below:

Fortunately, this only occurs after hitting Refresh and disappears after the next resize.

What Do You Need To Split Pages?

Now that we've succeeded in creating splittable documents inside Internet Explorer 4.0, let's stop a while and ask if there's a way of making it smooth and seamless.

The first consideration is that so far we haven't added splitting capability to Internet Explorer 4.0 but, instead, limited ourselves to making our documents splittable through scriptlets.

This seems to be the only way to go about getting such functionality from a browser today. However, you can make your own documents splittable—and this is not a bad result!

Basically, the two things we had to do were:

- Decide what page, or pages, we wanted to make splittable.
- Create a standard file to host them through the splitter scriptlet.

This standard file must fulfill a few other requirements. In particular, it must:

- Host a resizable splitter scriptlet.
- Assign it the file to display through the File property.
- Forward the onresize events it receives from the browser.
- Provides a way to set and reset the split-mode.

Let's say that, given a page you want to split, it's easy to create a wrapper for it that respects all these features. The drawback is that, this way, if you want to open **mypage.htm** in a splittable manner then you should resort to, for example, **splitpage.htm** which is **always** a file like this:

```
<html>

<script language=VBscript for="window" event="onload">
  Splitter1.File = … ' put here the file name you want to split, say mypage.htm
</script>

<script language=VBscript for="button" event="onclick">
  Splitter1.Enable = Not Splitter1.Enable
</script>

<script language=VBscript for="window" event="onresize">
  Splitter1.Resize
</script>

<body>
<img id=button src=splitter.bmp alt="Click to split/unsplit"></img>
<object id=Splitter1 data=splitter.htm type="text/x-scriptlet"
        width=1 height=1>
</object>
</body>
</html>
```

As you've probably guessed, the host page for splittable HTML documents has a fixed structure. The only parametric section of it is the name of the actual file to display and split! Consequently, if you have a file **mypage.htm** to view, then copy the above listing and replace:

```
Splitter1.File = …
```

with:

```
Splitter1.File = "mypage.htm"
```

The next figure shows the result.

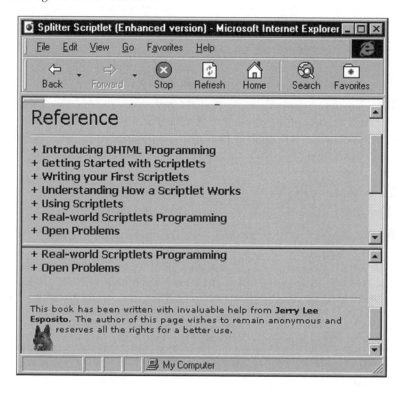

Summary

Splittable windows are a good and attractive result that you can obtain from an interesting use of frames. By combining them with scriptlets, you can make it reusable and far easier to handle as well. In this chapter, we presented three examples of scriptlets all of which relate to split-windows.

First, we discussed an embeddable viewer component you can insert in HTML pages and get to scroll and split other HTML content. Then we introduced the resizable attribute and examined the various issues you might face when attempting to fit your scriptlet into the available client area. Finally, this

enhanced component has become the core of a container page, allowing you to
get splittable documents through IE4 To summarize, the chapter covered:

- Using Frames in scriptlets
- Writing an embeddable HTML Viewer
- Creating splittable views in HTML documents
- Displaying splittable documents through IE4.

Further Reading

The topics covered in this chapter go back to advanced DHTML scripting and
frames. So if you need some further information, you should check out books
and articles that dig into the depths of HTML and DHTML. We have three
specific suggestions for you. The first one is our *Instant HTML Programmer's
Reference*. We recommend this book because in most cases what you need is to
know basic information about the syntax and semantics of all the tags and
attributes. The natural counterpart to this book is *Instant IE4 Dynamic HTML
Programmer's Reference* by Alex Homer and Chris Ullman.

Finally, to get even more inspiration—other than useful references—go to
Professional IE4 Programming. All these are Wrox books.

For little tips-and-tricks on everyday HTML and DHTML programming,
however, you might want to check out two monthly columns inn Microsoft
Internet Developer (MIND)—*Geek-To-Geek* by Robert Hess and *How It's Done* by
Michael Hyman.

Dynamic Methods and Inheritance

Scriptlets have been introduced to facilitate HTML code reuse. We live and work in a world more and more directed towards True Web Integration, where almost all computing can be seen as an extension of the internet, and the unceasing search for uniform—and possibly universal—ways of accessing everything (from databases to components). HTML is one of the very few things that represents certainty in a Web environment. Although we all know that what we call HTML today may well be superceded by Dynamic HTML tomorrow.

In the Microsoft vision of the Web, scriptlets are the missing link that could push DHTML forward as a fully-fledged development platform.

The official documentation for scriptlets emphasizes the concept of reusability, as opposed to flat procedures and lengthy modules. Scriptlets provide Web programmers with the capacity to design their own components following the most common guidelines for component development. This means self-contained objects that communicate with the outside world through methods, properties and events that together let you know about changes in their internal state through further events.

Up to this point, *Instant Scriptlets* hasn't really got away from a practical consideration of how scriptlets can simplify Web development. In this chapter, however, we attempt to do much more than this. We're about to enter unexplored territory, but persevere and you'll find out about mysterious but exciting topics such as:

- How to dynamically add new methods to existing scriptlets.
- How to derive scriptlets from standard objects.
- How to modify their public description interface.
- How to derive one scriptlet from another scriptlet.

Extending the Scriptlets Capabilities

In this chapter we will build examples which let you dynamically enable a new method in the scriptlet. This is done by passing in the name and the code to execute. Internally, the scriptlet will update its **public_description** object, therefore making the new automation symbol immediately available.

By exploiting the DHTML object model, you could also insert one scriptlet into another and make it visible to external callers. Think this over for a while: what would you call it? Inheritance? Aggregation? Delegation? Whatever the answer is, what matters is that you can "logically" import functionality from another component.

Three Ways to Extend

We identified three directions to take in order to extend the design capability of scriptlets. Firstly, you can add dynamic methods. This approach relies on the indirect code execution features we encountered in a previous chapter. (See Chapter 9—Making Callbacks with Scriptlets.) By "indirect code execution" we mean the possibility of executing some script code through the **window.execScript** method. It takes a string which denotes executable code as an argument and runs the argument.

Basically, adding dynamic methods requires an extension to the public interface of the component. We'll be discussing both the advantages and the drawbacks of this approach later.

Throughout this entire chapter, you must always keep in mind that topics like inheritance and run-time modifications of the exported interface are still very new. They are also topics for which an adequate support system does not always exist. This means that sometimes we have to accept compromises to get ahead.

A second way to extend scriptlets should not sound completely new to you, provided that you read Chapter 3—Writing the First Scriptlet—carefully, and in particular the section entitled *Little Games with public_description*. There we demonstrated how you can clone a Javascript object and have it in the form of a scriptlet. In this chapter we go further and extend such an object both statically and dynamically.

The third and final way we can go involves objects aggregation. By "aggregation" we mean the process of embedding a given object in another one. As a result, the outer is component enriched with new properties and methods.

What the user perceives is that he or she can set up new scriptlets exploiting the functions exposed by another one. This is obtained by embedding the base component into the new one and by exposing all its properties and methods through a sort of gateway that is actually the **document** object of the nested scriptlet.

Defining Dynamic Methods

What does defining dynamic methods mean? And how can you take advantage of it? Well, a dynamic method is a function that an object exports from at a given moment in time and not before. That is, at a certain point you add a completely new entry to the list of the public symbols of the object. From then on, the object exposes a different interface which applies both the old and the new functions. Dynamic methods aren't special. They behave and are perceived by the users in exactly the same way as static methods.

When can you take advantage of them? It's hard to say. Certainly, we don't think this is a feature you would place in your top ten fantasies. However, any highly interactive HTML-based environment might welcome such a feature. Defining a dynamic method, amongst other things, requires you to specify a string that denotes the code to execute. In some cases, you might think about adding just a specific dialog box to your application for updating a given component interactively. Of course, a scriptlet must offer a bit of cooperation to allow you to extend it in this way.

After all, the most important characteristic of the scriptlet's dynamic methods is that they allow forms of inheritance and aggregation!

The Simple New Method

To begin this argument, let's try to define what is needed from the architectural point of view in order to add a dynamic method to a Web component. First of all, we need an explicit means of accomplishing the extension. In other words, the scriptlet must export a method that takes care of properly updating the scriptlet's internal structures according to external instructions.

For example, let's consider the following—very minimal—scriptlet.

```
<html>
<head>
<title>Dynamic Scriptlet</title>
</head>

<script language="JScript">
public_description = new CreateDyn();

function CreateDyn() {
   this.AddMethod = AddMethod;
}

function AddMethod( name ) {
   // extend the public interface
}

function DoSomething () {
   alert( "I'm a new method" );
   return 1;
}
</script>

<body>
</body>
</html>
```

The component has a very limited public interface which is made up of just the **AddMethod** method. This method is undefined in the listing, but coming soon. Note that we also have a function called **DoSomething** that is not part of the scriptlet's public interface.

In this first example, we'll try to link that predefined, but unused, function to a public name that can be invoked by an external caller, although we will look at how to include new methods later.

Extending public_description

As we explained in Chapter 3, **public_description** is **almost** a keyword for scriptlet developers. You can avoid using it completely and choose the default description approach for declaring the public interface of the component. However, if you don't do it this way you must create a new JavaScript object called **public_description**. This approach means that you also have to pay careful attention to case.

As above, **public_description** plays a role very similar to a keyword, but actually is a JavaScript function object. So while it is important in the economy of a scriptlet, it doesn't bite. It works just like any other function object in JavaScript. What makes it special is that its name suggests a particular behavior to the browser.

In JavaScript you could have arrays with the most up-to-date syntax:

```
myArray = new Array(2);
```

or the older approach:

```
myArray = MakeArray(2);

function MakeArray( n )  {
  var i;
  this.length = n;
  for( i=1; i<=n; i++ )
    this[i] = ""

  return n;
}
```

The latter looks very much like the way you define the public interface of a scriptlet. As well as being able to modify the size and the content of an array dynamically, you can also modify the size and content of a scriptlet's public interface.

Given this, here's a possible implementation for the **AddMethod** method of the earlier component. This file is available on our Web site at **http://rapid.wrox.co.uk/books/138X** as **dynmeth1.htm**.

```
<html>
<head>
<title>Dynamic Scriptlet </title>
</head>

<script language="JScript">
public_description = new CreateDyn();
```

```
function CreateDyn() {
  this.AddMethod = AddMethod;
}

function AddMethod( name ) {
  s = "public_description."+name+" = DoSomething;"
  alert(s);  // for debug purposes only
  window.execScript( s, "JScript" );
}

function DoSomething () {
  alert( "I'm a new method" );
  return 1;
}
</script>

<body>
</body>
</html>
```

The method **AddMethod** receives the name of the new method as its only
parameter to add. Next, we format a string, adopting the following template:

```
public_description.<name> = DoSomething;
```

where **<name>** is the actual name of the new method. The screenshot below
shows the output produced by the:

```
alert(s);
```

that you can see in the above
listing. In the figure, we're passing
"NewMethod" as **<name>**.

Of course, formatting a code expression is not enough. We need to "execute"
that code. The best way to do it is use **window.execScript**. Note that it is
necessary here to ensure that the script language parameter is set to JScript or
JavaScript. Even if **execScript** also supports VBScript you must specify JScript
code. The reason for this is that the **public_description** object is handled
through JScript rules and in this specific context we're forced to use JScript.

New Features for the Public Interface

By executing script code like this:

```
public_description.<name> = DoSomething;
```

you can add new features to the scriptlet's prototype or even change a
predefined behavior by getting a method or property to point to a different
piece of code.

The following figure shows a demo page hosting a scriptlet. By clicking on the
page you cause a new method to be dynamically added to the scriptlet itself.

305

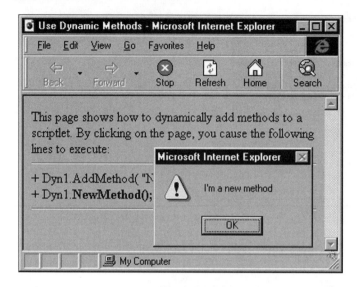

Here's the full source code for the page **usedyn1.htm**:

```
<html>
<head>
<title>Use Dynamic Methods</title>
</head>

<script language="JScript" for="document" event="onclick">
  Dyn1.AddMethod( "NewMethod" );
  Dyn1.NewMethod();
</script>

<body bgcolor="#C0C0C0">
This page shows how to dynamically add methods to a scriptlet.
By clicking on the page, you cause the following lines to execute:<hr>

+ Dyn1.AddMethod( "NewMethod" ); <br>
+ Dyn1.<b>NewMethod();</b><br>

<hr>

<object id="Dyn1" data="DynMeth1.htm" type="text/x-scriptlet"
style="display:none">
</object>

</body>
</html>
```

In particular, the page includes a hidden scriptlet

```
<object id="Dyn1" data="DynMeth1.htm" type="text/x-scriptlet"
style="display:none">
</object>
```

and handles the click on the visible area.

```
<script language="JScript" for="document" event="onclick">
  Dyn1.AddMethod( "NewMethod" );
  Dyn1.NewMethod();
</script>
```

In responding to the click we call the function **AddMethod** passing a string
"**NewMethod**". Then, we handle **NewMethod** as if it was (and actually now it is)
a regular method of the component. Note that if we swap the two calls and
execute them in reverse order then we'll definitely get an error.

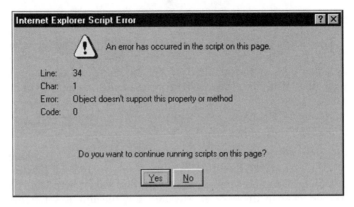

Executing:

```
Dyn1.AddMethod( "NewMethod" );
```

first modifies the public interface of the scriptlet and then allows us to call the
new method as a predefined attribute.

Getting Code for New Methods

The problem now is how to specify the code for the new method to execute?
In this first example, we are mainly limited to demonstrating that adding a new
method is possible. However, this won't always be enough. You must be able to
take advantage of this opportunity, otherwise, it remains a useless
demonstration!

In the previous example, we added a method by modifying the
public_description object.

```
s = "public_description."+name+" = DoSomething;"
window.execScript( s, "JScript" );
```

The name of the new object is passed on the command line and is rendered by
the variable **name** in the code above. But what about **DoSomething**? From the
syntax's standpoint it just represents the name of the internal procedure that
implements the method.

Conceptually, it is a piece of code that is strictly linked to the name and the
role of the new method. So it's perfectly reasonable that it is passed in through
AddMethod, along with the name. In addition, the body for this function
should be taken from the host page and must be external to the scriptlet.

Our first example provided a way to add a new dynamic method whose body
had been defined in the scriptlet since creation! You'll agree that this might be
good for demonstration purposes, but in a real-world context it doesn't make
sense at all.

307

Setting Dynamic Methods

The first aspect to change is the prototype of the **AddMethod** method. This method evolves to:

```
function AddMethod( name, code )
```

Now we have to pass on to the command line both the name, which we'd like to use to refer to it later, and the code that it will execute. Unfortunately, this is not enough. Looking at the required syntax for the **public_description** object you'll note that the r-value (right side) of the assignment must be a valid function name.

```
public_description.AddMethod = DoSomething
```

This means that whatever name we put on the right must be defined inside the scriptlet. What matters, however, is that the name of the internal procedure we associate with the method corresponds to a valid function within the scriptlet. Next we could change the code it executes, but the important thing to remember is that it is a scriptlet function.

This leads us to a compromise. We could define a certain maximum number of redefinable methods and create as many entries as needed in the scriptlet. When adding a new method, we simply assign a free slot (if any) to the new attribute and refuse it if there are no longer any seats available. Let's see how to implement this. The following scriptlet is called **dynmeth2.htm**.

```
<html>
<head>
<title>Dynamic Scriptlet</title>
</head>

<script language="JScript">
public_description = new CreateDyn();

function CreateDyn() {
   this.AddMethod = AddMethod;
}

var aCode = new Array(3)
var nMaxMethods = "3";
var nNextMethod = "1";

function AddMethod( name, code ) {
   if( nNextMethod > nMaxMethods )
      return 0;

   s = "public_description."+name+" = Executor"+nNextMethod+";"
   window.execScript( s, "JScript" );
   aCode[nNextMethod] = code;
   nNextMethod ++;
}

function Executor1 () {
   window.execScript( aCode[1], "JScript" );
   return 1;
}
function Executor2 () {
   window.execScript( aCode[2], "JScript" );
   return 1;
```

```
}
function Executor3 () {
  window.execScript( aCode[3], "JScript" );
  return 1;
}
</script>

<body>
</body>
</html>
```

We start off by defining the following three variables:

```
var aCode = new Array(3)
var nMaxMethods = "3";
var nNextMethod = "1";
```

The array has **nMaxMethods** entries and is intended to store the code
expressions for the upcoming new methods. Instead, **nNextMethod** denotes the
index of the next method to be inserted. The **AddMethod** method is rewritten
this way:

```
function AddMethod( name, code ) {
  if( nNextMethod > nMaxMethods )
      return 0;

  s = "public_description."+name+" = Executor"+nNextMethod+";"
  window.execScript( s, "JScript" );
  aCode[nNextMethod] = code;
  nNextMethod ++;
}
```

First we check for a free slot and return if the index of the next method is
greater than the maximum number of supported new methods. Next, we format
the code expression as above and execute it through **execScript**. The internal
name assigned to the new method is **ExecutorX**, where X is a number in the
range **1...nMaxMethods**.

The various procedures—Executor1, Executor2, ..., ExecutorN, are all predefined
in the scriptlet's code. They all have the same template:

```
function ExecutorX () {
  window.execScript( aCode[X], "JScript" );
  return 1;
}
```

As we have previously mentioned, **aCode** is an array of strings whose actual
content is the user-specified code expression for the i.th new method.

```
aCode[nNextMethod] = code;
nNextMethod ++;
```

The two lines above shows how the array is added a new code expression.

A Demo Page

In the above listing we presented a bare-bones scriptlet that only exposes the
method in order to add new methods to it. This is exactly what we're intending
to demonstrate here.

The following code shows how to instruct a scriptlet that can't, originally, do anything and get it to return to us the day, month and year of the current date. Let's see the **usedyn2.htm** page, available as usual on our Web site at **http://rapid.wrox.co.uk/books/138X**.

```
<html>
<head>
<title>Use Dynamic Methods</title>
</head>

<script language="JScript" for=document event=onclick>
  s = "d=new Date();alert(\"Day is \" + d.getDate());"
  Dyn1.AddMethod( "NewGetDate", s );
  s = "d=new Date();alert(\"Month is  \" + (1+d.getMonth()));"
  Dyn1.AddMethod( "NewGetMonth", s );
  s = "d=new Date();alert(\"Year is  \"+d.getYear());"
  Dyn1.AddMethod( "NewGetYear", s );

  Dyn1.NewGetDate();
  Dyn1.NewGetMonth();
  Dyn1.NewGetYear();
</script>

<body bgcolor="#C0C0C0">
This page will show you how to add up to three dynamic methods to a  scriptlet.
By clicking on the page, you cause the following lines to execute:<hr>
<code>
  s = "d=new Date();alert(\"Day is  \" + d.getDate());"<br>
  Dyn1.AddMethod( "NewGetDate", s );<br>
  s = "d=new Date();alert(\"Month is  \" + (1+d.getMonth()));"<br>
  Dyn1.AddMethod( "NewGetMonth", s );<br>
  s = "d=new Date();alert(\"Year is  \"+d.getYear());"<br>
  Dyn1.AddMethod( "NewGetYear", s );<br>
<b><br>
  Dyn1.NewGetDate();<br>
  Dyn1.NewGetMonth();<br>
  Dyn1.NewGetYear();<br>
</b>
</code>
<hr>

<object id="Dyn1" data="DynMeth2.htm" type="text/x-scriptlet"
style="display:none">
</object>

</body>
</html>
```

The page includes the scriptlet described above, and makes it invisible.

```
<object id="Dyn1" data="DynMeth2.htm" type="text/x-scriptlet"
style="display:none">
</object>
```

When the user clicks on the document the page ends up adding the following three new methods:

 NewGetDate

NewGetMonth

NewGetYear

```
<script language="JScript" for=document event=onclick>
  s = "d=new Date();alert(\"Day is  \" + d.getDate());"
  Dyn1.AddMethod( "NewGetDate", s );
  s = "d=new Date();alert(\"Month is  \" + (1+d.getMonth()));"
  Dyn1.AddMethod( "NewGetMonth", s );
  s = "d=new Date();alert(\"Year is  \"+d.getYear());"
  Dyn1.AddMethod( "NewGetYear", s );

  Dyn1.NewGetDate();
  Dyn1.NewGetMonth();
  Dyn1.NewGetYear();
</script>
```

The script defines the code expression and then invokes **AddMethod** for each of them. For example, the next fragment defines a method that returns a string like "Day is ..." plus the number of the current day.

```
  s = "d=new Date();alert(\"Day is  \" + d.getDate());"
  Dyn1.AddMethod( "NewGetDate", s );
```

Note that the semi colon (**;**) is used to explicitly terminate a JavaScript instruction, so that you can concatenate multiple instructions in a single string. When we invoke **NewGetDate**, we cause the following code to execute:

```
  d = new Date();
  alert(\"Day is  \" + d.getDate());
```

The final output of the demo page is shown below.

What's Next?

What we discussed here only scratches the surface of scriptlets software dynamic extension. There are two, more interesting and more powerful, innovations yet to explore. For example, you can create a scriptlet in just a few lines by cloning an existing JScript object. We have already mentioned this in a previous chapter. See Chapter 3—Writing the First Scriptlet.

What's new, in the light of our previous considerations, is that not only can you clone an existing object but you can add new methods as well! What do you call that, if not inheritance?

Deriving Scriptlets from Standard Objects

In Chapter 3 we discovered that you could avoid defining the public interface of a scriptlet completely from scratch. In fact, you can obtain the **public_description** object from a JScript standard object. We briefly discussed the following example:

```
<html>
<head>
<title>Date Scriptlet</title>
</head>

<script language="Javascript">
public_description = new Date();
</script>

<body>
</body>
</html>
```

The line

```
public_description = new Date();
```

creates a new instance of the JScript date object and assigns it to the **public_description** variable. You can then invoke the scriptlet, from an external module, exactly as if it was a JScript date object.

```
<html>
<head>
<title>Use Date</title>
</head>

<SCRIPT language=VBScript for=document event=onclick>
MsgBox Date1.getDate() & "/" & (1+Date1.getMonth()) & "/" & Date1.getYear()
</script>

<body bgcolor="#C0C0C0">
Test page.
<hr>
<object id="Date1" data="Date.htm" type="text/x-scriptlet"
        style="display:none">
</object>
</body>
</html>
```

The two components now expose an identical interface.

This would be a great result if JScript offered a certain number of reusable objects that it would make sense to extend and use as scriptlets. In practice, however, the Date object is the only one that is obviously worth exploiting. Can we write our own set of foundation objects?

The goal of the rest of the chapter is just to show how you can create a new scriptlet based on another one.

Extending a Standard Object

As we've seen earlier, we have the power to add new methods dynamically to virtually any running scriptlet. So why not to those derived from standard JScript objects? Let's look at the next example where we're attempting to create an enhanced date object. The file is **date.htm**.

```
<html>
<head>
<title>Date Scriptlet</title>
</head>
```

```
<script language="Javascript">
public_description = new Date();
public_description.getFormattedDate = FormatDate;

function FormatDate()  {
  d = public_description;
  return d.getDate() + "/" + (1+d.getMonth()) + "/" + d.getYear();
}
</script>

<body>
</body>
</html>
```

The new scriptlet has the same functions as the date object, plus a new method called **getFormattedDate**. This is provided by the following code:

```
public_description = new Date();
public_description.getFormattedDate = FormatDate;
```

The first instruction duplicates the date object and the second extends its public interface with a new method. Note that we're using the same approach seen in the previous chapter for dynamic methods.

getFormattedDate attempts to make up for a missing function in the date interface. In fact, while you have methods to find out the current day, month, year or time, there isn't a direct function that gives you a formatted string simpler than the one returned by the **toGMTString** method. We want just day, month, and year separated by a slash. Here's the function code.

```
function FormatDate()  {
  d = public_description;
  return d.getDate() + "/" + (1+d.getMonth()) + "/" + d.getYear();
}
```

When defining a scriptlet that inherits from an existing object you should find out a way to refer to the methods and the properties of the original object. For example, here we added a **FormattedDate** method that reasonably will need to access some standard Date's methods like **getDate** or **getMonth**.

You can't use **getDate** directly because IE4 will interpret it as if it is a scriptlet's function and that isn't the case. Actually, **getDate** is a method of the original object from which we cloned the present scriptlet. Consequently, **getDate** is a method of scriptlet but it is not defined in the current file! However, there's an easy and somewhat intuitive way to refer to it. Just use **public_description**. After all, **public_description** is a variable you can assign and treat like any other. When extending an existing object with new methods, you can refer base properties and methods through the **public_description** variable. This is exactly what we did above in the **FormatDate**'s source code. Remember that **FormatDate** is the name of the internal function implementing the **FormattedDate** method.

On the parent's side, we're still using the new method in a quite ordinary way as the following page **usedate.htm** demonstrates.

313

```html
<html>

<head>
<title>Use Date</title>
</head>

<body bgcolor="#C0C0C0">
This page shows a rudimental sample of scriptlet inheritance.
We derive our scriptlet from a Javascript's Date object, and add
new methods. By clicking on the page you'll run
<hr>
<code>
   MsgBox Date1.toGMTString(), vbInformation, "toGMTString"<br>
   MsgBox Date1.getFormattedDate(), vbInformation, "getFormattedDate"
</code>
<hr>
Note that the scriptlet works as an extended version of the date object and you
can call both original and new methods.

<object id="Date1" data="Date.htm" type="text/x-scriptlet"
style="display:none">
</object>

<SCRIPT language=VBScript for="document" event="onclick">
   MsgBox Date1.toGMTString(), vbInformation, "toGMTString"
   MsgBox Date1.getFormattedDate(), vbInformation, "getFormattedDate"
</script>

</body>
</html>
```

The next figure shows the effect of the page and illustrates the difference
between **toGMTString** and **getFormattedDate**.

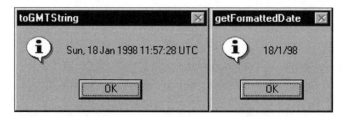

Note that the scriptlet works as an extended version of JScript's Date object,
and that you can call both original and new methods the same way.

Adding a New Property

So far, we've illustrated all the examples of how to extend a Web component
through methods. For the sake of completeness, let's now see that there's no
difference if you decide, or need, to add properties. After all, properties are
implemented by means of two hidden methods—one for reading and returning
the current value and one for storing a new one.

Let's try to make the same formatted date seen earlier available as a property
string, and also add the possibility of customizing the separator symbol for the
date. By default, this is a slash.

The following code shows how to change the scriptlet. The new file is called
date1.htm.

```
<html>
<head>
<title>Date Scriptlet</title>
</head>

<script language="Javascript">
var mSep = "/";
public_description = new Date();

public_description.get_FormattedDate = get_FormatDate;
public_description.get_Separator = get_Separator;
public_description.put_Separator = put_Separator;

function get_FormatDate() {
  d = public_description;
  return d.getDate() + mSep + (1+d.getMonth()) + mSep + d.getYear();
}
function get_Separator() {
  return mSep;
}
function put_Separator( s ) {
  mSep = s;
}
</script>

<body>
</body>
</html>
```

In this case, we're supposed to have a couple of properties: **FormattedDate**, which is a read-only attribute and **Separator**. The latter is a read/write property. To conclude this argument, let's see how a host page could handle such a component. The sample page is **usedate1.htm**.

```
<html>
<head>
<title>Use Date</title>
</head>

<body bgcolor="#C0C0C0">
This page shows a rudimental sample of scriptlet inheritance.
We derive our scriptlet from a Javascript's Date object, and add
new methods. By clicking on the page you'll run
<hr>
<code>
   MsgBox Date1.FormattedDate, vbInformation, "FormattedDate"<br>
   Date1.Separator = "-"<br>
   MsgBox Date1.FormattedDate, vbInformation, "FormattedDate"<br>
</code>
<hr>
Note that the scriptlet works as an extended version of the date object and you
can call both original and new methods.

<object id="Date1" data="Date1.htm" type="text/x-scriptlet"
style="display:none">
</object>

<SCRIPT language=VBScript for=document event=onclick>
   MsgBox Date1.FormattedDate, vbInformation, "FormattedDate"
   Date1.Separator = "-"
   MsgBox Date1.FormattedDate, vbInformation, "FormattedDate"
</script>

</body>
</html>
```

315

The page illustrates the use of the above
properties. The screenshot opposite
demonstrates how to modify the
separator for the date items.

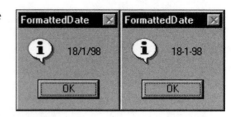

New Perspectives and Objectives

Being able to extend standard objects is a great result, even if it isn't
immediately exploitable. As mentioned earlier, you can do this mainly with
JScript objects. This happens because we rely on specific JScript features to
implement and register our extensions. All our examples assume and guarantee
the presence of a **public_description** object. However, we also sketched out
the possibility of using global public methods through both JScript and
VBScript.

Unfortunately, the standard JScript objects are not very numerous. By combining
dynamic methods and standard inheritance we got significant results, but still
didn't cross anything which could be considered a finishing line.

What's the next goal? Being able to inherit directly from existing scriptlets and
identifying them by name.

Deriving Scriptlets from Other Scriptlets

Suppose you write a scriptlet called **a.htm** and have it working perfectly.
Eventually, you need a specialized or extended version of it. You can make a
copy of the scriptlet's source code and modify it properly. What you get is a
scriptlet called **b.htm** which mainly consists of the code of **a.htm**. Again,
everything works fine

Next, you notice an error, or something that needs fixing, in the source code of
a.htm. You update it, but also need to change also the code of **b.htm** since it
is based on it and very likely it has the same error.

Wouldn't it be nice if you have a way to automatically include the source code
of **a.htm** inside **b.htm**? A possible solution might be the following:

```
<script language="Javascript" src="a.htm"></script>
```

However, for this to work, **a.htm** can only include script code. In fact you
should ensure that expanding the content of **src** doesn't violate the traditional
HTML syntax. A valid content for **a.htm** is

```
Function Name1() {
...
}
Function Name2() {
...
}
```

Of course, if **a.htm** is a scriptlet you would have a **<HTML>** and a **<BODY>** inside a **<SCRIPT>** tag.

This is not what we want here. Conceptually, we want to get the same result provided by

```
<script language="Javascript" src="a.htm"></script>
```

but have **a.htm** as a scriptlet. In other words—a way to force a given scriptlet to publicly inherit all the features of another. The only way to unambiguously identify scriptlets is by their names.

A possible way to code this scheme is by means of nesting. In practice, we insert scriptlet A into scriptlet B. This highlights the following, most important, issues:

 How to achieve nesting.

 How to make the nested object available.

Implementing Nested Scriptlets

At the current stage of the technology, nesting scriptlets seems to be the only way to gain a bit of inheritance and increased reusability. We need to find a way to dynamically insert an **<OBJECT>** tag into the scriptlet's body. Once we've done this, the final problem is how to make it available to the external callers of our base scriptlet.

Let's see an example of a scriptlet called **aggreg.htm**, which implements a special interface to support dynamic nesting.

```
<HTML ID=MyPage>
<HEAD>
<TITLE>Aggreg Scriptlet</TITLE>
</HEAD>

<SCRIPT language=VBScript>
  Function DoInsObject( name )
    Set coll = document.all("dynObject")
    if coll Is Nothing  Then
        s1 = "<object id=dynObject data="+name+" type="
        s2 = Chr(34) + "text/x-scriptlet" + Chr(34)
        s3 = " style=display:none></object>"
        s = s1+s2+s3
        document.body.insertAdjacentHTML "AfterBegin", s
        DoInsObject = 1
    else
        DoInsObject = 0
    end if
  End Function
</SCRIPT>

<SCRIPT language=Javascript>
public_description = new CreateAggreg();
var InScriptlet = (typeof(window.external.version)=="string");

function CreateAggreg() {
  this.get_dynObject = get_dynObject;
```

```
    this.Inherit = Inherit;
  }

  // INHERIT method
  function Inherit (name)  {
    return DoInsObject(name);
  }

  // OBJECT property (read-only)
  function get_dynObject()  {
    return document.all("dynObject");
  }
</SCRIPT>

<BODY bgcolor="cyan">
Hello, I'm a scriptlet called Aggregator!
</BODY>
</HTML>
```

This scriptlet exposes one method **Inherit** and a read-only property called **dynObject**.

```
function CreateAggreg()  {
  this.get_dynObject = get_dynObject;
  this.Inherit = Inherit;
}
```

The method **Inherit** takes an argument which is the **name** of another scriptlet. Then it modifies its body by embedding the specified scriptlet. Let's see an example:

```
<HTML>
<HEAD>
<TITLE>Aggregation Test Page</TITLE>
</HEAD>

<BODY>
<OBJECT id="Scriptlet1" data="Aggreg.htm" type="text/x-scriptlet">
</OBJECT>
</BODY>
</HTML>
```

The above simplest page just includes the **aggreg.htm** scriptlet seen earlier. This scriptlet has no functions of its own. However, it has got a method **Inherit** that allows it to dynamically import functionality from any other scriptlet. For example, let's see how this so far useless scriptlet can absorb the same methods and properties of another one. It suffices that we modify the page this way:

```
<HTML>
<HEAD>
<TITLE>Aggregation Test Page</TITLE>
</HEAD>

<SCRIPT language=VBScript for="window" event="onload">
    MsgBox "Inheriting from Date: " + CStr(Scriptlet1.Inherit( "date.htm" ))
</SCRIPT>

<BODY>
<OBJECT id="Scriptlet1" data="Aggreg.htm" type="text/x-scriptlet">
</OBJECT>
</BODY>
</HTML>
```

318

Now while the page is loading it executes such a line

```
Scriptlet1.Inherit( "date.htm" )
```

This causes the **date.htm** scriptlet to be inserted in the body of the
aggreg.htm scriptlet. This one, therefore, hosts another component and can
access its functions. But how can this be obtained? Through the previously
mentioned **dynObject** property. The following code shows that by clicking on
the document you have the **aggreg.htm** behaving like a date object.
The page is called **testaggr.htm**.

```
<HTML>
<HEAD>
<TITLE>Aggregation Test Page</TITLE>
</HEAD>

<SCRIPT language=VBScript for=window event=onload>
   MsgBox "Inheriting from Date: " + CStr(Scriptlet1.Inherit( "date.htm" ))
</SCRIPT>
```

```
  <SCRIPT language=VBScript for=document event=onclick>
    MsgBox Scriptlet1.dynObject.getFormattedDate(), 0, "Scriptlet1"
  </SCRIPT>
```

```
<BODY>
Click outside the Scriptlet area to get the current date.<br>
<OBJECT id="Scriptlet1" data="Aggreg.htm" type="text/x-scriptlet"
          width=100 height=100>
</OBJECT>
</BODY>
</HTML>
```

Now it's time to turn back to the code of **aggreg.htm**. The method **Inherit**
ends up calling an internal function called **DoInsObject**. It adds an **<OBJECT>**
tag into the body of the scriptlet.

```
Function DoInsObject ( name )
    Set coll = document.all("dynObject")
    if coll Is Nothing  Then
      s1 = "<object id=dynObject data="+name+" type="
      s2 = Chr(34) + "text/x-scriptlet" + Chr(34)
      s3 = " style=display:none></object>"
      s = s1+s2+s3
      document.body.insertAdjacentHTML "AfterBegin", s
      DoInsObject = 1
    else
      DoInsObject = 0
    end if
  End Function
```

The string that actually gets inserted looks like this:

```
<OBJECT id=dynObject data="file.htm" type="text/x-scriptlet"
style=display:none>
</OBJECT>
```

where **file.htm** is the supposed content of the argument **name**. (**file.htm**, of
course will be a scriptlet.) In this example, we choose to make the scriptlet
invisible. However, there's no particular reason for doing so and we could have
sized it any way we chose through the usual **WIDTH** and **HEIGHT** attributes. We
could also consider using the width and the height parameters of the
DoInsObject.

319

In the example seen above the string that gets included through **Inherit** is

```
<OBJECT id=dynObject data="date.htm" type="text/x-scriptlet"
style=display:none>
</OBJECT>
```

The subroutine **DoInsObject** is called via the public method **Inherit** and attempts to add an instance of the given scriptlet each time it gets invoked.

```
function Inherit (name)  {
   return DoInsObject(name);
}
```

This poses an immediate problem that relates to the way we intend to access the inner component.

Accessing the Inner Object

Once we host an external scriptlet, we must figure out a way to make it as accessible as if it were a native object of the main component. The easiest way to do this is to define a specific and new property that evaluates to the inner scriptlet. In the above listing we called it **dynObject**. Of course, it must be a read-only property. Through it, however, we can access and invoke all the features of the incorporated scriptlet. The property **dynObject** is defined this way:

```
function get_dynObject()  {
   return document.all("dynObject");
}
```

dynObject is also the ID we assigned to the added scriptlet.

In the **testaggr.htm** sample, by using **Scriptlet1.Inherit** we force **Scriptlet1** to incorporate another given component whose complete set of functions is made available through **Scriptlet1.dynObject**. The figure shows the page in action.

By making just a brief examination, it's clear that the proposed implementation of **dynObject** poses a potential problem. How do you handle possible multiple calls to **Inherit**? In fact, if you call the method **Inherit** more than once, then it ends up creating a collection of **dynObject** objects. Consequently the following code returns a reference to a collection and not a single object.

```
return document.all("dynObject");
```

Of course, this raises an error when you attempt to call the following code on the container's side

```
MsgBox Scriptlet1.dynObject.getFormattedDate()
```

In fact, to get at least two objects you should resort to something like this instead:

```
MsgBox Scriptlet1.dynObject.item(0).getFormattedDate ()
```

In the next paragraph we'll try to work around this apparent limitation.

Inserting Multiple Scriptlets

To import functionality from more than one scriptlet you can follow two steps:

1) Allow the **Inherit** method to accept a parameter through which you can refer the inserted scriptlet later.
2) Transform **dynObject** from a property to a method, and have it take the name of the referred scriptlet as the argument.

A scriptlet that supports the aggregation of other scriptlets must be done this way. The file is called **aggreg1.htm**.

```
<HTML>
<HEAD>
<TITLE>Aggreg Scriptlet</TITLE>
</HEAD>

<SCRIPT language=VBScript>
  Function DoInsObject( name, id )
    s1 = "<object id="+ id + " "+ "data="+name+" type="
    s2 = Chr(34) + "text/x-scriptlet" + Chr(34)
    s3 = " width=1 height=1></object>"
    s = s1+s2+s3
    document.body.insertAdjacentHTML "AfterBegin", s
    DoInsObject = 1
  End Function
</SCRIPT>

<SCRIPT language=JavaScript>
public_description = new CreateAggreg();
var InScriptlet = (typeof(window.external.version)=="string");

function CreateAggreg() {
  this.dynObject = dynObject;
  this.Inherit = Inherit;
}
```

```
function dynObject(id)  {
  return document.all(id);
}

function Inherit (name, id)  {
  return DoInsObject(name, id);
}
</SCRIPT>

<BODY bgcolor="cyan">
Hello, I'm a scriptlet called Aggreg1!
</BODY>
</HTML>
```

In practice, when a scriptlet is inserted it is no longer given a fixed ID like **dynObject**, but the same ID you specify as an argument of the **Inherit** method. This allows us to recover it easily through a new method called **dynObject** that replaces a previous property with the same name.

```
function dynObject(id)  {
  return document.all(id);
}
```

Let's see a test page for this. The file is called **testagg1.htm**.

```
<HTML>
<HEAD>
<TITLE>Aggregation Test Page</TITLE>
</HEAD>

<SCRIPT language=VBScript for="window" event="onload">
  Scriptlet1.Inherit "date.htm", "First"
  Scriptlet1.Inherit "time.htm", "Second"
</SCRIPT>

<SCRIPT language=VBScript for="document" event="onclick">
  MsgBox Scriptlet1.dynObject("First").getFormattedDate()
  MsgBox Scriptlet1.dynObject("Second").getFormattedTime()
</SCRIPT>

<BODY>
Click outside the Scriptlet area to get the current date.<br>
<OBJECT id="Scriptlet1" data="Aggreg1.htm" type="text/x-scriptlet"
        width=100 height=100>
</OBJECT>
</BODY>
</HTML>
```

It inherits from both **date.htm** and **time.htm**, that is two scriptlets representing exactly what their names suggest. Note that now to call the dynamically added methods we have to specify a string that identifies the component.

```
MsgBox Scriptlet1.dynObject("First").getFormattedDate()
MsgBox Scriptlet1.dynObject("Second").getFormattedTime()
```

A More Articulated Example

So far we inserted a scriptlet but have kept it hidden. In other cases, we want
to create a new scriptlet that maintains and show the user interface of the base
component, plus adding new functionality.

We're enhancing a basic object to make it clone the splitter object we created in
the previous chapter. Now the aggregate scriptlet expands until it covers the
entire area reserved to its parent in the host HTML page.

The following scriptlet is called **aggreg2.htm** and it can inherit from a single
component.

```
<HTML>
<HEAD>
<TITLE>Aggregation Scriptlet</TITLE>
</HEAD>

<SCRIPT language=VBScript for="window" event="onload">
  InitAggreg
</SCRIPT>

<SCRIPT language=VBScript>
  Sub InitAggreg
    document.body.style.margin = "0px"
  End Sub

Function DoInsObject( name )
  w = document.body.clientWidth
  h = document.body.clientHeight
  s1 = "<object id=dynObject "+ "data="+name+" type="
  s2 = Chr(34) + "text/x-scriptlet" + Chr(34)
  s3 = " width="+CStr(w)+" height="+CStr(h)+"></object>"
  s = s1+s2+s3
  document.body.insertAdjacentHTML "AfterBegin", s
End Function
</SCRIPT>

<SCRIPT language=Javascript>
public_description = new CreateAggreg();
var InScriptlet = (typeof(window.external.version)=="string");

function CreateAggreg() {
  this.get_dynObject = get_dynObject;
  this.Inherit = Inherit;
}

function Inherit (name) {
  return DoInsObject(name);
}

function get_dynObject() {
  return document.all("dynObject");
}
</SCRIPT>

<BODY>
</BODY>
</HTML>
```

Now the embedded scriptlet automatically expands to cover the maximum area.
The next figure illustrates a demo page that hosts the **aggreg2.htm** scriptlet.

323

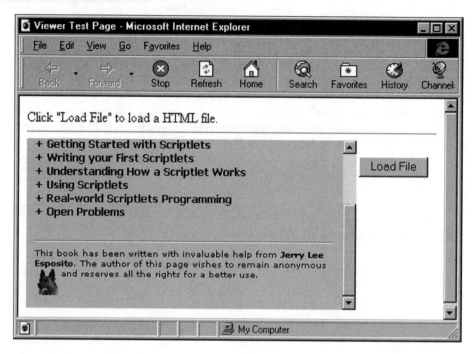

The screenshot shows a scriptlet that inherits the splitter component we've met in the previous chapter. The following listing shows the full source code of the host page. The page is **testvwr1.htm**.

```html
<html>
<head>
<title>Viewer Test Page</title>
</head>

<body>
Click "Load File" to load a HTML file.<hr>
<script language="VBScript" for="window" event="onload">
  View1.Inherit "splitter.htm"
</script>

<script language="VBScript">
Sub DoLoad
  View1.dynObject.File = "demo.htm"
End Sub
</script>

<object id="View1" data="Aggreg2.htm" align="left" width="400" height="200"
        type="text/x-scriptlet">
</object>

<p>
<input type="button" name="Load" value="Load File" language="VBScript"
        onclick="DoLoad">
</p>
</body>
</html>
```

During page loading we inherit from the splitter:

```
<script language="VBScript" for="window" event="onload">
  View1.Inherit "splitter.htm"
</script>
```

From now on the scriptlet inserted in the page through the traditional **<OBJECT>** tag is become quite similar to the splitter we've examined in Chapter 11.

To use the splitter component effectively we need to indicate which HTML file is to be displayed. We must set the **File** property according to the features of the splitter scriptlet. In the example, we force it to display a demo page called **demo.htm**.

```
View1.dynObject.File = "demo.htm"
```

At this point, all that remains to be done is to just see an example of how to add new functionality exploiting the existing methods and properties

Extending the New Scriptlet

What we've got so far is a scriptlet that has been enhanced to absorb both the functions and the user interface of a parent component. When you derive an object from a base component you usually need to customize existing functions, or add new ones for an enhanced behavior.

Now we have a splitter component that only allows you to set the document to view. So why not derive a new scriptlet with, say, a couple of predefined functions to return both the text and the HTML code? The point is, how to access the original scriptlet?

We've inserted it through an **<OBJECT>** tag with an ID of **dynObject**. So the object we need can be obtained via

document.all("dynObject")

Let's see how an enhanced version of the splitter, called **splitt2.htm** looks.

```
<HTML>
<HEAD>
<TITLE>Extended Splitter Scriptlet</TITLE>
</HEAD>

<SCRIPT language=VBScript for="window" event="onload">
  InitAggreg
  DoInsObject "splitter.htm"
</SCRIPT>

<SCRIPT language=VBScript>
  Sub InitAggreg
    document.body.style.margin = "0px"
  End Sub

  Function DoInsObject( name )
    Set coll = document.all("dynObject")
    if coll Is Nothing  Then
      w = document.body.clientWidth
      h = document.body.clientHeight
      s1 = "<object id=dynObject data="+name+" type="
```

```
          s2 = Chr(34) + "text/x-scriptlet" + Chr(34)
          s3 = " width="+CStr(w)+" height="+CStr(h)+"></object>"
          s = s1+s2+s3
          document.body.insertAdjacentHTML "AfterBegin", s
          DoInsObject = 1
      else
          DoInsObject = 0
      end if
  End Function
</SCRIPT>

<SCRIPT language=JavaScript>
public_description = new CreateAggreg();
var InScriptlet = (typeof(window.external.version)=="string");

function CreateAggreg() {
  this.get_dynObject = get_dynObject;
  this.Inherit = Inherit;

  // new functionality
  this.GetText = GetText;
  this.GetHTML = GetHTML;
}

function Inherit (name) {
  return DoInsObject(name);
}

function get_dynObject() {
  return document.all("dynObject");
}

function GetText() {
  return document.all("dynObject").innerDocument.body.innerText;
}

function GetHTML() {
  return document.all("dynObject").innerDocument.body.outerHTML;
}
</SCRIPT>

<BODY>
</BODY>
</HTML>
```

This scriptlet has two new methods: **GetText** and **GetHTML** that return
respectively the text and the HTML code of the page being viewed.
As you should remember, the splitter component also exposes an
innerDocument property that makes the **document** of the hosted file available.
The implementation of **GetText** and **GetHTML** is quite straightforward.

```
function GetText() {
  return document.all("dynObject").innerDocument.body.innerText;
}

function GetHTML() {
  return document.all("dynObject").innerDocument.body.outerHTML;
}
```

They simply access the embedded scriptlet and do the work of returning
innerText and **outerHTML**.

Here's the full source code of a test page called **testsp12.htm**.

```
<html>
<head>
<title>Extended Splitter Test Page</title>
</head>

<body>
Click on "Load HTML" to load a HTML file.<hr>

<script language="VBScript">
Sub DoLoad
  View1.dynObject.File = "demo.htm"
End Sub
</script>

<object id="View1" data="Splitt2.htm" align="left"
        width="400" height="200"
        type="text/x-scriptlet">
</object>

<p>
<input type="button" name="Load" value="Load HTML" language="VBScript"
       onclick="DoLoad">
<input type="button" name="GetText" value="Get Text" language="VBScript"
       onclick="MsgBox View1.GetText()">
<input type="button" name="GetHtml" value="Get HTML" language="VBScript"
       onclick="MsgBox View1.GetHTML()">
</p>
</body>
</html>
```

The next figure shows how this page will look once you've clicked on the Load
HTML button.

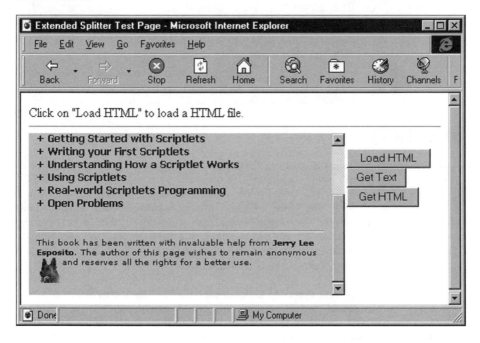

Note that we do need to use a gateway like **dynObject** to access the methods and properties of the base component. In fact, to set the splitter's **File** property we've used code like this:

```
View1.dynObject.File = "demo.htm"
```

Instead, this is not necessary (more, is wrong) when accessing properties and methods defined only by the aggregating object. If we had used:

```
MsgBox View1.dynObject.GetHTML()
```

instead of:

```
MsgBox View1.GetHTML()
```

then we would have got an error. The next figure shows the effect of the Get Text button.

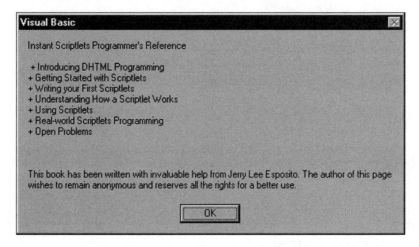

Summary

If you want to design a scriptlet that supports inheritance, then make sure it exposes a read-only property called **dynObject**, or something similar. This property will return a reference to the embedded object. Doing so, after all, is equivalent to making the entire inherited interface automatically public. Omitting such a property simply means that everything you inherit should be treated as private properties. Then it's up to you to decide how, and if, to make them visible to external callers. For example, you can wrap some inherited functions in new methods and expose them as your own.

In this chapter, we attempted to cover topics that at the moment are a bit beyond the traditional documentation. You could also think of it as an advanced use of the current scriptlets features. Our goal was to show you a way of setting up a structured mechanism (even if quite a rudimentary one) that gives us inheritance.

Inheritance is no simple matter, after all. We've shown how to:

- Add new methods to an existing scriptlet dynamically.
- Modify the public interface of a scriptlet at run-time.
- Embed a new scriptlet through its name.

Overall, what we have actually got is a way to incorporate existing functionality from other scriptlets, which is really not all that bad.

Further Reading

To comprehend the scope and the possibility of inheritance and dynamic modification of the interface thoroughly, you also need to know about functions and arrays in JavaScript. There are many books out there that cover the subject—some are better than others. We recommend *Instant JavaScript*, ISBN 1-861001-27-4 from Wrox Press as this covers all you need to know.

Chapter

13

A Dynamic HTML Toolbar

Scriptlets are an efficient way to set up user interface components and make them reusable and self-contained. Due to specialized mouse events it's pretty easy to detect and handle the most common circumstances in the user's activity. As in the Win32 programming world, a family of predefined components is a big help for the Web development community. In addition, DHTML lends itself well to writing active and interactive objects.

In the past chapters, we have discussed several brief examples of components that could enrich your HTML pages—such as expandable text (Chapter 7), bitmapped anchors (Chapter 3), scrollable images (Chapter 5) and many more.

In this section we will build a DHTML toolbar that looks like the IE4 and Windows 9x flat toolbars. In doing so, we will find a way to thoroughly examine how events are fired and received, and how to take advantage of the **<TABLE>** construct and the DHTML collections.

In particular, we're going to cover the most useful and interesting features of

- The HTML **<TABLE>** tag
- The **<IMG>** tag
- DHTML event handling
- The importance of element IDs

Overall, in this chapter we're presenting a complete real-world example of scriptlet programming and also providing you with a fully fledged toolbar ready to use in your own pages.

Designing a Dynamic HTML Toolbar

A toolbar is a window that aligns itself along a given border of a host window and provides buttons to speed up some common operations. A typical feature of a toolbar is that, as a user, you can identify and run functions through small—and sometimes animated—bitmaps. Toolbars have been a regular presence in any desktop Windows application for the last few years. So why not HTML pages?

Since Web pages are evolving from simply static information tables to the more active role of application user interface modules, you should consider them as a new stream of output for your programs. An HTML page is more and more comparable with a dialog box or a traditional window and should, therefore, be ready to host any feature of a desktop software component. The toolbar is the first in line for the following reasons:

- A Web page provides functions to choose
- A Web page will tend to fuse to desktop applications

From the beginning of the World Wide Web, an HTML page has offered a lot of interactive functionality, most of which was implemented through hyperlinks. Then things evolved and images (including animated images) have become the rule on all Web-based projects. Through images developers can set up colorful and attractive interfaces for the users. For example, by clicking a question mark you can get more information, or clicking on a picture of a hard-drive you can start a download operation.

There was a great effort to create a user interface that looked like the one we were all used to in Windows. HTML's basic immobility (the fact that it is fundamentally static and read-only), however, has proved a significant drawback. All the possible changes and all the possible ways to gain interactivity and action must be coded in advance. The only possible way to do this is to exploit animated logos or specialized controls.

A completely new range of choices and opportunities are made available by DHTML. Now the HTML page is composed of objects whose state may vary quite a bit during user activity. Put another way, now the users (and the programmers) have the chance to create user interface objects that are akin to those we find in any desktop Windows program.

What are Toolbars?

Many HTML pages present a strip of pseudo-buttons along the top of the page. A classic example of this can be found on the Microsoft site. There, we can see commands that refer to permanently-enabled functions such as Write Us or Search, Support, Products and so on and so forth. The next screenshot shows what we mean.

If you look at the source code for such a page, you'll realize that what appears to be a black ribbon of strings is actually a **<TABLE>** tag and, therefore, any item in there is a table cell. Given this, it's fairly easy to code a self-contained component, such as a scriptlet, that encapsulates all this functionality.

When rewriting existing pieces of HTML or DHTML code in the form of scriptlets, we must always keep in mind that scriptlets aren't windowless yet. This means that any reference to the **window** object that could exist in the scriptlet's source code actually points to an inner window object and not directly to the host page. Using pure DHTML code allows you to draw on the straight container page. This fact sometimes poses difficulties. Typically, this difference prevents us from having transparent backgrounds in the scriptlets.

Speaking in terms of Win32 programming—a toolbar is a collection of buttons. The displayed bitmaps are frames of a longer strip of bitmaps. In some cases elements are also taken from an image list. A toolbar is not a collection of button controls, as you might suppose. Instead, it is a window whose content is drawn as if it was given by a real series of buttons. Similarly, a toolbar in HTML is a collection of images and by using a table we can seamlessly display them as a strip.

The TABLE tag

Turning back to the code of the page illustrated above, let's examine it and see how it can be enhanced.

```
<TABLE WIDTH="100%" CELLPADDING=0 CELLSPACING=0 BORDER=0 bordercolor=yellow
  BGCOLOR=BLACK>
<TR>
  <TD WIDTH=459 ROWSPAN=2 VALIGN=TOP
      NOWRAP onmouseover="turnRed()" onmouseout="turnWhite()"><NOBR>
      <FONT FACE="Arial, Helvetica" SIZE=1><A HREF="/">
      <IMG SRC="home.gif" WIDTH=103 HEIGHT=21 ALT="Microsoft Home" BORDER=0></
A>
      <IMG SRC="prod.gif" WIDTH=81 HEIGHT=21 ALT="Products" BORDER=0></A>
      <IMG SRC="search.gif" WIDTH=68 HEIGHT=21 ALT="Search" BORDER=0></A>
      <IMG SRC="support.gif" WIDTH=74 HEIGHT=21 ALT="Support" BORDER=0></A>
      <IMG SRC="shop.gif" WIDTH=55 HEIGHT=21 ALT="Shop" BORDER=0></A>
      <IMG SRC="write.gif" WIDTH=78 HEIGHT=21 ALT="Write Us" BORDER=0></A>
      </FONT></NOBR>
  </TD>

  <TD BGCOLOR="#000000" WIDTH="100%" HEIGHT=20>
      <IMG SRC="1ptrans.gif" WIDTH=1 HEIGHT=1 ALT="" BORDER=0></TD>
  <TD WIDTH=91 ROWSPAN=2 ALIGN=RIGHT VALIGN=TOP>
      <FONT FACE="Arial, Helvetica" SIZE=1><A HREF="/" TARGET="_top">
      <IMG SRC="msft.gif" WIDTH=91 HEIGHT=21 ALT="Microsoft Home" BORDER=0></A>
      </FONT></TD>
  </TR>
  </TABLE>
```

If you have access to Microsoft's pictures, this first block of code produces the output you can see in the following figure.

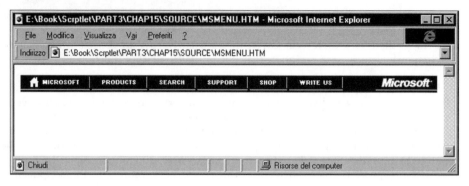

The code has been cleaned up and all the portions that referred to the server specific features have been removed, although the pictures themselves and their hyperlinks remain. What remains is the code that is of interest to us—the toolbar's implementation. The toolbar is nothing more than a `<TABLE>` tag enriched with images and some necessary anchors. The code above is pure DHTML. When you specify that the table should have:

```
WIDTH=100%
```

then this setting really applies to the whole available horizontal space. However, in the case of scriptlets it only applies to the site assigned to the component.

Why Use a Table?

Using a table gives us a lot of more flexibility. First of all, we can decide on the text alignment of any cell. Furthermore, tables offer automatic borders and can contain any kind of HTML data. Undoubtedly, using a table instead of concatenated text makes formatting a lot easier.

Making the Toolbar Interactive

Displaying something that more or less resembles a toolbar is fairly simple, making it interactive requires a bit of DHTML programming. Let's see an example of what you can do. The code shown next is taken from the HTML code for a standard Microsoft toolbar.

```
<!--TOOLBAR_START-->
<SCRIPT LANGUAGE="JScript">
<!--
function turnRed() {
what = window.event.srcElement;
if (what.tagName == "IMG") {
  what.src = what.src.substring(0,(what.src.indexOf(".gif"))) + "-red.gif";
  window.event.cancelBubble = true;
  }
}

function turnWhite () {
what = window.event.srcElement
if (what.tagName == "IMG") {
  what.src = what.src.substring(0,(what.src.indexOf("-red.gif"))) + ".gif";
  window.event.cancelBubble = true;
```

```
        }
    }
    //-->
    </SCRIPT>
```

In a previous code snippet, we encountered lines like these:

```
<TD WIDTH=459 ROWSPAN=2 VALIGN=TOP NOWRAP
    onmouseover="turnRed()" onmouseout="turnWhite()">
```

As you can see, there are two JavaScript procedures linked to two basic mouse events such as **onmouseover** and **onmouseout**. The source code for these functions is listed above. Basically, it consists of a dynamic replacement of the **src** attribute for the underlying **<IMG>** tag. Once the procedure detects the **onmouseover** event it verifies that the element involved has an **<IMG>** tag and then adds a **-red** suffix to its file name. In practice, if the original file was named **prod.gif**, then when the mouse passes over the specified HTML image element, the image to display becomes **prod-red.gif**. The original setting is then restored when the mouse exits. Changing the **src** attribute of an **<IMG>** tag results in an immediate change on the screen. The final result is a toolbar that indicates when one of its elements enters or exits a hot or a selected state.

Our goal here is a bit more ambitious: we would like to produce a DHTML toolbar with much the same look and feel as the Internet Explorer 4.0 top-level toolbars. By combining the DHTML object model with the power of the **<TABLE>** construct then we are almost certain of success.

Showing and Hiding Cells

A toolbar has a variable number of buttons or items. You can add them once for all and even modify its layout at run-time. Putting a scriptlet toolbar into an HTML sample page is as simple as typing in the following code:

```
<HTML>
<BODY>
<OBJECT id="Toolbar1" data="Toolbar.htm" width=120 height=240
        type="text/x-scriptlet">
</OBJECT>
</BODY>
</HTML>
```

Of course, this creates an empty toolbar assuming that the toolbar is implemented in the **toolbar.htm** file. This code looks much simpler and more readable than the code we examined above which was taken from the Microsoft pages. Creating a toolbar as a scriptlet, however, poses an additional problem— how to get the toolbar to grow and host the desired number of items. In fact, when you write a DHTML page you know how many buttons you need to implement and you can design the table accordingly. On the other hand, if you're developing a general component then you might be using it in several different contexts and so you should be ready to design a flexible object that can be adapted quickly and easily to the specific needs.

A typical—and indispensable—feature is that the toolbar should provide a method to allow the users to add (and possibly remove) new items. Put in terms of DHTML, this means that we need to figure out a way to programmatically add new cells to a given table.

Adding New Cells

A possible way to build a table is by concatenating pieces of text in order to format a series of **<TD>** tags. The following is a possible code snippet for adding a new cell to the DHTML toolbar.

```
function DoAddItem( img_n, img_h, img_d, img_g ) {
   s1 = "<IMG id=item src="+img_n+" normal="+img_n+" hot="+img_h+" gray="+img_g
   s2 = " down="+img_d+" pos="+mItemCount+"></IMG>";
   document.all("Row").innerHTML += s1+s2;
   mItemCount ++;
   return;
}
```

We have a function accepting as arguments the names of four files that will be used to render the four basic states of a toolbar item. A toolbar item can be in a normal, selected, grayed or pressed state. In particular, when the button is under the mouse, the 'hot' state is selected and indicates that the button is clickable. This behavior is typical of the new flat toolbar boasted by Internet Explorer 4.0 and the 95 family of Microsoft products. Based on the above code, all this data originates a DHTML code like this:

```
<IMG id=item src=img_n normal=img_n hot=img_h gray=img_g down=img_d pos=X></
IMG>
```

where the items in italic are the actual file names to use and the X is the ordinal number of the toolbar item we're referring to. It will be 1 for the first item, and so forth. As you can see we're saving all this specific information through non-standard attributes of the **<IMG>** tag such as **normal**, **hot**, and the like.

The code above also locates an element with an ID of **Row**. This element might correspond to a **<TD>** tag. Initially, the inner HTML code is empty and is then replaced by the strings seen above. This is a possible HTML body for the scriptlet.

```
<BODY>
  <TABLE WIDTH=100% BGCOLOR="#C0C0C0">
  <TR>
    <TD ROWSPAN=2 id=Row>
    <!-The code inserted through DoAddItem goes here-->
    </TD>
  </TR>
  </TABLE>
</BODY>
```

Each time you add an item to the toolbar a string like the one shown above is inserted at the end of the **<TD>** body.

We will discuss the details in a while. For now, let's remember that we need to associate non-standard information with an **<IMG>** tag. This non-standard information is new and specific attributes that characterize a toolbar item in terms of an image. In the lines above, in fact, we assigned special attributes such as:

- normal
- hot
- gray
- down
- pos

to a traditional HTML image. To build an object like the Microsoft toolbar you don't need to resort to such complications, but a simpler:

```
<IMG id=item src=img_n>
</IMG>
```

will suffice. Instead, additional information is needed to create flat toolbars like the Office 97 ones just because we want to manage more states for each item and consequently need more images for each item.

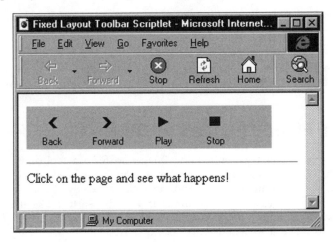

The screenshot represents the output produced by the following HTML source code:

```
<HTML>
<HEAD>
<TITLE>Fixed-Layout Toolbar Test Page</TITLE>
</HEAD>

<SCRIPT language=VBscript for="window" event="onload">
  Menu1.AddItem "Back", "Prev_N.gif", "Prev_H.gif", "Prev_D.gif", "Prev_G.gif"
  Menu1.AddItem "Forward", "Next_N.gif", "Next_H.gif", "Next_D.gif",
"Next_G.gif"
  Menu1.AddItem "Play", "Play_N.gif", "Play_H.gif", "Play_D.gif", "Play_G.gif"
  Menu1.AddItem "Stop", "Stop_N.gif", "Stop_H.gif", "Stop_D.gif", "Stop_G.gif"
</SCRIPT>

<BODY>
<OBJECT id="Toolbar1" data="Toolbar.htm" width=300 height=60 type="text/x-
scriptlet">
</OBJECT>
```

```
<HR>
Click on the page and see what happens!
</BODY>
</HTML>
```

Our toolbar has four buttons denoting part of a classic VCR-like interface. For each of them we invoke a scriptlet's method called **AddItem**. It takes as arguments the name of the images that will denote its four different states— normal, selected, grayed and pressed. In the Microsoft example, the name of the file for each state different from normal is identified by a special naming convention (that is, adding a **-red** suffix to the actual file name). Here we could do the same, but we have chosen to pass all the names required on the command line. However, a possible convention might be to have the file name followed by

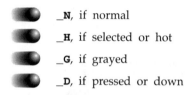

_N, if normal

_H, if selected or hot

_G, if grayed

_D, if pressed or down

as shown above. The file **toolbar.htm**—referenced in the listing—is what we have to examine right away. For now you got an idea of what we're aiming to produce.

Using a Fixed Number of Cells

Concatenating **<TD>** tags embedding images to form a toolbar is just a possible approach. We could use a fixed maximum number of cells as well. Whichever way you do it, the underlying handling code is exactly the same. We'll examine briefly what changes have to be made if you choose to make use of a fixed and maximum number of table cells. Next, we'll concentrate on what is required to make a toolbar behave as expected.

If we utilize a fixed table construct then we predefine the entire **<TABLE>** tag in the scriptlet's body and then use (or don't use) the cells as necessary. To avoid nasty user interface effects we also hide the **<IMG>** tags we aren't using. For example, the body of such a toolbar scriptlet might look like this

```
<BODY>
<TABLE WIDTH=100% BGCOLOR="#C0C0C0">
<TR id=Row>
  <TD ALIGN=center>
    <IMG style="display:none" id=item pos=1 src=""><BR>
    <FONT size="1" face="MS Sans Serif">
    <SPAN id=text></SPAN></IMG></FONT></TD>
  <TD ALIGN=center>
    <IMG style="display:none" id=item pos=2 src=""><BR>
    <FONT size="1" face="MS Sans Serif">
    <SPAN id=text></SPAN></IMG></FONT></TD>
  <TD ALIGN=center>
    <IMG style="display:none" id=item  pos=3 src=""><BR>
    <FONT size="1" face="MS Sans Serif">
    <SPAN id=text></SPAN></IMG></FONT></TD>
  <TD ALIGN=center>
```

```
        <IMG style="display:none" id=item  pos=4 src=""><BR>
        <FONT size="1" face="MS Sans Serif">
        <SPAN id=text></SPAN></IMG></FONT></TD>
    <TD ALIGN=center>
        <IMG style="display:none" id=item  pos=5 src=""><BR>
        <FONT size="1" face="MS Sans Serif">
        <SPAN id=text></SPAN></IMG></FONT></TD>
    <TD ALIGN=center>
        <IMG style="display:none" id=item  pos=6 src=""><BR>
        <FONT size="1" face="MS Sans Serif">
        <SPAN id=text></SPAN></IMG></FONT></TD>
    <TD ALIGN=center>
        <IMG style="display:none" id=item  pos=7 src=""><BR>
        <FONT size="1" face="MS Sans Serif">
        <SPAN id=text></SPAN></IMG></FONT></TD>
    <TD ALIGN=center>
        <IMG style="display:none" id=item  pos=8 src=""><BR>
        <FONT size="1" face="MS Sans Serif">
        <SPAN id=text></SPAN></IMG></FONT></TD>
    <TD ALIGN=center>
        <IMG style= display:none" id=item  pos=9 src=""><BR>
        <FONT size="1" face="MS Sans Serif">
        <SPAN id=text></SPAN></IMG></FONT></TD>
    <TD ALIGN=center>
        <IMG style="display:none" id=item  pos=10 src=""><BR>
        <FONT size="1" face="MS Sans Serif">
        <SPAN id=text></SPAN></IMG></FONT></TD>
</TR>
</TABLE>
</BODY>
```

The table has a **WIDTH** attribute set to 100% and this means that the toolbar will cover the entire width of the scriptlet's window. The table has a single row of cells identified by the **Row** string, which is the tag's **id**. Any toolbar button is rendered through the following **<TD>**:

```
<TD ALIGN=center>
    <IMG style="display:none" id=item pos=1 src=""><BR>
    <FONT size="1" face="MS Sans Serif">
    <SPAN id=text></SPAN></IMG></FONT></TD>
```

The image is initially hidden, but has an **id** of **item**. The only special feature is the **pos** attribute set to the index number of the item. We decided to have these numbers start from 1. Furthermore, we have a short string of text to denote the label of the button. These strings are identified through an **id** of "**text**". The block is completed by the font specifications that contribute to making this DHTML toolbar as similar as possible to the standard Win32 common control.

Implementation Differences?

Let's consider some differences between having an empty table that grows as long as you add **<TD>** tags or fixed layout table. Notice that the two solutions discussed so far produce the same HTML code—but in the first case it is more difficult to get a label to appear centered below the image, as shown in the last figure.

When we approached the problem of creating a DHTML toolbar, our first idea was to make it dynamically expandable through a new **<TD>** tag for each new button. This solution worked well enough but it does have a drawback—it's quite impossible to add a text label below the button. You might expect the text to appear there if you just concatenate it to the **<IMG>** tag and place a break in the middle. Feel free to try it, but it simply doesn't work!

However, the same code works perfectly—and allows you to put text labels—if you just define the table at design-time. This is the second approach that requires you to fix a maximum number of buttons to be made visible as soon as you need them.

However, as we're going to demonstrate, there's a strategic error in the background. Conceptually, an element of a table is no different from a new HTML page. So you should be able to format it without affecting the other cells. If this is not happening, there's something wrong somewhere.

In the rest of the chapter, we'll define the programming interface of our DHTML toolbar and build it from scratch—learning from previous errors. By the end, we'll have a component that is easier to use than the previously mentioned Microsoft toolbar and, above all else, a reusable HTML object. Once we've created a horizontal toolbar we'll make it vertical for our grand finale!

The Toolbar Programming Interface

There are a minimum set of functions any toolbar should provide. Among them, you will certainly find a method to add new buttons and other methods to manipulate the text labels and the state of each item. In addition, any button should present itself differently according to its internal state. This means a set of bitmaps to reflect the various stages. The following is a table of the functions that our DHTML toolbar will provide.

Function	Description
addItem()	Adds a new button to the toolbar. You specify the text label and the four bitmaps to reflect the various states: normal, selected, pressed and grayed.
getState()	Returns a boolean value to denote whether the specified item is enabled or disabled. The items are identified by their ordinal 0-based position. We can't define this attribute through a property because we need an additional argument (the index) for both the *get* and the *put* function.
setState()	Sets the current state of the button through a boolean value corresponding to the given 0-based index. The state can be enabled or disabled.
getTitle()	Returns the text label that corresponds to the specified button. Again, the item is identified via a 0-based index.
setTitle()	Sets a new text label for the given button.
cursor	Sets a string property that refers to a standard shape for the mouse cursor. Feasible values are those valid for the DHTML **style** object.

Function	Description
`onitemclick`	Event raised when a toolbar button has been clicked.
`onitemdown`	This event is fired when a toolbar button has been pressed and is drawn in the down state.
`onitemhot`	Event raised when the mouse has just entered the area relating to a given toolbar button.
`onitemout`	Event raised when the mouse has just left the area relating to a given toolbar button.

Those shown above are a small but sufficient set of functions. Others that you might want to implement include removing buttons, assigning them non-standard IDs, drawing separators, toggling text labels on and off, tooltips and so on. Plus, there might be other, merely 'cosmetic', functionality that you wish to add. For example, you could dynamically modify and decide the background color, the cell spacing, the color and the thickness of the border and even the docking capability or the capacity to automatically cover the entire width of the parent's client area.

Once we've coded our simple toolbar, we have really covered all the basic difficulties. Thus, you can improve the example to make it much more attractive and powerful.

Our DHTML Toolbar

As mentioned earlier, we have so far followed the wrong approach to get a scriptlet working as a toolbar. In fact, we've always considered the toolbar as a `<TABLE>` object and defined it in the body of the scriptlet itself. This is not flexible enough and only works in the short term. If you aren't using text labels, then you could easily add new table columns as long as you need them. We showed this code earlier, in the section "Adding New Cells".

Concatenating `<TD>` tags and inserting them in a predefined table row causes a problem that leads us to get a table that actually has just one single column! In fact, to insert HTML text we need an element that supports `innerHTML` or `insertAdjacentHTML` methods. Unfortunately, neither `<TABLE>` nor `<TR>` recognize them!

If we write code like this:

```
<TABLE id=Table>
<TR Id=Row>
:
</TR>
</TABLE>
```

and then attempt to invoke `innerHTML` or `insertAdjacentHTML` on a `<TABLE>` or `<TR>` element we get an error. Such methods, in fact, aren't supported. So we need to use a `<TD>` or a `<DIV>` element to wrap all the columns.

341

```
<TABLE id=Table>
<TR >
  <TD id=Row>
   :
  </TD>
</TR>
</TABLE>
```

and this results in the table having a single column, which in turn divides up into **n** other columns. So if you use break **
** tags you shift all the text down and not just a single cell.

The problem is caused by the wrapper element. However, if we don't use it, we don't have a handle to insert new and dynamic HTML text.

To work around this we could use tables with a fixed number of rows and columns, showing and hiding the cells as needed. This works well, but does lack something in terms of elegance and flexibility.

The Scriptlet's Body

The approach that uses a fixed table works better because we can define an HTML table with a standard and correct structure.

```
<TABLE id=Table>
<TR>
  <TD>...</TD>
   :
  <TD>...</TD>
</TR>
</TABLE>
```

We could hard-code this in a scriptlet, or even better, create the entire table dynamically—including the **<TABLE>** and the **<TR>** elements.

Our scriptlet, therefore, must have a completely empty body. Calling **AddItem** doesn't change anything in the scriptlet structure and user interface: it just formats a string with all the **<TD>** tags. Then, by calling a new method **SetButtons**, we give the scriptlet a body like the one shown above. So we have created an HTML table dynamically, according to our actual and real needs.

The listing doesn't include the various procedures yet, but does show the layout of the toolbar scriptlet.

```
<HTML>
<HEAD>
<TITLE>Toolbar Scriptlet</TITLE>
</HEAD>

<SCRIPT language=VBScript for="window" event="onload">
  InitToolbar
</SCRIPT>

<SCRIPT language=VBScript for="document" event="onmouseover">
</SCRIPT>
```

```
<SCRIPT language=VBScript for="document" event="onmousedown">
</SCRIPT>

<SCRIPT language=VBScript for="document" event="onmouseup">
</SCRIPT>

<SCRIPT language=VBScript for="document" event="onmouseout">
</SCRIPT>

<SCRIPT language=VBScript>
  Sub InitToolbar
    document.body.style.margin = "0px"
  End Sub
</SCRIPT>


<SCRIPT language=JScript>
public_description = new CreateToolbar();
var InScriptlet = (typeof(window.external.version)=="string");
var mItemCount = 0;
var mCursor = "";
var mItems = "";

function CreateToolbar()  {
  this.AddItem = DoAddItem;
  this.SetButtons = DoSetButtons;
  this.get_Cursor = DoGetCursor;
  this.put_Cursor = DoSetCursor;
  this.GetState = DoGetState;
  this.GetTitle = DoGetTitle;
  this.SetState = DoSetState;
  this.SetTitle = DoSetTitle;

  this.event_OnItemClick = "";
  this.event_OnItemDown = "";
  this.event_OnItemHot = "";
  this.event_OnItemOut = "";
}
</SCRIPT>

<BODY>
</BODY>
</HTML>
```

Properties of a Toolbar Item

A toolbar item has a series of specific attributes such as state, position or
command ID, and the various images corresponding to the different internal
states.

```
function DoAddItem(text, img_n, img_h, img_d, img_g)  {
  mItemCount ++;
  s0 = "<TD ALIGN=center>"
  s1 = "<IMG id=item src="+img_n+" normal="+img_n+" hot="+img_h+" gray="+img_g
  s2 = " down="+img_d+" state=1 pos="+mItemCount+" alt=\""+text+"\""
  s3 = " align=absmiddle></IMG>";
  s4 = "<BR><SPAN id=text><FONT FACE=\"Ms Sans Serif\" SIZE=1>"+text
  s5 = "</BR></SPAN></FONT></TD>"
  mItems += s0+s1+s2+s3+s4+s5;
  return 1;
}
```

The code shows what happens when a user attempts to add a new item to the toolbar. The final result is that we format a global string **mItems** given by the concatenation of the following blocks of HTML code:

```
<TD ALIGN=center>
   <IMG id=item src="…" normal = "…" hot="…" down="…" gray="…"
        state=1 pos="…" alt="…" align=absmiddle>
   </IMG>
   <BR>
   <SPAN id=text><FONT FACE="MS Sans Serif" SIZE=1>
   …
   </SPAN>
   </BR></FONT>
</TD>
```

Any cell is centered horizontally and is made up of an image and some text. All the images have an **id** of '*item*' and all the texts have '*text*' as their global identifier. The presence of a **
** tag causes the label to appear under the image. However, by omitting the **
** tag you can have a list-toolbar, just like the ones shown by Internet Explorer 4.0. (See the Internet Explorer 4.0 *Links* toolbar, below for a concrete example.)

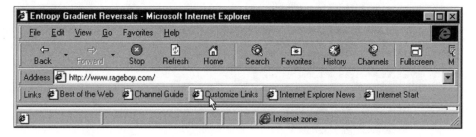

The text is drawn with the Windows standard font—which is the MS Sans Serif, 8-point size. The **<IMG>** tag defines new and specific attributes to keep track of the information associated with any toolbar item. In particular, the **pos** attribute uniquely identifies the button. It is an integer value that starts with 1. All the events related to the toolbar items use this convention to refer to a specific button. For example, the event fired when the 3rd button has been pressed and released (that is a click occurred), contains as an argument the value of **pos** for that element. By using it, a container page that hosts such a toolbar can detect which button caused the click event. Finally, **state** denotes whether the button is active or not.

Internal Collections

Having a certain number of items with the same ID means that you have created a custom collection of objects.

```
Set cItems = document.all("item")
Set cTexts = document.all("text")
```

This code returns two collections, pointing respectively to the **<IMG>** and the labels (identified by **<SPAN>** elements) of the toolbar. We'll be using them to return and set the button labels text and the state.

Detecting the Right Events

Our goal is to have a toolbar that works just like a flat Internet Explorer 4.0 toolbar. This is a result that we can achieve by combining the proper images with the right mouse events.

The picture above shows four sample images for a "Play" button. The first frame is a flat button with the symbol in the middle. The second and third frames show how the button will appear when the mouse passes over it—making it selected—and when the button is clicked. The final frame renders the button when it is disabled and unavailable to the user. To get a more attractive effect you might want to choose a monochrome image for the normal and disabled state and a colorful palette for the others.

There are four events to hook for:

- `onmouseover`
- `onmousedown`
- `onmouseup`
- `onmouseout`

The first one indicates that the mouse is moving over a given button, so you might want to change the bitmap to reflect that the item is now selectable. This is also a good time to set a new cursor—say, a pointing finger.

onmousedown and **onmouseup** are raised to notify that the button has been clicked down and up. At this point, you can still change the source of the `<IMG>` tag. At last, when the **onmouseout** arrives then it's time to restore the original bitmap—the one for the normal state.

```vbscript
<SCRIPT language=VBScript for="document" event="onmouseover">
  if window.event.srcElement.id="item" then
    if window.event.srcElement.state=1 Then
      Set cItems = document.all("item")
      window.event.srcElement.style.cursor = mCursor
      window.event.srcElement.src = cItems.item(window.event.srcElement.pos-
1).hot
      fireEvent "OnItemHot"
    end if
    window.event.cancelBubble = True
  end if
</SCRIPT>

<SCRIPT language=VBScript for="document" event="onmousedown">
  if window.event.srcElement.id="item" then
    if window.event.srcElement.state=1 Then
      Set cItems = document.all("Item")
      window.event.srcElement.src = cItems.item(window.event.srcElement.pos-
1).down
      fireEvent "OnItemDown"
    end if
    window.event.cancelBubble = True
  end if
</SCRIPT>
```

```
<SCRIPT language=VBScript for="document" event="onmouseup">
  if window.event.srcElement.id="item" then
    if window.event.srcElement.state=1 Then
      Set cItems = document.all("Item")
      window.event.srcElement.src = cItems.item(window.event.srcElement.pos-
1).hot
      fireEvent "OnItemClick"
    end if
    window.event.cancelBubble = True
  end if
</SCRIPT>

<SCRIPT language=VBScript for="document" event="onmouseout">
  if window.event.srcElement.id="item" then
    if window.event.srcElement.state=1 Then
      Set cItems = document.all("Item")
      window.event.srcElement.style.cursor = ""
      window.event.srcElement.src = cItems.item(window.event.srcElement.pos-
1).normal
      fireEvent "OnItemOut"
    end if
    window.event.cancelBubble = True
  end if
</SCRIPT>
```

The event must be caught at the document level, but afterwards we need to check for the ID of the element that originated the event. We do this through the **window.event.srcElement.id**. For the **onmouseover** event, for example, we could set a different cursor.

```
window.event.srcElement.style.cursor = mCursor
```

To change the actual bitmap displayed you simply access the image involved via its ID.

```
window.event.srcElement.src = cItems.item(window.event.srcElement.pos-1).hot
```

We use a -1 because any collection starts from 0, while the values for the **pos** attribute start from 1. If required, we fire an event to the container page. The value passed as an argument is the position, or the command ID, for the button.

```
function fireEvent (ev_name) {
  if( InScriptlet && !window.external.frozen ) {
    window.external.raiseEvent( ev_name, window.event.srcElement.pos );
  }
}
```

A container page which intercepts such events could easily assign a certain behavior to any button.

Identifying the Item Underneath the Mouse

By executing this kind of code for such events you can easily reproduce the flat-style of the most recent toolbars. In this implementation of the toolbar we have chosen to associate any possible contextual information directly with the images. Note that we detect all the events when they reach the **document** object. So the first step to take is to make sure that the specified mouse event is one which is of great interest to us. Due to the structure of the body—given by an HTML table—if the source element of the event is an **<IMG>** tag then we can be certain that the event involves one of the toolbar buttons.

Now the problem is, which button? We have two possible approaches. The first one is a sort of brute-force approach. It consists of defining an event handler for each possible button. Of course, this solution requires lots of code and, furthermore, must be coded dynamically as long as you add new buttons.

A better way to do this is to assign the image itself an identifier that looks like the command ID of the Win32 toolbar's items. In this way—whatever the highlighted button—once we get its reference we can seamlessly ask it for the command ID given by the **pos** attribute.

Working around this obstacle smooths the way ahead to a complete and functional implementation of our DHTML toolbar.

Firing Events to the Container

The only event that we really need to raise is the click on a button. For the sake of completeness we could let the host environment know about each single change of state that involves any button. As already mentioned, these events all relate to the mouse movements over and out of the various cells. In any case, we are always forced to pass the unique identifier of the button—our own **pos** attribute. The events indicate when a button becomes selectable, when it is held down, when it gets released, and when the mouse leaves its area.

Coding a Click Event

In our implementation, we don't just want a click event to be triggered. If so, we could have detected the specific **onclick** event at the scriptlet's document level and forwarded it to the host page to let it know that the button was clicked. A more flexible way to arrange all the event handling is by coding the click event ourselves. Logically, a click is produced by an **onmouseup** event that follows an **onmousedown** notification. If you aren't convinced, then think of what happens in Windows at the SDK programming level. You don't have a "**mouse button-click**" event, just "**mouse button-down**" and "**mouse button-up**" messages. The click is a sort of abstraction built on top of these two basic events.

Thus, in our toolbar's implementation we fire an **onitemclick** event only when we catch an **onmouseup** event on the specified button. However, we couldn't have relied on the standard **onclick** event alone, because we must pass some specific data down to the container page. The basic DHTML event, in fact, is a simple notification and doesn't include any arguments.

To fire our events, we're using a helper routine (the source code is shown above) that always assumes it is invoked after an event caused by an image element with a **pos** attribute defined.

The Complete Toolbar

At this point we can take a closer look at the complete source code for the toolbar. The file is **toolbar.htm**.

```
<HTML>
<HEAD>
<TITLE>Toolbar Scriptlet</TITLE>
</HEAD>

<SCRIPT language=VBScript for="window" event="onload">
  InitToolbar
</SCRIPT>

<SCRIPT language=VBScript for="document" event="onmouseover">
  if window.event.srcElement.id="item" then
    if window.event.srcElement.state Then
      Set cItems = document.all("item")
      window.event.srcElement.style.cursor = mCursor
      window.event.srcElement.src = cItems.item(window.event.srcElement.pos-
1).hot
      fireEvent "OnItemHot"
    end if
    window.event.cancelBubble = True
  end if
</SCRIPT>

<SCRIPT language=VBScript for="document" event="onmousedown">
  if window.event.srcElement.id="item" then
    if window.event.srcElement.state Then
      Set cItems = document.all("Item")
      window.event.srcElement.src = cItems.item(window.event.srcElement.pos-
1).down
      fireEvent "OnItemDown"
    end if
    window.event.cancelBubble = True
  end if
</SCRIPT>

<SCRIPT language=VBScript for="document" event="onmouseup">
  if window.event.srcElement.id="item" then
    if window.event.srcElement.state Then
      Set cItems = document.all("Item")
      window.event.srcElement.src = cItems.item(window.event.srcElement.pos-
1).hot
      fireEvent "OnItemClick"
    end if
    window.event.cancelBubble = True
  end if
</SCRIPT>

<SCRIPT language=VBScript for="document" event="onmouseout">
  if window.event.srcElement.id="item" then
    if window.event.srcElement.state Then
      Set cItems = document.all("Item")
      window.event.srcElement.style.cursor = ""
      window.event.srcElement.src = cItems.item(window.event.srcElement.pos-
1).normal
      fireEvent "OnItemOut"
    end if
    window.event.cancelBubble = True
  end if
</SCRIPT>

<SCRIPT language=VBScript>
```

```
   Sub InitToolbar
     document.body.style.margin = "0px"
   End Sub
</SCRIPT>

<SCRIPT language=JavaScript>
public_description = new CreateToolbar ();
var InScriptlet = (typeof(window.external.version)=="string");
var mItemCount = 0;
var mCursor = "";
var mItems = "";

function CreateToolbar () {
  this.AddItem = DoAddItem;
  this.SetButtons = DoSetButtons;
  this.get_Cursor = DoGetCursor;
  this.put_Cursor = DoSetCursor;
  this.GetState = DoGetState;
  this.GetTitle = DoGetTitle;
  this.SetState = DoSetState;
  this.SetTitle = DoSetTitle;

  this.event_OnItemClick = "";
  this.event_OnItemHot = "";
  this.event_OnItemOut = "";
  this.event_OnItemDown = "";
}

// AddItem method
function DoAddItem(text, img_n, img_h, img_d, img_g) {
  mItemCount ++;
  s0 = "<TD ALIGN=center>"
  s1 = "<IMG id=item src="+img_n+" normal="+img_n+" hot="+img_h+" gray="+img_g
  s2 = " down="+img_d+" state=1 pos="+mItemCount+" alt=\""+text+"\"";
  s3 = " align=absmiddle></IMG>";
  s4 = "<BR><FONT FACE=\"Ms Sans Serif\" SIZE=1><SPAN id=text>"+text
  s5 = "</SPAN></FONT></BR></TD>"
  mItems += s0+s1+s2+s3+s4+s5;
  return 1;
}


// SetButtons method
function DoSetButtons() {
  s0 = "<TABLE bgcolor=#C0C0C0><TR>";
  s1 = "</TR></TABLE>";
  document.body.insertAdjacentHTML( "AfterBegin", s0+mItems+s1 );
}

// CURSOR Property
function DoGetCursor() {
  return mCursor;
}
function DoSetCursor( curs ) {
  mCursor = curs;
  return 1;
}

// GetState method
function DoGetState(item) {
  cItems = document.all("Item");
  return cItems.item(item-1).state;
}

// SetState method
function DoSetState(item, bState) {
  cItems = document.all("Item");
  cTexts = document.all("Text");
```

```
    cItems.item(item-1).state = bState;
    if( bState ) {
      cItems.item(item-1).src = cItems.item(item-1).normal;
      cTexts.item(item-1).style.color = "";
    }
    else {
      cItems.item(item-1).src = cItems.item(item-1).gray
      cTexts.item(item-1).style.color = "gray";
    }
    return 1;
  }

  // GetTitle method
  function DoGetTitle(item)  {
    cTexts = document.all("Text");
    return cTexts(item-1).innerText;
  }

  // SetTitle method
  function DoSetTitle(item, text)  {
    if( text.length==0 )
      text = " ";

    cTexts = document.all("Text");
    cTexts(item-1).innerHTML = text;
    return 1;
  }

  // helper function
  function fireEvent (ev_name)  {
    if( InScriptlet && !window.external.frozen ) {
      window.external.raiseEvent( ev_name, window.event.srcElement.pos );
    }
  }
}
</SCRIPT>

<BODY>
</BODY>
</HTML>
```

So far we've discussed all the details of the basic engine that cause the toolbar
to work. However, there are a number of accessory functions that allow you to
set and get the text labels for the buttons, as well as the state or the cursor for
a given item.

All these methods exploit the two collections we've built to keep track of the
label list and the images. For example, to get the text associated with a given
element of the toolbar, we do:

```
function DoGetTitle(item)  {
  cTexts = document.all("Text");
  return cTexts(item-1).innerText;
}
```

For all these functions we assume the **item** argument to be 1-based.

However, when we're looking at the method used to dynamically set a label
there's a little snag to face. If the string to set has a null length, then the image
will be centered in the cell and lose the alignment with the other buttons. The
next figure shows just this.

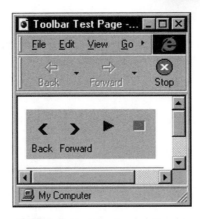

To avoid this effect you should force the text to have a non-null length, say a space. That's why we added a specific test in the code. The space character in HTML is rendered by '* *'. Note that at least in this case is absolutely necessary to use **innerHTML** instead of **innerText**. (**innerText**, in fact, won't be able to handle HTML special characters properly.)

```
function DoSetTitle(item, text)  {
  if( text.length==0 )
    text = " ";

  cTexts = document.all("Text");
  cTexts(item-1).innerHTML = text;
  return 1;
}
```

For the item's state, all that changes is the collection we work with. The code to return the current state of a given item is almost identical to the previous one, except for the collection used—which is **document.all("item")**.

When we update the state of an element, we also need to modify the bitmap that renders it to reflect the new logical state. It makes sense to replace the **src** attribute with the bitmap stored by the **gray** attribute, if the state to set is disabled (a boolean value of False).

```
function DoSetState(item, bState)  {
  cItems = document.all("Item");
  cTexts = document.all("Text");

  cItems.item(item-1).state = bState;
  if( bState )  {
    cItems.item(item-1).src = cItems.item(item-1).normal;
    cTexts.item(item-1).style.color = "";
  }
  else  {
    cItems.item(item-1).src = cItems.item(item-1).gray
    cTexts.item(item-1).style.color = "gray";
  }
  return 1;
}
```

On the other hand, when the state to set is normal we restore the bitmap indicated by the **normal** attribute. To make things more attractive, we could also change the color of the label text to reflect the grayed state.

```
cTexts.item(item-1).style.color = "";
```

An empty string means the default color, while "gray" assigns the text the dark gray color which is common for disabled items.

A Demo Page

Let's see now how to take advantage of such a component in a test page. The page is **tsttoolb.htm**.

```
<HTML>
<HEAD>
<TITLE>Toolbar Test Page</TITLE>
</HEAD>

<SCRIPT language=VBscript for="window" event="onload">
  Toolbar1.AddItem "Back", "Prev_N.gif", "Prev_H.gif", "Prev_D.gif",
"Prev_G.gif"
  Toolbar1.AddItem "Forward", "Next_N.gif", "Next_H.gif", "Next_D.gif",
"Next_G.gif"
  Toolbar1.AddItem "Play", "Play_N.gif", "Play_H.gif", "Play_D.gif",
"Play_G.gif"
  Toolbar1.AddItem "Stop", "Stop_N.gif", "Stop_H.gif", "Stop_D.gif",
"Stop_G.gif"
  Toolbar1.Cursor = "hand"
  Toolbar1.SetButtons
  Toolbar1.SetState 4, False
</SCRIPT>

<SCRIPT language=VBscript for="Toolbar1" event="onscriptletevent(n,item)">
  if n="OnItemClick" Then
    if item=3 Then
        Toolbar1.SetState 3, False
        Toolbar1.SetState 4, True
    else
        Toolbar1.SetState 3, True
        Toolbar1.SetState 4, False
    end if

    MsgBox "Clicked item No. " + CStr(item)
  end if
</SCRIPT>

<BODY>
<OBJECT id="Toolbar1" data="Toolbar.htm" height=60 type="text/x-scriptlet">
</OBJECT>

<HR>
The DHTML toolbar in action!
</BODY>
</HTML>
```

The page of code shown above produces a screen like the one shown below. We can see a toolbar made by four buttons whose bitmaps change while the mouse moves over them.

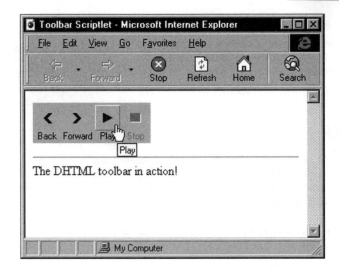

By clicking on the
buttons Play and Stop
you could toggle their
state and see how
SetState works.

```
if item=3 Then
    Toolbar1.SetState 3, False
    Toolbar1.SetState 4, True
else
    Toolbar1.SetState 3, True
    Toolbar1.SetState 4, False
end if
```

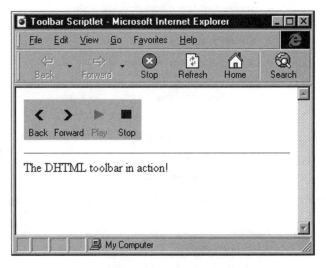

From the user's
standpoint the items
follow a natural
indexing which starts
from 1. The screenshot
opposite shows how the
toolbars look after you
click on Play.

A typical use for the toolbar is executing some action when the user clicks on a
button. Here is how to proceed.

```
<SCRIPT language=VBscript for=Menu1 event=onscriptletevent(n,item)>
    if n="OnItemClick" Then
        MsgBox "Clicked item No. " + CStr(item)
    end if
</SCRIPT>
```

The value stored in the argument **item** is the command ID of the clicked button. If you click on a button in the previous sample, you'll get a message like this.

Adding Tooltips

Any toolbar has tooltips, and ours follows the rule. Almost all HTML tags support tooltips through the **title** attribute. However, for **<IMG>** tags we must resort to the **alt** attribute. In the toolbar scriptlet seen above we initialize this attribute to the same text that appears to be the label text.

To allow dynamic change of the tooltips we need to add a new couple of methods, like **GetTooltip** and **SetTooltip**. The scriptlet declaration updates to this:

```
function CreateToolbar()  {
   this.AddItem = DoAddItem;
   this.SetButtons = DoSetButtons;
   this.get_Cursor = DoGetCursor;
   this.put_Cursor = DoSetCursor;
   this.GetState = DoGetState;
   this.GetTitle = DoGetTitle;
   this.GetTooltip = DoGetTooltip;
   this.SetState = DoSetState;
   this.SetTitle = DoSetTitle;
   this.SetTooltip = DoSetTooltip;

   this.event_OnItemClick = "";
   this.event_OnItemHot = "";
   this.event_OnItemOut = "";
   this.event_OnItemDown = "";
}
```

The new methods are simple wrappers around the **alt** attribute of the specified button.

```
function DoGetTooltip(item)  {
  cItems = document.all("Item");
  return cItems(item-1).alt;
}

function DoSetTooltip(item, tooltip)  {
  if( tooltip.length >0 )  {
    cItems = document.all("Item");
    cItems(item-1).alt = tooltip;
  }
  return;
}
```

To make use of these methods, just write code like this

```
Toolbar1.SetTooltip 4, "Stop the Player"
```

By adding such a line to the demo page seen earlier you should get the following output.

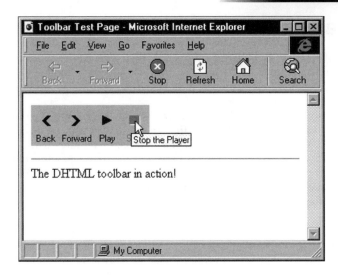

A Vertical Toolbar

At this point, getting a vertical toolbar is only one step away. Since the toolbar is heavily based on an HTML table, to get a vertical component we just need to arrange a vertical table. All the accessory code remains completely unchanged. The following listing shows the layout of a vertical table.

```
<TABLE>
   <FONT size="1" face="MS Sans Serif">
<TD>
   <TR>
     <IMG align=absmiddle
       style="id=item pos=1 state=1 src=""></IMG><SPAN id=text></SPAN>
   </TR>
   :
</TD>
```

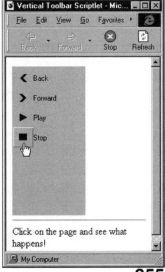

What's important is the value of the **ALIGN** attribute. This attribute should be **absmiddle** to cause the text to be vertically centered in relation to the image.

Summary

Overall, DHTML is a powerful innovation that succeeds in introducing HTML as a new development platform. Creating a Win32-style toolbar in pure HTML code was previously a dream. Now it has come true in all its reusable glory.

We started this chapter by looking at the source code used in some Microsoft Web pages. The typical toolbar we find in most of the pages is actually a table construct. To extract it and insert it into our pages requires a delicate cut-and-paste. Above all, it requires you to adjust—if not reinvent—the wheel each time.

Scriptlets save you from most of this work. They require you, however, to pay particular attention when designing a fairly complex component—like a toolbar.

The results, however, are encouraging and rather exciting. By the end of this chapter, we've got a toolbar object to insert and configure in our future Web pages. It is not an ActiveX control either, but a pure HTML module.

In this chapter, we dealt with the major issues inherent in the development of a toolbar component in DHTML. In particular, we covered:

- The **TABLE** construct
- The events to handle
- Adding custom attributes to image elements
- Using custom collections of objects

We created and discussed three different types of toolbar. The first has a fixed layout and hides or shows the buttons as it needs them. Then we showed you how to work around the limitations of this approach and to create a better one that creates a new table completely from scratch. Finally, we modified it slightly to make it vertical instead.

Packaging Scriptlets

Throughout this book you've learnt that scriptlets are made up of DHTML code and that they are nothing more than Web pages with a particular structure, that follow a special naming convention, and so forth. In short, what has become most prominent is the fact that scriptlets are pages rather than anything else. Even if many programmers—probably even many of you—are developing Internet-oriented applications, very few have ever faced the problem of automatically packaging Web-based modules. Believe it or not, this becomes a central issue with scriptlets. While specialized tools exist to arrange setup applications almost automatically for Windows programs, the same kind of support is missing for anything that relates to HTML. When it comes to HTML, in fact, it seems that packaging isn't a problem—or rather, it is not a primary problem.

At most, we could accept this approach for standard HTML applications but not for scriptlets. Scriptlets are special HTML documents. They have been introduced as being reusable and redistributable. This automatically assigns the problem of packaging components an important and fundamental role. Scriptlets exist to be deployed—once you have finished writing and testing them. Furthermore, since scriptlets are single and separate components you cannot think of installing them manually for each customer that buys them. (Sometimes, however, this might be reasonable for complete and totally customized applications.)

The first solution that comes to mind is putting all the files required in a directory and then, when it's time to distribute the component, packaging the whole folder. There's nothing wrong in this approach, and it will certainly work. However, throughout this book we've developed several scriptlets and they were often simple ones. Nevertheless, sometimes we have lost files along the hard disk. Time after time we had to move samples from folder to folder, manage, and reorganize them, and this kind of work was not always seamless. The most common error was forgetting some accessory files such as GIF or inner HTML pages. This made obvious the necessity of a piece of code with a double aim:

 Help us to automatically package the scriptlet

 Help the scriptlet to automatically check for all the required files

Wouldn't it be nice if you could have a development environment where you could create a new project, add new files and then have it generate on demand a zipped file ready to deploy? At the moment we're far from this, but could do something ourselves by scanning the DHTML code and searching for dependencies.

In this chapter, we will be discussing the details of the code that returns the list of all the files a scriptlet need to work properly. Doing so will provide us with a good opportunity to talk about:

- Scanning the files that form an HTML page

- Having a closer look at the DHTML object model

- Designing a setup program for scriptlets

- Using the WebBrowser control and DHTML in Visual Basic 5

The chapter is ideally divided in two parts. The first one is focused on the problem of finding out which files form a scriptlet. We will make use of a tool and discuss how to exploit it to package and distribute your own components. The second part emphasizes the code behind this and discusses how we have built such a tool in Visual Basic 5. If you're not interested in DHTML programming with Visual Basic feel free to skip that section and go directly to the next chapter.

The Origins of the Problem

The problem of packaging components arises with the concept of a software component. If you have a piece of code that, by design, can be plugged into an existing application, or into a program that is currently under construction, then you need to figure out how to deploy it in a safe and seamless way. An obvious parallel that springs to mind is—yet again—with hardware components. If you buy, for example, a sound card—what you get is a package with the hardware board, maybe a floppy or a CD and possibly a reference guide. All this is wrapped in a single envelope (or box) that you can order, or pick up straight from the shelf.

For scriptlets—and more generally for software components—it is the same. When you buy a graphic library or an ActiveX control, what you get is a package with some form of storage support—say a CD—and a reference guide. Typically, the software is made up of a variety of files that need special treatment (things like registering, unzipping, initialization, and so on).

Described in this way, a scriptlet is almost identical to an ActiveX control. It doesn't require special treatment such as registering or licensing just yet, but it is often composed of several helper files (images or sounds), other scriptlets or simply linked local pages.

However, what ultimately makes a scriptlet require a packaging process is the fact that it is a software component. In addition, a scriptlet is HTML-based and

HTML documents are usually compound documents that host a variety of files in a number of formats.

Of course making use of a special tool for packaging a component is not mandatory at all. Nothing prevents you from creating ZIP files manually and carefully scanning all the dependency-list of HTML files. Developing your whole project in a single directory helps, but in any case remember that you're working manually, while an integrated solution would be better.

HTML Pages Are Rich Documents

HTML pages represent, by design, a way to view and browse information. Originally, an HTML page included the text to be shown in its own body plus some links to external, and mostly remote, documents or sites. In recent times, however, an HTML page has seen its role changing and becoming more and more akin to a container of other objects. This change is somewhat related to the introduction of "Active Content" and the increased growth of the Web. This has had a double effect—the content of an HTML page has become richer and the information to be shown has been distributed among different pages.

To put it another way, HTML has evolved to become a surface capable of containing literally any kind of data. Today, if you download a page (or if you save a page while browsing on the Internet) you will, almost certainly, get just the template of the page or a sort of layout for it. Each of today's Web pages is filled with several images, applets, various objects and references to other local or remote pages.

This is especially true for Intranet-based applications and, more generally, for those applications that adopt a Web-based interface, or are somehow tightly bound to the Internet.

Scriptlets are HTML pages that take their place in just this context. Scriptlets are commonly rich in images, might contain ActiveX controls, other scriptlets, or links to other HTML pages. Packaging is clearly not a secondary issue since scriptlets are also reusable and distributable.

Dynamic HTML Collections

The DHTML object model helps considerably in analyzing and reporting the inner structure of an HTML page. A document object reference allows you to find out everything about it. To form a meaningful idea of what we're talking about, let's consider a Win32 executable module. An executable module—be it an EXE or a dynamic library—may be provided by several distinct libraries. Unless such links are only defined at run-time, you can examine the details of these subsidiary modules by looking at the file format structure. There are system libraries and tools that help to do this. As a result, you can be informed of all the modules that concur to the correct working of a program simply by examining the structure of the file itself.

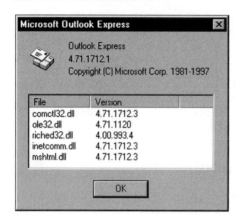

The screenshot on the left shows the About dialog box displayed by Microsoft Outlook Express. As you can see, it lists the modules that actually form the program and make it run. The information displayed in the dialog box is available inside a special section in the main executable file for the application.

In this chapter we'll attempt to code similar behavior for scriptlets. Our intention is to stroll through the scriptlet object model and indicate all the external files that may be considered part of the component. The component which you need to distribute as necessary accessories.

In reaching this result, we can rely on the various types of collection that populate the DHTML object model. By using them, we could obtain the result shown above for a Win32 executable.

We're talking mainly about scriptlets, but what we demonstrate in the next section also applies to any HTML page.

The Content of a HTML Document

There are a certain number of different file types that can be found in a Web page. Among them are:

- Images (GIF, JPEG, Bitmap, PCX, FIF, PNG and more)
- Sounds and Videos
- ActiveX Controls, plugins and applets
- Scriptlets
- Other HTML pages

A scriptlet can have any of these files as constituent components. All of them have a place in one of the DHTML collections. Links, frames and images all have specific lists of elements. For applets and controls there's the global collection of all the elements in a page.

In any case, through the DHTML object model we are able to gather information about all the files used throughout the page.

Designing an Examining Tool

When writing a scriptlet you can make use of a set of external files. When you have finished, you need to create a distributable package. For example, you might want to gather all the required files and create a CAB or a ZIP file. In other cases, you could use the list to create an InstallShield project, use another application distribution tool, or attach all of them as resources in a Win32 executable.

The tool we would like to design and build takes a given HTML file as its input, and returns all the files that actually compose it. The tool will use the DHTML object model to get the information. In particular, it checks the page tag by tag and stores each file name found.

For simplicity, we will create this tool—called HTML X-Ray—using Visual Basic 5. The next picture shows the tool in action.

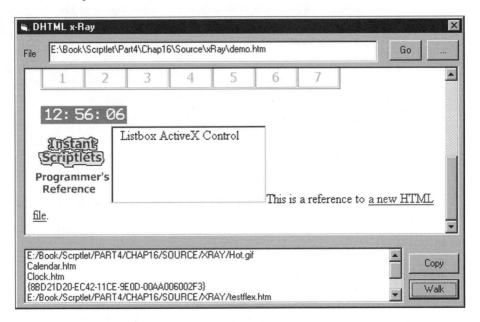

Using the Tool

The tool has a window to provide a preview of the file it is working on. In addition, it has an address bar and a couple of buttons to navigate to the specified URL or local file. It includes a browsing button to run an Open file dialog too. A user of this DHTML X-Ray utility would click on the browsing button (the one with ... as text) or type in the name of the HTML file to be analyzed. By clicking the Go or the browsing button, he or she will cause the specified Web document to be loaded and displayed through a WebBrowser control.

Furthermore, we need something to keep track of all the files that appear to contribute to the smooth running of the scriptlet. A listbox would be fine. We'll fill it in as soon as we've progressed through the DHTML object model and know about nested files. Finally, a Copy button will allow us to save the results to the clipboard.

The screenshot above shows how it will look when we have finished loading a file called **demo.htm**. The source code for this page is the following:

```
<html>
<head>
<title>A Demo Page</title>
</head>

<script language="VBscript" for="window" event="onload">
   Listbox1.AddItem "Listbox ActiveX Control"
</script>

<body>
<object data="Calendar.htm" width=400 height=250 type="text/x-scriptlet">
</object>
<object data="Clock.htm" width=120 height=40 type="text/x-scriptlet"
       align="absbottom">
</object>

<br>

<img src="Hot.gif" width="100" height="100" align="absmiddle">
<object id="Listbox1" width="196" height="96"
       classid="clsid:8BD21D20-EC42-11CE-9E0D-00AA006002F3">
</object>

This is a reference to <a href="testflex.htm">a new HTML file</a>.
</body>
</html>
```

It contains two scriptlets (the calendar and the clock), a GIF image, an ActiveX control, and a link to an external page.

At this point, all that remains to be done is to get a reference to the document object model and analyze it via collections and other means. By clicking on the Walk button, we do just this.

The listbox you can see below the page in the previous screenshot contains the list of the dependencies found. That is, the list of the files you need to distribute in order to have the page reproduce perfectly.

How the Tool Works

Let's now examine the details of how the tool works in an example. Remember that a scriptlet is basically an HTML file so the tool will work well on both scriptlets and ordinary Web pages.

The **demo.htm** page shown contains:

 The calendar and the clock scriptlet (we know from a previous chapter)

 A link to an HTML file (another scriptlet, to be precise)

 An Image

 An ActiveX control (it's the standard Listbox control you should have
installed with IE4)

When we run the tool it starts by enumerating the images. This causes the file
hot.gif to be added to the result listbox. The code scans the **<IMG>** collection
as well as the body background image.

Next, it's the turn of the objects, which include scriptlets and ActiveX controls.
The demo page has three objects in total: two scriptlets and an ActiveX control.
The first one our search meets is the scriptlet **calendar.htm**. It is added to
the list and analyzed for recursive references. The same occurs with
clock.htm.

The next entry is the CLSID of the ActiveX control. From this we could
manually go up to the file **fm20.dll**, say through the Registry Editor, as
shown next. That file is where the control is actually coded. You should have
this control installed if you run IE4.

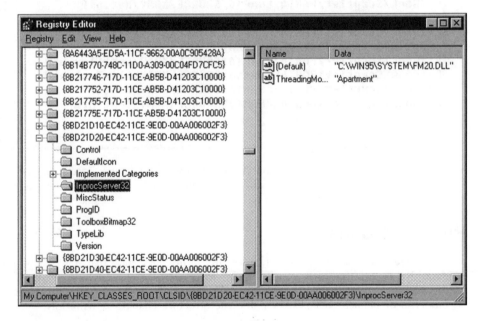

It's reasonable to suppose that this file has a dependency-list too. However, we
need specialized tools and specific algorithms to walk through the export
section of a Win32 executable module, be it a DLL, an OCX or a EXE. (See
Further Reading for suggestions.)

Finally, we enumerate the links. The demo page we're considering includes a
single link. To be precise, it is:

```
<a href="testflex.htm">a new HTML file</a>.
```

The referenced document is an HTML page containing a scriptlet we designed
and built in an earlier chapter. To refresh your memory—it is the expandable

textbox given by a line of text, a picture and a nested scriptlet. See Chapter 7 for more information about its structure and internal details.

The search procedure adds the file **testflex.htm** to the result listbox. Then it gets recursively analyzed and causes the **FlexText.htm** scriptlet to be added. A further examination extracts all the files that form the scriptlet. They are:

- **Flextext.htm**—the scriptlet itself
- **Dn.gif**—the default push button of the above scriptlet
- **Text.htm**—an "empty" and embedded component

The Copy button allows you to copy the entire content of the listbox to the clipboard for a possible further use. Here's what's copied:

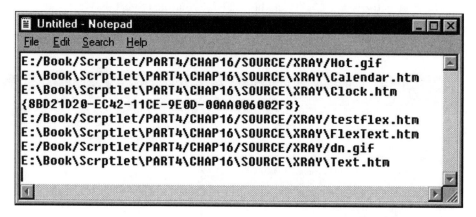

You can also copy a single line of the listbox to the clipboard. To do so, just highlight the desired item and press *Ctrl-C*. Immediately the text will be pasted to the clipboard ready for further use.

Pros and Cons

Before we start analyzing the details of this utility, let's state that it won't be the definitive routine for such a task. Firstly, we'll be covering a significant—but incomplete—subset of all the possible HTML tags. Secondly, the DHTML object model is of no help whatsoever if the file structure changes dynamically.

The traditional way to find out about the HTML dependency-list is to go through the DHTML collections and attributes. However, if you're considering a scriptlet that changes its user interface dynamically—adding or removing images, sounds, or even controls—then you won't be able to trace all the files required. Or rather, you can't complete the task simply by going through the element collections. Instead, (supposing this was possible), you ought to examine, character by character, the whole body and the single instructions of the HTML file.

In conclusion, our DHTML X-Ray tool helps to extract a subset of the file names that you need to package before deploying your scriptlet component.

However, once the tool has finished working there might be other files to take into account. The only category of files that might need further examination is those referred through **<OBJECT>**: ActiveX controls and scriptlets.

Principles of Working

The idea behind the working of such a tool is based on the following steps:

- Load the file to be examined
- Get its document object
- Scan some 'interesting' collections
- Add each file encountered to the result listbox

There might be other HTML files among the files found. In this case, we promptly recall the entire process recursively using a hidden WebBrowser control to load and examine the new documents.

The 'interesting' collections mentioned before are the images, the objects and the links. These aren't all the DHTML collections, but they are the only ones that could contain references to external files.

From now on we will concentrate on the inner details of the tool, and discuss how we have built it and how you could enhance its functionality. If you're only interested in using it, then this chapter ends here and you're ready for the next. However, if you want to look at a real-world example of DHTML programming with Visual Basic, keep on reading.

What follows might be of interest even to design a DHTML script procedure to call during the loading of your scriptlets to make sure that all the required files are available.

Implementing the Tool

The listing that follows illustrates the basic behavior of the tool. However, what's important—the core of the tool—is still to come.

```
Option Explicit

Private Sub cmdGo_Click()
  WebBrowser1.Navigate2 Text1.Text
End Sub

Private Sub cmdCopy_Click()
  Dim s As String
  Dim i As Integer

  For i = 0 To List1.ListCount - 1
    s = s + List1.list(i) + vbCrLf
  Next
  Clipboard.SetText s
End Sub
```

```
Private Sub cmdOpen_Click()
On Error GoTo ErrExit
  CommonDialog1.ShowOpen
  Text1.Text = CommonDialog1.filename
  cmdGo_Click
ErrExit:
End Sub

Private Sub cmdWalk_Click()
  List1.Clear
  DoWalkElements WebBrowser1.Document, List1
End Sub

Private Sub WebBrowser1_DocumentComplete(ByVal pDisp As Object, URL As Variant)
  cmdWalk.Enabled = True
  cmdCopy.Enabled = True
End Sub

Private Sub DoWalkElements(ByVal doc As HTMLDocument, ByVal list As ListBox)
  EnumerateImages doc, list
  EnumerateObjects doc, list
  EnumerateLinks doc, list
End Sub
```

Everything that the DHTML X-Ray utility does is concentrated in the
DoWalkElements subroutine. As shown above, it ends up calling three
enumeration functions, like **EnumerateImages**, **EnumerateObjects**, and
EnumerateLinks. The task of examining the HTML elements can be carried
out only once the document has finished loading. This state of things is notified
through the WebBrowser's **DocumentComplete** event. After receiving this
message, we enable the Walk and the Copy buttons.

```
cmdWalk.Enabled = True
cmdCopy.Enabled = True
```

As you can imagine, all the enumerative functions have the same structure and
the same prototype. They all take two arguments. The first is a reference to the
document object to consider, while the second is a listbox object to output to.

Having an **HTMLDocument** argument allows you to transparently handle two or
more WebBrowser controls. In practice, we use the main (and visible)
WebBrowser to perform a first scan of the document. For each HTML file we
find we need a recursive call. That's why we need to have a second (and
possibly invisible) WebBrowser control to load the inner HTML documents and
return the document object for further processing. Using an argument like this
saves us from duplicating the code of the **DoWalkElements**'s subroutines.

The WebBrowser control returns us a reference to the object model of the
viewed document through its property **Document**. For HTML files this coincides
with the DHTML object model. However, if you're viewing a Word document,
that property returns an entry-point to Word's hierarchy of objects. There is
more on WebBrowser in the two extra chapters of this book, available on our
web site at **http://rapid.wrox.co.uk/books/138X**.

Displaying the Results

As long as we get file names for the final scriptlet packaging, we store these names in a listbox (whose reference we're passing in and out through the various subroutines). In particular, we're using a specialized function to add a new file name to the list. Before adding the name this function performs some actions. For example, it checks whether the name already exists and whether the file name is an HTML document. In this case, it adds the name to the list but runs a recursive routine to process its content.

```
Public Const LB_FINDSTRINGEXACT = &H1A2
Declare Function SendMessageString Lib "user32" Alias "SendMessageA" ( _
        ByVal hwnd As Long, _
        ByVal wMsg As Long, _
        ByVal wParam As Long, _
        ByVal lParam As String _
    ) As Long


' Add subroutine
Private Sub Add(ByVal list As ListBox, ByVal s As String)
  Dim errCode As Integer

  errCode = SendMessageString(list.hwnd, LB_FINDSTRINGEXACT, -1, s)
  If errCode = -1 Then
    list.AddItem s
    If InStr(1, s, ".htm") > 0 Then
      If InStr(1, s, "/") = 0 Or InStr(1, s, "\") = 0 Then
        s = App.Path + "\" + s
      End If
      WebBrowser2.Navigate s
    End If

  End If
End Sub
```

By means of the **LB_FINDSTRINGEXACT** message we can check whether the specified string already exists in the listbox. To do so, we make use of a specialized version of the Win32 API function **SendMessage**. In this case, we re-declared its fourth argument and transformed it into **As String** instead of **As Any**. To avoid conflicts, we also declared an alias for this function.

```
Declare Function SendMessageString Lib "user32" Alias "SendMessageA" ( _
        ByVal hwnd As Long, _
        ByVal wMsg As Long, _
        ByVal wParam As Long, _
        ByVal lParam As String _
    ) As Long
```

This normally occurs in Visual Basic programming and represents the Visual Basic counterpart of a well-known mechanism called 'type-casting'.

Using the **LB_FINDSTRINGEXACT** message means that you must specify a couple of parameters. The first one—known as **wParam**—is the starting position for the search. If you pass −1 then the search begins from the first item in the listbox. The second argument—usually referred to as **lParam**—is now the string to search for. The function returns −1 if it fails. A failure means that the specified item doesn't exist in the listbox, so we can add it safely.

369

Scanning nested pages

Immediately after inserting a new item into the listbox, we check the file name for a substring like **.htm**. In practice, we try to find out whether the file is an HTML document. If it is, then we also need to scan it, in a recursive manner. ·

```
If InStr(1, s, ".htm") > 0 Then
    If InStr(1, s, "/") = 0 Or InStr(1, s, "\") = 0 Then
        s = App.Path + "\" + s
    End If
    WebBrowser2.Navigate s
End If
```

As shown in the above listing—we apply recursion by using a second but hidden WebBrowser control. In the example, we added the current directory to the file name. This is needed to enable the WebBrowser to successfully navigate to the URL. While this is quite rare you ought to make sure, however, that the file name doesn't already include a path. To test whether a path is included, we must verify if a slash or a backslash is present somewhere in the string.

When the second WebBrowser control completes the loading of the specified page, it raises a **DocumentComplete** event. We handle it this way:

```
Private Sub WebBrowser2_DocumentComplete(ByVal pDisp As Object, URL As Variant)
    DoWalkElements WebBrowser2.Document, List1
End Sub
```

As you can see, we call **DoWalkElements** again (this is recursion!) but specify the **document** object of the hidden control and the same listbox as before for displaying the results.

The application's current path is given by **App.Path**. You could also use the Win32 API function **GetCurrentDirectory** to find out about the current system directory.

Path and Protocol in File Names

You should consider that, even if the HTML source code doesn't include a path, you can locate one (and a protocol prefix) when you access an element through the DHTML object model.

For example, let's look at the following HTML code snippet:

```
<BODY>
This is a reference to <a href="testflex.htm">a new HTML file</a>.
</BODY>
```

This page includes a link to the local file **testflex.htm**. As you can see, there is no path and no protocol inside the file name. The **document.links** collection returns, however, when you load the page through WebBrowser and access its object model:

```
file:///c:/path/testflex.htm
```

as its first element. Note that the file name now includes the full original path and also a string denoting the protocol to access it. In this case, since it is a local file, we have **file://**. In addition, note that the slash has replaced all the backslashes that are more usual in a path name.

This kind of processing takes place for all the elements recognized through the DHTML object model. All the elements apart from the scriptlets, that is. In fact, if your page includes a scriptlet then the **data** attribute that stores the name of the component remains unchanged. If you specify a relative path for the scriptlet you will use backslashes as usual. But then in the result listbox you can observe path names with a mix of slash and backslashes!

Walking through the Object Model

When enumerating the images that actually make up an HTML page, we can rely on a built-in collection exposed by the **document** object. As explained earlier, any DHTML collection enriches the name of the files with its original path and protocol. Our purpose here is to arrange a packaging procedure for scriptlets. So we're interested in all the files that contribute to the correct working of the scriptlet itself. Plus, we want to identify all the local files. In fact, if the scriptlet refers to a remote image or control you don't need to distribute it, but can rely on the browser's capabilities to download it and register it properly.

For a more readable user interface we remove the protocol from the actual file name. As has been previously mentioned, all the files we're working with are local.

Enumerating the Images

The enumeration touches three main categories of elements—images, objects and links. Images are the simplest to handle. We only have to consider the collection of the **<IMG>** tags and the background image.

Even if the DHTML object model exposes a collection called **document.images** it will not include all the possible images. In fact, such a collection is limited to the files referenced through an **<IMG>** tag. On the other hand, an image used as the page background is, in effect, an image and must be considered. (For scriptlets, however, having a background image is a rarity.)

```
Private Sub EnumerateImages(ByVal doc As HTMLDocument, ByVal list As ListBox)
On Error Resume Next
    Dim i As Integer
    Dim s, temp As String

    ' <IMG> tag elements
    For i = 0 To doc.images.length - 1
        ' remove file:///
        s = doc.images.Item(i).href
        temp = Left$(s, 8)
        If temp = "file:///" Then
            s = Right$(s, Len(s) - 8)
        End If

        Add list, s
    Next
```

```
    ' BACKGROUND image, if any
    s = doc.body.getAttribute("BACKGROUND")
    If Len(s) > 0 Then
        ' remove file:///
        temp = Left$(s, 8)
        If temp = "file:///" Then
            s = Right$(s, Len(s) - 8)
        End If

        Add list, s
    End If
End Sub
```

The source code above first scans the **<IMG>** collection and then checks for the background image. A background image is defined as an attribute of the body object. In particular, you need to verify the:

```
s = doc.body.getAttribute("BACKGROUND")
```

BACKGROUND attribute. In this case, the name—complete with path and protocol—will be returned only if the path and protocol are actually coded in the HTML source. The following is typical code for a background image:

```
<body background="yellow_grad.gif">
...
</body>
```

Enumerating the Objects

We don't have a built-in collection for the elements rendered through an **<OBJECT>** tag. So we must arrange a dynamic collection starting from the generic **document.all** collection.

Like ActiveX controls, scriptlets are coded through the **<OBJECT>** tag. To distinguish between them we must use the **classid** and the **data** attributes. They are mutually exclusive and both concur to identify the component uniquely. In the former case, **classid** refers to the object CLSID—that is a 128-bit identifier that points to a registry location for the actual file name. The **data** is the name of the HTML file implementing the scriptlet.

```
Private Sub EnumerateObjects(ByVal doc As HTMLDocument, ByVal list As ListBox)
On Error Resume Next
    Dim i As Integer
    Dim s As String
    Dim obj As IHTMLElementCollection

    Set obj = doc.all.tags("OBJECT")

    ' <OBJECT> tag elements
    s = ""
    For i = 0 To obj.length - 1
        s = obj.Item(i).getAttribute("classid")
        If Len(s) = 0 Then
            s = obj.Item(i).getAttribute("data")
        Else
            ' remove "clsid:" and bracket between {}
            s = "{" + Right$(s, Len(s) - 6) + "}"
        End If
```

```
        If Len(s) > 0 Then
            Add list, s
        End If
    Next
End Sub
```

The picture shows the CLSID of the listbox control contained in the demo page.

Getting an ActiveX Control's File Name

While the name of the scriptlet is clear and readable, any ActiveX control hosted in an HTML page is indirectly referenced through its unambiguous CLSID. We saw previously how to extract the CLSID from an HTML **<OBJECT>** element. Now we must face the problem of recovering the actual OCX or DLL file name from the CLSID.

ActiveX controls are registered in special locations in the Windows registry. At least, this is what occurs under Win32-compliant platforms. Elsewhere, we have system objects that resemble and simulate the Win32 registry.

In Win32, therefore, ActiveX information is stored under the

```
HKEY_CLASSES_ROOT\
    CLSID\
        {...}\
            InProcServer32
```

key, where {...} denotes a string like the one highlighted in the previous screenshot.

Once you have the CLSID as a string, it's relatively easy to read the actual library name from the registry. You could also do it programmatically by the means of some Win32 API functions. (See the Further Reading section, later in this chapter.) However, as explained earlier, by hitting *Ctrl-C* when the CLSID is selected you can copy it to the clipboard and use it for a search with the Registry Editor.

*The Registry Editor, we also mentioned earlier, is a standard part of Windows 95 and Windows NT 4.0. The program name is **regedit.exe** and it is located in the Windows directory.*

Enumerating the Links

An HTML file can contain links to a variety of sources. A link might point to an e-mail address, a local file, a section later in the same page, or to a remote site through several protocols. So enumerating all the links is easy in one way, because we just need to resort to the built-in collection **document.links**, but it is complex too, because we must distinguish between the different types of links.

In short, we're developing a tool that needs to know how many—and what type of—files are necessary to a given scriptlet. More precisely, we're interested in all those files that we need to distribute along with the scriptlet for it to work properly. For this purpose, we're only interested in local references. In fact, suppose your scriptlet includes a link to a remote URL, say **http://www.something.com/index.htm**. You don't need to distribute that file together with the scriptlet. Even when a customer of yours is developing or using an application the scriptlet will still point to that URL through IE4. Things are quite different if the link refers to a page on your computer. That page won't be on the customer hard-disk, unless you distribute it with the scriptlet.

In particular, we'll be discarding all the links, except those that begin with **file://**.

```
Private Sub EnumerateLinks(ByVal doc As HTMLDocument, ByVal list As ListBox)
On Error Resume Next
   Dim i As Integer
   Dim s, temp As String

   ' <A> tag elements
   For i = 0 To doc.links.length - 1
       s = doc.links.Item(i).href

       ' remove file:///
       temp = Left$(s, 8)
       If temp = "file:///" Then
           s = Right$(s, Len(s) - 8)
       End If

       Add list, s
   Next
End Sub
```

The links we're primarily interested in for scriptlets raise the problem of recursive search. In fact, links point to other HTML files that are needed to enable the component to function correctly. In addition, these linked HTML files have their own content with other files that might be needed to enable them to work correctly, and so on.

Enumerating the Frames

This utility doesn't cover frames. However, a routine like *EnumerateFrames* is not difficult to write. It will scan the **document.frames** collection and read the **src** attribute for each item. What follows is a possible implementation:.

```
Private Sub EnumerateFrames(ByVal doc As HTMLDocument, ByVal list As ListBox)
On Error Resume Next
  Dim i As Integer

  For i = 0 To doc.frames.length - 1
      Add list, doc.frames.Item(i).src
  Next
End Sub
```

The object referenced through:

```
doc.frames.Item(i).src
```

is an HTML file name corresponding to the file that is actually hosted in the given frame. The discussed architecture will recursively examine the internal files one by one. To add frames support to the utility you just have to invoke such a procedure within the **DoWalkElements** subroutine.

```
Private Sub DoWalkElements(ByVal doc As HTMLDocument, ByVal list As ListBox)
    EnumerateImages doc, list
    EnumerateObjects doc, list
    EnumerateLinks doc, list
    EnumerateFrames doc, list
End Sub
```

A Few Curiosities

While developing this DHTML X-Ray utility we have come across a number of interesting features and shortcomings. In particular, there are a couple which warrant further investigation. The first one refers to the **onscriptletevent** event.

Suppose you write an HTML page that hosts a scriptlet and detects and handles its custom events. For example, you could consider the following **event.htm** page.

```
<html>
<head>
<title>A Demo Page</title>
</head>

<body>
<script language="VBscript" for="window" event="onload">
  Toolbar1.AddItem "Back", "Prev_N.gif", "Prev_H.gif", "Prev_D.gif",
"Prev_G.gif"
  Toolbar1.AddItem "Forward", "Next_N.gif", "Next_H.gif", "Next_D.gif",
"Next_G.gif"
  Toolbar1.AddItem "Play", "Play_N.gif", "Play_H.gif", "Play_D.gif",
"Play_G.gif"
  Toolbar1.AddItem "Stop", "Stop_N.gif", "Stop_H.gif", "Stop_D.gif",
"Stop_G.gif"
  Toolbar1.Cursor = "hand"
```

```
        Toolbar1.SetButtons
    </script>

    <script language="VBscript" for="Toolbar1" event="onscriptletevent(n,o)">
      if n="OnItemClick" Then
        MsgBox "Clicked item " + o
      end if
    </script>

    <object id="Toolbar1" data="Toolbar.htm" align="baseline" border="0"
            width="300" height="60" type="text/x-scriptlet">
    </object>
    </body>
    </html>
```

The page includes the toolbar scriptlet we saw in the previous chapter. If you
run the page from within Internet Explorer 4.0 and click the toolbar's buttons,
you get a message box informing you of the number of the button clicked.
However, if you run the page from within a Visual Basic utility that uses the
WebBrowser control, you won't be able to catch any of the **onscriptletevent**
events. To get those notifications you must resort to the Scriptlet Control. (We
covered this in Chapter 8.)

However, hosting scriptlet-based documents in a WebBrowser control doesn't
seem to provide the same functionality as the whole Internet Explorer 4.0.

Detecting Dynamically Referenced Files

There are scriptlets that have an empty body that is only filled out at run-time.
So if you scan the scriptlet page, as you see it in a browser, you often won't
get all that much. To understand what we mean try displaying the well-known
toolbar.htm file through IE4 and observe the results. Then, display a page
that scripts the component (like the one listed above) and—again—see what
happens. According to the content of the script instructions, the toolbar will
show some images. How can you get the name of these files? If you want to
know all the files that compose a given page, then you can't discard them—
even if they are not explicitly part of the scriptlet.

There is, however, a subtler circumstance. A scriptlet, like the expandable text
component discussed above and presented in Chapter 7, includes two bitmaps:
one for the collapsed state and one for the expanded. Only one (or even none)
of them is explicitly defined in the body. Consequently, only one bitmap is
caught by scanning routines. Nevertheless, both are undoubtedly part of the
scriptlet.

How to get at them? This is a problem quite similar to statically identifying the
DLLs a Windows program can load dynamically.

Unfortunately, there isn't a definitive and totally reliable solution. Something is,
however, possible if the component exposes its own **document** object. In this
way, we could try to work around the problem by analyzing *that* document
object. More specifically, the document object which renders the state of the
scriptlet, as modified by the script code of the host page.

The object identified by:

```
Set obj = doc.All.tags("OBJECT")
s = obj.Item(i).document
```

is not the document object of the *i.th* object, but the host page's document object.

This isn't a very workable solution, after all. The best and safest approach is to add these files to the package manually!

Creating a Self-Contained Cabinet

A tool like DHTML X-Ray automatically gives you a list of files to be distributed with your component. However, in some cases, these files are not the only ones required.

At this point you might want to enhance the tool by adding some capability to create zipped files or, better yet, a cabinet file. A cabinet file may be seen as a folder including a set of files in a compressed format. CAB files are an efficient way to package and distribute applications and software components. But they are also a format for which IE4 offers a great support. In fact, IE4 is able to download and install a component packaged as a cabinet.

The SDK for creating cabinet (*.cab) files is available on the Microsoft SiteBuilder site, where you can find the necessary documentation as well. The url is **http://www.microsoft.com/intdev/cab/cabdl.htm**.

The Necessity of an IDE

In this chapter we have discussed the details of a tool that should help you to realize a setup procedure for scriptlets components. We can get significant results through the DHTML object model but there are significant drawbacks too.

After all, the optimal solution for packaging scriptlets is the creation of a fully-fledged development environment (IDE). There you could create project files and store a link to all the components that are really needed. From this standpoint, arranging a setup wizard is relatively straightforward. Arranging such a product requires a valuable effort. This is a hint that hopefully Microsoft—or any other company—will hear.

Summary

Scriptlets are new pieces of technology, which have been developed in an extremely short space of time and bundled in with Internet Explorer 4.0 "as is". Behind scriptlets lie interesting previews of a possible new way of programming. The concept of software component arrives on the Web through DHTML. When it comes to Web components, however, you must worry about things like deployment. Scriptlets are just HTML pages—no specialized tool exists (at the time of writing) that supports them as a real development platform.

For example, we would expect a full-fledged IDE—possibly integrated with the Developer Studio environment—and an automatic wizard to arrange a setup procedure for distributing scriptlets across the Internet and beyond.

The packaging of scriptlets is a topic that, today, represents a major shortcoming. In this chapter, we have tried to address the main points for developing such a tool. Furthermore, we proposed a utility that analyzes any HTML page and returns the names of the required files. This utility—called DHTML X-Ray—is not perfect but it is clearly amendable and, therefore, open to improvement. Nevertheless, it highlights what such a packaging tool should do. What we have done here is:

- Presented an automatic tool to scan any HTML file for dependencies
- Detailed what it solves and what still remains to be solved
- Found the right design approach to arrange an automatic procedure
- Exploited recursion and browsing objects to enumerate the embedded files

Our hope is that someone will make available a fully-fledged IDE for developing scriptlets with the same ease as Visual Basic or Developer Studio.

Further Reading

Microsoft Interactive Developer (MIND) published a piece devoted to some shell extensions for DHTML files in the February 98 issue. In particular, the article shows how to extract some content information from an HTML file. The approach is different from the one discussed here. Firstly, the language used is C++ and the goal isn't the same as here. In fact, the article shows how to set up a namespace extension to walk into the content of a Web page directly from Windows Explorer. A namespace extension is a piece of software that extends Explorer allowing you to customize the way it handles some files or directories. However, many of the accessory topics covered in this article are also useful when enhancing this DHTML X-Ray tool. The first example that comes to mind is extracting the DLL file name from a CLSID. The article is published in the Cutting Edge column.

To learn more about the Win32 executable file format, you might want to check out the Under The Hood column in Microsoft System Journal, run by Matt Pietrek. It's likely that there you could find just the tool you need. In particular, we recommend you read the February 97 issue where you can find a description of a small utility to walk the export section of Win32 executables.

Remote Scripting and the Microsoft Scripting Library

Working with the Web requires a complete interaction between the user and the server. When you are browsing for a remote site, or viewing and downloading pages, it is easy to disregard the interaction taking place beneath the surface between you and the server. In fact, as a user, you are probably concentrating on the browser and its menus and toolbars. However, there are Web pages with "active" content that require you to issue commands outside the traditional interface of your favorite browser.

To put it another way, as a Web user you are always interacting with some kind of server—whatever action you take; be it a click on the Refresh button or a click on a given page hyperlink. Even by clicking on the Back or Forward buttons (if the page your moving to isn't in your cache) you risk becoming involved in a client/server conversation.

What's the problem with this anyway? It's just that each time the server is contacted, the client must wait for several seconds, instead of milliseconds. Another side-effect is that the page being viewed must completely reload once the server's response is ready to be displayed.

As you can imagine, these two circumstances make working through the Web time consuming and not as seamless and smooth as one would desire. The conversation is never continuous and this is even reflected on the user interface presented by the browser. Here there are jumps and flickers in what the user sees while working.

With DHTML things started to change for the better, at least for what is inherent to the client side of the matter. Internet Explorer 4.0 builds up an intermediate layer of code that is responsible for buffering all the changes the user intends to carry out on the currently viewed page. To use terminology typical of other programming contexts—the browser behaves like a proxy in relation to the displayed page and the user. Everything you want to change is sent to this layer and everything that has been changed is made available to you through this proxy. A proxy module works like a broker and provides the caller module with an interface that makes it quite transparent the callee is local or remote.

This intermediate level of code is the DHTML object model, a hierarchy of objects that render the entire content of the page itself in a standard and programmable way. DHTML, however, is only the first step towards a more powerful interaction between the client and the server in a Web environment. In this chapter, we will introduce and discuss the Microsoft Scripting Library, which is an interesting new proposal to work around some of today's drawbacks in the interaction between the client applications and the Web servers. In particular, we'll cover:

- What is and how to get the Microsoft Scripting Library
- How it is implemented and works
- What the Microsoft Scripting Library offers and how to take full advantage of its features

Finally, we'll discuss in more detail the most important of these features— Remote Scripting technology.

Before going on let's clarify a point. What do the Scripting Library and Remote Scripting have to do with scriptlets? The primary connection point is the fact that Remote Scripting allows us to define a scriptlet on the server and drive it transparently from the client. But there's a second—more general—point. Both Remote Scripting and the Microsoft Scripting Library are a kind of increment beyond DHTML and go in the direction of making Web development simpler and more powerful. This is the same direction as scriptlets.

Why do you need the Microsoft Scripting Library?

This is a very good question. Let's start by saying that we all need something that is able to extend the capability of Web computing and ferry us to the same smooth usability that we get with desktop applications. The greatest difference between the desktop and the Web world is in the response-time (and the consequent interface) of the running application. If you consider a traditional Windows program, all you have to do is click on a toolbar button (or alternatively select a menu command) and the function, associated with that toolbar or menu, will start. The output produced then appears visually. Typically, it fills out a container control, displays in a message box, or runs a new module. Anyway, all of this occurs within the same operational context and, for the users, it represents the natural consequence of their previous action.

This continuity is missing when we move to the Web world. An Internet-based (or even an Intranet-based) application presents a user interface with selectable commands and active objects. However, in the majority of cases, the business logic resides outside the client page we're working with. Therefore, some kind of bridge is needed to carry our request down to the server and bring the next response back to us.

In principle, the sequence of actions is the same in both computing worlds. Nevertheless, on the Web side it appears to be a discontinuous sequence—as if we had switched between two different, albeit similar, applications. To be honest, this is exactly what happens! Is there a way to remove this difference and gain the maximum control over the events from the client side? Will we ever be capable of obtaining the same smooth behavior for Web applications— the same speed and productivity—as we have today for desktop programs?

This same concept can be expressed in a much more impressive way. Will we ever be capable of using the underlying net (be it the Internet or an Intranet) as a transparent component of the software architecture? By taking this a step forward, we would enter a new age for Web computing and could finally state that the Web had, indeed, come of age.

Dynamic HTML Is a First Step

Technically speaking, the main cause of the actual differences between desktop and Web applications is that the latter rely on the HTTP protocol to communicate. As you probably know, the HTTP (the HyperText Transfer Protocol) is a stateless protocol. In other words, the interaction that takes place over the Web is based on transactions between a client and a server. But any of these transactions is independent and separate from the others. Consequently, there's no native and natural way for the server to remember what previously occurred. Each thread of conversation has no history. There's a server that responds to requests and multiple clients that send queries. Each of these communications is treated as a single and self-contained unit that always requires a separate session. Sending and receiving data is accomplished through HTML pages. Any page the server sends back ends up overriding the previous one. For the user this results in flickering and a pointless wait.

Unless we completely change the computing model, there's no way to alter this behavior. This means that the server will always keep sending pages. The client, on the other hand, will receive and display them through a browser. Thus, we have a new page that gets drawn for each message, or block of data, received from the server.

Given this, DHTML is a first step forward. In fact, DHTML allows you to be in the middle when data is exchanged between the client and the browser. With DHTML, the server isn't involved yet, but we have a layer that works as a proxy for anything that goes in and out of the current page. In addition, this layer makes you capable of modifying the content of the page without resorting to refreshes or more radical reloading.

What Happens When You Submit A Page

DHTML is a kind of machinery placed under the page that interprets and executes what the script code requires. With the current implementation of DHTML all the activity is limited to the client side. Hence, a page including buttons to submit requests to some remote server needs to somehow refer to pages created on a remote URL and send back a response. The following diagram shows what happens.

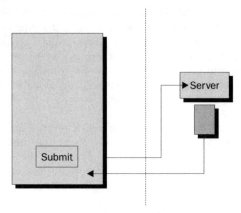

Once the server has prepared the resulting HTML page, the browser must show it by replacing the current page, which is the one that originated the request. There are tricks to ensure that a minimum of state is maintained between the pages, but undoubtedly, it is a logically unique session broken into by quite separate and independent communications.

We need a mechanism to connect the remote server and the client page in such a way that the script written on the client side can also automate a remote server. Finally, the data the server returns back can be shown in the current page via DHTML.

From Dynamic HTML to the Scripting Library

Basically, we need to figure out a way to specify, from a client page, some code to be executed on a remote server. In addition, we want to maintain the possibility of updating the current page and not loading a new one from scratch. In other words, our goal is have one or more local objects linked to remote servers, in order to drive it and handle its results from JScript or VBScript client code. In this way, pseudo-code like the following sounds perfectly reasonable

```
<SCRIPT language=VBScript for=btnSubmit event=onclick>
  Set remoteObj = GetRemoteObjectFromUrl(url)
  Set resultObj = remoteObj.Method1
  MsgBox resultObj.Text
</SCRIPT>
```

We'd like to specify a remote URL (for example, an ASP page) whose nested code will return an object to the client page. In the code snippet above, such a function is called **GetRemoteObjectFromUrl**. The local link to a remote object is represented by **remoteObj**. By 'return an object' we're using a quite generic sentence. We'll detail this later. Once we have correctly instantiated this object, we can start using it just like any other local object—be it an ActiveX control, a DHTML Scriptlet, a JavaScript function and so on.

By doing so, we have opened a session with a server and are talking to it without explicitly sending new pages back and forth. In a word, such an interface allows us to control the interaction with the server without ever

leaving the current page. Furthermore, we can exploit the DHTML object model
to update the user interface and avoid flickering and other possible nasty
effects.

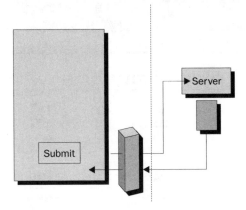

The diagram above shows how the Microsoft Scripting Library changes the
traditional browsing model by introducing a hidden layer of code that works as
a client-side broker between the browser and the server.

The Scripting Library

What is outlined above is exactly what the new Microsoft Scripting Library has
been designed for. More precisely, the Microsoft Scripting Library is a collection
of functions built beyond the DHTML object model with the purpose of
simplifying—and making more powerful—the interaction between the client and
the server.

Remote Scripting technology is what allows us to dialog with the server
through automation. It's an important part of this library, but it is not the only
component. There are a number of aspects of Web programming covered by the
Scripting Library. We will examine these in the paragraphs that follow.

For the moment, let's try to understand a bit more about the essence of the
Microsoft Scripting Library. To start with—do you know how to get it?

How to get the Microsoft Scripting Library

At the time of writing the Microsoft Scripting Library is available in beta
version from the Microsoft site devoted to scripting. You can find it at:

`http://www.microsoft.com/scripting`

By clicking on the 'Using the Microsoft Scripting Library to Improve Web
Applications' link on the page, you can download the current beta version of the
Microsoft Scripting Library. Once it is downloaded you have a self-extracting
file—**msl.exe**—that occupies about 50 KB. After unzipping it, you'll find the
following files on your hard drive:

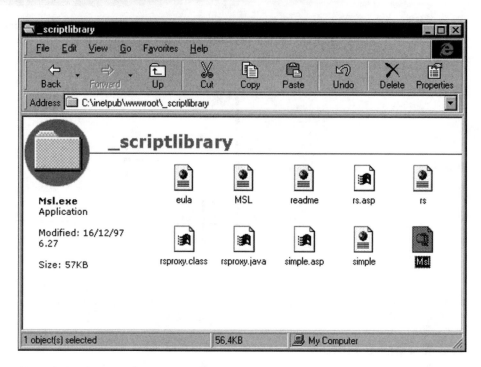

The whole library is concentrated in a pair of HTML pages to be used on the client and the server side respectively. They are:

- rs.htm, for the client side
- rs.asp, for the server side

The package also includes a couple of Java files called **rsproxy.class** and **rsproxy.java** that implement the Remote Scripting proxy module. Bundled in with the library there are also both the JScript and the Java version of the Remote Scripting objects to be used on the client and the server side.

At the moment, the Microsoft Scripting Library is distributed in sources and it is expected to work as a run-time library, although this might change in the future. Microsoft, in fact, suggests considering these releases as intermediate versions that pursue the objective of making users familiar with this new technology. By using and studying this implementation of Remote Scripting and the Microsoft Scripting Library you can get started with the technology and be ready to take advantage of it when it's finally made available as a development tool.

The Advantage of the Microsoft Scripting Library

Before continuing the discussion of the current state of the technology and its future perspectives, let's spend a while focussing on the advantages of the Microsoft Scripting Library by concentrating on the following questions: What has this library got to offer? Why should you use it? What points does it address and resolve?

First of all, the Microsoft Scripting Library is a small enhancement that increases the flexibility of the DHTML object model. The key aspect of the library is Remote Scripting—the ability to issue remote calls (like the Remote Procedure Call protocol does) and wait for an answer.

As mentioned earlier, Remote Scripting is the most important plus point, however, it is not the only one. The advantages of the library can be outlined in this way:

Technology	Description
Remote Scripting	Lets the client interact with the server without navigating to a new page. Through it you can issue remote calls without ever leaving the client page.
Closures	Lets the developer gather a method of a specified object into a single new object. In this way you can use it as you would any other variable.
Object Unevaluation	Returns a string representation for a given object. Now it is a valid input for the traditional script evaluation methods.
Miscellaneous Utilities	Provides facilities for more precise detection of object types and the manipulation of the ADO recordsets.

In a nutshell, the Microsoft Scripting Library provides some functionality that extends the DHTML object model and makes it richer and more flexible. The added features all lead in the direction of a better and closer interaction between the client and the server. For more information see the documentation on the Microsoft Scripting web site.

The State of the Art

By combining the Microsoft Scripting Library and DHTML you should be able to exploit the best of Internet Explorer 4.0. The most important point that emerges is that by mixing these two Web-oriented technologies, you are given the opportunity to create distributed Web applications with the same power and ease of well-established desktop development environments (Visual Basic).

The current implementation is nothing more than a technology preview. In the future, the Microsoft Scripting Library will become part of Visual InterDev.

For now, it's all reduced to a couple of HTML and ASP pages that must reside on the client and the server respectively. Since they are made up of pure JScript code, and heavily exploit that syntax to implement the features, it's fine to use Internet Explorer 4.0 to see Remote Scripting in action.

By snooping in the **rs.htm** and **rs.asp** files, we can see how Remote Scripting and Object Unevaluation are actually implemented.

Setting Remote Scripting to Work

To see Remote Scripting in action you first need to check out a short list of requirements. The Microsoft Scripting Library package includes a file called **simple.htm**. This file is the client side of a very simple Remote Scripting example. **simple.asp** is its server side counterpart. The next screenshot shows how it looks on the client.

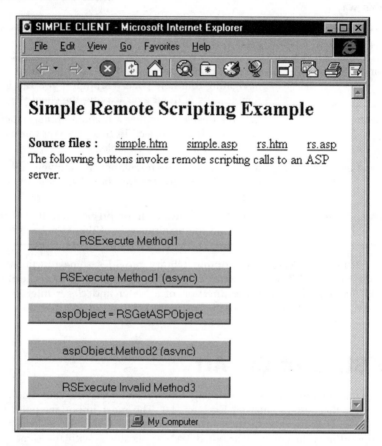

To test Remote Scripting you need to run a Web server that supports Active Server Pages. Internet Information Server (IIS) and the Personal Web Server (PWS) are both valid for testing. IIS is a standard part of Windows NT 4.0, while the PWS comes with Microsoft FrontPage. The server side files—those with an ASP extension—must reside in the **_ScriptLibrary** directory. This is found in the root folder of the Web server. In most cases this will be **\wwwroot**. The next screenshot illustrates the first screen of the **msl.exe** self-extractor program.

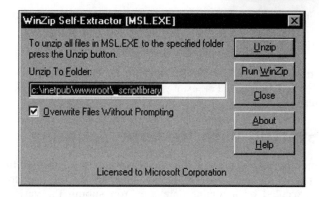

This program attempts to unzip the cabinet into a folder named:

```
c:\inetpub\wwwroot\_ScriptLibrary
```

Of course, it doesn't have to be exactly the same path shown in the dialog. What's important is that it is the right directory on the server.

Remote Scripting Technology

Remote Scripting technology is not the only component of the Microsoft Scripting Library, but it certainly is the key component. It makes use of Active Server Pages on the server-side to implement some objects that are driven from the client without navigation.

Closely connected to this is the concept of automation scripts. At the moment, there's no public documentation but we can think of them as being lightweight components hidden in client pages that take care of setting up remote conversations with the specified server.

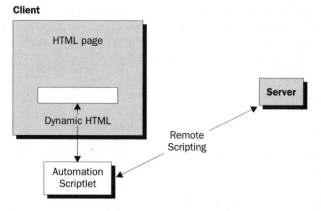

The figure above shows a possible diagram for automation scriptlets. In practice, they should be a way to encapsulate remote scripting logic and make it available at a higher abstract level. Since we are talking about a mixture of DHTML and Remote Scripting, a good solution is to build extremely specialized scriptlets that preserve the same client programming metaphor. At the same time, these scriptlets could provide the advanced communication facilities of the remote scripting technology.

The automation script objects should logically be lighter than the others due to their more limited purpose. For example, they don't need to provide support for the user interface.

Getting Started with Remote Scripting

To understand the importance of Remote Scripting let's consider the following example. Suppose we have an HTML page that allows the user to design a query to be executed on a remote database. You submit the various edit fields— say in an SQL string—and wait for a response. It doesn't matter how you set up a conversation with the server. Whatever approach you choose, the server will always reply through an HTML page with a given interface. On the client side, you must load a new page to display the results of the query. Often, you can arrange things in such a way that the final page appears to be almost identical to the previous one—but often you can't. Furthermore, even if you can decide the look of the resulting page, the user always perceives a refreshing screen. This never occurs with desktop development tools. Here you can set up a "silent" conversation with a database server and have a code layer in the middle that allows you to manipulate the output and present it without radical changes to the application's user interface.

We have consciously chosen a typical everyday example—just to emphasize that Remote Scripting really can help you enhance your Web-based modules and make them functionally equivalent to desktop applications.

What Changes with Remote Scripting

With Remote Scripting, what changes is the code that executes when you submit your query. First of all, you connect to a remote server through an Active Server Page and invoke a specified method on that remote server. This method does something meaningful and produces an output to be sent back to the caller. When the server has finished, the client is informed and receives the results. At this point, the client can update its own user interface through DHTML without loading a new page and without navigating to the server page.

Lookup Requests

Remote Scripting is a general way for a client to issue commands that a given server will execute. This could happen at any time. For example, we could asynchronously validate a field accessing a remote database without leaving the current page. In fact, another interesting application for Remote Scripting is the implementation of lookup requests, for example, to validate data entered on the client page. Doing this with today's methods requires a lot of programming work and—above all—setting up a direct communication with the server. Consequently, this will have a visual effect on the change of the page.

Get in touch with the Server

We've spent a large part of this chapter explaining that, through Remote Scripting, you can connect to a server with the same programming approach needed for another local object. As you can imagine, however, there's a great difference between working with modules that are remote to working with modules that are not. The difference is all in the response time and in the latent state in which our request could lie for a while.

This consideration leads us to distinguish between two kinds of remote calls: synchronous and asynchronous. In the former case, the function—we're calling to get in touch with the server—only returns when the whole transmission has completed. At this point we might want to check the result of the transaction and do something with the returned data.

In the latter, however, the function returns immediately. Alternatively, for asynchronous calls we're required to specify a callback script function too. Of course, this routine gets called automatically when the server has done with its work.

Synchronous Calls

In a remote invocation of script code we can identify three distinct steps:

- Establish a connection with some server code
- Get the results of that code execution
- Transmit the results back to the client

We distinguish synchronous and asynchronous calls from the vicinity in which the above steps take place.

A typical synchronous call is when all three steps occur inside the same client instruction. That is, we call a function specifying a URL and the name of the method to execute. The function takes care of connecting and running the given method and then passing back an instance of a new object for further local use. One line later, we are ready to modify the client user interface according to the result of the operation and the data received. As you can see, this requires nothing more than the usual notion of synchronous execution.

```
<SCRIPT language=Javascript>
  var serverURL = "simple.asp";
  var co = RSExecute ( serverURL,"Method1" );
  myCallBack ( co );
</SCRIPT>
```

The code above illustrates a synchronous call. The code snippet is taken from the file **simple.htm**; one of the demo examples provided with the beta version of the Microsoft Scripting Library. The function **RSExecute** is defined in the Remote Scripting client-side source code. We can find it in the **rs.htm** file. **myCallback** is just a function defined in **simple.htm** that processes the data returned by **RSExecute**.

For a synchronous call we just need to pass in the server name and the name of the method to execute. In the above example, the server is an ASP file whose source code (see the file **simple.asp**) defines a function called **Method1**. This is expanded on later in the chapter.

Executing the method causes the creation of an object. It is then returned and saved to the variable **co**. That value is then passed to a client function to be used.

Asynchronous Calls

To implement asynchronous calls we need to change the previous code slightly. In particular, we'll be using the same **RSExecute** function to issue the call, even if with more arguments.

```
<SCRIPT language=Javascript>
    var serverURL = "simple.asp";
    RSExecute( serverURL, "Method1", myCallBack );
</SCRIPT>
```

Now the function is called with a new parameter, but it is the same function we used to manipulate the results in the previous case. Later on we'll discuss the details of its prototype.

Let's see what happens now. The connection takes place and then the server method is called and produces the same results as before. Up to this point there's no difference from the synchronous case. However, the **RSExecute** function now returns immediately after being called. The code to be executed in response to the server reply is contained in the third argument, which is a local function. The same **RSExecute** function is now responsible for invoking the client code when finished.

Choosing between synchronous or asynchronous calls is completely up to you. We have seen two examples earlier and so now it would probably be helpful to determine which is the better. To send a query to a database server you could take a synchronous call into account. However, for a lookup request an asynchronous access appears to be far better. In fact, in this way the user could go on filling a series of fields while other edit boxes are validated in the background. The whole application would be far more responsive.

How the Interaction Takes Place

Let's now look in a bit more detail at how the interaction between the client and the server takes place through Remote Scripting. Basically, there are a couple of ways through which the client code and a remote server could communicate. The functions involved are:

 **RSExecute**

RSGetASPObject

The first one executes commands in an indirect way, be it synchronous or asynchronous. That is, you specify to the ASP server reference the method to invoke—possibly a callback procedure—and the Remote Scripting library does the rest. On the client side it's all reduced to one line of code.

The second approach lends itself to the creation of local objects that have a dual nature. They live locally and are accessed and driven by the page scripts—though they have a remote counterpart that actually executes the commands. In practice, we instantiate and use a client component as if it was an ActiveX control or a DHTML Scriptlet. In reality, it is the client-side of a remote object built into an ASP page on a given server. The **RSGetASPObject** function returns an object that is functionally equivalent to a scriptlet. In fact, it can expose methods and properties. What changes for the programmers? Simply, you have a tangible object to work with and no need to resort to callback functions to execute the necessary operations.

Enabling the Remote Scripting Engine

Remote Scripting requires a conversation between a client; that resides locally on a specific machine and a server, which can be placed somewhere in the world. This kind of communication is based on a proxy module that takes care of buffering the client requests and transforming them into concrete server calls. Of course, this proxy needs to be initialized to get Remote Scripting to work properly.

```
<HTML>
<HEAD>
<TITLE>SIMPLE CLIENT</TITLE>
</HEAD>

<BODY>
<script language="JavaScript" src="rs.htm"></script>
<script language="JavaScript">RSEnableRemoteScripting();</script>

<h2>Simple Remote Scripting Example</h2>
```

The code shown above is taken from the file **simple.htm** included in the Microsoft Scripting Library package. Notice the first two instructions in the **<BODY>** tag. The first one specifies the file with the full implementation of Remote Scripting. In this case, we're assuming that the client library files reside in the same folder as the example. Such a line includes the entire **rs.htm** content in the current page as a **<SCRIPT>** block.

```
<script language="JavaScript" src="rs.htm"></script>
```

The next line invokes the execution of the function **RSEnableRemoteScripting** immediately after entering the **<BODY>** tag. Such a function is defined in **rs.htm**. If we don't do this, we'll get an error when attempting to call the Remote Scripting engine.

But what do we mean by "enabling the Remote Scripting engine?" Let's find out in the next paragraph.

The Remote Scripting Proxy

As mentioned earlier, **RSEnableRemoteScripting** enables the Remote
Scripting proxy, and puts it to work. Let's take a look at its source code right
away.

```
function RSEnableRemoteScripting()
{
  if ((secondSlash = (mslRoot = window.location.pathname).indexOf("/",1)) != -
1)
      mslRoot = mslRoot.substring(0,secondSlash);
  s1 = "<APPLET name=RSAspProxyApplet codebase=";
  s2 = "/_ScriptLibrary code=RSProxy.class height=0 width=0></APPLET>";
  document.write( s1 + mslRoot + s2 );
}
```

In fact, it consists of adding a line of code to the current document's body
through DHTML. It inserts a reference to a Java applet that works as the proxy.
This applet is the **rsproxy.class** file bundled with the Microsoft Scripting
Library source. Overall, what is added looks like the following:

```
<APPLET name=RSAspProxyApplet
  codebase=/e:\msl\simple.htm/_ScriptLibrary
  code=RSProxy.class
  width=0 height=0>
</APPLET>
```

The **codebase** attribute denotes the path through which we can access the
body of the applet. Supposing we have copied everything in the **e:\msl**
directory, then the above listing is what the function adds to the page's body.
This is sufficient to enable the Remote Scripting proxy. If you're interested in
what the proxy does then you might want to look at the file **rsproxy.java**
which presents its source code. Here's the heading of the file.

```
import java.applet.*;
import java.awt.*;

import java.net.URL;
import java.io.InputStream;
import java.io.IOException;

public class RSProxy extends Applet implements Runnable
{
  ...
}
```

Briefly, it handles a list of requests and runs a new thread for each one. When
the thread completes, the **RSProxy** class holds a response to notify. The body
of the thread is given by the request string sent by the caller.

The remote proxy exposes a public method called **startRequest**. This is used
by the client Remote Scripting methods to establish a link through the
<APPLET> tag added previously. The applet works as a junction point between
the client page and the remote server.

The following code snippet shows the body of the **startRequest** method.

```
// RSProxy class constructor
public RSProxy()
{
  m_requestLock = new Object();
  m_responseLock = new Object();
}

// initiates a request given a request string and a URL
public void startRequest(String requestID, String url_context, String url, int
mode)
{
  Object[] request = newRequest(requestID, url_context, url, mode);
  insertRequest(request);
  Thread thread = new Thread(this, requestID);
  request[REQUEST_THREAD] = thread;
  thread.start();
}
```

The Remote Scripting Client Objects

At the beginning of any Remote Scripting page an applet is dynamically
defined through the function **RSEnableRemoteScripting**. The applet serves
the purpose of creating a link between the client page and the proxy module.
This one, therefore, will take care of satisfying any issued request and will
return the available data.

The client side of Remote Scripting relies on a hidden object that maps the
proxy methods one by one, as we discussed earlier. When we call the high-level
functions like **RSExecute** and **RSGetASPObject**, we're delegating a kind of
local proxy to establish a connection with the remote proxy and carry out the
request.

```
function RSExecute( url, method )
{
var cb, ecb, context;
var params = new Array;
var pn = 0;
var len = RSExecute.arguments.length;
for (var i=2; i < len; i++)
        params[pn++] = RSExecute.arguments[i];

return MSLRS.processRequest(url, method, params);
}
```

Let's see the source code for the **RSExecute** function. As you can see, it does
no more than prepare—and then issue—a call to the method **processRequest**
of a hidden object called **MSLRS**. **MSLRS** is a JavaScript object implemented in
rs.htm.

RSExecute is a JavaScript function. For all JavaScript functions, you can learn
about the command line through **arguments[]**. However, from the above
prototype the entire set of acceptable parameters is not evident. The real syntax
for the **RSExecute** function is the following:

```
function RSExecute( url, method, p1 ... pn, cb, ecb, context )
```

In a bit more detail, the various arguments have the following roles:

Url	The ASP file containing the remote script.
Method	Name of the method to be invoked in the ASP file.
P1...Pn	Any number of parameters required by the method.
Cb	Optional callback routine. Ignored if the call is synchronous.
Ecb	Optional callback routine for error handling. Ignored if the call is synchronous.
Context	An optional user context.

As you can see, apart from the first two parameters, all the others can have a variety of meanings. For example, the third argument might be the first parameter required by the specified method and the callback routine.

To work round this, all the arguments beyond the second are packaged into a variable-length array. The **arguments.length** property informs you of the real number of parameters passed.

```
var len = RSExecute.arguments.length;
for (var i=2; i < len; i++)
   params[pn++] = RSExecute.arguments[i];
```

When it's time to use the arguments, for the sake of clarity, their roles are determined through the type returned by JavaScript's built-in **typeOf** function.

Obtaining a Remote Object

If you have to reference the same object many times then you might want to create an explicit and local instance of it. To do so we need to call **RSGetASPObject** and pass the URL to an ASP page as an argument.

This function returns a server object for an ASP file. The object is completely described by its public description and is, therefore, very much like the scriptlets we have seen so far.

```
function RSGetASPObject(url)
{
  var cb, ecb, context;
  var params = new Array;
  var request = MSLRS.startRequest(url,"GetServerProxy",params,cb,ecb,context);

  if (request.status == MSLRS.S_COMPLETED)
  {
    var server = request.return_value;
    server.location = url;
    server.exec = MSLRS.processRequest;
    return server;
  }

  alert("Failed to create ASP object for : " + url);
  return null;
}
```

Let's examine this code to learn more about the interaction between the client and the remote server. The function is expected to return an object obtained as the result of a remote connection. This server is a kind of proxy, since it must be used on the client side to issue multiple requests and get them resolved.

Note that in the case of **RSGetASPObject**, we don't have anything to execute. Thus, the method called is:

```
MSLRS.startRequest(url,"GetServerProxy",params,cb,ecb,context);
```

instead of **MSLRS.processRequest**. In practice, we're asking the URL to execute the method **GetServerProxy**. This method is not defined directly in the ASP page referenced in the call. This happens because **GetServerProxy** is a Remote Scripting method.

The ASP page we nominated as the desired URL usually begins with something like the following:

```
<%@ LANGUAGE=VBSCRIPT %>
<% RSDispatch %>

<SCRIPT RUNAT=SERVER Language=javascript>
<!--#INCLUDE FILE="../../_ScriptLibrary/rs.asp"-->
```

We note that a **RSDispatch** procedure and the **rs.asp** file are included. In particular, **RSDispatch** is a function placed at the top of the ASP page and which handles Remote Scripting from the server side. It is responsible for dispatching all the methods that get called from the clients to a valid object on the server. Furthermore, it sends the return value back to the client.

What's a valid object on the server? And what do we mean by calling a method? Actually, we have a scriptlet on the server. So the valid object on the server whose methods we're calling is a scriptlet, with its own **public_description** and methods.

Inside the source code for **RSDispatch** there is a specific branch to handle the occasion when the method to be dispatched is **GetServerProxy**.

What is returned is the **public_description** object of the ASP file referenced as the URL. The next code excerpt shows how to enumerate all the methods in the object obtained. This code executes on the client page that wants to issue remote calls.

```
function handleRSGetASPObject ()
{
  var serverURL = "simple.asp";

  aspObject = RSGetASPObject(serverURL);
  var msg = "aspObject public_description:\n";
  for (name in aspObject)
msg += "    " + name + "\n";
  alert(msg);
}
```

397

Getting the Return Value

Each time we use Remote Scripting we run a request from the client side and wait for a response to arrive. Then we have the problem of transforming this reply into a usable and programmable object.

Executing Remote Scripting commands, instead of local ones, forces us to check the result of the operation before using the returned data.

```
var url = "simple.asp"

Server = RSGetAspObject(url);
callobject = Server.method(p0, … , pX);
if (callobject.Status == 'success')
  result = callobject.return_value;
```

In the above example, we obtained a remote object and used it to call a given method. What we get in return is not immediately the data we were waiting for. The **callobject** we can see in the listing is an object that has a property **Status** to be checked in order to ascertain the failure or success of the operation. Only at this point is it safe to store the returned data somewhere. This data is rendered by the property **return_value**.

We have, therefore, examined the case of an explicit object. However, things work much the same even if we're executing direct Remote Script code.

```
callobject = RSExecute(url, method, p0, … , pX);
if (callobject.Status == 'success')
  result = callobject.return_value;
```

There are a variety of reasons why a remote call might not be regularly completed. Just for this, you should make sure of the result of the entire operation before trying to access the returned value.

An Example of Remote Scripting

At this point, all that is missing is an example that illustrates how a remote scripting call is handled from the client and the server side. We're considering an example based on the **simple.htm** demo; which is located along with the source code of the Microsoft Scripting Library. However, on the Microsoft site dedicated to scripting you can download a few other samples. Find them at:

http://www.microsoft.com/scripting

The example we'll discuss in a while is composed of a couple of files: **simple.htm** that works locally and **simple.asp** that specifies the code to execute on the server. In addition to this, we need the files that represent the client and server implementation of Remote Scripting: **rs.htm** and **rs.asp**.

```
<HTML>
<HEAD>
<TITLE>SIMPLE CLIENT</TITLE>
</HEAD>

<BODY>
```

```html
<script language="JavaScript" src="rs.htm"></script>
<script language="JavaScript">RSEnableRemoteScripting();</script>

<h2>Simple Remote Scripting Example</h2><br>
The following buttons invoke remote scripting calls to an ASP server.<br>

<form>
<input type=button name=btnRSExecute value="RSExecute Method1"
      onclick="handleRSExecute()" style="width:250;height:25"><br>
<input type=button name=btnRSExecuteAsynch value="RSExecute Method1 (async)"
      onclick="handleRSExecuteAsync()" style="width:250;height:25"><br>
<input type=button name=btnRSGetASPObject value="aspObject = RSGetASPObject"
      onclick="handleRSGetAspObject()" style="width:250;height:25"><br>
<input type=button name=btnASPObject value="aspObject.Method2 (async)"
      onclick="handleAspObject()" style="width:250;height:25"><br>
<input type=button name=btnInvalidCall value="RSExecute Invalid Method3"
      onclick="handleInvalidCall()" style="width:250;height:25">

<SCRIPT LANGUAGE="javascript">
var serverURL = "simple.asp";
var aspObject;

function myCallBack(co)
{
      alert( co.return_value );
}

function errorCallBack(co)
{
      alert( co.status );
}

function handleRSExecute()
{
  var co = RSExecute(serverURL,"Method1");
  myCallBack(co);
}

function handleRSExecuteAsync()
{
  RSExecute(serverURL,"Method1",myCallBack,"RSExecute");
}

function handleRSGetAspObject()
{
  aspObject = RSGetASPObject(serverURL);
  var msg = "aspObject public_description\n";
  for (name in aspObject)
        msg += "    " + name + "\n";
  alert(msg);
}

function handleAspObject()
{
  aspObject.Method2(myCallBack,errorCallBack,"aspObject");
}

function handleInvalidCall()
{
  var co = RSExecute(serverURL,"Method3",myCallBack,
          errorCallBack,"Invalid RSExecute");
}

</SCRIPT>
</form>

</BODY>
</HTML>
```

399

The source code listed above produces the following figure.

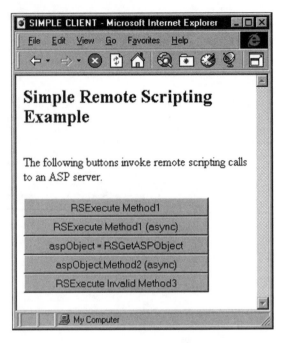

In the source code we can see five buttons that allow us to test the various possibilities of Remote Scripting. The methods invoked on the server **simple.asp** are called **Method1** and **Method2**. The function calls are issued both synchronously and asynchronously. The last button shows what happens if you attempt to call a method—**Method3**—that doesn't exist.

The code that actually gets executed in response to the user clicking on the page buttons is coded in the file **simple.asp**.

```
<%@ LANGUAGE=VBSCRIPT %>
<% RSDispatch %>

<SCRIPT RUNAT=SERVER Language=javascript>
<!--#INCLUDE FILE="../../_ScriptLibrary/rs.asp"-->

function Description()
{
  this.Method1 = Method1;
  this.Method2 = Method2;
}
public_description = new Description();

function Method1()
{
  return new Date;
}

function Method2()
{
        return new Array( "blue", "red", "green", "yellow", "orange", "purple",
                          "cyan", "magenta" );
}

</SCRIPT>
```

The ASP page defines a **public_description** object and shapes a remote object whose functionality is available to clients. The code shown by the ASP server is identical to a scriptlet. When the example calls **Method1** the server creates a new date object. By contrast, **Method2** causes the creation of a new array. Both the date and the array are returned to the client to be processed through a callback function.

Other Characteristics of the Microsoft Scripting Library

So far we have focused mainly on Remote Scripting and discarded other features of the Microsoft Scripting Library. While Remote Scripting is the key technology in such a library, other interesting and important characteristics make the Microsoft Scripting Library attractive to Web developers.

A couple of these important characteristics will be discussed in the following paragraph. In particular, we'll discuss closures and object unevaluation. The final section of this paragraph will be dedicated to a few other minor enhancements that have been announced, but not yet implemented, in the preliminary version of the library we considered.

Closures

The concept of closure is nothing new to the world of software. Originally, it was introduced with functional (and mostly academic) programming languages. More recently, however, closures have become part of some advanced scripting languages like Borland's cScript—the language used to program the Borland C++ IDE. Even the C++ Builder provides support for them.

In brief, closures are a way to gather into a single programming object both a function and its arguments. In practice, a closure renders an execution context for that function. Moving this concept to an object-oriented reality, it's natural to identify it with a pair given by an object (or a class) and one of its public methods.

A Typical Use of Closures

In Windows programming, you often need to specify a function address to be used as a callback procedure by another module. For example, to enumerate all the windows active in the system at a certain moment in time you can call the **EnumWindows** function and pass the address of a routine. This function will be called next on each window's handle found. If you're programming in C, this doesn't pose any problem. The same holds true if you're developing with C++ and don't pretend to use a class method as the callback function. In fact, a method of any C++ class requires a hidden argument on the stack that is the pointer to the instance of the class. Such a pointer is called **this**. Because of this peculiarity you cannot use a class method as a callback function, unless you declare it as a **static** member of the class. In this case, however, you won't be able to access the class private or public interface. So, why the closures? An environment that supports closures allows us to specify closures instead of simpler function address and automatically calls the method in the context of the object.

Scripting and Closures

We have seen how closures can help in any object-oriented language thought to support Windows programming. Now, let's shift our focus to scripting. Inside the Microsoft Scripting Library, a closure looks something like this:

```
<SCRIPT language=Javascript>
  document.onclick = closure(Scriptlet1, "DoSomething");
</SCRIPT>

<BODY>
  <OBJECT data="scriptlet.htm" id=Scriptlet1 type="text/x-scriptlet">
  </OBJECT>
</BODY>
```

The closure function returns something like an object given by a pair of components—the reference to an existing object and a string that evaluates to the name of an existing method of the previous object. In the example above, in fact, we assigned the **onclick** event of the current page a method called **DoSomething** on the **Scriptlet1** object. This means that each time the user clicks on the document, the following code executes:

```
Scriptlet1.DoSomething();
```

It is equivalent to:

```
<SCRIPT language=Javascript for=document event=onclick>
  Scriptlet1.DoSomething();
</SCRIPT>

<BODY>
  <OBJECT data="scriptlet.htm" id=Scriptlet1 type="text/x-scriptlet">
  </OBJECT>
</BODY>
```

As you can see, the closures allow more compact solutions. If the method forming part of the closure requires some parameters, what you have to do is particularly simple—just invoke the closure object with the required arguments. For example:

```
MyClosure = closure(Scriptlet1, "DoSomethingWithParams");
```

is a typical closure declaration. The following code shows how to use the closure passing in some arguments.

```
MyClosure( 1, "This is a text" );
```

This is done assuming that the method enclosed in the closure required two parameters, a number and a string. Calling **MyClosure** is a shortcut for invoking **Scriptlet1.DoSomethingWithParams**—it doesn't matter how many (if any) parameters are required.

Closures partially resume what we have already discussed in chapter 11 of this book about callbacks and scriptlets. At present, the Microsoft Scripting Library implements closures through JavaScript arrays. However, this might change when the final version gets shipped—just like any other current implementation detail.

Unevaluation Objects

In the previous chapters (in particular, Chapter 11) we discovered the power and the flexibility of the **window.execScript** method in the DHTML object model. It allows us to specify the code to be executed as a string. This feature, however, is strictly tied to the late-bound nature of the scripting languages. For JavaScript, for example, there's a built-in function that provides this functionality. The function is called **eval**. The following is, for example, acceptable code.

```
<HTML>
<SCRIPT language=Javascript>
  var s1 = "var d=new Date;";
  var s2 = "alert(d.getYear());";
  eval(s1+s2);
</SCRIPT>
</HTML>
```

It composes in a string the commands:

```
var d=new Date;
alert( d.getYear() );
```

and then executes them. The result is shown in the screenshot below that shows the year of the current date.

Together with this evaluation mechanism, the Microsoft Scripting Library introduces the reverse—an unevaluation engine. This means that the library is given the capacity to flatten out an object as a descriptive string. After all, the JavaScript **eval** function takes a string and creates an object. More precisely, it takes a string and evaluates it as script code.

The uneval function

The new **uneval** function, by contrast, does the reverse. It takes a JavaScript object and converts it to a string representation. It maintains the state of the object. Of course, the format of the string is such that passing it to **eval** allows us to obtain a perfect copy of the original. As an immediate consequence, we can pass objects back and forth between clients and servers in a string format. Any kind of complex data structure can be translated in a universal format and transmitted over a network. So this function works as a sort of converter to exchange data across the client/server boundaries.

In the file **rs.asp** the **uneval** function is implemented like this.

```
function uneval(obj)
{
  if (!unevalInitialized)
  {
    initUneval();
    unevalInitialized = true;
  }
  unevalNextID = 0;
  var s = "var undefined;" + unevalDecl(obj) + unevalInst(obj);
  unevalClear(obj);
  return s;
}
```

Of course, the code above only shows the skeleton of the function. It needs some sort of initialization and then each object flattens the declaration and the current instance to export.

To have an idea of what **uneval** produces, then you need to include the **rs.asp** file to your HTML page before call it. To make it simpler, we have extracted from **rs.asp** only the portion related to the **uneval** function and called it **rsuneval.htm**.

The following page shows an example. The file is called **uneval.htm**.

```
<HTML>
<HEAD>
<TITLE>UnEval Sample</TITLE>
</HEAD>
Click to see an example of <b>uneval</b>.

<script language="JavaScript" for="document" event="onclick">
d = new Date();
s = uneval( d );
alert( s );
</script>

<BODY>
<script language="JavaScript" src="rsuneval.htm"></script>
</BODY>
</HTML>
```

Here we're defining an object like a date

```
d = new Date();
s = uneval( d );
alert( s );
```

and then ask the **uneval** function to convert it to a string. The next figure shows the output.

It's natural at this point to verify that **uneval** is the exact opposite of **eval**.
Let's modify the page and save it as **uneval1.htm**.

```
<HTML>
<HEAD>
<TITLE>UnEval and Eval Sample</TITLE>
</HEAD>
Click to see an example of <b>uneval</b> and <b>eval</b>.

<script language="JavaScript" for=document event=onclick>
d = new Date();
s = uneval( d );
alert( s );

d = eval( s );
alert( d.getYear() );
</script>

<BODY>
<script language="JavaScript" src="rsuneval.htm"></script>
</BODY>
</HTML>
```

Now we take the string returned by **uneval**
and let **eval** to work with it. We should get
back a Date object. So it is. In fact, the figure
shows the current year again.

Miscellaneous Facilities

The Microsoft Scripting Library white papers tell us about a couple of other
interesting facilities that we haven't yet encountered in the source code. The first
one refers to an improved object introspection capability, while the second is
specific to the Active Data Object (ADO) programming; the new standard way
to access databases.

In particular, the Microsoft Scripting Library should include a new function
called **TypeOf**. This new function is an improvement over the built-in **typeof**
JavaScript function and will provide a more accurate recognition capability for
the type of the various objects. Often, in fact, the standard **typeof** (note the
lowercase) returns a generic "Object" as the object's type. The **TypeOf** will be
able to distinguish better. This will be especially true for arrays.

ADO Recordsets as Arrays

The Active Data Object is a way to access databases that mediates the
characteristics of the DAO and RDO technologies. A recordset is a collection of
records extracted from a given database, say as the result of a query. The ADO
object model allows the programmers to examine the recordset through a series
of navigational methods, such as **MoveFirst**, **MovePrevious**, **MoveNext** and
the like. However, there might be circumstances in which you prefer to scan the
recordset as if it was an array.

405

The Microsoft Scripting Library will provide a variety of ways to transform ADO recordsets into more easily usable JavaScript objects. Once you have a JavaScript object it's easy to flatten it out to a string and send it across the network from a server to a client or viceversa.

At the moment, we're supposed to have three different ways of converting ADO recordsets: lists, arrays and objects. For a bit more detail, let's look at the following table:

Function	Description
`RecordSetAsList`	This function is supposed to extract a given field name from the recordset. We will be returned a one-dimensional array whose items are the values of the field contained in the recordset.
`RecordSetAsArray`	This function is supposed to realize a full conversion from the recordset into an array. The resulting object is a two-dimensional array, which represents the table of data. The number of columns is the same as the record's fields, while the number of rows match the size of the recordset. We can also include an additional line at the top for the column headings.
`RecordAsObject`	The current record of the recordset becomes a JavaScript object through this function. The transformation creates a new object that exposes all the fields as properties.

Even this aspect of the Microsoft Scripting Library is subject to change in the future, perhaps by the time you read this. For your convenience, don't forget to check out the Microsoft Scripting site frequently at the following address:

`http://www.microsoft.com/scripting`

Summary

In this chapter, we have breathed the air of work in progress. In fact, we have discussed the content of the Microsoft Scripting Library—which is a small-code enhancement over the DHTML object model. However, what makes the library really interesting are the key points it addresses now and those it will focus on tomorrow.

There are a group of powerful technologies inside: first and foremost, Remote Scripting. The ability to establish a connection with a remote server without leaving the current page is a great improvement. Now we really do have enough flexibility to design and realize Web-oriented applications that work with the same productivity and user-friendliness as the desktops'. But putting aside Remote Scripting, we touched on a few other enhancements that contribute to making scripting programming easier and more powerful. The true goal of the library seems to be to make the world of script languages evolve towards a more active and conscious role—becoming a full development environment for applications.

In the chapter, we discussed the most important features of Remote Scripting technology and the other characteristics of the Microsoft Scripting Library. In particular:

- The practical advantages of Remote Scripting
- How Remote Scripting is implemented
- How the interaction between the client and the server takes place
- Hightlights of the source code
- What closures are and how to use them
- The meaning of object unevaluation
- The transformation of ADO recordsets

The whole of this chapter is instilled with an air of the indefinite, because of the preliminary version of the library we have examined. However, some key points are evident and come out clearly—even in a beta version.

Chapter

Server Scriptlets

So far we've discussed all aspects of programming scriptlets. In doing so we have pointed out drawbacks and shortcomings, as well as key features such as reusability, components and so forth. The scriptlet technology, however, is continuously evolving. Just consider that, for example, when I started writing this book, in the fall of 1997, scriptlets had only just been introduced and there was no "public" idea of what things like Remote Scripting might be.

However, we have already covered Remote Scripting and now we're about to introduce a completely new and exciting application of scriptlet technology. Its official name is Server Scriptlets, but you might also find them referred to through the more evocative name of COM Scriptlets. Basically, Server Scriptlets are scriptlets with a more flexible syntax that behave like a COM server. From the programmer's standpoint, Server Scriptlets are COM servers written in any of the available script languages.

In this chapter we're going to examine the various language backdrops and then delve into the following details in more depth:

- Structure of the file
- Differences with DHTML scriptlets
- Registration Information
- Defining a Public Interface
- Using Server Scriptlets in applications

At the time of writing Server Scriptlets were still under beta testing. Consequently, some of the topics discussed here may change by the time of the final release. The latest and most up-to-date news is available from the following address:

`http://www.microsoft.com/scripting`

At the same address you can also find a useful FAQ on the subject of Server Scriptlets.

Despite the fact that Server Scriptlets and DHTML Scriptlets have a great deal in common title wise, conceptually they are quite different. In particular, Server Scriptlets are perceived from external applications such as COM objects. This means that they need to follow special behaviors and specific conventions that simply don't apply to DHTML Scriptlets. In this chapter, we're going to refer to aspects of programming that will not always be entirely familiar to Web developers. I have, however, tried to make the unknown as pleasant as possible and have always tried to provide the simplest explanations. However, it is important to be aware of the advanced nature of this chapter

A good understanding of the COM model would be useful—although you don't need to be an expert COM programmer. Let's say that this chapter assumes that you have a reasonably precise idea of what a COM server is and how it works. This kind of knowledge is required because, after all, a Server Scriptlet is just a COM object. To know more about COM, you might want to consider flicking through "*ActiveX COM Control Programming*" by Sing Li and Panos Econopoulos ISBN 1-861000-37-5 published by Wrox Press.

What's a Server Scriptlet Anyway?

In the previous chapter, when we talked about Remote Scripting we used a term like server-side scriptlet. In this chapter we're facing a very similar expression—"Server Scriptlet". Are they different? Yes, they differ quite a lot. What we called server-side scriptlets were JavaScript function objects defined and executed on the server. What Microsoft have called Server Scriptlets are, instead, scriptlets that appear to be functionally equivalent to COM servers.

When you think of a COM server what usually comes to mind is a kind of black-box exposing a number of methods and properties. These methods and properties can be called from within a Visual Basic form, or an HTML page, or any other development tool that is COM-aware. With Server Scriptlets you have such a component, but it is written in a script language such as VBScript, JavaScript, or even PerlScript or Python.

The DHTML Scriptlets we've discussed so far do, however, expose the automation interface made up of properties and methods—so what's different with Server Scriptlets? There's one big difference: Server Scriptlets are *already* real COM objects and can be exploited from any development environment just as they are. You make use of them in the same way that you would use any other COM component. That is—you create a new instance of the given object and identify it through its name. To be precise, this name is known as **ProgID**. Usually it is a string like **Name.Something**.

From this it is possible to identify other differences that exist between Server and DHTML Scriptlets. First and foremost, Server Scriptlets require registration and are identified through a CLSID in addition to a ProgID. There are more differences but these will be addressed later in the chapter. For now let's move up to a higher level.

*Despite use of the word "Server", a Server Scriptlet is not specifically related
to any topics inherent to Active Server Pages (ASP). Therefore, we have to
conclude that the name chosen is just misleading. The name actually comes
from the word 'Server', which denotes that the component works as a server
and 'scriptlet', which emphasizes its construction from script code.*

Why Server Scriptlets?

If you consider the evolution of scripting over the last few months, you'll notice
a kind of continuity that makes the next step appear perfectly natural, given all
the previous ones. This evolution began with the advent of DHTML. DHTML
highlighted the need for a more powerful development platform to increase the
level of code reusability. This need is the very origin of scriptlets, or to be more
precise, DHTML Scriptlets.

Such components are nothing more than Web pages with a special layer of
script code that shapes a public interface through methods and properties. Most
of these features are accomplished through JavaScript's built-in functions. In
addition, you need a kind of external engine to host scriptlets in both HTML
pages and Visual Basic forms.

The next step is a generalization of this external engine which transforms it into
a run-time module capable of providing a full-fledged COM interface to the
external callers. In this way, DHTML Scriptlets become a special case of Server
Scriptlets. In other words, Server Scriptlets are a superset of the functionality of
the existing scriptlets. This will be particularly evident when we take a look at
the source code of Server Scriptlets and make a comparison with DHTML
Scriptlets.

So to answer the original question—why Server Scriptlets? It is mainly because
they are the next step in the evolutionary process. Server Scriptlets encompass
DHTML Scriptlets and provide the same functionality through a more general
and powerful interface.

Differences from DHTML Scriptlets

Today it could take you until the official release of Server Scriptlets to find all
the many differences that exist between the two scriptlet forms. First of all,
DHTML Scriptlets and Server Scriptlets are different objects and cannot, in all
cases, be interchanged. Secondly, at least in this beta release, Server Scriptlets
are simple automation objects and, therefore, don't have any user interface
elements, be it a body, an HTML tag or even the ability to run a message box.
Finally, a Server Scriptlet needs additional information to be stored in the file
and has a different file layout. Let's now see all these features in more detail.

DHTML Scriptlets and Server Scriptlets

To start off let's consider a bare-bone scriptlet with just one method and
compare its implementations as a DHTML and a Server Scriptlet. In this way
we can observe the differences at source code level. Suppose we call it **Time**
and assign a method called **GetCurrentTime** that returns just the current time.

411

Writing it as a DHTML scriptlet is really rather easy. The file is **dhtime.htm**.

```
<html>
<body>

<script language=JScript>
public_description = new Time;

var public_description = new Time;
var mTime = "";

function Time() {
  this.GetCurrentTime = GetCurrentTime;
}

function GetCurrentTime() {
  mTime = new Date;
  return mTime.getHours() + ":" + mTime.getMinutes();
}

</script>
</body>
</html>
```

We can test this document by using the following page **tstdtime.htm**.

```
<html>
<body>
Click on the page to test the Time DHTML Scriptlet.<hr>

<script language=Javascript for="document" event="onclick">
  alert( obj.GetCurrentTime() );
</script>

<object id="obj" data="dhtime.htm" style="display:none"
        type="text/x-scriptlet">
</object>

</body>
</html>
```

Of course a DHTML scriptlet can have a user interface but in this case we don't actually need one, so we hide the scriptlet. All works well and by clicking on the page we get the current time expressed in hours and minutes.

Let's now see if we can write a Server Scriptlet with the same degree of functionality. The file is called **sstime.sct**. A Server Scriptlet is, in fact, a text file with an **.sct** extension.

```
<scriptlet>

<Registration
    Description="Time"
    ProgID="Time.Scriptlet"
    Version="1.00"
    ClassID="{51eb18c0-98a7-11d1-83d1-f46705c10000}"
>
</Registration>

<implements id=Automation type=Automation>
    <method name=GetCurrentTime>
    </method>
</implements>
```

```
<script language=JScript>
var mTime = "";

function GetCurrentTime() {
  mTime = new Date;
  return mTime.getHours() + ":" + mTime.getMinutes();
}

</script>
</scriptlet>
```

The only aspect they have in common is the **<SCRIPT>** tag. We will discuss thoroughly the structure of a Server Scriptlet file in an upcoming section. For now, let's limit ourselves to noting the HTML-like syntax and a bunch of new tags such as **implements**, **Registration**, **scriptlet** and **method**.

If you're even a tiny bit familiar with COM modules, you won't find it hard to recognize in the above listing all the information that features a COM server, such as an ActiveX control. If you don't know anything about COM servers, then consider that such a module exposes its functionality implementing a certain number of interfaces. An interface may be seen as a table of functions with a given name. The tag **implements** is where this Server Scriptlet lets us know which interface is actually being implemented.

Unfortunately, this first beta only supports the automation interface so we can't do a different example. However, if you're planning to develop Server Scriptlets it's quite likely that you're also thinking about using them with HTML pages or Visual Basic forms. If so what you need, in most cases, is just the automation interface.

Calling a Server Scriptlet

The **Registration** tag defines all the key information that will allow you to identify a COM object. Once we have the CLSID (that is a number that uniquely identifies a COM object—we'll see more about how to get a CLSID soon), we can set up a regular **<OBJECT>** tag as shown in the following file. The page **tststim1.htm** is a valid test page for our Server Scriptlet. Here we're treating it as an ActiveX control.

```
<html>
<body>
Click on the page to test the Time Server Scriptlet.<hr>

<script language=Javascript for="document" event="onclick">
  alert( obj.GetCurrentTime() );
</script>

<object id=obj classid="clsid:51eb18c0-98a7-11d1-83d1-f46705c10000"
        style="display:none">
</object>

</body>
</html>
```

Of course, the CLSID is the same as the one encountered in the previous listing for the Server Scriptlet. We use this number instead of the file name to identify the component. The association between this code and the actual file name is stored in the Windows registry during the registration process. More on this later.

413

If we run this page, we get a message (see the figure) that reminds us that using ActiveX controls might well be dangerous.

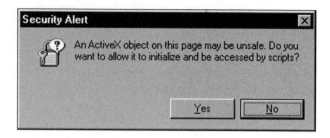

We can either choose to initialize it, or not make it available to the scripts. If we choose Yes then all the scripts contained in the page will execute properly and the current time will be displayed with a click.

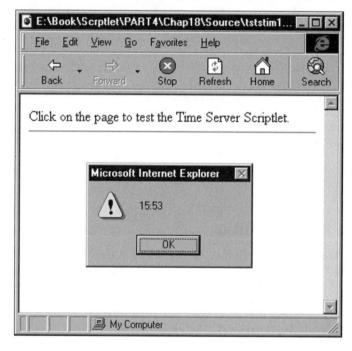

Checking ActiveX Controls for scripting

In the above example, we were using our scriptlet as if it was an ActiveX control (remember that an ActiveX control is also a COM object). In fact, Internet Explorer 4.0 verifies whether it is safe for scripting and then alerts us. An ActiveX control may cause harm when used through scripting. Given this, the author sometimes "marks" his control as safe for scripting, that is, the author asserts that invoking the control's methods will never result in any kind of damage for the host system. Usually this is done through the implementation of a specific COM interface or by adding specific keys to the registry. However, as explained before, the beta we have at the moment only supports the automation interface and, therefore, we can't add support for a specific COM interface. This feature is supposed to appear in future versions of the package.

Calling a Server Scriptlet as a DHTML Scriptlet

Earlier, we said that a Server Scriptlet and a DHTML Scriptlet cannot be interchanged in all cases. In fact, if we try to call the Server Scriptlet defined above, specifying the scriptlet's MIME type and the **data** attribute, all we get is a run-time error. Let's look at the following file, which is **tststim2.htm**.

```
<HTML>
<BODY>
Click on the page to test the Time Server Scriptlet.<hr>

<SCRIPT language=Javascript for="document" event="onclick">
alert( obj.GetCurrentTime() );
</SCRIPT>

<OBJECT id=obj data="sstime.sct" style="display:none"
        type="text/x-scriptlet">
</OBJECT>

</BODY>
</HTML>
```

Running this page and clicking anywhere on it causes the following message.

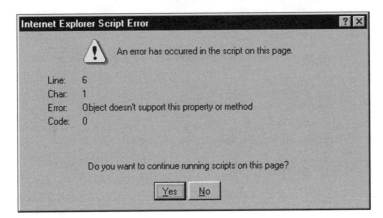

The line;

```
alert( obj.GetCurrentTime() );
```

is invalid and refers to a method that the object doesn't expose. Nevertheless, the file is exactly the same as before. The problem is with the following code:

```
<OBJECT id=obj data="sstime.sct" style="display:none"
        type="text/x-scriptlet">
</OBJECT>
```

In this we're telling IE4 that **sstime.sct** is a DHTML Scriptlet. This means that IE4 will recognize, as public members, all the functions that have the **public_** prefix, or those exposed through an object called **public_description**. We covered this in Chapter 3. The Server Scriptlet, however, has no **public_description** variable. Nothing, however, prevents us from defining such a variable. The presence of a **public_description** object won't affect the behavior of the Server Scriptlet when we use it as a real COM object. So let's change the Server Scriptlet code this way:

```
<SCRIPTLET>

<REGISTRATION
    Description="Time"
    ProgID="Time.Scriptlet"
    Version="1.00"
    ClassID="{51eb18c0-98a7-11d1-83d1-f46705c10000}"
>
</REGISTRATION>

<IMPLEMENTS id=Automation type=Automation>
    <method name=GetCurrentTime>
    </method>
</IMPLEMENTS>

<SCRIPT language=JScript>
var mTime = "";

var public_description = new Time;
function Time() {
  this.GetCurrentTime = GetCurrentTime;
}

function GetCurrentTime() {
  mTime = new Date;
  return mTime.getHours() + ":" + mTime.getMinutes();
}

</SCRIPT>
</SCRIPTLET>
```

This new component is called **sstime1.sct**. Now it is interchangeable and can be used as both an ActiveX Control and a DHTML Scriptlet.

User interface differences

For the moment, a Server Scriptlet cannot have any user interface elements and cannot call message box functions. All that it can do is perform background operations and calculations. From this point of view, a Server Scriptlet could be usefully employed in middle-tier business logic units or used in the accessing of databases. This is fundamentally different from DHTML Scriptlets. DHTML Scriptlets, by contrast, are heavily based on the DHTML object model and are Web pages with a graphical content to display.

If you add a line like

```
alert( "This is a message" );
```

to a Server Scriptlet, it will be ignored or an error will be displayed. In the same way, you can't include a body or an **<HTML>** tag. A Server Scriptlet can **only** be made of script.

Development differences

Writing a DHTML Scriptlet and a Server Scriptlet means writing two different files, whose only common code might well be just the **public_description** object. But again, defining a **public_description** object for a Server Scriptlet is optional. However, if one is present it does also make the Server Scriptlet usable as a DHTML Scriptlet.

The differences don't end here. A Server Scriptlet uses a different way to expose its properties and methods and needs to be registered before using. The registration step ensures that IE4 will be capable of retrieving the actual file name starting from the CLSID. Furthermore, the registration also ensures that a host environment like Visual Basic can create such an object through its name (that is, its **ProgID**).

After this quick tour of the differences between Server Scriptlets and DHTML Scriptlets, we're ready to go into more depth, analyzing in detail the structure of Server Scriptlet files, how they work behind the curtain, and finally how to host them in real-world applications.

To start experimenting, however, you need the tools. So let's see where and how you can get the Server Scriptlet Package.

The Server Scriptlet Package

The Server Scriptlet Package is available from the Microsoft's Web site at the usual address:

http://www.microsoft.com/scripting

Once you download it, you have an auto-extracting file called **scp10en.exe**. It installs, by default, in:

C:\Program Files\Common Files\System\Server Scriptlets

You are, of course, completely free to choose whichever path your heart desires.

The Server Scriptlet Package consists of three basic components:

- The Microsoft Scriptlet Wizard
- The run-time engine for Server Scriptlets
- A few HTML pages of documentation

The wizard is quite similar to the one we built and presented in Chapter 4. There are, however, some differences which will be dealt with in due course. This wizard helps you write both Server Scriptlets and DHTML scriptlets.

The run-time engine is a DLL called **scrobj.dll** that installs in the Windows\System directory. This module is responsible for interpreting the source code of the scriptlet and works as a broker between the clients and the Server Scriptlets. It provides a COM-based interface and builds a wrapper around the script code to make it appear as a compiled and self-contained COM component. It is, therefore, practically undistinguishable from an ATL server or a Visual Basic ActiveX control.

The next figure shows us how the Server Scriptlet Package will appear once installed.

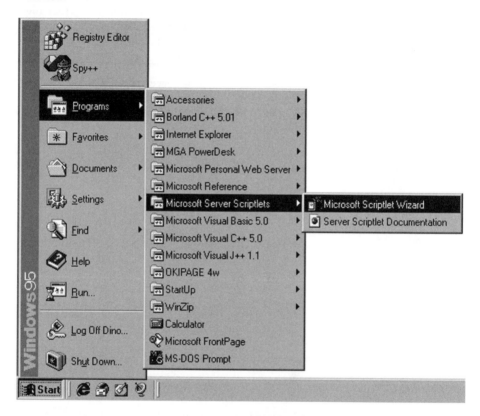

The Microsoft Scriptlet Wizard

Bundled with the package you'll find a wizard that lets you create Server Scriptlets as well as DHTML scriptlets. It consists of a few basic steps through which you enter general information about the component, and the list of its properties and methods. The next figure shows its first screenshot.

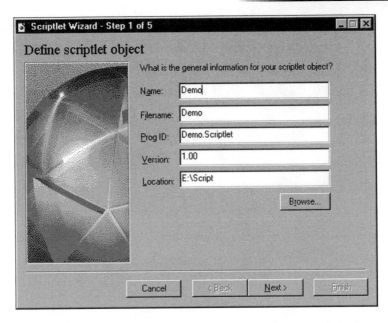

Here you specify the name and the path of the scriptlet, as well as its **ProgID** and version number. Next, you will be required to indicate which kind of component to generate and the language you'd like to use. Even if it's possible to write code in more than one script language, mixing, say VBScript and JScript, to avoid performance slow down, you should decide once and for all on one language, and then use it throughout that page.

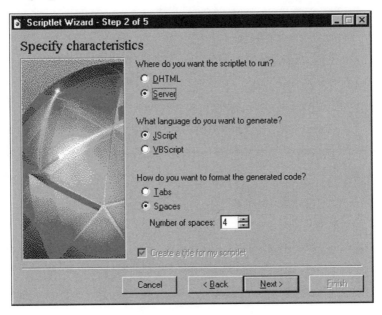

To list the required properties and methods the wizard offers an expanding listbox where you can enter the name of the property, its default value and even read/write, read-only or write-only.

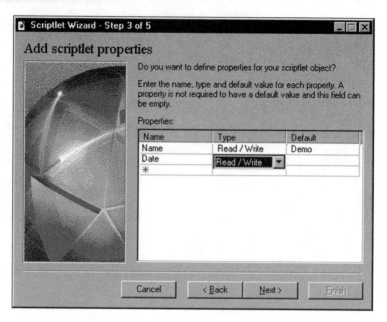

For the methods you need to indicate their names, and list the parameters. Each parameter name must be separated with a comma. For example, if you have a method called **Say** that takes in input a string called **text** and a number called **numRepeat** then the string to enter is:

```
text, numRepeat
```

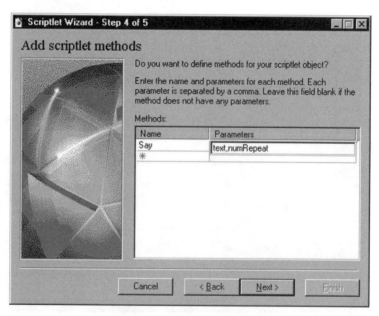

Of course, you can leave it blank if that method requires no argument. The final step displays a summary of your choices.

420

If you choose to create a DHTML Scriptlet instead of a Server Scriptlet, then there's a further step where you can check the standard events you want the component to forward. This doesn't make sense for Server Scriptlets since they have no user interface and only interact with the user through methods and properties.

Comparing this Wizard with our own

The goals of the Microsoft Scriptlet Wizard and the one we introduced in Chapter 4 are similar. This one supports Server and DHTML Scriptlets at the same time. However, the code generated for DHTML Scriptlets has some redundancies—it includes the **<SCRIPTLET>** tag anyway, which is, instead, the kernel of a Server Scriptlet. When we generate a Server Scriptlet we also get the public_description for free so it can also be used as a DHTML Scriptlet.

Even in terms of options provided they are similar. Our own, however, provides slightly superior support for a few stock properties, but doesn't allow you to specify a prototype for the methods you add.

So, in conclusion, you can choose between two quite similar tools if you need DHTML Scriptlets (there is only one choice for Server Scriptlets). Our suggestion is to consider our wizard if you just need to work with DHTML Scriptlets but to otherwise choose Microsoft's.

The Run-Time Engine for Server Scriptlets

A Server Scriptlet is a script file that works as a real COM object. In fact, a Server Scriptlet is still a script file—but one which is interpreted by a run-time module that eventually implements the needed and referred COM interfaces. This module takes care of creating the standard layer of code for all the COM-aware development tools and all the COM-aware applications .

Without this run-time engine—called **scrobj.dll**—you simply don't have a COM scriptlet. Of course, when planning how to distribute your Server Scriptlet you should make sure that such a library is available on the client machine. However, personally, I think that by the time the Server Scriptlet Package gets released Microsoft will include a Setup Wizard or include the needed file with Internet Explorer.

To understand the role of this run-time engine, let's consider how a method gets called in a DHTML and Server Scriptlet. In the first case, the container—be it IE4 or the Microsoft Scriptlet Control used in Visual Basic—is aware that the object being referred to is a scriptlet. Therefore, it knows about its **public_description** object and its public methods and so it's easy for it to invoke the right script function.

As explained above, a Server Scriptlet can act as a traditional DHTML Scriptlet if you add a **public_description** object and insert it in an HTML page—specifying the scriptlet's MIME type. However, a Server Scriptlet can also be exploited through its COM automation interface. You can create an instance of it with the following syntax:

```
Set obj = CreateObject( "Time.Scriptlet" )
```

When next you attempt to invoke its methods and properties the underlying environment will completely ignore the fact that it's made of JScript or VBScript code. What matters is that the **ProgID** passed in (the string **Time.Scriptlet** in the above example) links to a COM server regularly registered in the client machine. From the **ProgID** the executor of the code will go up to the CLSID of the server. This information is stored in the registry. The next figure shows where and how.

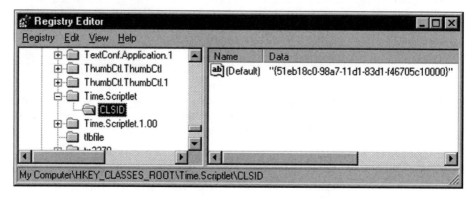

When it's time to execute a method on that object,

```
Set obj = CreateObject( "Time.Scriptlet" )
obj.GetCurrentTime
```

there's no more **public_description** variable to take care of. The CLSID points to a library name to be loaded. The next figure demonstrates that the **scrobj.dll** is the library associated with the CLSID assigned to the Time Server Scriptlet seen above. Note the correspondence between the CLSID shown in the figure and the one in the source code of **sstime.sct**.

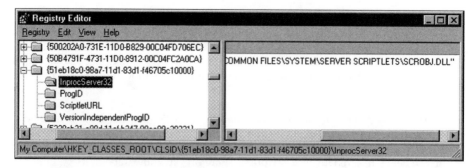

scrobj.dll is a common interface for all the Server Scriptlets. A COM-aware development tool attempts to use such a component, it accomplishes the same steps as for any other COM object. It's up to **scrobj.dll** to map any call it receives to the right scriptlet URL. The diagram shows the role played by this run-time module. It implements the COM interfaces necessary to talk to the clients and translate the calls back to the specific SCT file whose name is coded in the **ScriptletURL** key of the registry.

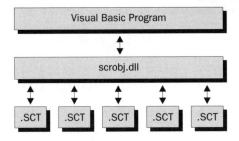

In other words, this run-time module works as an interpreter between the client (say, a Visual Basic program) and the server (say, a Server Scriptlet).

Invoking a method the COM way actually results in calling the **Invoke** function of the **IDispatch** or **IDispatchEx** interfaces. A Scriptlet doesn't know anything about it, but **scrobj.dll** does, and proceeds to translate the call into something that the Scriptlet can understand.

The code sufficient to implement an automation interface with methods and properties is stored inside **scrobj.dll**. This module at the moment only offers support for the dispatch interfaces mentioned above. A COM server could do much more and may need other interfaces to be implemented. For any COM interface that you want your Server Scriptlet to support, you need a kind of interface handler, that is, a module (mostly written in C++) which takes care of exposing the interface pointers to the clients and turning back to the script code for the actual code execution. As I have already mentioned, we have only **scrobj.dll** that handles the **IDispatch** interface needed for automation at the moment. In the future, however, we can expect both Microsoft and third-party companies to provide other specialized interface handlers.

An interface handler is a COM server with a predefined behavior. It will work in conjunction with (and not replace) the **scrobj.dll**. Actually, it is helpful to think of an interface handler as an extension of the run-time module. There is no documentation yet for writing interface handlers, but it will surely be available in the months to come.

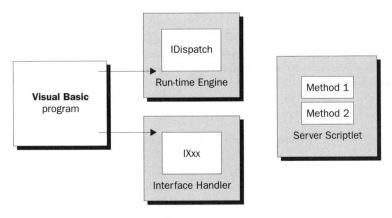

The previous figure shows a more detailed view of the Server Scriptlet's architecture. In the next section, we'll start examining the inner structure of a Server Scriptlet and have a closer look at the new tags.

Structure of a Server Scriptlet File

A Server Scriptlet file is not an HTML file. In fact it doesn't contain the **<HTML>** tag or body. Nevertheless, it **looks** like a "traditional" HTML file. Moreover, it contains **<SCRIPT>** tags just like any "normal" HTML file. After all, a Server Scriptlet file is just a text given by a mix of script code and XML. XML is a kind of further evolution of HTML and is based on the same layout that is found behind the IE4 channels file (CDF—Channel Definition Format). XML is also used in the OSD format for Open Software Distribution. A complete reference guide for CDF and OSD may be found in our *Professional IE4 Programming* – ISBN 1-861000-70-7.

Before going into any more depth with the new tags just defined for Server Scriptlet, let's have a quick tour of the XML features.

An overview of XML

XML is an acronym that stands for eXtensible Markup Language and represents a more general way of defining text-based documents. XML descends from SGML (Standard Generalized Markup Language) and is specifically targeted for use with the Web. The greatest difference between HTML and XML is the flexibility of the allowable tags. In HTML any tag you can use must be taken from a fixed subset. An XML-based document, instead, can define its own tags, as well as include a set of tags defined by a third-party.

This kind of flexibility relies on a parser that reads a document type definition (DTD) for a specific XML document if one is available. By defining a new DTD you establish a set of rules and a set of tags creating *de facto* a new markup language. This may become very useful for those applications that need to deal with very complex data structures. A DTD is a text file that describes the syntax of the tags you're using in that class of documents.

However, you don't need to always define a new DTD. The IE4 XML object model allows you to take in any XML document and climb it as if it were a tree. In this way, you can examine all the tags and their nesting. This is what **scrobj.dll** does when registering the Server Scriptlet, or invoking one of its methods or properties. More information on XML may be found in the Internet Client SDK available at:

http://www.microsoft.com/msdn/sdk/inetsdk

Alternatively, an FAQ on XML is available at **http://www.ucc.ie/xml/**.

XML and Server Scriptlets

A Server Scriptlet **.sct** file contains three main tags. These tags are the following:

- **<SCRIPTLET>**

- **<REGISTRATION>**

- **<IMPLEMENTS>**

REGISTRATION and **IMPLEMENTS** include some other more specific tags, while **SCRIPTLET** plays the same role as the **<HTML>** for HTML documents—namely it is the main wrapper that encompasses all the information. In addition, we have a well-known **<SCRIPT>** tag that—as expected—contains the script code to be executed.

The **<SCRIPTLET>** tag denotes the beginning and the end of a SCT document and doesn't support any additional attributes. Everything included between the **<SCRIPTLET>** and **</SCRIPTLET>** tags is part of the Server Scriptlet document. A Server Scriptlet can rely on three categories of information:

- Registration information such as **ProgID, CLSID, Version**

- Implemented interfaces

- Script code written in a variety of script languages

Let's see them in detail.

Adding registration information

Registration information is required to put your Server Scriptlets to work as a real COM object. Basically, it allows any COM server to be retrieved and invoked by clients at run-time. There are two fundamental pieces of registration information—a **ProgID** and a CLSID. Both of these allow any client application to get in touch with the server and work with it. This information must be public and stored in an easily accessible location Under the Win32 platform this is the system registry.

A **ProgID** is a string usually composed by two or more words separated by dots. When you use the VBScript's **CreateObject** function to instantiate a new object, what you are actually doing is passing it a **ProgID** string. A COM server is uniquely identified by a number called CLSID. The CLSID is what you're requested to indicate when using ActiveX Controls in your HTML pages.

Even when the function you're using requires a **ProgID** then it gets translated into the corresponding CLSID. In a previous figure, we presented a screenshot of the Windows registry where a given **ProgID** entry had its own CLSID key.

What's a CLSID?

A CLSID should be a globally unique number—that is you should make sure that there are no other COM objects with the same ID! Microsoft provided a couple of utilities to generate CLSIDs. All these utilities rely on an algorithm capable of generating random and different numbers for any machine. The next figure shows one of these utility programs called **guidgen.exe**. It comes with any version of Microsoft Visual C++ from 4.0 onwards.

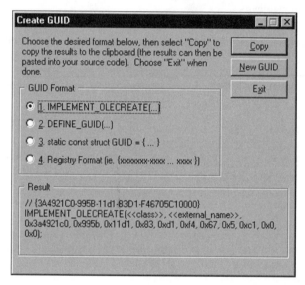

Another command-line tool that does the same is **uuidgen.exe**. This is also available through the same Visual C++ channel. The latter, however, has no user interface. Other non-Microsoft development environments allow you to generate a new CLSID within the IDE by just hitting a key combination. This is the case with Delphi 3, where—by pressing *Ctrl-G*—you can ask the program to create a CLSID for you.

> *A CLSID often is also referred to with the word GUID, which stands for Globally Unique IDentifier.*

If you don't have any of these tools, then the Microsoft Scriptlet Wizard we examined earlier provides this capability. Any time you create a Server Scriptlet it returns a new CLSID.

Even if we are accustomed to seeing it as a series of numbers enclosed in curly brackets—and actually looking like a string—a CLSID is a number. It is, in fact, a 128-bit number with a variety of possible representations. The most frequently used is the one with curly brackets and dashes to isolate inner components. Something very much like this in fact:

```
{51eb18c0-98a7-11d1-83d1-f46705c10000}
```

Always assign a CLSID

You could avoid specifying a CLSID when creating the Server Scriptlet. In doing so, you're implicitly asking the registration code inside **scrobj.dll** to generate a CLSID for you when it's time to register a given Server Scriptlet. While this approach is perfectly legitimate, it has a subtle drawback. Your component, in fact, will not have the same CLSID on all client machines. Due to the internal machinery of the GUID generator, algorithms executing the program on different machines at different moment in time will surely produce different numbers. Naturally, this behavior is by design and not a bug.

On the other hand, having the same component registered differently on different machines is not necessarily a problem. This is, however, a potentially risky situation because some development tools may cache the CLSID of the COM components they're using and get confused if you register again.

Always remember that a CLSID unambiguously identifies a COM object, but it is just a number and its generation process has nothing to do with any aspect of the COM server file (name, size, date, or other).

Version and Description

Besides the ProgID and the CLSID you might want to add other two fields to the **<REGISTRATION>** tag. These are **Version** and **Description** and are both strings. The number version is usually a string of the form:

n.nn

The version string is also appended to the **ProgID** for those applications that require the creation of a version-dependent instance of the object. The description text—as well as all this data—will be stored in the registry and made available to those development tools that require a description for the COM objects in use.

The required syntax

The layout for registration information is the following:

```
<REGISTRATION
      ProgID="ProgID"
      ClassID="{CLSID}"
      Description="Description"
      Version="Version"
>
</REGISTRATION>
```

In a concrete case this layout will originate such a code:

```
<REGISTRATION
    ProgID="Time.Scriptlet"
    ClassID="{51eb18c0-98a7-11d1-83d1-f46705c10000}"
    Description="Time Server Scriptlet"
    Version="1.00"
>
</REGISTRATION>
```

The order of the various attributes is completely free.

Adding Script Code in the Registration Tag

When you register the Server Scriptlet (we'll cover this later) the registration information which has been added here is read and interpreted. If you have any reason to detect and process this event, you can insert a **<SCRIPT>** tag inside the **<REGISTRATION>**, as shown below.

```
<REGISTRATION
    ProgID="Time.Scriptlet"
    ClassID="{51eb18c0-98a7-11d1-83d1-f46705c10000}"
    Description="Time Server Scriptlet"
    Version="1.00"
>

<SCRIPT LANGUAGE="JScript">
function Register() {
  alert( "Scriptlet registered." );
}

function Unregister() {
  alert( "Scriptlet unregistered." );
}
</SCRIPT>
</REGISTRATION>
```

By defining two functions named **Register** and **Unregister** you will be notified when the scriptlet is registered and then unregistered. The registration process is governed by the run-time module **scrobj.dll** which will call back such routines if you define them.

Public Interface of a Server Scriptlet

The XML tag that allows you to shape the public interface of a Server Scriptlet is **<IMPLEMENTS>**. A DHTML Scriptlet is a piece of code that exposes methods and properties. That's all.

A Server Scriptlet, instead, is a piece of code that implements interfaces—one of which is the automation interface that allows a scriptlet to expose methods and properties. From this emerges how a Server Scriptlet is a more general object than a DHTML scriptlet.

All the COM interfaces the scriptlet implements must be declared in the **<IMPLEMENTS>** section and must have an interface handler—that is a run-time module which handles the requests from the clients and transmit them for execution down to the scriptlet. As explained above, at present only an interface handler has been developed to handle the **IDispatch** interface. This handler is built inside **scrobj.dll**. By using it we can create a scriptlet that acts as a real COM object that supports automation.

Given today's limited support to COM interfaces, you could think that there's not such a great difference between DHTML Scriptlets and Server Scriptlets, at least for the code inside the scriptlet. Today you would be right, but as soon as but as soon as more interface handlers become available (or rather the documentation to write them) Server Scriptlet will boast an edge in flexibility over the DHTML Scriptlets.

The <IMPLEMENTS> tag

The `<IMPLEMENTS>` tag for any Server Scriptlets you can write today begins like this:

```
<IMPLEMENTS TYPE=Automation ID=automation>
:
</IMPLEMENTS>
```

where you indicate the type of the interface you're implementing, as well as some specific information. The **ID** attribute has the same level of importance as it does in DHTML code. It allows you to reference the interface handler as an object. As has already been mentioned, the current version of the Server Scriptlets Package only supports the automation interface. In this case, the additional information you need to provide are the exposed methods and properties. The following is the syntax layout:

```
<IMPLEMENTS TYPE=COMhandlerName ID=internalHandlerName>
    <PROPERTY name="name"/>
    <METHOD name="name"/>
</IMPLEMENTS>
```

The `<IMPLEMENTS>` tag accepts child tags named `<PROPERTY>` and `<METHOD>`. Both follow a special XML-specific syntax that doesn't require the end-tag. Instead of:

```
<PROPERTY name="Age">
</PROPERTY>
```

you can write it all through a single command

```
<PROPERTY name="Age"/>
```

replacing the end-tag with a final **/**. You can use this convention only if the tag doesn't contain nested tags.

Object's Properties

There are two ways through which you can expose a property—simple values or functions. In other words, you can define a global variable and make it public or define a couple of **get**/**put** functions to gain more control over how the property is read or written. The DHTML Scriptlets provide only the function-based approach, while the Server Scriptlets provide both options.

Exposing Properties through Variables

Conceptually, a property is a variable so you should find it quite natural to implement it with a global buffer—freely accessible from both internal scripts and external callers. In most development tools, instead, you implement properties with a pair of functions which handle the reading and the writing separately. The variable-based approach is simpler to code but somewhat violates the encapsulation of the object. However, this is what you need to do to implement properties in terms of a variable.

```
<IMPLEMENTS ID=automation TYPE=Automation>
    <PROPERTY name="Age" internalname="mAge" />
    <PROPERTY name="Address" />
</IMPLEMENTS>
```

The tag **\<PROPERTY>** includes two attributes, **name** and **internalname**. The latter is optional. By **name** you determine the externally visible name of the variable. Instead, **internalname** denotes the name of the variable used internally to hold the value of the property. If you omit the internal name then the value is stored in a variable with the same name as the property.

In the example above, we defined a property called **Age** but implemented it through a global variable called **mAge**. We also defined an **Address** property without an internal name. In this case, we absolutely need to declare and initialize a variable called **Address**.

```
<SCRIPT language=JScript>
  mAge = 32
  Address = "30 Lincoln Road, Olton, Birmingham"
</SCRIPT>
```

Exposing Properties through Functions

The second way to declare properties is nearly identical to what we're used to doing with DHTML Scriptlets. That is—we must specify a function to return the value of the property and another one to allow the user to set a new content. This approach has two advantages:

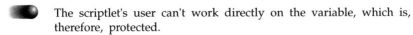

The scriptlet's user can't work directly on the variable, which is, therefore, protected.

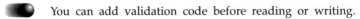

You can add validation code before reading or writing.

In addition, we also gain in flexibility since we can now decide which access rights a property can have—read/write, write-only or read-only. In the first case, we specify a **Get** and a **Put** function. In the other two instances we omit the **Get** and the **Put** functions respectively. The **Get** and the **Put** functions of a property are equivalent to the internal functions we met in Chapter 3. In was here where we first described how to assign properties to a DHTML Scriptlet.

Here's how to re-declare the above two **Age** and **Address** properties in terms of **Get**/**Put** functions assuming both properties are read/write.

```
<IMPLEMENTS ID=automation TYPE=Automation>
  <PROPERTY name="Age">
    <GET internalname="getAge"/>
    <PUT internalname="putAge"/>
  </PROPERTY>
  <PROPERTY name="Address">
    <GET />
```

```
<PUT />
</PROPERTY>
</IMPLEMENTS>
```

There are a few things to notice in the above code. The first is the fact that the **<PROPERTY>** tag is closed with the usual end-tag **</PROPERTY>**. As explained earlier, this occurs because now the tag contains other tags, specifically **<GET>** and **<PUT>**. These tags, which can be equated to the leaves of the tree, render the **<IMPLEMENTS>** tag and prevent the end-tag from exploiting the XML syntax facilities.

The <GET> and <PUT> tags

The **<GET>** and **<PUT>** tags allow us to specify the name of the internal functions that actually provide the expected behavior. To define a property in DHTML Scriptlets **Name** we are used to writing:

```
this.get_Name = getInternalName;
this.put_Name = putInternalName;
```

where **getInternalName** and **putInternalName** are the names of the functions that will be called. By assigning a property **get_Name** to the **this** object we specify that our scriptlet has a read-enabled property called **Name**. Alternatively, by assigning a property **put_Name** we mean to enable external callers to write a property through the name **Name**.

The **<GET>** and **<PUT>** tags are an equivalent and more general way to get the same result. By specifying such tags (or even only one of them)

```
<GET internalname="getAge"/>
<PUT internalname="putAge"/>
```

we enable the Server Scriptlet to add reading and writing capability to the property. In other words, the completely valid lines above are equivalent to the following for DHTML Scriptlets:

```
this.get_Age = getAge;
this.put_Age = putAge;
```

Again, **internalname** is an optional attribute.

```
<PROPERTY name="Address">
    <GET />
    <PUT />
</PROPERTY>
```

If you avoid it, then the names of the working functions are assumed to be given by the exposed name of the property prefixed by **get_** or **put_**. In the case above, we need to implement functions named necessarily **get_Address** and **put_Address**.

Of course, the **Get** function must not take any argument and return the current value of the property. By contrast, the **Put** function needs a single parameter—the new value—and doesn't need to return anything.

Object's Methods

Methods and properties exposed through **Get**/**Put** functions follow much the same pattern, at least from a syntax point of view. To declare a method you need to use the following notation:

```
<IMPLEMENTS TYPE=Automation ID=automation>
   <METHOD name="methodName" internalname="functionName">
   </METHOD>
</IMPLEMENTS>
```

Even in this case, **name** denotes the public name of the method while **internalname**—which is an optional attribute—indicates the name of the function that internally implements the method. A method called **Speak** would be coded this way:

```
<IMPLEMENTS TYPE=Automation ID=automation>
   <METHOD name="Speak" internalname="DoSpeak">
   </METHOD>
</IMPLEMENTS>
```

It will be called **Speak** externally but internally implemented in **DoSpeak**. By omitting the **internalname** attribute we assume that the internal function has the same name as the method. At this point there's no need to declare the prototype of the method.

The Scriptlet's Script Code

Both the **<REGISTRATION>** and the **<IMPLEMENTS>** tags have no internal code—except for the registration callbacks discussed before. All the script code that provides the scriptlet's behavior should be defined in a **<SCRIPT>** section outside the above tags. Unless you're planning to use more than one script language you don't need multiple **<SCRIPT>** sections. Don't forget, however, that using more scripting engines (VBScript, JScript, PerlScript, and so forth) can slow down the performance of your component. This is due to the fact that the run-time engine might be changing the parser continuously.

Unless you want your Server Scriptlet to be DHTML compatible—used as a DHTML Scriptlet—you don't need to include a **public_description** object.

A Complete Server Scriptlet

At this point let's build an example of a Server Scriptlet and discover how to make use of it in various development environments like Visual Basic and Delphi 3. Server Scriptlets cannot have a user interface. We need to create one that can provide services to other modules. We have, therefore, chosen to create a Server Scriptlet that works as a Date Calculator. It exposes four methods and a property.

Function	Description
`DateAsDDMMYYYY()`	Returns the current date formatted as *dd/mm/yyyy*. The separator is the character stored in the Separator property.
`Add( dateString, days )`	Adds the specified day to a given date. The date is specified through a valid string. The return value is always a string of the form *Month day, year*.
`Diff( dateString1, dateString2 )`	Calculates the difference in days between the two dates expressed in strings. If the second date is greater than the first returns –1.
`IsGreaterThan( dateString1, dateString2 )`	Returns a boolean value denoting whether the first date string is greater than the second one.
`Separator`	A property that denotes the separator character to be used for the date returned by DateAsDDMMYYYY().

The scriptlet exposes methods to calculate the difference in days between two dates and also the specified number of days to a given date. The dates are expressed through strings. All the formats recognized by the JScript's Date object are valid. For example, September 23, 1995 or the number of milliseconds since the start date of 1/1/1970. Check out *Instant JavaScript* by Nigel McFarlane ISBN 1-861001-27-4 for more details.

In addition, we have added a method to compare two date strings and another one to return the current date formatted as *dd/mm/yyyy* where we can set the separator through a property.

The source code for this server is in the file **datecalc.sct**. I created the CLSID using **guidgen.exe** (we talked about it earlier).

```
<SCRIPTLET>

<REGISTRATION
  ProgID = "DateCalculator.Scriptlet"
  Version = "1.00"
  Description = "Date Calculator"
  ClassID = "{70AE1C41-99A4-11d1-83D1-F46705C10000}"
>
</REGISTRATION>

<IMPLEMENTS ID=Automation TYPE=Automation>
    <METHOD name="Diff" internalname="DoDiff" />
    <METHOD name="Add" />
    <METHOD name="IsGreaterThan" />
    <METHOD name="DateAsDDMMYYYY" />
    <PROPERTY name="Separator" internalname="mSep" />
</IMPLEMENTS>

<SCRIPT language=JavaScript>

var mSep = "/";
var g_msPerDay = 1000*60*60*24;
var g_aMonths = new Array( "Jan", "Feb", "Mar", "Apr", "May", "Jun", "Jul",
"Aug", "Sep", "Oct", "Nov", "Dec" );
```

```
// Add method (Month day, year)
function Add( sDate, nDays )  {

  d1 = new Date( sDate );
  ms1 = d1.getTime();
  ms2 = nDays * g_msPerDay;

  d2 = new Date( ms1 + ms2 );
  s = g_aMonths[d2.getMonth()] + " " + d2.getDate() + ", ";

  nYear = d2.getYear();
  if( nYear < 2000 )
    nYear += 1900;

  return  s + nYear;
}

// Diff method
function DoDiff( sDate1, sDate2 )  {

  d1 = new Date( sDate1 );
  d2 = new Date( sDate2 );
  ms1 = d1.getTime();
  ms2 = d2.getTime();

  if( ms2 > ms1 )
    return -1;

  ms = (ms1 - ms2);
  nDays = ms/g_msPerDay;
  x = parseInt( nDays, 10 );
  if( nDays > x )
    nDays = x+1;

  return nDays;
}

// IsGreaterThan method
function IsGreaterThan( sDate1, sDate2 ) {

  d1 = new Date( sDate1 );
  d2 = new Date( sDate2 );

  ms1 = d1.getTime();
  ms2 = d2.getTime();

  return (ms1 > ms2);
}

// DateAsDDMMYYYY method
function DateAsDDMMYYYY() {

  d = new Date();
  nMonth = 1 + d.getMonth();
  nYear = d.getYear();
  if( nYear < 2000 )
    nYear += 1900;

  return d.getDate() + mSep + nMonth + mSep + nYear;
}
</SCRIPT>

</SCRIPTLET>
```

What this code does has been explained in the table above, so we aren't going to detail it here.

Once we finish writing a Server Scriptlet we are still far from testing. There is one significant step to take before we can check our work—registering the scriptlet. This registration allows any COM-aware development tool to retrieve and use our server. We can't test this scriptlet until we register it.

The built-in JScript date object already supports the year 2000. In fact if you add a number of days so that it exceeds Dec 31, 99 then the year returned is 2000 and not 99 or 98 as can happen.

Registering a Server Scriptlet

Once you have installed the Server Scriptlet Package, and right-clicked on any SCT file in the Windows Explorer you get a context menu like below.

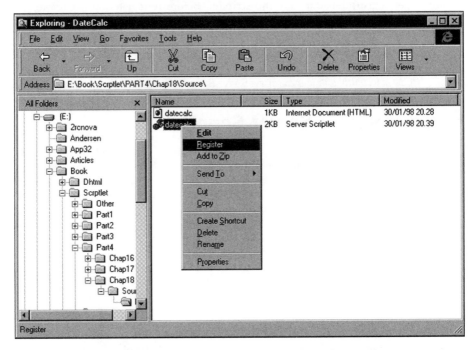

By clicking on it, you should get a message box like this that informs you that all went well.

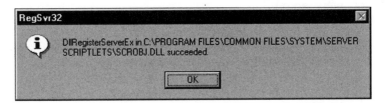

While writing this book, however, I often got the following message box instead:

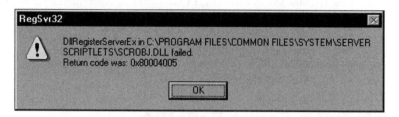

Despite the presence of the unintelligible message all is not lost. I discovered that this message is sent when you attempt to re-register a scriptlet. You might want to do so because, for example, you changed the CLSID or the **ProgID** or any other registration data for the scriptlet. Before re-registering, therefore, you must unregister the scriptlet.

Note that a Server Scriptlet can only be successfully registered if it doesn't have an <HTML> tag or a body. You cannot register a DHTML Scriptlet as a COM object although you can use a Server Scriptlet as a DHTML scriptlet.

Unregistering a Server Scriptlet

Usually the registration for a COM component is accomplished in two ways—by the component itself through a function called DllRegisterServer (or DllRegisterServerEx) or by the means of a utility called **regsvr32.exe** which is located in the Windows directory. To be honest, even the utility ends up calling the **DllRegisterServer** function.

The Server Scriptlet Package comes with its own copy of the utility, so you don't have to worry about it—just install the package!

The syntax for registering a Server Scriptlet is straightforward:

```
regsvr32.exe sct_filename
```

where *sct_filename* is the name of the SCT file you want to register. This is because **regsvr32** is a well-known utility for COM developers. I then need to take a look at the content of the Windows registry under the key:

HKEY_CLASSES_ROOT
  .sct

There you will learn that everything that defines the context menu for the SCT files is stored under another key: (see the figure)

HKEY_CLASSES_ROOT
  scriptletfile

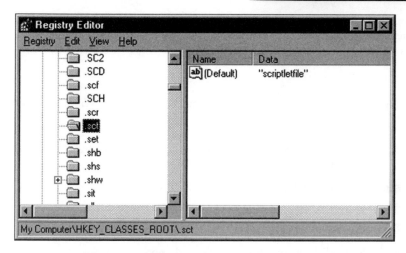

Under such a registry key there should be a subtree called **Shell** that looks like in the screenshot below. All the subkeys defined here correspond to items added to the context menu for the scriptlets file. As you can see, there are two items—Edit and Register. Compare this figure with the one showing the context menu, that we encountered earlier. The key **Command** for each item defines the program that actually executes after the click.

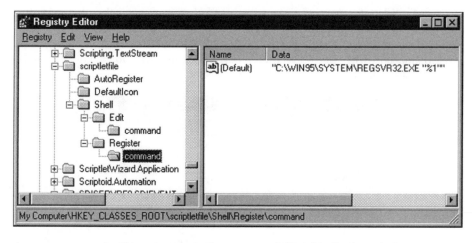

As you can see in the screenshot, the command line for Register is just:

```
c:\win95\system\regsvr32.exe "%1"
```

Of course the Windows path refers to my home computer. The "%1" means that the utility will receive the file currently highlighted in Windows Explorer. In other words, the file you have just right-clicked.

How to Unregister

If you've used regsvr32.exe then you should know that by calling it this way:

```
regsvr32.exe /u filename
```

437

you will be able to unregister a COM object from the registry. The next step, therefore, is essential. You need to add a new "Unregister" item to the context menu with the following **Command** string:

```
regsvr32.exe /u "%1"
```

Using the Registry Editor (**regedit.exe**, located in the Windows directory) the next steps are pretty straightforward.

- Open the Registry Editor. The easiest way to do it is by typing **regedit** in the Run box.

- Expand the HKEY_CLASSES_ROOT node.

- Search for the **scriptletfile** key and expand it.

- Expand its **Shell** node.

- Right-click on the **Shell** item and choose New|Key.

- Type in Unregister.

- Right-click on the just added **Unregister** item and choose New|Key again.

- Type in Command.

- Select the new **Command** item, and double-click on the **Default** string in the right-hand pane.

A dialog box will appear. Type in regsvr32.exe /u "%1". To make sure prefix with the actual path of your Windows\System directory.

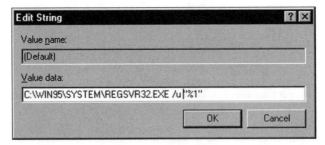

Once this is completed turn back to Explorer and right-click on an SCT file. The context menu should now be the following.

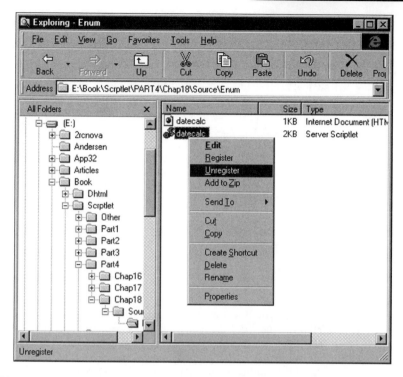

In this way you can register and unregister a Server Scriptlet with the greatest of ease. The next figure shows that unregistering this way really works!

Note that there's an error in what the beta version of the Server Scriptlet Package writes in your registry. It does not store the name of the application that will run if you right-click on the Edit voice. If you highlight the Edit key in the same subtree discussed here, you'll note that it attempts to run notepad.exe but from the System directory. This is an error, since Notepad resides in the Windows directory. To correct this, edit the corresponding Default string on the right-hand pane and remove the System subdirectory from the path.

Making use of a Server Scriptlet

Now we have created and registered a Server Scriptlet, we're ready to test it. First of all, let's see if all is well when we call it from an HTML page. For this purpose, we prepared a page called **datecalc.htm**. The Server Scriptlet must be inserted as if it was an ActiveX control.

```
<HTML>
<BODY>
Click on the page to test the Date Calculator Server Scriptlet.<hr>

<SCRIPT language=Javascript for="document" event="onclick">
  s1 = "May 4, 1998";
  s2 = obj.Add( s1, 2 );
  alert( s2 );

  s3 = obj.Diff( s2, s1 );
  alert( s3 );

  s4 = obj.IsGreaterThan( s2, s1 );
  alert( s4 );

  obj.Separator = "-";
  alert( obj.DateAsDDMMYYYY() );
</SCRIPT>

<OBJECT id=obj classid="clsid:70AE1C41-99A4-11d1-83D1-F46705C10000"
        style="display:none">
</OBJECT>

</BODY>
</HTML>
```

By clicking on the page you'll see a message box that displays a date 2 days after my next birthday. Then the difference in days between the two dates (again, it is 2). The page also adds a few lines to test the other functions of the scriptlet. Note that we're using the property **Separator** but we implemented it through a variable with another name. The only link between **Separator** and the variable **mSep** (see the previous listing) is established in the **<IMPLEMENTS>** section.

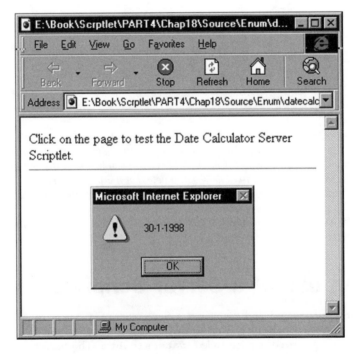

The figure shows the date formatted with a dash instead of the common slash. It follows the notation dd-mm-yyyy.

Testing HTML pages with Server Scriptlets

It is, on the whole, best to start testing a Server Scriptlet with an HTML page, as we did above. Writing an HTML page is quite straightforward and quicker than Visual Basic. However, there's a possible nasty side effect, which does need to be pointed out. It seems that you need to close IE4 before testing a modified scriptlet. In other words, you write your scriptlet and run an HTML page to test it. Then you find out there's a bug or something you want to fix. So you switch to your favorite editor and enter the changes. However, you can't simply refresh IE4 for the updates to take place.

There's a reason for this. A DHTML Scriptlet is a far simpler object, really nothing more than an HTML page. With this in mind, by refreshing the IE4 window you could force the browser to consider the most recent version of it. Things aren't so smooth with Server Scriptlets. A Server Scriptlet is a COM object—or rather it is accessed through a real COM object. Loading and unloading a COM object, say an ActiveX control, poses a number of problems. In practice the object remains locked and gets freed only when you close IE4 or—probably—when you open so many documents that it's put out of the browser's cache. Only then is a COM object unloaded from memory. If you're using a tool like Visual Basic, Visual C++ or Delphi at this point you can delete or recompile it. If you're using Server Scriptlets, however, only now can you have it reloaded again from scratch with all the new changes to the XML and script code.

> With the first beta of Server Scriptlets, if you're using a scriptlet and have an error then the JScript parser remains hanging. You need to close your development tool (say Visual Basic) before re-testing the scriptlet. This is due to a bug which will probably be fixed by the time you read this.

Using Server Scriptlets in Visual Basic

Once you have written a Server Scriptlet you have, inadvertently, written a COM component. Hence, you can call it through any tool that supports COM components. Visual Basic is certainly the first in line. Our Date Calculator module must be instantiated in Visual Basic code using the **CreateObject** function.

```
Dim g_sctDateCalc As Object
Set g_sctDateCalc = CreateObject("DateCalculator.Scriptlet")
```

The following code shows how to create such an object. From now on, the **g_sctDateCalc** variable can be used to invoke the methods and properties of the scriptlet following the usual object-oriented syntax.

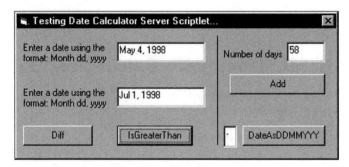

Notice that unlike the DHTML Scriptlets you don't require additional ActiveX control to exploit Server Scriptlets. The figure shows a sample program you can download from our Web site. The file is called **vbsct.zip**. It uses the Date Calculator Server Scriptlet to make date additions and subtractions. Once you download the file you actually find two files—a project file and a form. The source code of the **.frm** form file is the following:

```
Dim g_sctDateCalc As Object

Private Sub cmdAdd_Click()
   txtDate2.Text = g_sctDateCalc.Add(txtDate1.Text, Val(txtDays.Text))
End Sub

Private Sub cmdDate_Click()
   g_sctDateCalc.Separator = txtSep.Text
   MsgBox g_sctDateCalc.DateAsDDMMYYYY("")    ' Pay attention here!!!
End Sub

Private Sub cmdDiff_Click()
   txtDays.Text = g_sctDateCalc.Diff(txtDate2.Text, txtDate1.Text)
End Sub

Private Sub cmdGreater_Click()
   b = g_sctDateCalc.IsGreaterThan(txtDate2.Text, txtDate1.Text)
   If b Then
     MsgBox "<" + txtDate2.Text + "> is greater than <" + txtDate1.Text + ">"
   Else
     MsgBox "<" + txtDate1.Text + "> is greater than <" + txtDate2.Text + ">"
   End If
End Sub

Private Sub Form_Load()
   Set g_sctDateCalc = CreateObject("DateCalculator.Scriptlet")
End Sub

Private Sub Form_Unload(Cancel As Integer)
   Set g_sctDateCalc = Nothing
End Sub
```

Notice that the scriptlet is instantiated during the form load and released while unloading. The sample program adds the number of days to the first date field and displays the resulting date in the second field. It also subtracts the first date field from the second and places the result, in days, in the correspondent edit box. Furthermore, it compares the two dates and displays the current date—formatted as *dd/mm/yyyy*—using the specified separator.

In the source above there's a comment in the correspondence of the line:

```
MsgBox g_sctDateCalc.DateAsDDMMYYYY("")    ' Pay attention here!!!
```

If you look back at the source code for this method you will notice that it doesn't take any parameter as input. So why exactly are we passing an empty string in the Visual Basic call? I must confess that the reason for this is beyond me, however, if you call it omitting that "additional" argument what you get is

instead of the following (what we'd like to have):

The same didn't occur in our previous HTML test page.

This is a known bug in the first beta version. It will be fixed in the second beta release of the package.

Using Server Scriptlets in Delphi

In Chapter 8 we talked about the limited support that the Microsoft Scriptlet Control provides outside the Visual Basic and the IE4 environments. In particular, we pointed out that DHTML Scriptlets couldn't be successfully used in Delphi programs due to certain scriptlet control shortcomings.

Server Scriptlets, however, are ready to be used in Delphi since they are real COM objects. No matter what the run-time module does behind the curtains. What other applications see is a COM object. And what's important is that you can write it in JavaScript!

To demonstrate this, let's see how our Date Calculator scriptlet works in a Delphi 3 program.

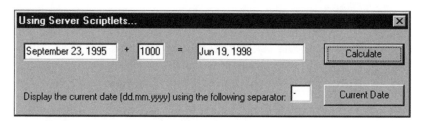

The key instruction is the creation of the COM automation object This requires a quite similar approach to that in Visual Basic.

```
g_sctDateCalc := CreateOleObject('DateCalculator.Scriptlet');
```

The full source code is the following:

```
unit d3sslet;

interface

uses
  Windows, Messages, SysUtils, Classes, Graphics, Controls, Forms, Dialogs,
  StdCtrls, OleAuto;

type
  TForm1 = class(TForm)
    Button1: TButton;
    Edit1: TEdit;
    Label1: TLabel;
    Edit2: TEdit;
    Label2: TLabel;
    Edit3: TEdit;
    Button2: TButton;
    Label3: TLabel;
    Edit4: TEdit;
    procedure Button1Click(Sender: TObject);
    procedure FormCreate(Sender: TObject);
    procedure Button2Click(Sender: TObject);
  private
    { Private declarations }
  public
    { Public declarations }
  end;

var
  Form1: TForm1;
  g_sctDateCalc: Variant;

implementation

{$R *.DFM}

{ Button: Current Date }
procedure TForm1.Button1Click(Sender: TObject);
begin
  g_sctDateCalc.Separator := Edit4.Text;
  ShowMessage( g_sctDateCalc.DateAsDDMMYYYY() );
end;

{ Button: Calculate }
procedure TForm1.Button2Click(Sender: TObject);
begin
  Edit3.Text := g_sctDateCalc.Add( Edit1.Text, StrToInt(Edit2.Text) );
end;

procedure TForm1.FormCreate(Sender: TObject);
begin
  Edit1.Text := 'September 23, 1995';
  Edit2.Text := '1000';
  Edit3.Text := '';
  g_sctDateCalc := CreateOleObject('DateCalculator.Scriptlet');
end;

end.
```

The entire Delphi 3 project is available from our site. The file to download is **d3sslet.zip**. With Delphi, we get the same strange behavior we have in Visual Basic when calling methods with no parameters.

444

Summary

Server Scriptlets are the most recent evolution of scripting technology. They bring to light two key topics that will play a pivotal role in Web technology in the months to come—scriptlets and XML. Scriptlets are reusable objects made up of script code. XML is an HTML-like syntax that allows you to describe virtually any kind of complex data structure with a natural and very expressive language. By combining scriptlets and XML we have a new file format that can be exploited to define a high-level interface for a COM object.

Server Scriptlets are just this. Pieces of script code with a layer of information which is interpreted at run-time by a specialized module. This run-time library shields the details of the script code and exposes a table of functions to the external world through the usual COM conventions.

From within Visual Basic applications (and not only them) you can now call a piece of script code using the same COM approach you're already familiar with. This is the first step towards the time when you can use a script language to implement any COM interface. But there's another equally impressive feature—the opportunity to write your own generic COM servers with script code. This feature is still to come. Today, at least, we can't yet define a totally new COM interface.

The current beta version of the Server Scriptlet Package allows us only to implement COM interfaces for which a run-time module (called interface handler) that provides the COM-based interaction with clients exists. Overall, the implementation is far from being complete but it looks really superb so far!

In this chapter, we provided an overview of the Server Scriptlet technology paying particular attention to a comparison between Server Scriptlets and DHTML Scriptlets (the main focus of this book). In particular, we covered:

- What Server Scriptlets are
- Differences with DHTML Scriptlets
- The XML-based syntax of a Server Scriptlet
- Registering and unregistering
- How to implement a Server Scriptlet
- How to use it in HTML, Visual Basic and Delphi applications

Server Scriptlets are a comprehensive technology that encompass DHTML Scriptlets—in our opinion they will continue living side-by-side at least for the next few months, maybe for the next couple of years. However, none of us have magical powers (as far as I'm aware) and software is a very hard field to forecast.

Final Thoughts

This book has been developed primarily to let you know about Scriptlets, the latest DHTML innovation. Scriptlets are self-contained, reusable and distributable Web components made up of script code. They exploit many of the inner features of the JavaScript language but you can even write them with VBScript.

Next, going steadily on down the development road, Microsoft changed the platform where scriptlets were based. The DHTML-based scriptlets we covered throughout this book suddenly became a special case of a more generalized layout, called Server Scriptlets or—maybe more intuitively—COM Scriptlets. This sounds like a small step but it opens up a whole new world for Web developers and others. How many of you know how to arrange a COM server—dealing with **IUnknown**, **IClassFactory**, **IDispatch** and all those strange interfaces? Now things start to simplify, and you can even use JavaScript or VBScript to set up *real* COM objects.

They called it Server Scriptlets but the scope of this technology is far wider than DHTML Scriptlets. This book stands in the middle of all these changes. It starts by presenting a detailed explanation of DHTML Scriptlets, and ends by addressing the changes which are still ongoing at the time of publication. In our opinion the chapter dedicated to Server Scriptlets is more like the first chapter of a new book than the last chapter of this one!

At the moment Scriptlets are only supported by the final released version of IE4 or higher and we don't know anything about the future of DHTML. At the moment, we can only try to guess the release date for Windows 98.

As you will certainly have noted, there too many "at the moment"s to be totally certain of anything... at the moment!

What does it all mean? It means that the Web computing model is changing and becoming more and more powerful and easy to use. It is gaining in flexibility, but also in robustness, quality and performance. This transformation will pass through DHTML. The next—mandatory—step is the introduction of some kind of reusability. Then a universal scripting language and finally a better integration with the most popular operating systems.

All these steps are outlined in the book, but we can't be sure today whether what we have discussed here will be the right way to go, even in the months to come.

The current DHTML object model and scriptlets have still to gain a wide acceptance. By the end of 1998, we're expecting approval of the DHTML standard. This is the key event. Then, we certainly will have something like Scriptlets and something like Remote Scripting. Hopefully, we will have universal solutions not tied to any specific product or language. And then—maybe—we'll need to rewrite a book like this.

The Browser Object Model

The Dynamic HTML Object Model contains 14 **objects**. Most of these are organized into a strict hierarchy that allows HTML authors to access all the parts of the browser, and the pages that are loaded, from a scripting language like JavaScript or VBScript.

The Object Model in Outline

The diagram shows the object hierarchy in graphical form. It is followed by a list of the objects and collection, with a brief description. Then, each object is documented in detail, showing the properties, methods, and events it supports.

Note that not all the objects and collections are included in the diagram. Some are not part of the overall object model, but are used to access other items such as dialogs or HTML elements.

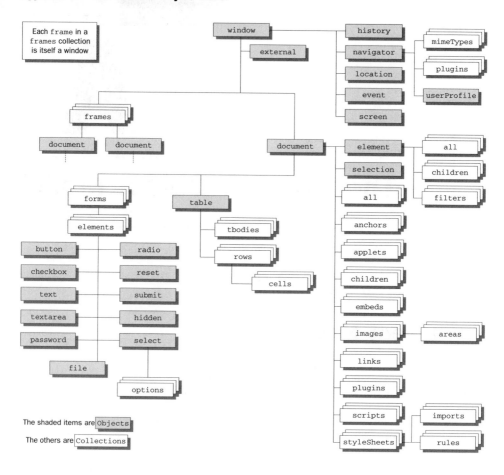

The Document Object

Exposes the entire HTML content through its own collections and properties, and provides a range of events and methods to work with documents.

PropertyName	AttributeName	CSSName	Description
activeElement			Identifies the element that has the focus.
alinkColor	**ALINK**		The color for active links in the page - i.e. while the mouse button is held down.
bgColor	**BGCOLOR**	**background-color**	Specifies the background color to be used for an element.

PropertyName	AttributeName	CSSName	Description
body			Read-only reference to the document's implicit body object, as defined by the `<BODY>` tag.
charset			Sets or returns the character set of the document.
cookie			The string value of a cookie stored by the browser.
defaultCharset			Sets or returns the default character set for the document.
domain			Sets or returns the domain of the document for use in cookies and security.
expando			Prevents script from creating arbitrary properties for objects, such as a mis-spelled property name
fgColor	TEXT		Sets the color of the document foreground text.
lastModified			The date that the source file for the page was last modified, as a string, where available.
linkColor	LINK		The color for un-visited links in the page.
location			Reference to the location object, also returns the full document URL.
parentWindow			Returns the parent window that contains the document.
readyState			Specifies the current state of an object being downloaded.
referrer			The URL of the page that referenced (loaded) the current page.
selection			Read-only reference to the document's selection object.
title	TITLE		Provides advisory information about the element, such as when loading or as a tooltip.

PropertyName	AttributeName	CSSName	Description
url	URL		Uniform Resource Locator (address) for the current document or in a **META** tag.
vlinkColor	VLINK		The color for visited links in the page.

Collection	Description
all	Collection of all the tags and elements in the body of the document.
anchors	Collection of all the anchors in the document.
applets	Collection of all the objects in the document, including intrinsic controls, images, applets, embeds, and other objects.
children	Collection of all the direct descendent or contained elements of this element.
embeds	Collection of all the embed tags in the document.
forms	Collection of all the forms in the page.
frames	Collection of all the frames defined within a **FRAMESET** tag.
images	Collection of all the images in the page.
links	Collection of all the links and **AREA** blocks in the page.
plugins	An alias for collection of all the embeds in the page.
scripts	Collection of all the **SCRIPT** sections in the page.
styleSheets	Collection of all the individual style property objects defined for a document.

MethodName	Description
clear	Clears the contents of a selection or document object.
close	Closes a document forcing written data to be displayed, or closes the browser window.
createElement	Creates an instance of an image or option element object.
createStyleSheet	Creates a new style sheet and inserts it into the stylesheets collection.
elementFromPoint	Returns the element at the specified x and y coordinates with respect to the window.
execCommand	Executes a command over the document selection or range.
open	Opens the document as a stream to collect output of **write** or **writeln** methods.

MethodName	Description
`queryCommandEnabled`	Denotes if the specified command is available for a document or TextRange.
`queryCommandIndeterm`	Denotes if the specified command is in the indeterminate state.
`queryCommandState`	Returns the current state of the command for a document or TextRange object.
`queryCommandSupported`	Denotes if the specified command is supported for a document or TextRange object.
`queryCommandValue`	Returns the value of the command specified for a document or TextRange object.
`showHelp`	Opens a window to display a Help file.
`write`	Writes text and HTML to a document in the specified window.
`writeln`	Writes text and HTML to a document in the specified window, followed by a carriage return.

EventName	Description
`onafterupdate`	Occurs when transfer of data from the element to the data provider is complete.
`onbeforeupdate`	Occurs before transfer of changed data to the data provider when an element loses focus or the page is unloaded.
`onclick`	Occurs when the user clicks the mouse button on an element, or when the value of a control is changed.
`ondblclick`	Occurs when the user double-clicks on an element.
`ondragstart`	Occurs when the user first starts to drag an element or selection.
`onerrorupdate`	Occurs when an **onbeforeupdate** event cancels update of the data, replacing the **onafterupdate** event.
`onhelp`	Occurs when the user presses the *F1* or *Help* key.
`onkeydown`	Occurs when the user presses a key.
`onkeypress`	Occurs when the user presses a key and a character is available.
`onkeyup`	Occurs when the user releases a key.
`onmousedown`	Occurs when the user presses a mouse button.
`onmousemove`	Occurs when the user moves the mouse.
`onmouseout`	Occurs when the mouse pointer leaves the element.
`onmouseover`	Occurs when the mouse pointer first enters the element.

EventName	Description
onmouseup	Occurs when the user releases a mouse button.
onreadystatechange	Occurs when the readyState for an object has changed.
onrowenter	Occurs when data in the current row has changed and new values are available.
onrowexit	Occurs before the data source changes data in the current row.
onselectstart	Occurs as soon as the user starts to make a selection with the mouse.

The Event Object

The global object provided to allow the scripting language to access an event's parameters. It provides the following properties:

PropertyName	Description
altKey	Returns the state of the *ALT* key when an event occurs.
button	The mouse button, if any, that was pressed to fire the event.
cancelBubble	Set to prevent the current event from bubbling up the hierarchy.
clientX	Returns the *x*-coordinate of the mouse pointer in relation to the window client area.
clientY	Returns the *y*-coordinate of the mouse pointer in relation to the window client area.
ctrlKey	Returns the state of the *CTRL* key when an event occurs.
fromElement	Returns the element being moved from for an **onmouseover** or **onmouseout** event.
keyCode	ASCII code of the key being pressed. Changing it sends a different character to the object.
offsetX	Returns the *x* coordinate of the mouse pointer when an event occurs, relative to the containing element.
offsetY	Returns the *y* coordinate position of the mouse pointer when an event occurs, relative to the containing element.
reason	Indicates whether data transfer to an element was successful, or why it failed.
returnValue	Allows a return value to be specified for the event or a dialog window.
screenX	Returns the *x* coordinate of the mouse pointer when an event occurs, in relation to the screen.
screenY	Returns the *y* coordinate of the mouse pointer when an event occurs, in relation to the screen.

PropertyName	Description
shiftKey	Returns the state of the *SHIFT* key when an event occurs.
srcElement	Returns the element deepest in the object hierarchy that a specified event occurred over.
srcFilter	Returns the filter that caused the element to produce an **onfilterchange** event.
toElement	Returns the element being moved to for an **onmouseover** or **onmouseout** event.
type	Returns the name of the event as a string, without the 'on' prefix, such as 'click' instead of 'onclick'.
x	Returns the x coordinate of the mouse pointer relative to a positioned parent, or otherwise to the window.
y	Returns the y coordinate of the mouse pointer relative to a positioned parent, or otherwise to the window.

The External Object

Provides access to an external object model when the browser is hosted in another application.

MethodName	Description
addChannel	Opens a dialog for adding or changing settings of a CDF file specified by URL
isSubscribed	Indicates if the CDF file at URL is already subscribed to.

The Filter Object

Provides access to a filter object within an element's filters collection.

PropertyName	Description
duration	The amount of time the filter occurs over.
status	Whether the effect has completed or not.

MethodName	Description
addAmbient	Adds an ambient light of color r,g,b, and intensity strength to a Light filter.
addCone	Adds a cone light at a specified position, and with a specified color, strength and spread, to a Light filter.
addPoint	Adds a point light source at a specified position and with a specified color and strength to a Light filter.

MethodName	Description
apply	Applies a transition filter to an object.
changeColor	Changes the color of a Light filter, either as an absolute value or an increment.
changeStrength	Changes the strength of a Light filter, either as an absolute value or an increment.
clear	Removes all lights associated with a Light filter.
moveLight	Changes the position of a Light filter, either as an absolute value or an increment.
play	Plays a transition filter for an object.
stop	Stops the playing of a transition filter.

The History Object

Contains information about the URL's that the client has visited, as stored in the browser's History list, and allows the script to move through the list.

PropertyName	Description
length	Returns the number of elements in a collection.

MethodName	Description
back	Loads the previous URL in the browser's History list.
forward	Loads the next URL in the browser's History list.
go	Loads the specified URL from the browser's History list.

The Location Object

Contains information on the current URL. It also provides methods that will reload a page.

PropertyName	AttributeName	Description
hash		The string following the # symbol in the URL.
host		The hostname:port part of the location or URL.
hostname		The hostname part of the location or URL.
href	HREF	The entire URL as a string.
pathname		The file or object path name following the third slash in a URL.

PropertyName	AttributeName	Description
port		The port number in a URL.
protocol		The initial substring up to and including the first colon, indicating the URL's access method.
search		The contents of the query string or form data following the ? (question mark) in the complete URL.

MethodName	Description
assign	Loads another page. Equivalent to changing the **window.location.href** property.
reload	Reloads the current page.
replace	Loads a document, replacing the current document's session history entry with its URL.

The Navigator Object

This object represents the browser application itself, providing information about its manufacturer, version, and capabilities.

PropertyName	Description
appCodeName	The code name of the browser.
appMinorVersion	The minor version number of the browser.
appName	The product name of the browser.
appVersion	The version number of the browser.
browserLanguage	Returns the ISO language code of the browser.
connectionSpeed	Returns the current browser connection speed value.
cookieEnabled	Indicates if client-side cookies are enabled in the browser.
cpuClass	Returns the class of the processor in use, i.e. "Alpha", "x86", etc.
online	If False, indicates if the browser is in 'Work Offline' mode. True does not mean that the browser is actually on line.
platform	Indicates the OS that the browser is running on, i.e. "Win32", "WinCE", etc.
plugins	An array of plugins available in the browser. Returns an empty collection in IE4.
systemLanguage	Returns the ISO language code of the current operating system.

PropertyName	Description
userAgent	The user-agent (browser name) header sent in the HTTP protocol from the client to the server.
userLanguage	Returns the ISO language code for the current user.
userProfile	Reference to the userProfile object for the browser.

Collection	Description
plugins	An alias for collection of all the embeds in the page.

MethodName	Description
javaEnabled	Returns True or False, depending on whether a Java VM is installed and enabled.
taintEnabled	Returns False, included for compatibility with Netscape Navigator

The Screen Object

This object provides information to the scripting language about the client's screen resolution and rendering abilities.

PropertyName	Description
bufferDepth	Specifies if and how an off-screen bitmap buffer should be used.
colorDepth	Returns the number of bits per pixel of the user's display device or screen buffer.
height	Returns the height of the user's display screen in pixels.
updateInterval	Sets or returns the interval between screen updates on the client.
width	Returns the width of the user's display screen in pixels.

The Selection Object

Returns the active selection on the screen, allowing access to all the selected elements including the plain text in the page.

PropertyName	AttributeName	Description
type	TYPE	Specifies the type of list style, link, selection, control, button, MIME-type, rel, or the CSS language.

MethodName	Description
clear	Clears the contents of a selection or document object.
createRange	Returns a copy of the current selection in the document.
empty	Deselects the current selection. Sets selection type to none and the item property to null.

The Style Object

This provides access to the individual style properties for an element. These could have been previously set by a style sheet, or by an inline style tag within the page.

PropertyName	AttributeName	CSSName	Description
background	BACKGROUND	background	Specifies a background picture that is tiled behind text and graphics.
backgroundAttachment		background-attachment	Defines if a background image should be fixed on the page or scroll with the content.
backgroundColor		background-color	Specifies the background color of the page or element.
backgroundImage		background-image	Specifies a URL for the background image for the page or element.
backgroundPosition		background-position	The initial position of a background image on the page.
backgroundPositionX			The x-coordinate of the background image in relation to the containing window.

PropertyName	AttributeName	CSSName	Description
`backgroundPositionY`			The *y*-coordinate of the background image in relation to the containing window.
`backgroundRepeat`		`background-repeat`	Defines if and how a background image is repeated on the page.
`border`	BORDER	`border`	Specifies whether a border will be drawn around the element, and its thickness.
`borderBottom`		`border-bottom`	Used to specify several attributes of the bottom border of an element.
`borderBottomColor`		`border-bottom-color`	The color of the bottom border for an element.
`borderBottomStyle`		`border-bottom-style`	The style of the bottom border for an element.
`borderBottomWidth`		`border-bottom-width`	The width of the bottom border for an element.
`borderColor`	BORDERCOLOR	`border-color`	The color of all or some of the borders for an element.
`borderLeft`		`border-left`	Used to specify several attributes of the left border of an element.
`borderLeftColor`		`border-left-color`	The color of the left border for an element.
`borderLeftStyle`		`border-left-style`	The style of the left border for an element.
`borderLeftWidth`		`border-left-width`	The width of the left border for an element.
`borderRight`		`border-right`	Used to specify several attributes of the right border of an element.
`borderRightColor`		`border-right-color`	The color of the right border for an element.
`borderRightStyle`		`border-right-style`	The style of the right border for an element.
`borderRightWidth`		`border-right-width`	The width of the right border for an element.

PropertyName	AttributeName	CSSName	Description
borderStyle		border-style	Used to specify the style of one or more borders of an element.
borderTop		border-top	Used to specify several attributes of the top border of an element.
borderTopColor		border-top-color	The color of the top border for an element.
borderTopStyle		border-top-style	The style of the top border for an element.
borderTopWidth		border-top-width	The width of the top border for an element.
borderWidth		border-width	Used to specify the width of one or more borders of an element.
clear	CLEAR	clear	Causes the next element or text to be displayed below left-aligned or right-aligned images.
clip		clip	Specifies how an element's contents should be displayed if larger that the available client area.
color	COLOR	color	The text or foreground color of an element.
cssText			The text value of the element's entire **STYLE** attribute.
cursor		cursor	Specifies the type of cursor to display when the mouse pointer is over the element.
display		display	Specifies if the element will be visible (displayed) in the page.
filter		filter	Sets or returns an array of all the filters specified in the element's style property.

PropertyName	AttributeName	CSSName	Description
`font`		`font,` `@font-face`	Defines various attributes of the font for an element, or imports a font.
`fontFamily`		`font-family`	Specifies the name of the typeface, or 'font family'.
`fontSize`		`font-size`	Specifies the font size.
`fontStyle`		`font-style`	Specifies the style of the font, i.e. normal or italic.
`fontVariant`		`font-variant`	Specifies the use of small capitals for the text.
`fontWeight`		`font-weight`	Specifies the weight (boldness) of the text.
`height`	`HEIGHT`	`height`	Specifies the height at which the element is to be drawn, and sets the `posHeight` property.
`left`		`left`	Specifies the position of the left of the element, and sets the `posLeft` property.
`letterSpacing`		`letter-` `spacing`	Indicates the additional space to be placed between characters in the text.
`lineHeight`		`line-height`	The distance between the baselines of two adjacent lines of text.
`listStyle`		`list-style`	Allows several style properties of a list element to be set in one operation.
`listStyleImage`		`list-` `style-image`	Defines the image used as a background for a list element.
`listStylePosition`		`list-style-` `position`	Defines the position of the bullets used in a list element.
`listStyleType`		`list-` `style-type`	Defines the design of the bullets used in a list element.

PropertyName	AttributeName	CSSName	Description
`margin`		`margin`	Allows all four margins to be specified with a single attribute.
`marginBottom`		`margin-bottom`	Specifies the bottom margin for the page or text block.
`marginLeft`		`margin-left`	Specifies the left margin for the page or text block.
`marginRight`		`margin-right`	Specifies the right margin for the page or text block.
`marginTop`		`margin-top`	Specifies the top margin for the page or text block.
`overflow`		`overflow`	Defines how text that overflows the element is handled.
`paddingBottom`		`padding-bottom`	Sets the amount of space between the bottom border and content of an element.
`paddingLeft`		`padding-left`	Sets the amount of space between the left border and content of an element.
`paddingRight`		`padding-right`	Sets the amount of space between the right border and content of an element.
`paddingTop`		`padding-top`	Sets the amount of space between the top border and content of an element.
`pageBreakAfter`		`page-break-after`	Specifies if a page break should occur after the element.
`pageBreakBefore`		`page-break-before`	Specifies if a page break should occur after the element.
`pixelHeight`			Sets or returns the height style property of the element in pixels, as a pure number rather than a string.

PropertyName	AttributeName	CSSName	Description
pixelLeft			Sets or returns the left style property of the element in pixels, as a pure number, rather than a string.
pixelTop			Sets or returns the top style property of the element in pixels, as a pure number, rather than a string.
pixelWidth			Sets or returns the width style property of the element in pixels, as a pure number, rather than a string.
posHeight			Returns the value of the height style property in its last specified units, as a pure number rather than a string.
position		position	Returns the value of the position style property, defining whether the element can be positioned.
posLeft			Returns the value of the left style property in its last specified units, as a pure number rather than a string.
posTop			Returns the value of the top style property in its last specified units, as a pure number rather than a string.
posWidth			Returns the value of the width style property in its last specified units, as a pure number rather than a string.

PropertyName	AttributeName	CSSName	Description
styleFloat		float	Specifies if the element will float above the other elements in the page, or cause them to flow round it.
textAlign		text-align	Indicates how text should be aligned within the element.
textDecoration		text-decoration	Specifies several font decorations (underline, overline, strikethrough) added to the text of an element.
textDecorationBlink			Specifies if the font should blink or flash. Has no effect in IE4.
textDecorationLineThrough			Specifies if the text is displayed as strikethrough, i.e. with a horizontal line through it.
textDecorationNone			Specifies if the text is displayed with no additional decoration.
textDecorationOverline			Denotes if the text is displayed as overline, i.e. with a horizontal line above it.
textDecorationUnderline			Denotes if the text is displayed as underline, i.e. with a horizontal line below it.
textIndent		text-indent	Specifies the indent for the first line of text in an element, and may be negative.
textTransform		text-transform	Specifies how the text for the element should be capitalized.
top		top	Position of the top of the element, sets the posTop property. Also returns topmost window object.

PropertyName	AttributeName	CSSName	Description
verticalAlign		vertical-align	Sets or returns the vertical alignment style property for an element.
visibility		visibility	Indicates if the element or contents are visible on the page.
width	WIDTH	width	Specifies the width at which the element is to be drawn, and sets the posWidth property.
zIndex		z-index	Sets or returns the z-index for the element, indicating whether it appears above or below other elements.

MethodName	Description
getAttribute	Returns the value of an attribute defined in an HTML tag.
removeAttribute	Causes the specified attribute to be removed from the HTML element and the current page.
setAttribute	Adds and/or sets the value of an attribute in an HTML tag.

The StyleSheet Object

This object exposes all the styles within a single style sheet in the styleSheets collection.

PropertyName	Attribute Name	Description
disabled	DISABLED	Sets or returns whether an element is disabled.
href	HREF	The entire URL as a string.
id	ID	Identifier or name for an element in a page or style sheet, or as the target for hypertext links.
owningElement		Returns the style sheet that imported or referenced the current style sheet, usually through a LINK tag.
parentStyleSheet		Returns the style sheet that imported the current style sheet, or null for a non-imported stylesheet.

PropertyName	Attribute Name	Description
readOnly	READONLY	Sets or returns whether an element's contents are read only, or that a rule in a style sheet cannot be changed.
type	TYPE	Specifies the type of list style, link, selection, control, button, MIME-type, rel, or the CSS language.

MethodName	Description
addImport	Adds a style sheet from url to the current document, optionally at index in the styleSheets collection.
addRule	Adds a new property rule to a style sheet.

Collection	Description
imports	Collection of all the imported style sheets defined for a styleSheet object.
rules	Collection of all the rules that are defined in a style sheet.

The TextRange Object

This object represents the text stream of the HTML document. It can be used to set and retrieve the text within the page.

PropertyName	Description
htmlText	Returns the contents of a TextRange as text and HTML source.
text	The plain text contained within a block element, a TextRange or an OPTION tag.

MethodName	Description
collapse	Shrinks a TextRange to either the start or end of the current range.
compareEndPoints	Compares two text ranges and returns a value indicating the result.
duplicate	Returns a duplicate of a TextRange object.
execCommand	Executes a command over the document selection or range.

MethodName	Description
expand	Expands the range by a character, word, sentence or story so that partial units are completely contained.
findText	Sets the range start and end points to cover the text if found within the current document.
getBookmark	Sets String to a unique bookmark value to identify that position in the document.
inRange	Denotes if the specified range is within or equal to the current range.
isEqual	Denotes if the specified range is equal to the current range.
move	Changes the start and end points of a TextRange to cover different text.
moveEnd	Causes the range to grow or shrink from the end of the range.
moveStart	Causes the range to grow or shrink from the beginning of the range.
moveToBookmark	Moves range to encompass the range with a bookmark value previously defined in String.
moveToElementText	Moves range to encompass the text in the element specified.
moveToPoint	Moves and collapses range to the point specified in x and y relative to the document.
parentElement	Returns the parent element that completely encloses the current range.
pasteHTML	Pastes HTML and/or plain text into the current range.
queryCommandEnabled	Denotes if the specified command is available for a document or TextRange.
queryCommandIndeterm	Denotes if the specified command is in the indeterminate state.
queryCommandState	Returns the current state of the command for a document or TextRange object.
queryCommandSupported	Denotes if the specified command is supported for a document or TextRange object.
queryCommandValue	Returns the value of the command specified for a document or TextRange object.
scrollIntoView	Scrolls the element or TextRange into view in the browser, optionally at the top of the window.

MethodName	Description
select	Makes the active selection equal to the current object, or highlights the input area of a form element.
setEndPoint	Sets the end point of the range based on the end point of another range.

The UserProfile Object

Provides access to the user's profile settings from within a script.

MethodName	Description
addReadRequest	Adds a request for an item of user information to the request queue.
clearRequest	Empties the request queue of any existing requests.
doReadRequest	Instructs the browser to process all the requests in the request queue.
getAttribute	Retrieves the value of an item after the requests have been processed.

The Window Object

This refers to the current window. This can be a top-level window, or a window that is within a frame created by a **FRAMESET** in another document.

PropertyName	AttributeName	CSSName	Description
clientInformation			A reference that returns the navigator object for the browser.
closed			Indicates if a window is closed.
defaultStatus			The default message displayed in the status bar at the bottom of the window.
dialogArguments			Returns the arguments that were passed into a dialog window, as an array.
dialogHeight			Sets or returns the height of a dialog window.
dialogLeft			Sets or returns the x coordinate of a dialog window.

PropertyName	AttributeName	CSSName	Description
dialogTop			Sets or returns the y coordinate of a dialog window.
dialogWidth			Sets or returns the width of a dialog window.
document			Read-only reference to the window's document object.
event	EVENT		The event that a script is defined for.
history			Read-only reference to the window's history object.
length			Returns the number of elements in a collection.
location			Reference to the location object, also returns the full document URL.
name	NAME		Specifies the name of the window, frame, element, control, bookmark, or applet.
navigator			Read-only reference to the window's navigator object.
offScreenBuffering			Specifies whether to use off-screen buffereing for the document.
opener			Returns a reference to the window that created the current window.
parent			Returns the parent window or frame in the window/frame hierarchy.
returnValue			Allows a return value to be specified for the event or a dialog window.
screen			Read-only reference to the global screen object.
self			Provides a reference to the current window.
status			Text displayed in the window's status bar, or an alias for the value of an option button.
top		top	Position of the top of the element, sets the posTop property. Also returns topmost window object.

MethodName	Description
alert	Displays an Alert dialog box with a message and an OK button.
blur	Causes a control to lose focus and fire its **onblur** event.
clearInterval	Cancels an interval timer that was set with the **setInterval** method.
clearTimeout	Cancels a timeout that was set with the **setTimeout** method.
close	Closes a document forcing written data to be displayed, or closes the browser window.
confirm	Displays a Confirm dialog box with a message and OK and Cancel buttons.
execScript	Executes a script. The default language is JScript.
focus	Causes a control to receive the focus and fire its **onfocus** event.
navigate	Loads another page (VBScript only). Equivalent to changing the **window.location.href** property.
open	Opens a new browser window and returns a reference to it.
prompt	Displays a Prompt dialog box with a message and an input field.
scroll	Scrolls the window to the specified x and y offset relative to the entire document.
setInterval	Denotes a code routine to execute repeatedly every specified number of milliseconds.
setTimeout	Denotes a code routine to execute a specified number of milliseconds after loading the page.
showHelp	Opens a window to display a Help file.
showModalDialog	Displays an HTML dialog window, and returns the **returnValue** property of its document when closed.

EventName	Description
onbeforeunload	Occurs just before the page is unloaded, allowing data bound controls to save their contents.
onblur	Occurs when the control loses the input focus.
onerror	Occurs when an error loading a document or image arises.
onfocus	Occurs when a control receives the input focus.
onhelp	Occurs when the user presses the *F1* or *Help* key.
onload	Occurs when the element has completed loading.
onresize	Occurs when the element or object is resized by the user.
onscroll	Occurs when the user scrolls a page or element.
onunload	Occurs immediately before the page is unloaded.

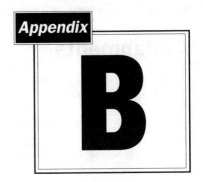
The VBScript Language

Array Handling

Dim—declares an array variable. This can be static with a defined number of elements or dynamic and can have up to 60 dimensions.

ReDim—used to change the size of an array variable which has been declared as dynamic.

Preserve—keyword used to preserve the contents of an array being resized. If you need to use this then you can only re-dimension the rightmost index of the array.

```
Dim strEmployees ()
ReDim strEmployees (9,1)

strEmployees (9,1) = "Phil"

ReDim strEmployees (9,2)               'loses the contents of element (9,1)
strEmployees (9,2) = "Paul"

ReDim Preserve strEmployees (9,3)   'preserves the contents of (9,2)
strEmployees (9,3) = "Smith"
```

LBound—returns the smallest subscript for the dimension of an array. Note that arrays always start from the subscript zero so this function will always return the value zero.

UBound—used to determine the size of an array.

```
Dim strCustomers (10, 5)
intSizeFirst = UBound (strCustomers, 1)     'returns SizeFirst = 10
intSizeSecond = UBound (strCustomers, 2)    'returns SizeSecond = 5
```

> The actual number of elements is always one greater than the value returned by **UBound** because the array starts from zero.

Assignments

Let—used to assign values to variables (optional).
Set—used to assign an object reference to a variable.

```
Let intNumberOfDays = 365

Set txtMyTextBox = txtcontrol
txtMyTextBox.Value = "Hello World"
```

Constants

Empty—an empty variable is one that has been created but not yet assigned a value.
Nothing—used to remove an object reference.

```
Set txtMyTextBox = txtATextBox        'assigns object reference
Set txtMyTextBox = Nothing            'removes object reference
```

Null—indicates that a variable is not valid. Note that this isn't the same as **Empty**.
True—indicates that an expression is true. Has numerical value –1.
False—indicates that an expression is false. Has numerical value 0.

Error constant:

Constant	Value
vbObjectError	&h80040000

System Color constants:

Constant	Value	Description
vbBlack	&h00	Black
vbRed	&hFF	Red
vbGreen	&hFF00	Green
vbYellow	&hFFFF	Yellow
vbBlue	&hFF0000	Blue
vbMagenta	&hFF00FF	Magenta
vbCyan	&hFFFF00	Cyan
vbWhite	&hFFFFFF	White

Comparison constants:

Constant	Value	Description
vbBinaryCompare	0	Perform a binary comparison.
vbTextCompare	1	Perform a textual comparison.
vbDatabaseCompare	2	Perform a comparison based upon information in the database where the comparison is to be performed.

Date and Time constants:

Constant	Value	Description
VbSunday	1	Sunday
vbMonday	2	Monday
vbTuesday	3	Tuesday
vbWednesday	4	Wednesday
vbThursday	5	Thursday
vbFriday	6	Friday
vbSaturday	7	Saturday
vbFirstJan1	1	Use the week in which January 1 occurs (default).
vbFirstFourDays	2	Use the first week that has at least four days in the new year.
vbFirstFullWeek	3	Use the first full week of the year.
vbUseSystem	0	Use the format in the regional settings for the computer.
vbUseSystemDayOfWeek	0	Use the day in the system settings for the first weekday.

Date Format constants:

Constant	Value	Description
vbGeneralDate	0	Display a date and/or time in the format set in the system settings. For real numbers display a date and time. For integer numbers display only a date. For numbers less than 1, display time only.

Table continued on following page

Constant	Value	Description
vbLongDate	1	Display a date using the long date format specified in the computers regional settings.
vbShortDate	2	Display a date using the short date format specified in the computers regional settings.
vbLongTime	3	Display a time using the long time format specified in the computers regional settings.
vbShortTime	4	Display a time using the short time format specified in the computers regional settings.

File Input/Output constants:

Constant	Value	Description
ForReading	1	Open a file for reading only.
ForWriting	2	Open a file for writing. If a file with the same name exists, its previous one is overwritten.
ForAppending	8	Open a file and write at the end of the file.

String constants:

Constant	Value	Description
vbCr	Chr(13)	Carriage return only
vbCrLf	Chr(13) & Chr(10)	Carriage return and linefeed (Newline)
vbLf	Chr(10)	Line feed only
vbNewLine	-	Newline character as appropriate to a specific platform
vbNullChar	Chr(0)	Character having the value 0
vbNullString	-	String having the value zero (not just an empty string)
vbTab	Chr(9)	Horizontal tab

Tristate constants:

Constant	Value	Description
TristateTrue	-1	True
TristateFalse	0	False
TristateUseDefault	-2	Use default setting

VarType constants:

Constant	Value	Description
vbEmpty	0	Un-initialized (default)
vbNull	1	Contains no valid data
vbInteger	2	Integer subtype
vbLong	3	Long subtype
vbSingle	4	Single subtype
vbDouble	5	Double subtype
vbCurrency	6	Currency subtype
vbDate	7	Date subtype
vbString	8	String subtype
vbObject	9	Object
vbError	10	Error subtype
vbBoolean	11	Boolean subtype
vbVariant	12	Variant (used only for arrays of variants)
vbDataObject	13	Data access object
vbDecimal	14	Decimal subtype
vbByte	17	Byte subtype
vbArray	8192	Array

Control Flow

For...Next—executes a block of code a specified number of times.

```
Dim intSalary (10)
For intCounter = 0 to 10
    intSalary (intCounter) = 20000
Next
```

For Each...Next Statement—repeats a block of code for each element in an array or collection.

```
For Each Item In Request.QueryString("MyControl")
   Response.Write Item & "<BR>"
Next
```

Do...Loop—executes a block of code while a condition is true or until a condition becomes true.

```
Do While strDayOfWeek <> "Saturday" And strDayOfWeek <> "Sunday"
   MsgBox ("Get Up! Time for work")
   ...
Loop

Do
   MsgBox ("Get Up! Time for work")
   ...
Loop Until strDayOfWeek = "Saturday" Or strDayOfWeek = "Sunday"
```

If...Then...Else—used to run various blocks of code depending on conditions.

```
If intAge < 20 Then
   MsgBox ("You're just a slip of a thing!")
ElseIf intAge < 40 Then
   MsgBox ("You're in your prime!")
Else
   MsgBox ("You're older and wiser")
End If
```

Select Case—used to replace **If...Then...Else** statements where there are many conditions.

```
Select Case intAge
Case 21,22,23,24,25,26
   MsgBox ("You're in your prime")
Case 40
   MsgBox ("You're fulfilling your dreams")
Case 65
   MsgBox ("Time for a new challenge")
End Select
```

Note that **Select Case** can only be used with precise conditions and not with a range of conditions.

While...Wend—executes a block of code while a condition is true.

```
While strDayOfWeek <> "Saturday" AND strDayOfWeek <> "Sunday"
   MsgBox ("Get Up! Time for work")
   ...
Wend
```

Functions

VBScript contains several functions that can be used to manipulate and examine variables. These have been subdivided into the general categories of:

 Conversion Functions

 Date/Time Functions

- Math Functions
- Object Management Functions
- Script Engine Identification Functions
- String Functions
- Variable Testing Functions

For a full description of each function, and the parameters it requires, see the VBScript Help file. This is installed by default in your **Docs/ASPDocs/VBS/ VBScript** subfolder of your IIS installation directory.

Conversion Functions

These functions are used to convert values in variables between different types:

Function	Description
Asc	Returns the numeric ANSI code number of the first character in a string.
AscB	As above, but provided for use with byte data contained in a string. Returns result from the first byte only.
AscW	As above, but provided for Unicode characters. Returns the **Wide** character code, avoiding the conversion from Unicode to ANSI.
Chr	Returns a string made up of the ANSI character matching the number supplied.
ChrB	As above, but provided for use with byte data contained in a string. Always returns a single byte.
ChrW	As above, but provided for Unicode characters. Its argument is a **Wide** character code, thereby avoiding the conversion from ANSI to Unicode.
CBool	Returns the argument value converted to a **Variant** of subtype **Boolean**.
CByte	Returns the argument value converted to a **Variant** of subtype **Byte**.
CDate	Returns the argument value converted to a **Variant** of subtype **Date**.
CDbl	Returns the argument value converted to a **Variant** of subtype **Double**.
CInt	Returns the argument value converted to a **Variant** of subtype **Integer**.
CLng	Returns the argument value converted to a **Variant** of subtype **Long**
CSng	Returns the argument value converted to a **Variant** of subtype **Single**

Table continued on following page

Function	Description
CStr	Returns the argument value converted to a **Variant** of subtype **String**.
Fix	Returns the integer (whole) part of a number.
Hex	Returns a string representing the hexadecimal value of a number.
Int	Returns the integer (whole) portion of a number.
Oct	Returns a string representing the octal value of a number.
Round	Returns a number rounded to a specified number of decimal places.
Sgn	Returns an integer indicating the sign of a number.

Date/Time Functions

These functions return date or time values from the computer's system clock, or manipulate existing values:

Function	Description
Date	Returns the current system date.
DateAdd	Returns a date to which a specified time interval has been added.
DateDiff	Returns the number of days, weeks, or years between two dates.
DatePart	Returns just the day, month or year of a given date.
DateSerial	Returns a **Variant** of subtype **Date** for a specified year, month, and day.
DateValue	Returns a **Variant** of subtype **Date**.
Day	Returns a number between **1** and **31** representing the day of the month.
Hour	Returns a number between **0** and **23** representing the hour of the day.
Minute	Returns a number between **0** and **59** representing the minute of the hour.
Month	Returns a number between **1** and **12** representing the month of the year.
MonthName	Returns the name of the specified month as a string.
Now	Returns the current date and time.
Second	Returns a number between **0** and **59** representing the second of the minute.
Time	Returns a **Variant** of subtype **Date** indicating the current system time.

Function	Description
TimeSerial	Returns a **Variant** of subtype **Date** for a specific hour, minute, and second.
TimeValue	Returns a **Variant** of subtype **Date** containing the time.
Weekday	Returns a number representing the day of the week.
WeekdayName	Returns the name of the specified day of the week as a string.
Year	Returns a number representing the year.

Math Functions

These functions perform mathematical operations on variables containing numerical values:

Function	Description
Atn	Returns the arctangent of a number.
Cos	Returns the cosine of an angle.
Exp	Returns **e** (the base of natural logarithms) raised to a power.
Log	Returns the natural logarithm of a number.
Randomize	Initializes the random-number generator.
Rnd	Returns a random number.
Sin	Returns the sine of an angle.
Sqr	Returns the square root of a number.
Tan	Returns the tangent of an angle.

Object Management Functions

These functions are used to manipulate objects, where applicable:

Function	Description
CreateObject	Creates and returns a reference to an ActiveX or OLE Automation object.
GetObject	Returns a reference to an ActiveX or OLE Automation object.
LoadPicture	Returns a picture object.

Script Engine Identification

These functions return the version of the scripting engine:

Function	Description
ScriptEngine	A string containing the major, minor, and build version numbers of the scripting engine.
ScriptEngineMajorVersion	The major version of the scripting engine, as a number.
ScriptEngineMinorVersion	The minor version of the scripting engine, as a number.
ScriptEngineBuildVersion	The build version of the scripting engine, as a number.

String Functions

These functions are used to manipulate string values in variables:

Function	Description
Filter	Returns an array from a string array, based on specified filter criteria.
FormatCurrency	Returns a string formatted as currency value.
FormatDateTime	Returns a string formatted as a date or time.
FormatNumber	Returns a string formatted as a number.
FormatPercent	Returns a string formatted as a percentage.
InStr	Returns the position of the first occurrence of one string within another.
InStrB	As above, but provided for use with byte data contained in a string. Returns the byte position instead of the character position.
InstrRev	As InStr, but starts from the end of the string.
Join	Returns a string created by joining the strings contained in an array.
LCase	Returns a string that has been converted to lowercase.
Left	Returns a specified number of characters from the left end of a string.
LeftB	As above, but provided for use with byte data contained in a string. Uses that number of bytes instead of that number of characters.
Len	Returns the length of a string or the number of bytes needed for a variable.
LenB	As above, but is provided for use with byte data contained in a string. Returns the number of bytes in the string instead of characters.
LTrim	Returns a copy of a string without leading spaces.

Function	Description
Mid	Returns a specified number of characters from a string.
MidB	As above, but provided for use with byte data contained in a string. Uses that numbers of bytes instead of that number of characters.
Replace	Returns a string in which a specified substring has been replaced with another substring a specified number of times.
Right	Returns a specified number of characters from the right end of a string.
RightB	As above, but provided for use with byte data contained in a string. Uses that number of bytes instead of that number of characters.
RTrim	Returns a copy of a string without trailing spaces.
Space	Returns a string consisting of the specified number of spaces.
Split	Returns a one-dimensional array of a specified number of substrings.
StrComp	Returns a value indicating the result of a string comparison.
String	Returns a string of the length specified made up of a repeating character.
StrReverse	Returns a string in which the character order of a string is reversed.
Trim	Returns a copy of a string without leading or trailing spaces.
UCase	Returns a string that has been converted to uppercase.

Variable Testing Functions

These functions are used to determine the type of information stored in a variable:

Function	Description
IsArray	Returns a **Boolean** value indicating whether a variable is an array.
IsDate	Returns a **Boolean** value indicating whether an expression can be converted to a date.
IsEmpty	Returns a **Boolean** value indicating whether a variable has been initialized.
IsNull	Returns a **Boolean** value indicating whether an expression contains no valid data

Table continued on following page

Function	Description
IsNumeric	Returns a **Boolean** value indicating whether an expression can be evaluated as a number.
IsObject	Returns a **Boolean** value indicating whether an expression references a valid ActiveX or OLE Automation object.
VarType	Returns a number indicating the subtype of a variable.

Variable Declarations

Dim—declares a variable.

Error Handling

On Error Resume Next—indicates that if an error occurs, control should continue at the next statement.
Err—this is the error object that provides information about run-time errors.

Error handling is very limited in VBScript and the **Err** object must be tested explicitly to determine if an error has occurred.

Input/Output

This consists of **Msgbox** for output and **InputBox** for input:

MsgBox

This displays a message, and can return a value indicating which button was clicked.

```
MsgBox "Hello There",20,"Hello Message","c:\windows\MyHelp.hlp",123
```

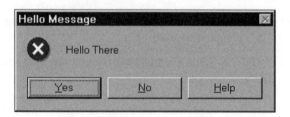

The parameters are:
"Hello There"—this contains the text of the message and is obligatory.
20—this determines which icon and buttons appear on the message box.

"Hello Message"—this contains the text that will appear as the title of the message box.

"c:\windows\MyHelp.hlp"—this adds a Help button to the message box and determines the help file that is opened if the button is clicked.

123—this is a reference to the particular help topic that will be displayed if the Help button is clicked.

The value of the icon and buttons parameter is determined using the following tables:

Constant	Value	Buttons
vbOKOnly	0	OK
vbOKCancel	1	OK Cancel
vbAbortRetryIngnore	2	Abort Retry Ignore
vbYesNoCancel	3	Yes No Cancel
vbYesNo	4	Yes No
vbRetryCancel	5	Retry Cancel
vbDefaultButton1	0	The first button from the left is the default.
vbDefaultButton2	256	The second button from the left is the default.
vbDefaultButton3	512	The third button from the left is the default.
vbDefaultButton4	768	The fourth button from the left is the default.

Constant	Value	Description	Icon
vbCritical	16	Critical Message	
vbQuestion	32	Questioning Message	
vbExclamation	48	Warning Message	
vbInformation	64	Informational Message	

Constant	Value	Description
vbApplicationModal	0	Just the application stops until user clicks a button.
vbSystemModal	**4096**	Whole system stops until user clicks a button.

To specify which buttons and icon are displayed you simply add the relevant values. So, in our example we add together **4 + 16** to display the Yes and No buttons, with Yes as the default, and to show the **Critical** icon.

You can determine which button the user clicked by assigning the return code of the **MsgBox** function to a variable:

```
intButtonClicked = MsgBox ("Hello There",35,"Hello Message")
```

Notice that brackets enclose the **MsgBox** parameters when used in this format. The following table determines the value assigned to the variable **intButtonClicked**:

Constant	Value	Button Clicked
vbOK	1	OK
vbCancel	2	Cancel
vbAbort	3	Abort
vbRetry	4	Retry
vbIgnore	5	Ignore
vbYes	6	Yes
vbNo	7	No

InputBox

This accepts text entry from the user and returns it as a string.

```
strTextEntered = InputBox ("Please enter your name","Login","John Smith",500, 500)
```

"Please enter your name"—this is the prompt displayed in the input box.
"Login"—this is the text displayed as the title of the input box.
"John Smith"—this is the default value displayed in the input box.
500—specifies the x position of the input box.
500—specifies the y position of the input box.

As with the **MsgBox** function, you can also specify a help file and topic to add a Help button to the input box.

Procedures

Call—optional method of calling a subroutine.
Function—used to declare a function.
Sub—used to declare a subroutine.

Other Keywords

Rem—old style method of adding comments to code.
Option Explicit—forces you to declare a variable before it can be used.

Visual Basic Run-time Error Codes

The following error codes also apply to VBA code and many will not be appropriate to an application built completely around VBScript. However, if you have built your own components then these error codes may well be brought up when such components are used.

Code	Description	Code	Description
3	Return without GoSub	49	Bad DLL calling convention
5	Invalid procedure call	51	Internal error
6	Overflow	52	Bad file name or number
7	Out of memory	53	File not found
9	Subscript out of range	54	Bad file mode
10	This array is fixed or temporarily locked	55	File already open
11	Division by zero	57	Device I/O error
13	Type mismatch	58	File already exists
14	Out of string space	59	Bad record length
16	Expression too complex	61	Disk full
17	Can't perform requested operation	62	Input past end of file
		63	Bad record number
18	User interrupt occurred	67	Too many files
20	Resume without error	68	Device unavailable
28	Out of stack space	70	Permission denied
35	Sub or Function not defined	71	Disk not ready
		74	Can't rename with different drive
47	Too many DLL application clients		
		75	Path/File access error
48	Error in loading DLL	76	Path not found

Table continued on following page

Code	Description
322	Can't create necessary temporary file
325	Invalid format in resource file
380	Invalid property value
423	Property or method not found
424	Object required
429	OLE Automation server can't create object
430	Class doesn't support OLE Automation
432	File name or class name not found during OLE Automation operation
438	Object doesn't support this property or method
440	OLE Automation error
442	Connection to type library or object library for remote process has been lost. Press OK for dialog to remove reference.
443	OLE Automation object does not have a default value
445	Object doesn't support this action
446	Object doesn't support named arguments
447	Object doesn't support current locale setting
448	Named argument not found
449	Argument not optional
450	Wrong number of arguments or invalid property assignment
451	Object not a collection
452	Invalid ordinal
453	Specified DLL function not found

Code	Description
454	Code resource not found
455	Code resource lock error
457	This key is already associated with an element of this collection
458	Variable uses an OLE Automation type not supported in Visual Basic
481	Invalid picture
500	Variable is undefined
501	Cannot assign to variable
1001	Out of memory
1002	Syntax error
1003	Expected ':'
1004	Expected ';'
1005	Expected '('
1006	Expected ')'
1007	Expected ']'
1008	Expected '{'
1009	Expected '}'
1010	Expected identifier
1011	Expected '='
1012	Expected 'If'
1013	Expected 'To'
1014	Expected 'End'
1015	Expected 'Function'
1016	Expected 'Sub'
1017	Expected 'Then'
1018	Expected 'Wend'
1019	Expected 'Loop'
1020	Expected 'Next'
1021	Expected 'Case'
1022	Expected 'Select'
1023	Expected expression
1024	Expected statement
1025	Expected end of statement
1026	Expected integer constant

Code	Description
1027	Expected 'While' or 'Until'
1028	Expected 'While', 'Until' or end of statement
1029	Too many locals or arguments
1030	Identifier too long
1031	Invalid number
1032	Invalid character
1033	Un-terminated string constant
1034	Un-terminated comment
1035	Nested comment
1036	'Me' cannot be used outside of a procedure
1037	Invalid use of 'Me' keyword
1038	'loop' without 'do'
1039	Invalid 'exit' statement
1040	Invalid 'for' loop control variable
1041	Variable redefinition
1042	Must be first statement on the line
1043	Cannot assign to non-ByVal argument

For more information about VBScript, visit Microsoft's VBScript site at:

`http://www.microsoft.com/vbscript/us/techinfo/vbsdocs.htm`

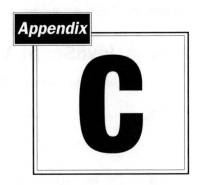

JavaScript Reference

General Information

JavaScript is included in an HTML document with the **`<SCRIPT>`** tag. Here's an example:

```
<HTML>
<HEAD>

<!-- wrap script in comments
<SCRIPT LANGUAGE = "JavaScript">
script code goes here
</SCRIPT>
-->

</HEAD>
<BODY>
HTML goes here
</BODY>
</HTML>
```

The following points should be kept in mind when programming in JavaScript:

- The main core of your JavaScript code should be put in the <HEAD> section of the document. This ensures that all the code has been loaded before an attempt is made to execute it. "On-the-fly" scripts that generate HTML at specific parts of the document can be placed exactly as required.

- The script code should be wrapped in a comment tag, as this stops older (non-JavaScript) browsers from trying to read the code.

- JavaScript is case-sensitive.

- In Javascript, semicolons (;) are used to separate statements when they are on the same line. If the statements are not on the same line, semicolons are optional.

New in JavaScript Version 1.2

The changes to the language that appear in version 1.2 are:

- The statement **new Array**(*value*) creates a new array with the first element (indexed zero) set to the specified value. You can create a new array with several elements by listing them in the brackets separated by commas, using **new Array**(*value0*, *value1*, *value2*, **...**).

- The **Number** object now returns **NaN** (not a number) if a string being converted is not a legal number, rather than an error.

- The equality operators **==** and **!=** no longer try and convert the values to the same type before comparison. They are just compared 'as is'.

- The new **break** and **continue** statements can be used to jump out of a loop or other construct, and continue execution at a specific line:

```
while (count < 4)
{
  if (anothervalue == 2 ) break skipitall;
  somevalue = somevalue + anothervalue;
}
skipitall :
//execution continues here outside the loop
```

```
while (count < 4)
{
  if (anothervalue == 2 ) continue skipit;
  somevalue = somevalue + anothervalue;
  skipit :
  //execution continues here within the loop
}
```

- JavaScript now contains the **do..while** construct and the **switch** construct:

```
do
  somevalue = somevalue + anothervalue;
while (anothervalue != 2 );
```

```
switch (language)
{
  case "Java" :
    alert("One program for all.");
    break;
  case "C" :
    alert("Speed is king.");
    break;
  case "VB" :
    alert("Anyone can do it.");
}
```

- The **String** object has three new methods, **charCodeAt**, **fromCharCode**, and **substr**. **charCodeAt** returns the ASCII code of the character at the specified position, **fromCharCode** constructs a string from a comma-separated list of ASCII code values, and **substr** returns a specified number of characters from a string:

```
MyString = "ABCDE";
alert(MyString.charCodeAt(2))     // produces 66 (decimal).
```

```
MyString.fromCharCode(65, 66, 67)     // returns "ABC"
```

```
MyString = "ABCDE";
MyString.substr(2, 5)     // returns "BCD"
```

Other changes are:

- the **substring** method no longer swaps over the indexes when the first is greater than the second
- the **sort** method now works on all platforms and converts undefined elements to null and sorts them to the top of the array
- the **split** method now removes more than one white-space character when splitting a string
- the **toString** method now converts the object or array into a string literal

Values

JavaScript recognizes the following data types:

- **strings**—"Hello World"
- **numbers**—both integers (86) and decimal values (86.235)
- **boolean**—true or false

A null (*no value*) value is assigned with the keyword **null**.

JavaScript also makes use of 'special characters' in a similar way to the C++ programming language:

Character	Function
\n	newline
\t	tab
\f	form feed
\b	backspace
\r	carriage return

You may 'escape' other characters by preceding them with a backslash (\), to prevent the browser from trying to interpret them. This is most commonly used for quotes and backslashes, or to include a character by using its octal (base 8) value:

```
document.write("This shows a \"quote\" in a string.");
document.write("This is a backslash: \\");
document.write("This is a space character: \040.");
```

Variables

JavaScript is a **loosely typed** language. This means that variables do not have an explicitly defined variable type. Instead, every variable can hold values of various types. Conversions between types are done automatically when needed, as this example demonstrates:

```
x = 55;     // x is assigned to be the integer 55
y = "55"; // y is assigned to be the string "55"
y = '55';   // an alternative using single quotes

z = 1 + y;
<!-- even though y is a string, it will be automatically
 converted to the appropriate integer value so that 1 may
 be added to it. -->

document.write(x);
<!-- the number 55 will be written to the screen. Even
 though x is an integer and not a string, Javascript will
 make the  necessary conversion for you. -->

n = 3.14159;  // assigning a real (fractional) number
n = 0546;     // numbers starting 0 assumed to be octal
n = 0xFFEC;   // numbers starting 0x assumed to be hex
n = 2.145E-5; // using exponential notation
```

Variable names must start with either a letter or an underscore. Beyond the first letter, variables may contain any combination of letters, underscores, and digits. JavaScript is case sensitive, so **this_variable** is not the same as **This_Variable**.

Variables do not need to be declared before they are used. However, you may use the **var** keyword to explicitly define a variable. This is especially useful when there is the possibility of conflicting variable names. When in doubt, use **var**.

```
var x = "55";
```

Assignment Operators

The following operators are used to make assignments in JavaScript:

Operator	Example	Result
=	x = y	x equals y
+=	x += y	x equals x plus y
-=	x -= y	x equals x minus y
*=	x *= y	x equals x multiplied by y
/=	x /= y	x equals x divided by y
%=	x %= y	x equals x modulus y

Each operator assigns the value on the right to the variable on the left.

```
x = 100;
y = 10;
x += y;   // x now is equal to 110
```

Equality Operators

Operator	Meaning
==	is equal to
!=	is not equal to
>	is greater than
>=	is greater than or equal to
<	is less than
<=	is less than or equal to

Other Operators

Operator	Meaning
+	Addition
–	Subtraction
*	Multiplication
/	Division
%	Modulus
++	Increment
––	Decrement
–	Unary Negation

Operator			Meaning
&	or	**AND**	Bitwise AND
|	or	**OR**	Bitwise OR
^	or	**XOR**	Bitwise XOR
<<			Bitwise left shift
>>			Bitwise right shift
>>>			Zero-fill right shift
&&			Logical AND
||			Logical OR
!			Not

String Operators

Operator	Meaning
+	Concatenates strings, so **"abc" + "def"** is **"abcdef"**
>	Compare strings in a case-sensitive way. A string is 'greater' than
>=	another based on the Latin ASCII code values of the characters,
<	starting from the left of the string. So **"DEF"** is greater than **"ABC"**
<=	and **"DEE"**, but less than **"abc"**.

Comments

Operator	Meaning
// a comment	A single line comment
/* this text is a	
multi-line comment */	A multi-line comment

Input/Output

In JavaScript, there are three different methods of providing information to the user, and getting a response back.

Alert

This displays a message with an OK button.

```
alert("Hello World!");
```

Confirm

Displays a message with both an OK and a Cancel button. True is returned if the OK button is pressed, and false is returned if the Cancel button is pressed.

```
confirm("Are you sure you want to quit?");
```

Prompt

Displays a message and a text box for user input. The first string argument forms the text that is to be displayed above the text box. The second argument is a string, integer, or property of an existing object, which represents the default value to display inside the box. If the second argument is not specified, "<undefined>" is displayed inside the text box.

The string typed into the box is returned if the OK button is pressed. False is returned if the Cancel button is pressed

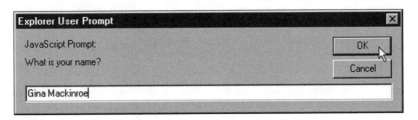

```
prompt("What is your name?", "");
```

497

Control Flow

There are two ways of controlling the flow of a program in JavaScript. The first involves **conditional** statements, which follow either one branch of the program or another. The second way is to use a **repeated iteration** of a set of statements.

Conditional Statements

JavaScript has one conditional statement:

if..then..else—used to run various blocks of code—depending on conditions. These statements have the following general form in JavaScript:

if (*condition*)
    {
  code to be executed if condition is true
    }
else
    {
  code to be executed if condition is false
    };

In addition:

- The **else** portion is optional.
- **if** statements may be nested.
- Multiple statements must be enclosed by braces.

Here is an example:

```
person_type = prompt("What are you ?", "");
if (person_type == "cat")
  alert("Here, have some cat food.")
else
{
  if (person_type == "dog")
    alert("Here, have some dog food.")
  else
  {
    if (person_type == "human")
      alert("Here have some, er, human food!");
  };
};
```

Notice that the curly brackets are only actually required where there is more than one statement within the block. Like many other constructs, they can be omitted where single statements are used. The final semi-colon is mandatory:

if (*condition*)
  code to be executed if condition is true
else
  code to be executed if condition is false;

Loop Statements

for—executes a block of code a specified number of times.

```
for (i = 0; i = 10; i++)
{
  document.write(i);
}
```

while—executes a block of code while a condition is true.

```
while (condition)
{
  statements to execute ...
}
```

break—will cause an exit from a loop regardless of the condition statement.

```
x = 0;
while (x != 10)
{
  n = prompt("Enter a number or 'q' to quit", "");
  if (n == "q")
  {
    alert("See ya");
    break;
  }
}
```

continue—will cause the loop to jump immediately back to the condition statement.

```
x = 0;
while (x != 1)
{
  if (!(confirm("Should I add 1 to n ?")))
  {
    continue;
    // the following x++ is never executed
    x++;
  }
  x++;
}
alert("Bye");
```

Built-in Functions

JavaScript provides a number of built-in functions that can be accessed within code.

Function	Description
escape(*char*)	Returns a string of the form **%***XX* where *XX* is the ASCII encoded value of *char*.
eval(*expression*)	Returns the result of evaluating the numeric expression *expression*
isNaN(*value*)	Returns a Boolean value of **true** if *value* is not a legal number.
parseFloat(*string*)	Converts *string* to a floating-point number.
ParseInt(*string, base*)	Converts *string* to an integer number with the base of *base*.
typeOf(*object*)	Returns the data type of *object* as a string, such as **"boolean"**, **"function"**, etc.

Built-in Objects

JavaScript provides a set of built-in data-type objects, which have their own set of properties, and methods—and which can be accessed with JavaScript code.

Array Object

The **Array** object specifies a method of creating arrays and working with them. To create a new array, use:

```
cats = new Array();      // create an empty array
cats = new Array(10);    // create an array of 10 items

// or create and fill an array with values in one go:
cats = new Array("Boo Boo", "Purrcila", "Sam", "Lucky");
```

Properties	Description
length	A read/write Integer value specifying the number of elements in the array.

Methods	Description
join([*string*])	Returns a string containing each element of the array, optionally separated with *string*.
reverse()	Reverses the order of the array.
sort([*function*])	Sorts the array, optionally based upon the results of a function specified by *function*.

Early versions of JavaScript had no explicit array structure. However, JavaScript's object mechanisms allow for easy creation of arrays:

```
function MakeArray(n)
{
  this.length = n;
  for (var i = 1; i <= n; i++)
    this[i] = 0;
  return this
}
```

With this function included in your script, you can create arrays with:

```
cats = new MakeArray(20);
```

You can then populate the array like this:

```
cats[1] = "Boo Boo";
cats[2] = "Purrcila";
cats[3] = "Sam";
cats[4] = "Lucky";
```

Boolean Object

The **Boolean** object is used to store simple yes/no, true/false values. To create a new Boolean object, use the syntax:

```
MyAnswer = new Boolean([value])
```

If **value** is **0**, **null**, omitted, or an empty string the new Boolean object will have the value **false**. All other values, *including the string* **"false"**, create an object with the value **true**.

Methods	Description
toString()	Returns the value of the Boolean as the string **"true"** or **"false"**.
valueOf()	Returns the primitive numeric value of the object for conversion in calculations.

Date Object

The **Date** object provides a method for working with dates and times inside of JavaScript. New instances of the **Date** object are invoked with:

```
newDateObject = new Date([dateInfo])
```

dateInfo is an optional specification for the date to set in the new object. If it is not specified, the current date and time are used. **dateInfo** can use any of the following formats:

milliseconds (*since midnight GMT on January 1st 1970*)
year, month, day (e.g. 1997, 0, 27 is 27th Jan 1997)
year, month, day, hours, minutes, seconds
month day, year hours:minutes:seconds
(e.g. September 23, 1997 08:25:30)

501

Methods	Description
`getDate()`	Returns the day of the month as an Integer between 1 and 31.
`getDay()`	Returns the day of the week as an Integer between 0 (Sunday) and 6 (Saturday).
`getHours()`	Returns the hours as an Integer between 0 and 23.
`getMinutes()`	Returns the minutes as an Integer between 0 and 59.
`getMonth()`	Returns the month as an Integer between 0 (January) and 11 (December).
`getSeconds()`	Returns the seconds as an Integer between 0 and 59.
`getTime()`	Returns the number of milliseconds between January 1, 1970 at 00:00:00 GMT and the current **Date** object as an Integer.
`getTimeZoneOffset()`	Returns the number of minutes difference between local time and GMT as an Integer.
`getYear()`	Returns the year (generally minus 1900 - i.e. only two digits) as an Integer.
`parse(`*dateString*`)`	Returns the number of milliseconds in a date string, since Jan. 1, 1970 00:00:00 GMT.
`setDate(`*dayValue*`)`	Sets the day of the month where *dayValue* is an Integer between 1 and 31.
`setHours(`*hoursValue*`)`	Sets the hours where *hoursValue* is an Integer between 0 and 59.
`setMinutes(`*minutesValue*`)`	Sets the minutes where *minutesValue* is an Integer between 0 and 59.
`setMonth(`*monthValue*`)`	Sets the month where *monthValue* is an Integer between 0 and 11.
`setSeconds(`*secondsValue*`)`	Sets the seconds where *secondsValue* is an Integer between 0 and 59.
`setTime(`*timeValue*`)`	Sets the value of a **Date** object where *timeValue* is an integer representing the number of milliseconds in a date string, since Jan. 1, 1970 00:00:00 GMT.
`setYear(`*yearValue*`)`	Sets the year where *yearValue* is an Integer (generally) greater than 1900.
`toGMTString()`	Converts a date from local time to GMT, and returns it as a string.
`toLocaleString()`	Converts a date from GMT to local time, and returns it as a string.
`UTC(`*year*, *month*, *day* `[,`*hrs*`] [,`*min*`] [,`*sec*`])`	Returns the number of milliseconds in a date object, since Jan. 1, 1970 00:00:00 Universal Coordinated Time (GMT).

Function Object

The **Function** object provides a mechanism for compiling JavaScript code as a function. A new function is invoked with the syntax:

```
functionName = new Function(arg1, arg2, ..., functionCode)
```

where **arg1**, **arg2**, etc. are the arguments for the function object being created, and **functionCode** is a string containing the body of the function. This can be a series of JavaScript statements separated by semi-colons.

Properties	Description
arguments[]	A reference to the **Arguments** array that holds the arguments that were provided when the function was called.
caller	Specifies the function that called the **Function** object.
prototype	Provides a way for adding properties to a **Function** object.

Arguments Object

The **Arguments** object is a list (array) of arguments in a **Function** object.

Properties	Description
length	An Integer specifying the number of arguments provided to the function when it was called.

Math Object

Provides a set of properties and methods for working with mathematical constants and functions. Simply reference the **Math** object, then the method or property required:

```
MyArea = Math.PI * MyRadius * MyRadius;
MyResult = Math.floor(MyNumber);
```

Properties	Description
E	Euler's Constant e (the base of natural logarithms).
LN10	The value of the natural logarithm of 10.
LN2	The value of the natural logarithm of 2.
LOG10E	The value of the natural logarithm of E.
LOG2E	The value of the base 2 logarithm of E.
PI	The value of the constant π (pi).
SQRT1_2	The value of the square root of a half.
SQRT	The value of the square root of two.

Methods	Description
abs(*number*)	Returns the absolute value of *number*.
acos(*number*)	Returns the arc cosine of *number*.
asin(*number*)	Returns the arc sine of *number*.
atan(*number*)	Returns the arc tangent of *number*.
atan2(*x, y*)	Returns the angle of the polar coordinate of a point *x, y* from the *x*-axis.
ceil(*number*)	Returns the next largest Integer greater than *number*, i.e. rounds up.
cos(*number*)	Returns the cosine of *number*.
exp(*number*)	Returns the value of *number* as the exponent of *e*, as in e^{number}.
floor(*number*)	Returns the next smallest Integer less than *number*, i.e. rounds down.
log(*number*)	Returns the natural logarithm of *number*.
max(*num1, num2*)	Returns the greater of the two values *num1* and *num2*.
min(*num1, num2*)	Returns the smaller of the two values *num1* and *num2*.
pow(*num1, num2*)	Returns the value of *num1* to the power of *num2*.
random()	Returns a random number between 0 and 1.
round(*number*)	Returns the closest Integer to *number* i.e. rounds up *or* down to the nearest whole number.
sin(*number*)	Returns the sin of *number*.
sqrt(*number*)	Returns the square root of *number*.
tan(*number*)	Returns the tangent of *number*.

Number Object

The Number Object provides a set of properties that are useful when working with numbers:

```
MyArea = Math.PI * MyRadius * MyRadius;
MyResult = Math.floor(MyNumber);
```

Properties	Description
MAX_VALUE	The maximum numeric value represented in JavaScript (~1.79E+308).
MIN_VALUE	The minimum numeric value represented in JavaScript (~2.22E-308).
NaN	A value meaning 'Not A Number'.
NEGATIVE_INFINITY	A special value for negative infinity ("-Infinity").
POSITIVE_INFINITY	A special value for infinity ("Infinity").

Methods	Description
toString(*[radix_base]*)	Returns the value of the number as a string to a radix (base) of 10, unless specified otherwise in *radix_base*.
valueOf()	Returns the primitive numeric value of the object.

String Object

The **String** object provides a set of methods for text manipulation. To create a new string object, the syntax is:

```
MyString = new String([value])
```

where **value** is the optional text to place in the string when it is created. If this is a number, it is converted into a string first.

Properties	Description
length	An Integer representing the number of characters in the string.

Methods	Description
anchor("*nameAttribute*")	Returns the original string surrounded by **<A>** and **</A>** anchor tags, with the **NAME** attribute set to "*nameAttribute*".
big()	Returns the original string enclosed in **<BIG>** and **</BIG>** tags.
blink()	Returns the original string enclosed in **<BLINK>** and **</BLINK>** tags.
bold()	Returns the original string enclosed in **<B>** and **</B>** tags.
charAt(*index*)	Returns the single character at position *index* within the **String** object.
fixed()	Returns the original string enclosed in **<TT>** and **</TT>** tags.
fontcolor("*color*")	Returns the original string surrounded by **<FONT>** and **</FONT>** tags, with the **COLOR** attribute set to "*color*".
fontsize("*size*")	Returns the original string surrounded by **<FONT>** and **</FONT>** anchor tags, with the **SIZE** attribute set to "*size*".
indexOf(*searchValue* [, *fromIndex*])	Returns the first occurrence of the string *searchValue* starting at index *fromIndex*.
italics()	Returns the original string enclosed in **<I>** and **</I>** tags.

Methods	Description
lastIndexOf(*searchValue* [,*fromIndex*])	Returns the index of the last occurrence of the string *searchValue*, searching backwards from index *fromIndex*.
link("*hrefAttribute*")	Returns the original string surrounded by **<A>** and **</A>** link tags, with the **HREF** attribute set to "*hrefAttribute*".
small()	Returns the original string enclosed in **<SMALL>** and **</SMALL>** tags.
split(*separator*)	Returns an array of strings created by separating the **String** object at every occurrence of *separator*.
strike()	Returns the original string enclosed in **<STRIKE>** and **</STRIKE>** tags.
sub()	Returns the original string enclosed in **_{** and **}** tags.
substring(*indexA*, *indexB*)	Returns the sub-string of the original **String** object from the character at *indexA* up to and including the one **before** the character at *indexB*.
sup()	Returns the original string enclosed in **^{** and **}** tags.
toLowerCase()	Returns the original string with all the characters converted to lowercase.
toUpperCase()	Returns the original string with all the characters converted to uppercase.

Reserved Words

The following are reserved words that can't be used for function, method, variable, or object names. Note that while some words in this list are not currently used as JavaScript keywords, they have been reserved for future use.

abstract	else	int	super
boolean	extends	interface	switch
break	false	long	synchronized
byte	final	native	this
case	finally	new	throw
catch	float	null	throws
char	for	package	transient
class	function	private	true
const	goto	protected	try
continue	if	public	typeof
default	implements	reset	var
delete	import	return	void
do	in	short	while
double	instanceof	static	with

Appendix

D

Support and Errata

One of the most irritating things about any programming book can be when you find that a bit of code you've just spent an hour typing simply doesn't work. You check it a hundred times to see if you've set it up correctly and then you notice the spelling mistake in the variable name on the book page. Grrrr! Of course, you can blame the authors for not taking enough care and testing the code, the editors for not doing their job properly, or the proofreaders for not being eagle-eyed enough, but this doesn't get around the fact that mistakes do happen.

We try hard to ensure no mistakes sneak out into the real world, but we can't promise you that this book is 100% error free. What we can do is offer the next best thing by providing you with immediate support and feedback from experts who have worked on the book and try to ensure that future editions eliminate these gremlins. The following section will take you step by step through how to post errata to our web site to get that help:

- Finding a list of existing errata on the web site
- Adding your own errata to the existing list
- What happens to your errata once you've posted it (why doesn't it appear immediately?)

and how to mail a question for technical support:

- What your e-mail should include
- What happens to your e-mail once it has been received by us

Finding an Errata on the Web Site

Before you send in a query, you might be able to save time by finding the answer to your problem on our web site, **http:\\www.wrox.com**. Each book we publish has its own page and its own errata sheet. You can get to any book's page by using the drop down list box on our web site's welcome screen.

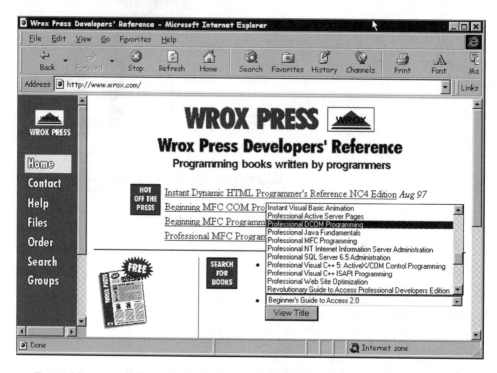

From this you can locate any book's home page on our site. Select your book and click View Title to get the individual title page:

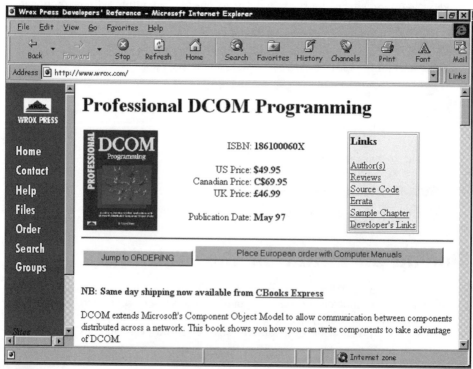

Each book has a set of links. If you click on the Errata link, you'll immediately be transported to the errata sheet for that book:

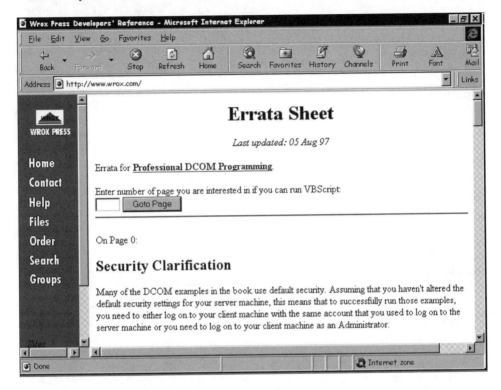

If you're using Internet Explorer 3.0 or later, you can jump to errors more quickly using the text box provided. The errata lists are updated on daily basis, ensuring that you always have the most up-to-date information on bugs and errors.

Adding an Errata to the Sheet Yourself

It's always possible that you may not find your error listed, in which case you can enter details of the fault yourself. It might be anything from a spelling mistake to a faulty piece of code in a book. Sometimes you'll find useful hints that aren't really errors on the listing. By entering errata you may save another reader some hours of frustration and, of course, you will be helping us to produce even higher quality information. We're very grateful for this sort of guidance and feedback. Here's how to do it:

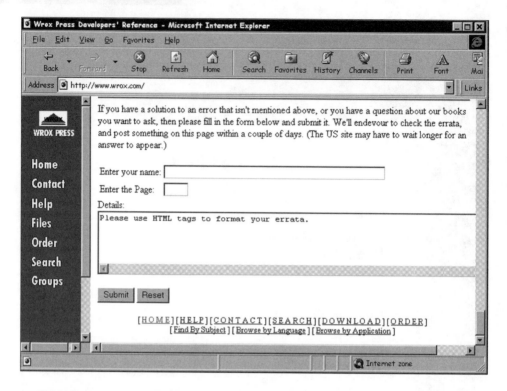

Find the errata page for the book, then scroll down to the bottom of the page, where you will see a space for you to enter your name (and e-mail address for preference), the page the errata occurs on and details of the errata itself. The errata should be formatted using HTML tags - the reminder for this can be deleted as you type in your error.

Once you've typed in your message, click on the Submit button and the message is forwarded to our editors. They'll then test your submission and check that the error exists, and that any suggestions you make are valid. Then your submission, together with a solution, is posted on the site for public consumption. Obviously this stage of the process can take a day or two, but we will endeavor to get a fix up sooner than that.

E-mail Support

If you wish to directly query a problem in the book with an expert who knows the book in detail then e-mail **support@wrox.com**, with the title of the book and the last four numbers of the ISBN in the Subject field of the e-mail. A typical e-mail should include the following things:

the page number of the errata

the title of the book

the last four numbers of the ISBN

the e-mail address

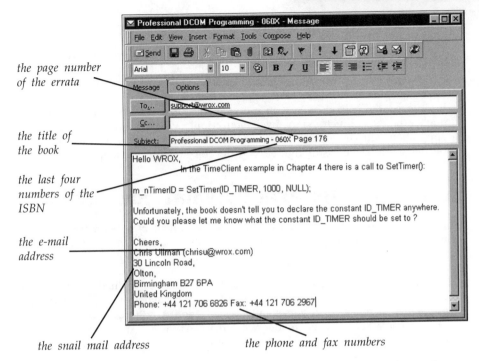

the snail mail address

the phone and fax numbers

We won't send you junk mail. We need details to help save your time and ours. If we need to replace a disk or CD we'll be able to get it to you straight away. When you send an e-mail it will go through the following chain of support;

Customer Support

Your message is delivered to one of our customer support staff who are the first people to read it. They have files on the most frequently asked questions and will answer anything immediately. They answer general questions about the books and web site.

Editorial

Deeper queries are forwarded on the same day to the technical editor responsible for that book. They have experience with the programming language or particular product and are able to answer detailed technical questions on the subject. Once an issue has been resolved, the editor can post the errata to the web site.

The Author(s)

Finally, in the unlikely event that the editor can't answer your problem, he/she will forward the request to the author. We try to protect the author from any distractions from writing. However, we are quite happy to forward specific requests to them. All Wrox authors help with the support on their books. They'll mail the customer and editor with their response, and again, all readers should benefit.

What we can't answer

Obviously with an ever growing range of books and an ever-changing technology base, there is an increasing volume of data requiring support. While we endeavor to answer all questions about a book, we can't answer bugs in your own programs that you've adapted from our code. So, while you might have loved the help desk system examples in our Active Server Pages book, don't expect too much sympathy if you cripple your company with a live application you customized from chapter 12. But do tell us if you're especially pleased with a successful routine you developed with our help.

How to tell us exactly what you think!

We understand that errors can destroy the enjoyment of a book and can cause many wasted and frustrated hours, so we seek to minimize the distress that they can cause.

You might just wish to tell us how much you liked or loathed the book in question. Or you might have ideas about how this whole process could be improved. In which case you should e-mail **feedback@wrox.com**. You'll always find a sympathetic ear, no matter what the problem is. Above all you should remember that we do care about what you have to say and we will do our utmost to act upon it.

INSTANT

DHTML Scriptlets

Index

Symbols

$(CurText) macro 72, 76
<...>. *See* **See specific tag**

A

absolute positioning 17
Active Data Object (ADO)
    recordsets 355, 373
Active Desktop 31, 35, 157
Active Server Pages
    ActiveX controls 14
    dynamism 14
    Remote Scripting 355, 356, 361
Active Template Library (ATL)
    34, 39, 40
    category IDs 42
    classes 15
ActiveDocument 61, 63
ActiveX controls
    Active Server Pages 14
    adding to Scriptlet 140
    CLSID 17, 40, 45, 166, 341
    compared to Server Scriptlets 382
    container object, Scriptlet 90
    Control Pad 37, 46
        ScriptWizard 50, 45
    data binding compared 18

Delphi 173
embedding 30, 44
events 39, 123
identification 40
information resources 51
languages 38
Microsoft Scriptlet Control 49, 175
naming conventions 27
OBJECT tag 23, 45
objects 11
outgoing interface 123, 125
packaging 328
parent properties 89
platforms supported 154
prototyping with Scriptlets 36
registration 40, 43, 341
reusability 30
safety 42, 43
Scriptlets compared 38
    events 39, 123
    identification and registration 40
    implementation 38
    non-HTML documents 36
    platform compatibility 41
    reusability 30
    security 42
    size and performance 40
security 42
size 34, 40
UserControl object 39
viewing in Developer Studio 59
Visual C++ 175

I

T

U

V

X

XML
  and Server Scriptlets 392

Z

z-index property 17
z-ordering 17